Fortunes of France

THE
BRETHREN

ROBERT MERLE

Translated from the French by
T. Jefferson Kline

PUSHKIN PRESS
LONDON

Pushkin Press
71–75 Shelton Street
London WC2H 9JQ

Fortunes of France: The Brethren first published
in French as *Fortune de France* in 1977

This translation first published by Pushkin Press in 2014

This book is supported by the Institut français
(Royaume-Uni) as part of the Burgess programme

ISBN 978 1 782270 44 7

Set in Monotype Baskerville by Tetragon, London

Printed and bound by
CPI Group (UK) Ltd, Croydon CRO 4YY

www.pushkinpress.com

Shall we never see France's fortunes reversed?
Or shall we remain for ever despised and downtrodden?

MICHEL DE L'HOSPITAL

FOREWORD

The Brethren is a chronicle situated in the second half of the sixteenth century, beginning two years before the death of François I (1547) and ending a year after the Meeting of Bayonne (1565).

It is a concentric tale, whose first circle is a family, second circle a province and third a kingdom, whose princes receive no more attention than is necessary to understand the happiness and unhappiness of those who, far away in their baronial courts, depended on their decisions.

The family which I have imagined (carefully feeding this fantasy with precise historical documents) was Protestant and lived in the southern part of the Périgord region, midway between two villages which were then called Marcuays and Taniès—the latter overlooking a small river which fed its mills. Parallel to this river there winds a road that led—and, indeed still leads—to Ayzies, now called les Eyzies. Mespech, the name of the castlery acquired by the Siorac family, comes from *mes*, the word for house in *langue d'oc*, and *pech*, hill.

I am not Protestant myself, so it is no Huguenot austerity that drove me to complete my documentation without aid of any kind. It was, rather, a kind of sensual pleasure: to ensure that I would miss none of the charming, vivid, horrible or savoury details that abound in the memoirs of this period.

The Brethren, as a story, forms a complete whole and can stand alone. I have not excluded the possibility of providing a sequel, yet refuse to commit to such a project in advance, desiring to preserve my liberty as long as possible, that is, until I begin the first page of my next book.

ROBERT MERLE, 1977

1

M Y FAMILY'S CLAIM to nobility does not extend very far back. In fact, it originates with my father. I say this without the least sense of shame. You must understand that if I were out to hide anything I would never have begun this story at all. My design is to write it straight out, without any deviation, the way you'd go about ploughing a field.

Some have dared to claim that my great-grandfather was a mere lackey: a falsehood which I shall be glad to prove to anyone who will listen. In fact, my great-grandfather, François Siorac, never served a day under anyone. He owned and worked with his own hands a rich piece of farmland near Taniès, in the Sarlat region. I cannot tell you the exact extent of his land, but it was neither small nor unproductive, judging by the fact that he paid the highest tithes to the king of any man in his parish. Nor was he a miser, since he gave ten sols a month to his curate so that his younger son Charles could study Latin, hoping, no doubt, to see him become a priest in his turn.

My grandfather Charles was a handsome man, whose beard and hair verged on red, like my half-brother Samson's. He learnt his Latin well, but preferred adventures to sermons: at eighteen he left his village to seek his fortune in the north.

He found it, apparently, since he married the daughter of an apothecary from Rouen, to whom he was apprenticed. I cannot imagine how, being an apprentice, he managed to study for his apothecary's exams, nor do I even know whether he passed them or not, but at the death of his father-in-law he took over his shop and did remarkably well. In 1514, the year my father was born, he was prosperous enough to acquire a mill surrounded by good farmland, some ten leagues from Rouen, which he named la Volpie. It was at this time that between "Charles" and "Siorac" the particle "de" was inserted to indicate nobility, an addition my father made much sport of, but maintained. And yet I've never seen on any of the documents preserved by my father the title "nobleman" preceding the signature "Charles de Siorac, lord of la Volpie": proof that my grandfather wasn't out to fool anyone, like so many bourgeois who acquire land only to lay claim to a title never granted them by the king. False nobles abound, as everyone knows. And, to tell the truth, when these bourgeois fortunes grow fat enough to merit an alliance, the real nobles don't look too closely.

My father, Jean de Siorac, was a younger brother, like his father Charles before him and like me. And Charles, remembering the costly Latin lessons old François Siorac had provided for him, sent Jean off to learn his medicine in Montpellier. It was a long journey requiring a lengthy stay and a great sacrifice of capital, even for an apothecary. As he grew older, however, Charles's great dream was—God willing—to see his eldest son Henri settled in his apothecary's shop, his younger son Jean established as a doctor in town, and the two of them, squeezing the patient from either side, prospering grandly. His three daughters counted but little for him, yet he provided each of them enough in dowry so that he should never be ashamed of their station.

My father received his bachelor's degree with a licence in medicine from the University of Montpellier, but he never defended his thesis. He was forced to flee the town two days before his defence, fearing that his last look would be heavenward as he dangled from a noose, after which he would be quartered and, as was the custom of the place, his quarters hung from olive branches at each of the town gates. This fact gave me cause to shudder when, in my turn, I entered Montpellier one sunny morn, thirty years later, and confronted the rotting remains of some women, hanged from the branches of these trees, shamelessly laden, as if with their own profusion of fruit.

Today, I have trouble imagining my father thirty years ago, just as wild as I am now, and no less attracted by a pretty skirt. Yet it is undoubtedly over some unworthy wench that my father fought an honourable duel and skewered the body of a petty nobleman who had provoked him. An hour later, spying the archers coming to arrest him in his attic, Jean de Siorac jumped from a rear window onto his horse (luckily still saddled), and galloped full tilt out of town. Bareheaded and dressed only in his doublet, with neither coat nor sword, he headed towards the hills of Cévennes. There he sought refuge with a student who was spending six months in the mountains preparing his medical exams for Montpellier. He later crossed the Auvergne region and headed to Périgord, where old François Siorac armed and clothed him at his own expense and sent him on to the home of his son Charles in Rouen.

By this time a formal complaint had been lodged with the parliament of Aix by the parents of the late petty nobleman. They succeeded in making such an enormous stir that even my grandfather's considerable influence as apothecary of Rouen did not make it safe for Jean de Siorac to show himself in daylight.

All of this transpired in the same year that our great king, François I, ordered the conscription of a legion of soldiers from each of the provinces of his kingdom. This was a wise decision, which, had it been continued, would have spared us the wartime use of the Swiss Guard, who fought bravely enough when they were paid, but, when they weren't, set about pillaging the poor peasants of France faster than our enemies could.

The Norman legion, a full 6,000 strong, was the first to be formed in all of France, and Jean de Siorac enlisted when the king promised to consider a pardon for the murder he had committed. Indeed, when François I inspected the regiment in May 1535, he was so happy that he granted my father's immediate pardon on condition that he serve five years in the army. "And so," as Jean de Siorac tells it, "it came to pass that, having learnt the art of healing my fellow men, I had taken up the trade of killing them."

My grandfather Charles was not a little chagrined to see his younger son recruited as a legionnaire after having spent so many écus to educate him to be a doctor in the town. His sorrow was compounded by his elder son Henry's behaviour. The future apothecary neglected his studies for drinking and merrymaking, and ended up in the Seine one night drowned (with a little help, evidently, since his pockets had first been carefully emptied).

My grandfather was greatly relieved that the daughter he had always called a "silly gossip", but who was not lacking in common sense, furnished him with a son-in-law capable of inheriting his shop. 'Tis strange indeed that his apothecary's shop was passed on for the second time not from father to son, but from father-in-law to son-in-law.

As for my father, Jean de Siorac, he was cast of a very different metal from his elder brother. He set about bravely advancing his fortunes in the legion. He was courageous, patient and tolerant, and, though he never breathed a word of his medical training (for fear of ending up in the medical corps, a role he would have disdained), he treated and bandaged his companions' wounds, which earned him the goodwill of his commanders and comrades alike.

In all, he served not five, but nine years in the legion, from 1536 to 1545, and in each campaign received a wound and a promotion. From centurion he rose to standard-bearer and from this rank to lieutenant. From lieutenant, in 1544, having been stabbed or shot in every part of his body but the vital ones, he was promoted to captain.

This rank was as high as any enlisted man could aspire to and meant the command of 1,000 legionnaires, pay of 100 livres during each month of a campaign and the lion's share of any booty pillaged from captured towns. It turned out to be an even greater privilege for my father, for it eventually led to his ennoblement as *écuyer*, or squire—justly and honourably won by valour rather than by wealth or advantageous marriage vows.

The day my father was named captain, they also promoted his friend and steadfast companion, Jean de Sauveterre. Between these two were woven, out of the hazards of battle and their many brushes with death from which each had saved the other, the ties of an affection so deep that neither time, misfortune nor even my father's marriage could damage it in the slightest. Jean de Sauveterre was about five years older than my father and was as swarthy as my father was blond, with brown eyes, a badly scarred face and a most reticent tongue.

My father didn't remain an *écuyer* for very long. In 1545, he fought so valiantly at Ceresole that he was knighted on the battlefield by his commander, the Duc d'Enghien. My father's joy was severely compromised, however, by the news that Jean de Sauveterre had received a leg wound so grave as to cause him to limp for the rest of his days. With the return of peace, the best Jean de Sauveterre could look forward to would be some stationary post in a fortress that would have separated him from the other Jean—a thought as unbearable to the one as to the other.

They were plunged in gloomy ruminations about their future when news reached them of the death of my grandfather Charles. He'd scarcely had time to enjoy all the attention his younger son's military successes had brought to the family. He had been announcing to all his friends in Rouen the upcoming visit of his son, the "Chevalier de Siorac", when he was overcome with a terrible intestinal pain—a *miserere*, or appendicitis, according to what I heard. He died, sweating and in terrible pain, before he could see his son, his sole surviving male heir and the only one of his children he had ever really loved, since, as I have said, he considered his daughters worthless.

Jean, Chevalier de Siorac, collected his part of the inheritance, which amounted to 7,537 livres, and, upon his return to camp, sequestered himself in his tent with Jean de Sauveterre to do their accounts. Since both had been careful with their expenses, addicted neither to wine nor to gambling, they had managed to save most of their pay and the greater part of their booty. Moreover, having entrusted the greater part of their savings to an honest Jew in Rouen, each had prospered through his usury and now found that together they possessed some 35,000 livres—a sum large enough to permit them to purchase a farm together, from which they agreed to share all profits and losses.

With the reluctant permission of the lieutenant general, the two Jeans left the Norman legion, taking with them their arms, their horses, their booty and three good foot soldiers in their service. One of these drove a cart bearing all their worldly goods, including an assortment of loaded pistols, blunderbusses and firearms confiscated from their enemies. From Normandy to Périgord, the roads were long and dangerous, and the small troop rode prudently, avoiding large groups of horsemen and cutting to pieces the petty thieves who dared demand payment for bridge crossings. After each band of these scoundrels was dispatched, they were relieved of arms and treasure, a part of the booty going to each of the three soldiers and the rest into the coffers of the two leaders.

On the road to Bergerac, just beyond Bordeaux, their troop over-took a gentle covey of nuns, each on her pony, preceded by a proud abbess in a carriage. At the sight of these five tanned, well-armed and bearded soldiers bearing down on them from the dusty road behind, the nuns began shrieking, thinking, perhaps, to have reached the end of their vows. But Jean de Siorac, riding up alongside the carriage, greeted the abbess with great civility, presented his respects and reassured her of their good intentions. She turned out to be a young woman of noble birth, far from diffident, whose sweetly fluttering eyelashes held out a certain promise, and who asked for escort as far as Sarlat. Now, my father was by reputation easy prey for all the enchantresses of this world, even those in nun's clothing, and was just about to agree when Jean de Sauveterre intervened. Polite, but stern, fixing his black eyes on the abbess, he pointed out that, at the rate the ponies were going, an escort would necessarily slow down their troop and expose them to many dangers of the road. In short, it was a service that couldn't be enjoyed for less than fifty livres. Abandoning her charms, the abbess haggled bitterly over this price, but Jean de Sauveterre stood his ground, and she ended up paying this sum right down to the last sol—and in advance.

I remember hearing this story told more than a hundred times when I was still a child, by Cabusse, one of our three soldiers (the other two were known as Marsal and Coulondre). And even though I loved this tale, I found it hard to understand the humour of Cabusse's closing words, inevitably accompanied by a great belly laugh: "One Jean handled the money and the other Jean handled the rest, God bless 'im!"

At Taniès, my great-grandfather, old François Siorac, had died, and Raymond, Charles's elder brother, had taken over the land. He received his nephew hospitably, though he was secretly terrified at the sight of five booted, bearded and well-armed men invading his house. But Jean paid his way, both room and board, and, since it was harvest time, the three soldiers rolled up their sleeves and pitched in. They were brave lads and though they served in the Norman legion, two of the three were natives of Quercy and the third—Cabusse—was Gascon.

Before deciding where or how to establish themselves, the two Jeans, astride their best horses and clad in their finest costumes, went from chateau to chateau to present their respects to the Sarlat nobility. Jean de Siorac was then twenty-nine, and with his blue eyes, blond hair and military bearing, he appeared to be in the bloom of his youth, but for a swipe on his left cheek which had scarred but not disfigured him—the rest of his wounds being hidden beneath his clothing. Jean de Sauveterre, at thirty-four, seemed almost old enough to be Siorac's father, as much because of his already grey-ing, stiffly combed hair and deep-set, jet-black eyes as because of his battle-scarred face. He limped, yet was still nimble, and his large shoulders suggested his great strength.

Neither the Chevalier de Siorac nor Jean de Sauveterre, Écuyer, took the trouble to hide their lowly origins, believing there was no disgrace in being so recently ennobled. Their openness on this matter was the surest sign of their sense of self-worth. Moreover, both men were eloquent speakers, without any trace of haughtiness, yet clearly not men to be lightly dismissed.

The natives of Périgord have the reputation of being amiable, and the two captains were well received wherever they went. Nowhere was their welcome warmer than from the family of François de Caumont, lord of Castelnau and Milandes. The magnificent Château de Castelnau, built by François de Caumont's grandfather, was then hardly fifty years old, and its Périgord stone still retained its ochre brilliance, especially in the sunlight.

Powerfully situated on a rocky promontory overlooking the entire Dordogne river basin, flanked by a broad circular tower, it seemed to the two captains as if it were impregnable—except perhaps by artillery, which, however, would be disadvantaged by having to fire from so far below its walls. They were also impressed, as they crossed the drawbridge, by two small cannon, set in embrasures, whose crossfire would seriously hinder the advance of any assailant. The two visitors began by complimenting Caumont warmly on this splendid, nearly impregnable castle, which so dominated the Dordogne valley. After these lengthy opening remarks (my father was not given to abbreviating formalities), there was a fulsome exchange of compliments.

François de Caumont had already learnt of his guests' exploits, and congratulated them on their courage in the service of the king. All of this had to be expressed in the pompous style practised by our fathers' generation, which I personally find tiring, and prefer the simpler language of our peasants.

François de Caumont (whose brother Geoffroy was to share some hair-raising experiences with me which we survived only by the greatest miracle) was small but powerfully built, with a deep voice and a bright and attentive expression. At twenty-five, he seemed to have the wisdom of a much older man, always inclined to weigh his options, inevitably wary and ready to retreat at the slightest sign of danger. After the ritual exchange of greetings, François sensed in his two visitors a pair of allies open to "the new opinion" of Protestantism, and sounded them out with a few delicate questions. Despite their prudent answers, François's suspicions proved to be well founded. He knew, of course, the enormous weight such men would lend to his party and immediately resolved to help us to get established in the region.

"Messieurs," said he, "you couldn't have come to a better place. In a week's time, the castlery of Mespech will be auctioned by sealed bids. As you will see, the place has fallen into disrepair since the death of its owner, but its lands are spacious and fertile and include some good grazing land and handsome hardwood forests.

The Baron de Fontenac, whose lands abut on the Mespech domain, would naturally like to round out his holdings as cheaply as possible, and he has done everything he can to delay the sale in hopes that the castle will fall into such disrepair that no other buyers would be tempted. However, despite the manoeuvrings of Fontenac, the authorities in Sarlat have finally decided in the interests of the heirs of Mespech to proceed to a sale. The auction will take place on Monday next at noon."

"Monsieur de Caumont," said Jean de Sauveterre, "do you count the Baron de Fontenac among your friends?"

"Absolutely not," answered Caumont. "No one here counts Fontenac as his friend, and he is friend to no man."

From the silence that followed, Sauveterre understood that there was a long history behind his words that Caumont preferred not to relate. Siorac would have pressed the matter, but at that very moment a gracious maiden entered the great hall, clothed in a very low-cut morning dress, her blonde hair falling freely about her shoulders. Since the beginning of his visits to the noble families of Sarlat, Siorac had seen a great many women whose necks were so bound in plaits and ruffles that their heads appeared to be served on platters. His heart gave a mighty leap at the sight of this white breast sculpted with the grace of a swan, while, for her part, the maiden returned his gaze with her large blue eyes. As he limped forward to exchange greetings with her, Sauveterre caught sight of a medallion on her breast which displeased him mightily.

"Isabelle," Caumont announced in his deep bass voice, "is the daughter of my uncle, the Chevalier de Caumont. My wife is forced to keep to her bed as a result of the vapours, otherwise she would herself have come down to honour our guests with her presence. But Isabelle will take her place. Although she is not without her own fortune, my cousin Isabelle lodges with us—a distinct honour and a pleasure, for she is perfection itself." This last was directed, accompanied by a significant look, at Siorac.

François added, jokingly, this time glancing at Sauveterre, "Really there is nothing one could reproach her for, except perhaps her strange taste in medallions."

Sparks flew from Isabelle's blue eyes as she replied with a petulant movement of shoulders and neck, "A taste shared, my cousin, by my king, Louis XI—"

"Who was a great king, despite his idolatry," interrupted Caumont gravely, though his eyes danced in merriment.

When the two Jeans arrived at the Château de Mespech the next morning, they were surprised to find the drawbridge raised. After repeated cries, a hairy head finally appeared on the ramparts, wild-eyed and face flushed with drink: "Go your way!" the fellow croaked. "I have orders to open to no man."

"What is this order?" asked Jean de Siorac. "And who has given it? I am the Chevalier de Siorac, nephew of Raymond Siorac de Taniès, and I wish to purchase the castlery with my friend and companion, Jean de Sauveterre. How can I make a purchase, my good man, if I cannot visit the premises?"

"Ah, Monsieur," whined the man, "I humbly beg your pardon, but my life and my family's lives would be worth nothing if I opened these gates."

"Who are you and what is your name?"

"Maligou."

"He seems to like his drink," muttered Sauveterre.

"Maligou," said Siorac, "are you a servant in this house?"

"Not on your life," answered Maligou proudly. "I have lands, a house and a vineyard."

"A large vineyard?" asked Sauveterre.

"Large enough, Monsieur, for my thirst."

"And how do you come to be here?"

"My harvest is in, and I agreed, for my misfortune, to serve as guard at Mespech for the heirs of the estate, for two sols a day."

"You seem to be earning them badly if you don't open the doors to prospective buyers!"

"Monsieur, I cannot," said old Maligou plaintively. "I have my orders. And I risk my life if I disobey them."

"Who gives these orders?"

"You know very well," said Maligou, his head hanging.

"Maligou," answered Sauveterre, knitting his brow, "if you don't lower the drawbridge, I will ride to Sarlat in search of the king's lieutenant and his archers! And they will hang you for refusing entry to us."

"I will certainly open the gates to Monsieur de La Boétie," Maligou sighed in relief, "but I don't think he'll hang me. Go find the lieutenant, Monsieur, before I am killed by the others. I beg you in the name of the Lord and all his saints!"

"The Devil take the saints," grumbled Sauveterre, "does this fool also wear a medallion to the Virgin?"

"Perhaps, but not in so beautiful and goodly a place," whispered Siorac. And, out loud, "Come, Sauveterre. Let's ride to Sarlat! We must hie ourselves all the way back to Sarlat thanks to this fool."

"Or thanks to those who've terrorized him," countered Sauveterre worriedly, spurring his horse. "My brother, we must consider this bad neighbour we shall likely have, if it's true that the lands of Fontenac border those of Mespech."

"But 'tis a beautiful chateau," replied Siorac, standing full up on his stirrups. "'Tis handsome and newly built. We will have much joy from living in a house so new as this. A pox on the narrow windows of the old fortresses with their blackened, moss-covered walls. Let me live instead in shining stone and with doubled windows which let in the sun!"

"And offer easy entry to our assailants…"

"If need be, we'll reinforce them on the inside with oak shutters."

"You're buying a pig in a poke, brother," growled Sauveterre. "We haven't even seen the fields."

"Today the house. Tomorrow and the day after the land," cried Siorac.

Anthoine de La Boétie, police lieutenant by authority of the seneschalty of Sarlat and of the domain of Domme, lived opposite the church in Sarlat. He had a beautiful new house, pierced with the double casement windows so admired by my father, who loved all the new ideas, whether in matters of religion, agriculture, military science or medicine. For Jean had continued his diligent study of the medical sciences. I recently found in his impressive library a treatise by Ambroise Paré entitled *The Method of Treating Wounds Made by the Blunderbuss and Other Firearms*, bought, according to my father's notation, from a book dealer in Sarlat on 13th July 1545, the year of this business concerning Mespech.

Monsieur de La Boétie was elegantly clad in a silk doublet and sported a carefully groomed moustache and goatee. Seated beside him on a low chair was a lad of about fifteen whose homeliness was offset by brilliant piercing eyes.

"My son, Étienne," Monsieur de La Boétie announced, not without a touch of pride. "Messieurs," he continued, "I am entirely aware of the machinations of Fontenac. He wants Mespech and will try to get it by any means—no matter how vile and dirty. I have learnt, though alas I cannot prove it, that a month ago he sent some men by night to scale the walls and dislodge some roofing stones so that water could get in and ruin the flooring, thus depreciating the value of the place. Fontenac has only 15,000 livres and knows that no one hereabouts would lend him a sol. So, unless he's the only bidder on Mespech, he won't be able to afford it. To prevent any further damage, the heirs to Mespech hired Maligou to stand guard, but Fontenac, having learnt of your interest—"

"So, he knows about us!" said Siorac.

"Like everyone else in Sarlat," smiled La Boétie, stroking his goatee. "You're the talk of every chateau and farm in the region. And everyone knows that Fontenac has threatened to roast Maligou and his wife and children alive in their house if he lets you in."

"And Fontenac is capable of such a thing?" asked Sauveterre.

"He has done much worse," replied La Boétie with a helpless gesture. "But he's as clever as a snake and has never left a trace of his foul play by which we could try him."

"We have some experience of war and command three good soldiers," said Sauveterre. "Lieutenant, what harm can this brigand baron do to us?"

"Post masked men in ambush on any wooded road in Périgord and attribute your deaths to the many armed bands that infest the countryside."

"And how many swords does Fontenac have at his disposal?"

"About ten good-for-nothing scoundrels whom he calls his soldiers."

"Ten?" sniffed Siorac haughtily. "That's precious few."

The moment of silence that followed this remark was broken by Anthoine de La Boétie: "But Fontenac has already begun a campaign of rumours to get at you by subtler means. The monster possesses a kind of venomous sweetness to sugar his plots. He has already advised the bishopric of Sarlat that you are both purported to be members of the reformed religion."

"We are neither of us members of the reformed congregation," replied Siorac after a moment of reflection, "and we attend Mass like everyone else."

Sauveterre neither confirmed nor denied this, but chose to remain silent. This difference did not go unnoticed by Anthoine de La Boétie. As for his son, Étienne, he rose, walked briskly to the window and turned, saying with equal indignation and eloquence, "Is it not shameful to question these gentlemen's attendance at Mass when they have shed their blood for ten years in the service of the kingdom? And who dares raise this question? This incendiary, this butcher, this wild animal, this dirty plague of a man who wears religion like a shield to cover his crimes! God preserve us from the worst tyranny of all which respects not our beliefs—"

"My son," broke in Anthoine with a mixture of affection and admiration, "I appreciate the feelings which incite your generous heart against oppression."

"Moreover, you express yourself admirably," said Siorac to Étienne. It had not escaped his notice that Étienne had said "in the service of the kingdom" and not "in the service of the king".

Étienne returned to his place on the stool beside Monsieur de La Boétie's chair and, blushing, took Anthoine's hand in a touching gesture that revealed his love for his father. His ardent look conveyed his immense gratitude for the approbation he had received. What good fortune that nature had united such a father and son, for their hearts could not be closer nor their wills more clearly intermingled.

"Ah, Father," exclaimed Étienne, tears in his eyes, "why do people accept tyranny so easily? I think about this every day God has given me to live. I cannot forget the infernal expedition undertaken last April against the poor Vaudois people of Luberon: 800 workers massacred, their villages burnt, their wives and daughters raped in the very church of Mérindol and then burnt inside, the old women who instead of being raped were torn asunder by gunpowder forced into their intimate parts, prisoners who were eviscerated alive to have their guts displayed on sticks! And the Pope's legate, witnessing these horrors at Cabrières, applauded them! And why did all this happen? Because these poor people, peaceful and hard-working as they are, refused to hear Mass, worship the saints and accept confession—just like the reformists whom they resemble so closely. As you know, Father, I am as good a Catholic as the next man (though I cannot approve of the corruption of the Roman Church), but I blush for shame that the Church of St Peter has steered the king of France towards such abominations…"

"My son," said Anthoine de La Boétie, glancing with embarrassment at his guests, "you know as I do that our king, François I, is a good man. He signed without reading them the letters ordering the Baron d'Oppède to execute the Act of the parliament at Aix against the Vaudois. But afterwards he was filled with such remorse that he has ordered an inquest against the men responsible for these massacres."

"Alas, it is too late now!" replied Étienne. But sensing his father's impatience, he sighed, lowered his eyes and fell silent.

Sauveterre broke the silence: "If I may return to this rascal Fontenac, may I ask if his word has any weight with the bishop?"

"I know not," replied La Boétie, who looked as if he knew all too well. "This scoundrel claims to be a good Catholic, although he's a miserable excuse for a Christian. He pays for Masses, and makes many charitable contributions…"

"And the bishop accepts these payments?"

"Well, the problem is that we don't have a bishop," rejoined La Boétie with a smile, all the while stroking his goatee with the back of his hand. "Our bishop, Nicolas de Gadis, appointed by Catherine de' Medici, is a Florentine, like his patroness, and lives in Rome where he awaits his cardinal's mitre."

"In Rome!" replied Siorac. "The tithes extracted from the sweat of the Sarlat workers have a long way to go to reach him!" At this exclamation, Étienne burst out laughing, and his sudden gaiety infused his melancholy countenance with youth.

"We have, of course, a coadjutor," La Boétie added, half seriously, half amusedly, "one Jean Fabri."

"But he lives in Belvès," noted Étienne, "since he finds the climate of Sarlat suffocating, especially in summer…"

"From Sarlat to Belvès," Siorac rejoined in the spirit of the moment, "the Church tithes have less far to travel than to Rome."

"But a few of these tithes must tarry in Sarlat," said Étienne, "for we have here a tertium quid, the vicar general, Noailles, who pretends to govern in their place."

This exchange had the effect of weaving a close complicity among these four men, barely masked by the apparent hilarity of their speech. La Boétie rose; as Étienne stood up, his father put his arm around his son's shoulders and, smiling, looked at his visitors as they rose too—Sauveterre with some difficulty due to his infirm leg.

"Gentlemen, if you want Mespech," he continued in that inimitable Périgordian jocular manner, which always masks some more serious or satirical intention, "you'll have to make some concessions. It may be too much to ask of you to make a gift to Anthoine de Noailles in honour of the Holy Virgin, for whom you have so long felt a special devotion…"

Siorac smiled but refrained from any response; Sauveterre remained impassive.

"Or perhaps you could manage to attend High Mass this Sunday at Sarlat. The vicar general will be presiding and could not fail to notice your presence."

"Indeed!" cried Siorac happily. "If Mespech is to our liking, we will not fail to be there!"

The king's lieutenant and his archers, followed by the two Jeans, had only to appear; the drawbridge of Mespech was lowered before them. Maligou, infinitely relieved to escape with a scolding, was sent home and four of La Boétie's men were stationed within the walls until the date of the sale. La Boétie obviously feared that a desperate Fontenac might try to set fire to the place, since, without the chateau itself, the vast acreage of Mespech would attract no buyer other than its powerful neighbour.

After La Boétie had taken his leave, Siorac and Sauveterre explored Mespech from top to bottom. The next day, Friday, they spent surveying the farmlands and woods belonging to the property. On Saturday they returned to Sarlat and there, in the presence of Ricou, the notary, they formally adopted each other and ceded each to the other all of his present and future worldly goods. From this moment on, the two Jeans became brothers, not only out of the mutual affection they had sworn, but now legally as well, heirs one of the other—and Mespech, should they acquire it, was to be their indissoluble property.

I have read this moving document. It is composed entirely in *langue d'oc* even though by this time all official acts were already written in French. But the notaries were the last to give in to this rule, since their clients more often than not could understand nothing of the northern tongue.

Word of the captains' brothering had spread in Sarlat, and it was quickly bruited about that the two worthies would purchase Mespech right from under Fontenac's nose. And this hypothesis was confirmed when they were sighted at High Mass the next morning.

Rumour also had it that after Mass they presented the vicar general, Anthoine de Noailles, with a gift of 500 livres "for the poor veterans of the king's armies who live within the diocese in feeble and crippled condition".

The arrival of the captains in Sarlat, that Sunday, was no trivial event: they passed through the la Lendrevie gate, escorted by their three soldiers, all five (except Coulondre) with pistols and swords drawn and at the ready. They paraded through the streets, Siorac and Sauveterre, eyes on the windows above them, their soldiers scrutinizing every passer-by. They did not sheathe their weapons until they dismounted in front of La Boétie's house. The lieutenant, alerted by the sound of horses' hooves in the street, immediately emerged to greet them, smiling and extending a welcoming hand, a gesture intended to impress upon those gathered in the square (as was their custom in good weather before Mass), the consideration accorded these newcomers by a royal officer.

There was a great to-do when the "Brethren" had withdrawn into La Boétie's house, much chatter and shaking of heads among the burghers, while the peasants crowded around the five purebred steeds tethered by the three soldiers, admiring their sweaty flanks and the military fittings, whose embroidered covers had been folded back to reveal the handles of their powerful firearms.

Fontenac was roundly detested by the burghers of Sarlat, as well as by the nobles in their chateaux, because of his many crimes and infinite excesses, yet the populace of the town favoured him since, with the profits of his various plunders, he occasionally paid for a religious procession supposedly to honour a saint, but which always ended up in a river of free wine and the usual street fight which La Boétie had to quell. Despite these all-too-frequent disruptions, many are of the opinion that the peasants, who must work from dawn to dusk for a pittance, cannot help loving the Church processions, since they provide a day of rest—the innumerable saints revered by the Catholic cult providing fifty holidays, not counting Sundays, year in, year out. Thus it has always been easy to excite the populace against members of the reformed religion because they are suspected of wanting to do away with these holidays by suppressing the worship of the very saints which occasion them.

Although the dialects of Quercy and Gascony are quite different from their own, these gawkers soon discovered that our soldiers spoke the *langue d'oc*. And so, as they patted the horses, admiring the saddles and the iron hook Coulondre wore in place of his left hand, they rattled off innumerable questions which only Cabusse, with his quick wit and ready tongue, seemed inclined to answer.

"Are your masters going to purchase Mespech?"

"We don't have masters. These gentlemen are our captains."

"Are your captains going to purchase the chateau?"

"Perhaps."

"Can they afford it?"

"I haven't inspected their coffers."

"It's rumoured that Fontenac has 15,000 livres."

"May God keep them for him."

"Do your captains have more?"

"You'll have to ask them."

"Suppose your captains do acquire Mespech. We hear that Monsieur de Fontenac won't stomach such an insult."

"May God preserve his digestion."

"You swear by God. Do you also swear by His saints?"

"Indeed so, by the saint of gawkers!"

"What religion are you?"

"The same as you."

"They say your captains are afflicted with the scourge of heresy."

"Only a fool would say such a thing."

Whereupon Cabusse rose up and shouted at the top of his lungs, "Good people, get out from under our horses' hooves and take your hands off our saddles!" And such is the authority of a large man with a loud voice that he was immediately obeyed.

As soon as the door closed behind La Boétie and his guests, the police lieutenant announced: "Gentlemen, I have just learnt from a spy that Fontenac intends to ambush you tonight at Taniès. If you wish, I will give you and your men lodging in my country house tonight and until the sale is completed."

"I thank you infinitely for your offer, Monsieur de La Boétie," replied Siorac, "but we cannot accept it. If Fontenac did not find us at Taniès, God knows what evil vengeance he would wreak on my uncle's family and their poor villagers!"

"Siorac is right," said Sauveterre, seemingly unperturbed by the fact that Siorac had spoken before consulting him. He added, "Thanks to you, Lieutenant, the surprise will not be ours tonight, but Fontenac's."

"Oh, he won't be there," cautioned La Boétie. "He's too clever for that."

"But if we eliminate his band," countered Siorac, "we'll dull his fangs a bit."

Taniès, home to about ten families whose houses cluster around a squat church tower, is built on a hill from which a steep road descends to the banks of the les Beunes river. Now, the river gets its plural name by reason of the canals and millraces which seem to double its course. The name also designates the little valley watered by this river as far as the village of Ayzies. A fairly well-paved road runs the length of this river—the only means of access to the Château de Fontenac.

At dusk, our captains posted Cabusse and Uncle Siorac's two sons at the foot of this hill, for they figured that their assailants would probably tether their horses there and creep on foot up the steepest and rockiest face of the hill leading to the village. Cabusse and his men were not to engage the enemy, but to let them pass by and, at the first sound of gunfire, to overpower anyone left on guard there and lead the horses to one of my uncle's barns nearby. This done, they were to return and lie in wait for any of the assailants who might try to flee that way and to shoot them as they reached the bottom of the hill.

Cabusse, who later recounted this adventure (for the Brethren disdained any talk of their own exploits) laughingly told me that the hardest part of the whole affair was not to enter battle but to convince the villagers to join in, so terrified were they of Fontenac. However, once their minds were made up, nothing could stem their fury. After the battle, they coldly put to death all of the wounded and immediately set to stripping them of their clothes and boots, vociferously demanding their share of the plunder, not only arms but horses, despite the fact that it was Raymond Siorac's two sons who, alone, had participated in their capture.

To each of these lads, the captains gave a horse and saddle, and to the village they presented another two horses to be shared by all in the fields. But the villagers, accustomed to the use of oxen, preferred to sell the horses and divide the money. The Brethren kept the rest, to wit, six handsome and powerful horses, as apt for working in the fields as for saddle riding and which would be useful when the time came to break ground at Mespech.

Without suffering a single casualty, they killed that night six of the outlaw baron's band. And they took one prisoner: the horse guard, whom Cabusse had knocked unconscious along the les Beunes river. When he was returned to the village, it was extremely difficult to prevent the villagers from tearing him apart. But one prisoner had to be kept alive in order to have someone to bear witness against

Fontenac. To judge by the number of horses, two of the assailants must have slipped away on foot in the darkness, despite the full moon. Of course, it must be pointed out that, once past les Beunes, the forest of chestnut trees provides a deep, well-shaded cover for the full five leagues that separate Taniès from Fontenac.

The following Monday, the date of the sale of Mespech, the captains had the bloodied bodies piled in a cart and delivered to La Boétie along with the prisoner. This latter was sequestered in the city jail, but La Boétie displayed the bodies at the gibbet in Sarlat, which stood in those days opposite the la Rigaudie gate. The populace immediately crowded around. The gawkers apparently included several young women, although the six ruffians were stark naked.

La Boétie lingered awhile nearby with the captains, not so much to enjoy the spectacle as to listen to the townspeople and note which of them seemed to recognize friends among the hanged bodies of Fontenac's men, with whom they had been drinking of late in the taverns of the town. And, indeed, as the winds began to shift against the robber baron, tongues began wagging.

As for the prisoner, the executioner began his inquisition an hour after arriving in Sarlat, and he told all and more than all. Indeed he revealed some well-nigh unbelievable atrocities committed two years previously, which weighed heavily on the conscience of this churl, clearly made of weaker stuff than his master.

In 1543, a rich burgher of Montignac, one Lagarrigue, had disappeared. A month later, his wife left the town alone on horseback never to reappear. The prisoner's confession shed sinister light on these disappearances. Fontenac had kidnapped Lagarrigue on the way from Montignac to Sarlat at dusk one evening, killing his two servants and sequestering his captive in his chateau. Then, secretly, he alerted the wife to her husband's plight. And, on condition that she breathe not a word of his whereabouts to a living soul, not even to her confessor, he promised to release the man for a ransom of 8,000 livres. She was to deliver this sum alone, and without anyone's knowledge.

This unfortunate lady, who nourished an extraordinary love for her husband and who trembled at the thought of losing him, was mad enough to believe the robber baron to be a man of his word. She obeyed him in all particulars. Once the great doors of the chateau had closed upon her, and the ransom money was counted and locked away in his coffers, Fontenac, a man of uncommonly good looks, education and manners, told the lady, in the sweetest of tones, to be patient and that she should soon be reunited with her husband. But no sooner was Lagarrigue dragged before him, bloodied and chained, than Fontenac changed his expression and his tune. He threw the lady down before his servingmen telling them to take their pleasure of her if they were so inclined. And so they did—within plain sight of Lagarrigue, who struggled in his bonds like a madman.

So that nothing should be lacking in the complete torture of the poor woman, he then ordered her husband strangled before her very eyes and threatened her with a similar fate. Still, he kept her alive for two or three days for the amusement of his soldiers. But as several among them expressed pity for her, since she had maintained a Christian composure and dignity throughout her abominable ordeal, Fontenac, as if to provide a lesson in cruelty, plunged his dagger into her heart, turning and twisting the blade, asking her with terrible blasphemies whether he gave her thus her pleasure. The two bodies were then thrown into the dry moat and burnt so that no trace of this horrible crime should survive. And Fontenac, watching from the ramparts above the acrid smoke rising towards him, remarked snidely that Lagarrigue and his lady should be happy that they were now finally reunited.

Fontenac got wind of his henchman's testimony and did not appear in Sarlat on that Monday at noon. Mespech was sold in broad daylight for 25,000 livres to Jean de Siorac and Jean de Sauveterre, a modest enough price for such a rich and extensive property, but not as low as Fontenac would have paid had he succeeded in his scheme to be the only bidder.

We might think that finally justice was about to be rendered on Fontenac in the form of capital punishment. But the prisoner who accused him died, poisoned in his jail two days later, and his death rendered ever more fragile the testimony brought against the robber baron. The parliament of Bordeaux called Fontenac to testify, but he refused to quit his crenellated hideout. He wrote to the president of the parliament a most courteous and elegant letter of regret, sprinkled, naturally, with erudite Latin phrases.

With profuse compliments, he regretted infinitely his inability to conform to their commandment, beset as he was with a grave malady which had him at death's very door, praying for recovery. Moreover, he claimed to be the victim of a heinous plot in which the awful hand of heretics could be discerned from beginning to end. While it was true that the six men hanged at Sarlat had been in his service, these villains, driven by shameful promises, had quit his household the previous day, stealing blunderbusses and horses for their dark purposes. They had, he claimed, hoped to sign on in the service of some religionaries, who, hiding their real beliefs, wanted to settle in that province and contaminate it. But as soon as his faithless servants arrived at their rendezvous with these devious and bloodthirsty Huguenots they were treacherously assassinated, both to give the impression that Fontenac had attacked them and to make off with arms and horses rightfully his. As for the prisoner, even if one were able to accept his testimony, since it was unique and unsupported (*testis unus, testis nullus*—a single witness is of no value), his tongue had obviously been bought by the Huguenots to besmirch the timeless honour of the Fontenac name. If Fontenac had been able to confront this miserable wretch, he surely would have recanted all his lies. But a very suspicious death (*fecit qui prodest*—he who profits from the crime must be its author) had intervened, ensuring his silence for the evident benefit of his accusers.

In sum, Fontenac demanded that the president of the Bordeaux parliament issue an injunction to Messieurs Siorac and Sauveterre stipulating the immediate return of his arms and his horses. So powerful was the spirit of partisanship in the last years of the reign of François I, and so general was the parliament's suspicion of any who even appeared to favour the heresy, that this brazen and specious letter from Fontenac shook the resolve of the Bordeaux president and his advisors despite Fontenac's execrable reputation throughout Guyenne. They immediately convoked not only our two captains, but also La Boétie, the two consuls of Sarlat, and François de Caumont, as delegate of the nobility, to establish the facts of the case. In addition, the parliament refused to hear the case unless the two captains agreed to submit to an interrogation of their beliefs. They consented to this stipulation on condition that their testimony be privately taken by the counsellor assigned to this interrogation.

This counsellor was a thoughtful, grey-haired gentleman of impeccable manners who apologized profusely to the two brothers before beginning his interrogation.

"Good Counsellor," said Siorac, "how can an accusation coming from such a thorough scoundrel be given any credence whatsoever?"

"Well, he is a good Catholic, however great his sins! He goes to Mass and to confession and takes Communion—he even attends retreats in a convent."

"What a pity that good works do not follow upon good words."

"I am happy," rejoined the counsellor, "to hear you speak of works. In your mind, is it by good works that a Christian can hope for salvation?"

Sauveterre's look darkened considerably, but Siorac responded without hesitation: "Certainly, that is how I understand the matter."

"You reassure me, Monsieur," smiled the counsellor. "But after all, I am not a great clerk and ask only the simplest questions which you can easily answer. Do you yourself regularly attend Mass?"

"Indeed so, Counsellor."

"Let us not stand on ceremony, I beg you. Do you mind answering simply 'yes' or 'no'?"

"As you wish."

"I shall continue, then. Do you honour the Holy Virgin and the saints?"

"Yes."

"Do your prayers invoke the intercession of the Virgin and the saints?"

"Yes."

"Do you respect the medallions, paintings, stained-glass windows and statues that represent them?"

"Yes."

"Do you accept spoken confession?"

"Yes."

"Do you believe in the real presence of God in the Eucharist?"
"Yes."

"Do you believe in Purgatory?"

"Yes."

"Do you believe that the Pope is the holy pontiff of the Roman, Apostolic, Catholic Church and that every Christian owes him obedience?"

"Yes."

"Do you worship the saints and the martyrs?"

"Yes."

"Next August in Sarlat, will you follow the procession in honour of the Virgin devoutly, bareheaded, candle in hand?"

"Yes."

The counsellor wanted to turn next to Sauveterre in order to pursue his inquisition, but Sauveterre rose and limped forward, speaking quite firmly and staring him down with his dark eyes: "Counsellor, my brother has responded excellently to all of your questions. Take his replies for my own. And pray conclude that our religion is in every respect the same as that of the king of France, whom we both served faithfully in the legion in Normandy."

This aggressive parry caught the counsellor quite off guard and he sensed that nothing was to be gained by pursuing the matter further. And yet he was not satisfied. For he was accustomed to the type of men who were drawn to the reformed religion like a nail to a magnet, and from this perspective the very virtues of the captains, their seriousness, knowledge and tranquil courage did not speak in their favour.

"These are honest men to be sure," the counsellor reported to the president of the parliament at the conclusion of his inquest. "They are free of any frivolity, weakness or faults of any kind. And yet they give lip service to the religion of the king. I detect a Huguenot odour about them."

"Despite your keen sense of smell," replied the president, "an odour is not sufficient to convict them. As long as they refrain from professing the plague of reform, they are not rebels against the king. Leave these questions of zeal to churchmen."

Whatever odour the parliament detected on Baron de Fontenac and whatever support this bandit received from them remained a mystery. "Lacking any material proof or irrefutable testimony", the

parliament ultimately banished him for twenty years from the seneschalty of Sarlat and from the domain of Domme, an act deemed
excessively clement throughout Guyenne.

On the way home, La Boétie left the consuls of Sarlat and
Caumont at their homes and then set out in advance to prepare
lodgings for the little company at Libourne, followed at some
distance by the "Brethren", as they were now popularly called,
touchingly joining them in a single noun as if they were one and
the same person.

"What a pity we are in such haste," remarked La Boétie, "for
otherwise we might have passed through Montaigne, and I could
have introduced you to a funny little twelve-year-old who has learnt
Latin from his father, and amazes everyone with his readings from
Ovid's *Metamorphoses*."

"This gentleman," said Siorac, "does very well to take the trouble
to instruct his son. We badly need knowledgeable men to lead us
out of our barbarism."

"Alas, knowledge and morality are not always sisters," lamented
La Boétie. "Fontenac is well enough educated."

"And the scoundrel used his letters well enough," cried Sauveterre.
"Twenty years of banishment for so many murders! My blood boils
at such evil."

"And he has only killed ten people," rejoined La Boétie. "What
should we do with the Baron d'Oppède, who has massacred the
peasants of Luberon by the hundred, confiscated their lands in the
name of the king and then secretly purchased them himself? He
is on trial now, but you can rest assured he'll emerge from it all as
white as the new-fallen snow."

"So it is in our sad world," said Sauveterre, "ceaselessly dragged
through blood and mire, and through the mendacious superstitions
that have corrupted the pure Word of God."

A silence followed these words. No one, not even Siorac, felt like picking up on Sauveterre's lead, least of all La Boétie.

"And who will occupy the barony of Fontenac for these twenty years of banishment?" asked Siorac.

"The baron's only son, Bertrand de Fontenac, who has just turned fifteen and is now of age." And La Boétie added after a moment's reflection: "Now you are rid of the old wolf, my friends, but there's still the cub. I have heard little good concerning this fellow, and since he's young, he may yet grow sharp teeth."

2

I WAS BORN on 28th March 1551, six years after the acquisition of Mespech by the Brethren, when its appearance had already considerably changed. Actually the captains made few changes in the chateau itself: it was a huge rectangular construction of two stories built around an interior courtyard and flanked at each corner by towers with machicolations, and these were joined by a crenellated battlement walk.

When they bought it, however, the chateau was surrounded only by an embryonic moat, scarcely a toise wide and so shallow that a small person, if thrown in, could easily regain his footing. Obviously, this was a ridiculous defence. Such a moat rendered the drawbridge leading to the chateau's fortified south gate totally superfluous. Any attacker could have easily waded across the moat and thrown up a ladder against the ramparts, anchoring it in the mud at the foot of the wall.

The technology and inventiveness that the captains dedicated to their modifications of these moats could not have succeeded without one lucky circumstance: the well dug in a corner of the interior courtyard at Mespech turned out to be inexhaustible. The Brethren discovered this when, a short time after the sale, they set about emptying the well to purify it. In the middle of August, during a severe drought, they began work in pairs with buckets, but since the water level remained constant, and the well's circumference

permitted it, the work crew expanded to three, to four, then five...
At eight men strong, the level began to recede somewhat, and they
redoubled their efforts. Ultimately the level was lowered enough to
reveal a split in the bedrock the size of a fist, through which water
gushed in a steady stream. The captains sounded a retreat before
this friendly assault and the water quickly rose to its usual level and
gushed into the conduit which empties into the moat.

Before beginning work on the moat, they would have to deviate
this overflow and this work would have to wait until after harvest
time, given the large numbers of men needed to dig the excavations
required by the captains' plans. In addition to our own soldiers, servants and neighbours, day labourers were hired and fed, the Brethren
sparing no expense to accomplish their grand project. Their idea
was to dig a veritable pond a toise deep and seven wide around the
entire circumference of Mespech. And thus, Mespech became an
island, linked to the continent by a scheme so ingenious, so beautiful and so well defended that I've never seen a visitor to our manor
who wasn't deeply impressed by it.

Indeed, the drawbridge and fortified gate do not connect to the
land, but instead to a small tower several toises shorter than the castle
gate. This little tower is surrounded by water and itself connects, by
means of a second drawbridge, to an island five toises square. This
island, surrounded by a high wall, pierced by loopholes, is made up
of outbuildings, including a shed for ploughs, ricks, harrows and
other cumbersome farm machinery, as well as a wash house built
on the side facing Mespech. Another tower at the far end of this
island, where the moat narrows, houses a third drawbridge, this one
giving access to "terra firma", as we now call it.

The narrowness of these three protected passageways elimi-
nates two-way traffic and slows the movement of our wagons when
we are harvesting, haying or bringing in the animals. At night,

everything must be brought within the courtyard of Mespech for protection—except of course the heavy machinery, which would be too cumbersome a nightly task and which is therefore stored on the island. But the extent and depth of the water surrounding us and the three drawbridges which separate us from the land all produce a very comforting sense of security which somehow contributes to the beauty of the place.

For a long time I believed this disposition, as pleasing to the eye as it was useful for defence, to be unique in France. But once when I was much older and was racing through hill and dale, hotly pursued by a band of savage, murderous Moors intent on taking my purse, my horse and my life, I caught sight of a chateau which greatly resembled Mespech in the layout of its moats and of the small towers which commanded its defence. I hardly had time to visit this place, however, given the band of twenty brigands on my heels. Though my valiant black steed delivered me from that fateful encounter, I was never able to retrace my path to this attractive dwelling whose resemblance to Mespech set my heart pounding, as if it weren't beating hard enough already from the danger I'd confronted. All I can say is that it's somewhere in the Bordeaux region, not far from the city itself.

On the far side of the moat, close to hand and easy to irrigate, we laid out the kitchen gardens and our fruit orchards, and, a little farther down the hill, so that they wouldn't spoil the view, our walnut trees. These last we planted plentifully, hoping to extract enough oil for our own use and for sale. The entire area, woods and gardens we enclosed with a high stockade of sharpened and fire-hardened chestnut stakes. We also laid out below the palisade rows of caltrops to catch any marauders who might attempt to steal our fruits and vegetables by night. Alas, the poverty of our poor Périgord region is now so acute, and so great the number of homeless driven by hunger out of the mountains of the Auvergne, that not a summer passes without finding some poor beggar in our orchards, barefoot and bleeding, mouth agape and fists clenched in pain, doggedly limping towards our gardens, knowing full well that feudal law condemns him to be hanged if caught.

My mother used to weep over these hangings, but the Brethren pointed out that, given the extreme weakness and hunger of these poor fellows, their trap wound would never heal, and that to allow them to wander off limping and bleeding merely condemned them to the agonies of a prolonged death. My mother finally got them to agree to knock these poor devils senseless before hanging them and not to leave their bodies to rot on the gallows as was the custom.

Since her intervention, we have given a decent burial to an entire cemetery full of these tramps in a rocky corner of our land where not even dandelions would grow. My mother used to go there the first Sunday of every month to pray for their souls, escorted by Barberine, the wet nurse who carried me in her arms, little Hélix, her inseparable daughter, and Cabusse, fully armed, since neither spouse nor children were allowed outside the walls of Mespech without escort. Later on, when these rules were relaxed, I used to play with Hélix in the marauders' field. These poor souls, who went so hungry throughout life, provided rich nourishment to our fields after their death. For now the grass there grows green, and in springtime the field is buried under a profusion of bright yellow daffodils which no one dares pick. It is said in these parts that when one of these flowers is picked it utters a baleful moan and that whoever picks it is condemned to a life of hunger.

One year after the purchase of Mespech, my father married Isabelle de Caumont, whose blue eyes, blonde hair and medallion had made such a lively impression on him when he and Sauveterre had visited Castelnau for the first time. At fifteen, Isabelle was in the flower of her youth, "tall in stature, with firm and sumptuous breasts, long legs and small feet". My father composed this description on the first page of his *Book of Reason*, begun on his marriage day, 16th September 1546. He noted as well that he was thirty-two years old, his wife but fifteen, that she was of sweet temperament, healthy in body, very pleasing company, of a gay and even disposition (although strong-minded at times), and a good Christian, despite her penchant for idolatry. "The wedding, bridal clothes, gifts to the clergy, dona-tions to the poor and the two dinners," I read subsequently, "cost 500 livres, a modest sum," my father concludes, "considering the noble customs of the day." To which Sauveterre, in his tiny spidery handwriting, added in the margin, "Still too much. Five hundred livres is the price of a handsome piece of work."

Not that the Brethren, on this occasion, were divided. Since he was now too old to marry, Jean de Sauveterre was content that Jean de Siorac should continue his line, so that at least one branch of the Brethren should take root, flourish and bear heirs to whom Mespech could be willed. But Isabelle's medallion disturbed him somewhat, as well as the sudden intrusion of so many women into Mespech. For Isabelle brought with her not only her chambermaid Cathau, but also, a year later, the wet nurse Barberine, with little Hélix, whom she nursed along with my mother's first child, my elder brother, François de Siorac.

Though very economical with the Brethren's wealth and most desirous of increasing it, Sauveterre could hardly complain that Isabelle came empty-handed to Mespech. For, besides her connec-tions to the Périgord nobility, she brought 2,000 écus, a beautiful forest of hardwood, a field large enough to graze two or three cattle along the road to Ayzies, and, just three leagues beyond it, an excel-lent and accessible sandstone quarry.

The Brethren always turned everything to good use, selling off surplus grain, hay, wool, honey, walnut oil, pork or horseflesh, and thus hoped to make a good profit from this quarry at a time when many burghers were starting to build chateaux outside the towns, as much for show as for convenience.

On the Sunday following the wedding, the captains had the town crier in Sarlat announce with great fanfare that any stonemason living in the town or its environs should present himself to the captains on the next Sunday before the church. But, the very next day, a bearded fellow appeared at our outer drawbridge, as tall in stature as he was broad of shoulder. His heavy linen shirt, tied at the waist, revealed a chest thickly matted with black hair and his sandals were laced to ankles and knees with leather thongs. He was heavily laden, wearing slung across his back an English longbow, and at his belt a large bowl, an impressive cutlass and a quiver full of arrows. In addition, a large wooden box was slung on a strap over his right shoulder. His large feet, bare except for the sandals, were covered with dust, but his head was covered by a pointed felt hat which he doffed the minute the captains appeared in the tower window above the drawbridge.

"Messieurs," he cried, "I am the stonecutter you're looking for. My name is Jonas."

"But you are to meet us in front of the church at Sarlat next Sunday," replied Sauveterre. "Couldn't you wait?"

"I could wait well enough!" cried Jonas. "It's my body that needs bread."

"What are you doing with an English longbow?"

"I hunt with it when townships and barons give me leave to do so."

"You wouldn't be a bit of a poacher, now, would you?"

"Surely not!" protested Jonas. "That's a capital crime! Never would I do such a thing! I've only got one throat and that's to drink with, to eat with and to breathe God's air with."

Siorac burst out laughing: "And what is this great box you carry on your back?"

With a dip of his shoulder, Jonas eased the chest to the ground and opened it. "My stonecutter's tools."

Standing, dark-skinned, black of beard, his large hands trembling slightly at the end of his brawny arms, he waited, gazing fixedly at the captains.

"Where are you from, Jonas?" asked Sauveterre, and, because the captain had addressed him by name, Jonas threw him a grateful look.

"From the mountains of Auvergne. My village is called Marcolès. The quarry I worked is all used up."

"Jonas," said Siorac, "are you a good marksman with that bow?"

"At your service, my good captains."

"Can you hit that crow who's just occupied the top of our walnut tree?"

Turning in search of the insolent crow, Jonas tested the air and replied, "'Tis as good as done, if the wind's not against me!" Seizing his weapon, he fit an arrow, steadied himself, bent the bow until the string touched the point of his nose and the tip of his chin, and, without seeming to aim, let fly his shaft. The arrow whistled through the air and the crow, pierced through, dropped through the branches with a great flutter of wings and leaves.

"Well done!" cried Siorac.

"The English," Sauveterre noted, "still maintain their companies of archers. Perhaps they're right. Jean, we've seen more than one battle lost because the rain has dampened the fuses of the arquebuses. So, my good Jonas," he continued, turning to this worthy, "are you as good a stonecutter as you are an archer?"

"Indeed so!" replied Jonas with pride. "I know my trade as well as any man alive, and I take pleasure in it. I can not only cut stone from the quarry, I know how to split it into roofing tiles. I can shape blocks for your walls and can round them for your towers. I can set a straight lintel in the ground for a door or a window; I can build you a semicircular arch or set a triple arch with every stone at the correct angle and drop in the keystone perfectly. I can construct transom windows or double-columned ones with capitals. And if I have to climb a ladder and place and mortar a stone as heavy as I am, I can do that too."

"Can you read and write?"

"Alas, no, but I can count, number stones and understand a design if it's got only figures on it. I can use a ruler, a compass, a plumb line and a square."

The two captains exchanged glances. "Jonas," announced Sauveterre, "we'll try you out for three months, with food and lodging. At the end of three months, if we hire you, you'll get two sols a day plus bed and board."

Those were honest enough conditions for the time, but thirty years later, with the cost of living considerably augmented—and the price of cut stone as well—Jonas still earned his two sols a day, with no hope of exhausting his quarry before it exhausted him, and yet professed himself happy enough, as he put it, to use his two large arms to nourish his large body, when there were so many in the region who had no work.

"Messieurs," rejoined Jonas, "before I came to you, I went to see your quarry. If the woods and the field above belong to you, I would like permission to hunt there. I'll give you three quarters of everything I bag, keeping one quarter for myself, which will save you that much salt beef which you would have given me for my board. Also, if you give me a she-goat for the field, I'll raise kids for you in return for the milk she'll provide me."

"We'll consider it," answered Sauveterre.

"In the quarry," continued Jonas, "I discovered a very deep cave. If you'd be so good as to furnish me a mattress of chestnut leaves, I'll live there summer and winter, so as not to lose time walking back and forth that would be better spent in my work. Anyway, who would guard my cut stone if I don't live where I work?"

Thus did Jonas give account of himself on the day he arrived, and so he is still today: more worried about his masters' interests than his own, having entered Mespech the way others enter a monastery. Not that our stonecutter was without a taste for life, or didn't enjoy a bottle at our Sunday table, a game or a story by the evening fire—nor was he unresponsive when a sorceress came to tempt him in his cave—but that is a story for another time.

My mother was five months pregnant with my elder brother when La Boétie returned from the capital, on 21st April 1547, with all manner of stories concerning the death of François I. Our police lieutenant had gone up to Paris with a large escort in order to solicit the king's favour regarding some matter of great importance to him, but which my father neglected to explain in the *Book of Reason*, although he wrote down everything else there: meetings, conversations, as well as the prices of things. I read there, for example, that on the preceding Saturday, my father journeyed to Sarlat to buy a hundred pins for my mother (five sols), shoes for Cabusse (five sols, two deniers) and shoes for his pony (two sols), and that he enjoyed "an excellent repast" at the Auberge de la Rigaudie for eight sols.

I quote this entry because it contrasts so dramatically with what follows. La Boétie found a great to-do at the court, sad faces and hopeful ones mingling together—the former all too obvious, the latter hypocritically disguised—none, however, sincere, except for the real suffering of the dauphin and the despair of Madame d'Étampes, the king's favourite, who was already packing her bags. As for the king himself, whom La Boétie only glimpsed from afar, he seemed much changed, his face thinned greatly, his body bent and his movements agonizingly slowed.

"Monsieur de La Boétie," said Siorac, "allow me to interrupt you. My brother is laid up in his room, in some distress from an old leg wound. Would you be willing to continue this narrative in his tower chambers? He would be greatly chagrined to have missed your story."

The east tower to which Siorac referred is reached by a winding staircase set in a smaller adjoining tower. Our chapel occupies the ground floor of this tower, Sauveterre's rooms the first. The room adjoining his bedroom is a small study, where our uncle spends much of his time; the chimney draws well and the window looks out onto the courtyard so that Sauveterre can keep an eye on the comings and goings of our servants. "'Tis nothing serious, Lieutenant," grimaced Sauveterre to his guest, unable to rise to greet him, "my leg cramps up once or twice a month and all will be well tomorrow."

"So I will hope with all my heart," answered La Boétie, settling himself with a groan. "My own posterior is sore enough from all the riding I have just done, which has brought me naught but vexation. I had scarcely arrived at court when the king decided to move. Despite his deplorable health, he seems unable to stay in one place. You'd think he felt death stealing about him, given his haste to flee from one chateau to the next: from Saint-Germain to la Muette, from la Muette to Villepreux-lès-Clayes, then on to Dampierre, to Limours, to Rochefort-en-Yvelines… All I could do was follow him about, unable to approach him, paying good money for my escort's lodgings to all the rascally innkeepers of the royal territories who charge two sols a day just for hay for the horses! What's more, they mock my guards' speech, which is as good as any man of theirs."

"Ah, to be sure," agreed Sauveterre. "Our speech is the purer!"

"At Rochefort-en-Yvelines I had a more hopeful moment," La Boétie continued. "The king was feeling better and mounted his horse to go hunting three days in a row. After which he ate and drank to excess as usual."

"He went riding with an abscess!" exclaimed Siorac. "What madness!"

"Perhaps," said La Boétie naively, "the king hoped the ride would drain the abscess. But after three days he was much the worse off and beset by a running fever. He ordered them to bring him to Rambouillet where, trying to deny the gravity of his illness, he said he wanted to 'take his pleasure in hunting and birding'. On 21st March I was finally admitted to the Château de Rambouillet, only to learn that they were operating on the king. Afterwards, he sank into the slow pangs of death. On 30th March the dauphin asked for his benediction, and while the king was giving it, the dauphin fainted on his bed and the king held him as closely as though he would die if he let go of him.

"Finally they led the dauphin Henri away into the dauphine's room where he threw himself face down on the bed with his boots on, stricken with grief. Catherine de' Medici, seeing her husband in this state, fell to the floor weeping and disconsolate. François de Guise, taking scarce more note of her than of his future king, paced stiffly back and forth in the room, a superb defiance on his face, his heels ringing on the floorboards. Diane de Poitiers, Henri's mistress, sat stiffly nearby, triumphant and smiling. Guise stopped his pacing long enough to address her, and, with a gesture in the direction of the king's room, sneered derisively, 'He's leaving us, the old fop!'"

"Did you get this incredible story on good authority?" stammered Siorac. "So much insolence towards his dying master? Is it possible?"

"I have it from an excellent source," replied La Boétie, somewhat testily, "and I can also assure you that the king, who was entirely in possession of his wits when he confessed, declared out loud—this has been confirmed by many different people—that he 'had no remorse on his conscience, never having done any injustice to anyone in this world'."

Sauveterre started violently in his chair. "Has he forgotten the massacres of the Vaudois of Luberon? Mérindol and Cabrières seemed to have slipped his mind!" he growled. "But he must be counting on Purgatory to purge him of these venial sins!" He pronounced "Purgatory" with a scornful irony that seemed to put La Boétie ill at ease.

"Monsieur de La Boétie," Siorac said hastily, "do you think Diane still holds sway over the new king? After all, Henri is twenty-eight, she is already forty-eight and the younger lionesses of the court might yet steal her prey."

"Ah, but Diane is still a beauty," replied La Boétie, happy to find himself on more familiar ground. "I can't guarantee the face, which shows a few cracks here and there despite all her artifices, but her body is superb, and the young king gawks at her like the day she deflowered him. Do you know that after dinner every night, he visits her to tell her of the day's affairs of state and sits on her lap? On her lap, I tell you! He plays her songs on the guitar, interrupting himself to exclaim to the constable as he fondles her breasts: 'Look, Montmorency, what a figure she cuts!' In truth, the new king is a gawking child. He looks at Diane as if he were completely surprised by her friendship. She'll do with him whatever she pleases."

"And whatever pleases Guise, the clergy and Montmorency," added Sauveterre sombrely. "Well, so much for peace in the kingdom of France. We are going to witness a very Spanish Inquisition in our poor country, with endless tortures."

"So I fear," agreed La Boétie, adding after a moment's reflection, "'Tis neither my duty nor my inclination to question your religious practices, but aren't you somewhat imprudent? The vicar general complains that he never sees you at Mass in Sarlat any more."

"For my part, I must complain that the 500 livres we donated to the Church expressly for the maimed veterans of this parish when we purchased Mespech have never found their way into their hands."

"I like you too well to echo these foolhardy words to anyone," cautioned La Boétie. "You'd never be forgiven."

"But truth be told," rejoined Siorac, whose smile lit up his eyes, "you may reassure the vicar general that we hear Mass every Sunday right here, thanks to the opening in the wall that communicates with the chapel beneath us in this very tower. We donate five sols every Sunday to the curate of Marcuays so that he will say Mass at noon every Sabbath. Madame de Siorac, the children and all our servants attend Mass in the chapel, and we are able to listen from this study where my brother is laid up, as you know, by his war wounds."

Sauveterre was only half mistaken. Henri II (or rather those who controlled his life, for he was only a plaything in their hands) did not succeed in creating a Spanish-style Inquisition in France, despite the Pope's pleas for one: the resistance of the great bodies of state was too fierce. But he multiplied the edicts and created within the Paris parliament the sinister *chambre ardente*, which imprisoned a great number of the reformed in the Conciergerie fortress before dragging them to their execution at the place Maubert. There they were tied to hastily erected stakes and burnt alive in great fires, their bodies consumed and reduced to ashes. I find in one of my father's entries in the *Book of Reason* of about this date an echo of the ongoing discussion between the two brothers as to whether they should openly declare their support for the Reformation. Sauveterre felt that the times required that they sign their faith in blood. Siorac held, on the contrary, that in making such a declaration during a period of persecution they would merely add to the list of martyrs without contributing in any way to the cause. It was much better, in his view, to wait until the party of the Huguenots had gained enough strength in the region and in the kingdom to allow some hope of vanquishing their enemies.

If Sauveterre had been left to his own devices, he would have taken up his cross without further ado, and run headlong to his own death, so great was his dislike of dissimulation, and so violent was his agitation at seeing the errors of the papists (as he called them) gain credence throughout the land. If he restrained himself, it was not out of any fear of the stake—his austere management of the wealth of Mespech was ample proof of his disdain for this world—but rather out of fear of making his way alone, and without his beloved brother, to the felicities of eternal life. I read in a touching marginal note added by Sauveterre to my father's entry of 12th June 1552, "I arose today at five o'clock and looked out of my window at the pure sky and the sun shining on the foliage, the birds singing by the thousands. And yet, what is all of this compared to the happiness and the glory we will know in Our Lord when we have left our mortal remains here below? Oh, Jean, how you do delay! Of course I know that you would feel a deep sadness in leaving behind Mespech and your family, but think only what measure of thing you leave behind in comparison to what you will receive in the life hereafter."

To which my father wrote in reply on the following day: "We did not take Mespech from the mouth of the wolf only to abandon it to the wolf cubs. The same goes for my wife and beloved children, François and Pierre." This is the first time that I am mentioned by name in the *Book of Reason*, along with my elder brother.

Continuing their dialogue on paper, my father later entered an argument which must have touched Sauveterre even more deeply:

"It is written in the Holy Book: 'If thou obeyst the voice of the Lord, blessed will be the offspring of thy cattle, blessed thy fruits and thy honey.' Certainly, in this respect, we have no reason to complain of Mespech. Is this not the proof that our house is seen as the house of God, since He makes us to prosper in this world, as is promised in the Scriptures? Must we think of destroying everything He has built and ourselves destroy the roof over our heads, our descendants, our servants and our flocks, giving ourselves to the stake and Mespech to the papists? No, my brother, we owe the truth in our hearts only to God, whereas to the enemies of God that we have encountered thus far we owe only ruses and lies: to the Devil go the fruits of the Devil..."

And so, every Sunday, while the curate of Marcuays said Mass to Isabelle de Siorac and to our servants in the chapel on the ground floor of the east tower, the two brothers, deaf to the Latin intonations of the Mass filtering through the grate from below, softly chanted the Psalms of David in their first-floor library.

In the midst of the many benedictions which the Lord rained down on Mespech, there were nevertheless a few afflictions, and among these were the premature deaths of three children, whose names are entered in the *Book of Reason*. But I must guard against any implication that these were punishments from on high. For there was no family in France of this century exempt from such grief, and some mourned more than half of the children they brought into this world.

In entries in the *Book of Reason* dated a few months before my birth, I read repeated notes from Sauveterre, "I pray for you, Jean," which of course excited my curiosity, especially since my father never answered them. What sickness did Jean de Siorac have that should provoke his brother's repeated prayers, and what sudden attack of ingratitude kept my father from ever thanking his brother for these orisons?

I must confess here what I but guessed during my childhood, and only fully understood much later. Between my father and my mother, almost from the first day of their marriage, there raged a small war of religion, which, whether latent or openly engaged, knew no respite. For Isabelle not only never consented to renounce the cult of her fathers, but also, on the strength of a thoughtless agreement concluded with Jean de Siorac before their marriage, declared her intention to raise her children according to the Catholic rites. When it was my turn to be born, my father wanted to give me a biblical name. Isabelle adamantly refused. Hardly had I uttered my first cry in this vale of tears when Barberine was sent to fetch the curate and she maliciously had me baptized Pierre, since upon this rock His Church had been built.

Doubtless she had other reasons for her scornful fury, since, but a short week after my own arrival, a girl in Taniès gave birth to a son whom Jean de Siorac named Samson, signifying that, by the grace of God, this lad would be bigger and stronger than any of his sons baptized in the Catholic faith. Which turned out to be true for my brother François, but not for me.

My half-brother Samson's mother was a shepherdess named Jehanne Masure, a beautiful and good girl, according to our nurse Barberine, but whose parents were dreadfully poor, if I am to judge by the many loans of grain, hay, salt pork and money that were sent their way by Jean de Siorac. These gifts coincide exactly with the entry in the *Book of Reason* in which Jean de Sauveterre first began to pray for his brother. As I flip through the pages of the book, this largesse seems to multiply—especially in lean years—and I find Sauveterre's pointed questions next to each notation of these loans: "To be repaid when?" To which my father invariably responded: "When it pleases me to ask." But it never pleased him to do so, for the loans continued over the months and years and were never repaid.

A few pages further, opposite the notation of a particularly generous sum, Sauveterre wrote: "Is this not shameful?" To which Siorac impatiently replied: "Jacob knew Leah, and then he knew Rachel and the servingwomen of his wives, and from these came forth the strongest and most beautiful tribe of the Hebrews ever to serve the Lord. Would it not be a greater shame to allow my son Samson to run barefoot, ill clad and hungry like a wolf? Rest assured that when the time is ripe for his education, Samson will live at Mespech with his brothers."

But Samson moved to Mespech sooner than anticipated, for in November of 1554—when we were both three years old—the plague broke out in Taniès, and, hearing this, my father had his horse saddled within the hour, galloped to Jehanne's house, bringing her enough nourishment for a month since the village would soon be quarantined for the duration of the epidemic. Jehanne begged my father to take Samson with him, which he did, burning all of the boy's clothes upon his return to Mespech and washing the child in hot water after rubbing him with ashes and cutting his hair.

A great commotion among our servants ensued, doubtless fomented by my mother's mercurial nature, against this intruder who was "bringing the contagion". But my father put a quick end to it by isolating himself with the boy in the west tower, nourishing him by his own hand for forty days, never once stepping beyond the threshold of the tower, where eating and reading matter were left each day according to his orders.

When Jean de Siorac finally emerged from his seclusion, it was only to learn that Jehanne Masure had died along with her entire family, the plague having carried off half the village. Among the victims was my uncle, Raymond Siorac, but his two sons were spared—the same who, on the eve of the purchase of Mespech, had helped Cabusse to exterminate the rascals from Fontenac down in les Beunes.

Samson emerged from the tower a strong and beautiful lad, with thick, curly hair, whose reddish-blond tint recalled his great-grandfather Charles's.

I was his age and size and I loved him from the minute I set eyes on him. The only thing I resented, though it surely wasn't his fault, was that Samson enjoyed from the outset the privilege of going to "hear Mass" with the Brethren upstairs in Sauveterre's study whereas I had to remain downstairs in the chapel with François, listening to the Latin verses, hanging on to Barberine's skirts. I had no other recourse than to make faces at little seven-year-old Hélix, who, hidden from her mother's view, returned grimace for grimace, a practice we laughingly continued through the years, for she was a little scoundrel, as the rest of my story will bear out.

The lovable shepherdess was no more, but the fruit of her womb lived on within the walls of Mespech, more handsome and shining with his milky complexion and red hair than any illegitimate child who ever lived. Every God-given day (doubtless the work of the Devil, as well, as a punishment for my father) Jean Siorac was assailed by a flood of marital discomforts. On one occasion he entered a melancholy quote from the Bible in his *Book of Reason*: "A querulous woman is like a rainy day." And added a bit further on: "A woman's hair is long, but longer still her tongue." And two pages later Isabelle's Catholicism sticks in his craw: "Oh the hard-headedness of woman! This terrible abscess in her will, which nothing has ever been able to pierce! And her fatal attachment to error!" To which Sauveterre adds in the margin, substituting for his usual ceremonial *"vous"* a fraternal *"tu"*: "Would it not have been wiser to marry a woman of your own faith? Though her breast lay underneath her medallion, it nevertheless hid her Catholic icon from your sight." This old complaint resurfacing on such an occasion blindsided my father from the left, while he was heavily besieged on the right. It was not a very wounding comment for all that, since one can just as well imagine an equally intractable Huguenot wife.

Good things don't always come easily, yet despite all the groans and opposition Samson was now among us, good looks and all, bringing to three the number of sons Siorac could count at his table. As streams flow into rivers, prosperity grows fat, sometimes even at others' expense. The plague, by carrying off half the families in Taniès, had left much property untended, which the Brethren were able to purchase at greatly advantageous prices.

What heir would have wanted to live in a village where sickness could flare up any day out of the infected soil or the evil vapours emanating from it? For less than 3,000 livres, Mespech grew piece by piece to half its size again in the hillsides of Taniès, including a wood of beautiful chestnut trees, now fully grown and ready for cutting, suitable for heavy beams or woodworking and easily worth double the price paid for the property. But the Brethren, always on the lookout for any providential occurrence that might add to its "basket and store" conceived by chance or by inspiration a project that was more profitable yet.

One Saturday, Sauveterre was doing his marketing at Sarlat, when he spied before him on the church square a little dark man limping along carrying a box on his back. "Greetings, friend," said Sauveterre, in a military but cordial way, "where did you catch that limp?" The dark little fellow turned in his tracks, looked long and hard at Sauveterre, placed his box on the ground and removed his cap. "I didn't catch it," he replied, "it caught me, and it was moving right smartly, the bullet that gave it to me at Ceresole."

"At Ceresole? So you were a soldier!"

"Ay, an armourer in the legion of Guyenne."

"And who was the commanding officer at Ceresole?"

This question was, of course, a trap, but the soldier replied evasively by naming the field general.

"D'Enghien."

"And did your captain give you honorary discharge?"

"That he did! The paper is in my box. Would you read it?"

"Soldier," replied Sauveterre, "you should not be so quick to show your papers. Someone might take them from you."

"Monsieur, you do not appear to be 'someone', or a thief."

"I am Captain de Sauveterre of the Norman legion. And I caught my limp in the same place and on the same day as yourself."

The soldier gaped in disbelief and then immediately in joy, so clearly did this meeting augur well for him.

"And what are you doing here, soldier?" continued Sauveterre.

"I am seeking a job as a cooper. They call me Faujanet and I'm twenty-nine years old." And opening his toolbox, he brought out a tiny barrel merely three inches high, but in every respect similar to a wine cask, with its casings and sluice hole. Handing it to Sauveterre, he announced, "Here is my work, Captain. And what I have done in miniature here, I can do full-size as well."

Sauveterre, fully enjoying the feel of it, turned the little cask in his hand. "Faujanet," he said (pronouncing it "Faujanette" in our Périgordian way), "this is good work and finely cut and it speaks well of you. But it's made of chestnut and not oak."

"No one makes casks of oak any more," replied Faujanet. "The wine growers won't have 'em. They claim oak gives the wine a bad taste."

Sauveterre stood for a long while contemplating Faujanet, who held his breath and swallowed hard given the gravity of the moment. He had been out of work for two months and had had nothing to eat since the night before, and only a bowl of oily soup and a fistful of beans the night before that, thanks to the charity of the town.

But he had been told that this was an act of generosity that would not be repeated, and that his entry permit to Sarlat would expire the next day, Sunday, at noon.

Slowly, carefully, Sauveterre examined the cooper, his build, his arms, his face, his robust neck and his honest expression. "Let me see your discharge," he requested. Faujanet fumbled through his box and held out the paper with a trembling hand. Sauveterre unfolded it and read it, one eyebrow registering his concentration. "Faujanet, have you received any aid from the Sarlat consuls?"

"To be sure, my captain, the day before yesterday when I showed them my discharge slip."

"And from the diocese?"

"Not a crumb."

"Well, you know the proverb," replied Sauveterre, lowering his voice somewhat, "monks and lice are never satisfied. To them everything tastes good, even crumbs."

"Right you are," agreed Faujanet. "Those people do more damage with their mouths than with their swords."

Sauveterre, laughing, handed Faujanet his paper and Faujanet began to feel that things might just be going his way. As his heart leapt, it brought with it the reminder of acute hunger.

"My chestnut trees are still standing, Faujanet," cautioned Sauveterre. "Can you play both lumberjack and sawmiller?"

"With help, yes I can."

"We'll give you a try for three months with room and board. After that, three sols a day. Agreed?"

"Agreed, Captain!"

"Cabusse!" called Sauveterre, and Cabusse came running, tall and brawny, his ruddy face barred with a formidable moustache. "Cabusse, this is Faujanet, a veteran of the legion of Guyenne. He's to be our cooper. Take him over to our wagon and wait for me there."

Cabusse, who stood a head taller than Faujanet, watched him limp along at his side pushing through the market-day crowds.

"That will make two with a limp at Mespech," he remarked. "Two peg legs and an iron arm."

"An iron arm?"

"Coulondre. He has a hook in place of his left hand. It's Siorac who had it made for him."

He relieved Faujanet of his box and had him clamber up beside him on the wagon. Once seated, Cabusse took from his sack a piece of bread and an onion and, knife in hand, began to eat deliberately, mute, his eyes glued to the horses' ears. Faujanet tried to keep from drooling. After a moment of feeling Faujanet's eyes on him, Cabusse turned to look at his companion. "Are you hungry?"

"Lord, yes!"

"The Lord gave you a tongue, soldier! You should have said so!"

Cabusse cut his bread and his onion and held out half of each to Faujanet. This latter took them so avidly that he neglected to thank his new friend.

"Don't gorge on an empty stomach," warned Cabusse, "lest it swell and burst your liver."

"You're right!" agreed Faujanet, but could scarce slow his pace or reduce the size of his mouthfuls. When he had finished, Cabusse offered him a gourd.

"You've stoked up too fast. Now you need to let the bottle keep you from your feed or you'll die from the blockage of your bowels."

Faujanet drank as fast as he had eaten, then sat up straight, squared his shoulders, threw out his chest and, from his perch atop the wagon, surveyed the market crowds below, like a swimmer who has just been pulled from the sea where he was drowning. Opening his big eyes wide, he took in the horse, his robust croup, Cabusse and his hefty trunk, the solid, new, handsome wagon on which he sat, and then looked proudly around him. He now belonged to the world of happy people: those who eat.

"How is the master?" he asked Cabusse in hushed tones.

"We have no master," replied Cabusse. "We have two captains. We: that's Coulondre, called Iron-arm, Cockeyed Marsal and me. We're all veterans of the Norman legion."

"So how are the captains?" repeated Faujanet. Cabusse gave a quick glance around.

"They don't pay better than the going wage," he said. "And as for the work, they're hard on themselves and hard on their people. But it's not a house in which the master eats good wheat bread and the servants eat rotten, pasty barley bread. We eat the same food and at the same table as the captains."

"This is a good thing," said Faujanet licking his lips.

"It's good for the paunch," rejoined Cabusse, "but not so good for your freedoms. You can't say anything you want at the captains' table, nor can you do anything you please. The captains have no truck with lechery."

"Oh well, as for that, you can taste beauty but you can't eat it," said Faujanet.

"Hunger doesn't just strike your stomach," replied Cabusse. "There's the other kind. And the poor beast can have too much bridle. Not so much as a gallant word to the chambermaid, nor a pinch either, and if you stumble on the wet nurse you'll be out of a job! Yet you surely wouldn't hurt yourself falling on her. Alas, they may well say 'A mouse without hole is soon caught,' but at Mespech it's not so," he smiled.

"And how is the other captain?" asked Faujanet, abstaining from any comment and not even daring to smile in response to this proverb.

"One is as good as the other when it comes to work. But as to the other matter, the second one would be more easy-going. He is married and has three children. No, four," he said, correcting himself with a smile and a wink.

So well made were Faujanet's barrels that five years later you could find his work throughout the Sarlat region and as far away as Périgueux. To their noble friends, who raised an eyebrow over this commerce, the Brethren pointed out that it was better to grow rich by selling casks and cut stone than by thievery and highway robbery as some barons did. Moreover, the captains avoided frequenting the expensive festivities given at the other chateaux, using Sauveterre's injury as their excuse, but, in reality, with an eye to the expense that would inevitably come from reciprocating such invitations. They did invite their friends, but always in small groups and for dinner only—no dancing, singing, games or wasted candles, a parsimony which annoyed my mother no little bit since she would have preferred more pomp and gaiety.

And yet, despite their prosperity, the Brethren had little reason to rejoice. Henri II's persecution of the reformers had not abated, quite the contrary. On his orders, many notable people were attacked who had until now been spared. For most of the Périgordians, the king was a distant character whom no one, except perhaps a few noblemen, would ever see, and who counted little in their daily lives, except when royal officers came collecting tithes. But for the reformers, whom he crushed mercilessly, Henri II was as real as the thongs, the gibbet, the stake, the flames that leapt from the pyre or the smoke that choked the cities with the awful smell of their burning flesh.

I see in the *Book of Reason* that the reformers or those who hid their Protestantism wondered much about Henri's character. But in truth, those who had approached him concluded that there was nothing to understand. As affectionate as a young dog, very attached to Diane and to Montmorency, to his children and even to his wife, at the age of thirty-eight Henri II was but a bearded and large-jawed boy, whose vacant eyes gaped stupidly at the world around him. He was cruel only through lack of imagination. Ten years of reigning had left him virtually unchanged from the lad who had been pulled in tears from the arms of his dying father. He excelled at tennis, hunting and jousting, but his mind had never been awakened and he depended on others for his ideas—even the simplest ones.

The king considered the Reformation like the "sickness of the plague". But even this metaphor wasn't his; he'd had to be prompted. He said as well that he wanted "to see his people cleaned and spared such a dangerous plague and vermin as these heresies". But this was the language of the priests and preachers he had heard thousands of times and which consequently he believed to be true. Fearing that this "sickness", or "vermin", or "plague" might spread throughout the kingdom and endanger the royal power, he sought to root it out by edicts, torture chambers, imprisonment, inquisition and fire. As books coming from abroad might also carry this contagion, they were burnt. The tongues of the most resolute Protestant martyrs had to be cut lest, from atop their funeral pyres, their professions of faith contaminate the populace. The king could not understand how this "sickness", despite all such remedies, continued to spread and find purchase among the royal officers, the nobles, the great lords and even in the parliaments which were supposed to combat it.

Ten years of persecution had taught the king nothing about those he persecuted. Lacking reflection or dignity, he lived dully in the rut of his habits, between his wife, Catherine de' Medici, and Diane de Poitiers, now fifty-nine years old. The two women, each fearful of the other, had decided to make their peace and to share the king amicably. When Henri forgot about Catherine on Diane's lap, dazzled as if for the first time by her sexagenarian breasts, Diane would firmly remind him of his conjugal duties and push him into bed with his wife.

As for politics, unable to decide anything alone, the king lent one ear to Montmorency and the other to the Duc de Guise. He preferred the constable, probably because he instinctively felt him to be as artless as himself. But Guise often prevailed. The king followed one or the other depending on the season, and since their designs were contradictory, his policies were inevitably confused.

My father notes in his *Book of Reason* that Henri had no real reason to break the Peace of Vaucelles in 1557, since it guaranteed his conquest of the house of Austria. Yet Guise, who had distinguished himself by defending Metz against Charles V, dreamt of refurbishing his honour by undoing Felipe II of Spain. He had defeated the father and now needed to defeat the son. Guise, in his nonchalance, forgot one new element: Felipe II was consort to the queen of England, Mary Tudor—France would have to face two powerful kingdoms and to wage war on all of its frontiers.

Yet the king was inclined to follow Guise because, as a great jouster, he loved war, which his feeble imagination reduced to a superb tourney between two sovereigns in which each must, by a deft stroke of the lance, knock the other out of his stirrups. My father observed that during his previous war against Charles V, the king had no idea how to use his army of 50,000 men, except to line them up and march them in full parade dress with banners and fanfare in front of the emperor's camp at Valenciennes. Since Charles's army never broke ranks, the king thought the emperor must consider himself defeated according to the rules of chivalry. Consequently, without having fired a single shot, the king beat a retreat, ravaging the countryside in his path, friend and foe alike.

In this year of 1557, the Brethren feared the worst for the kingdom, and the worst, indeed, occurred when Henri, unprovokedly tearing up the Treaty of Vaucelles, declared war on Spain on 31st January and when Mary Tudor, in turn, declared war on Henri on 7th June of the same year.

The kingdom was invaded from the north. A powerful army, assembled in the Low Countries, besieged Saint-Quentin, while Guise struggled unsuccessfully against Felipe II's soldiers in Italy. Saint-Quentin was marvellously defended by Coligny with but a handful of men, but Montmorency, coming to his rescue with the royal army, managed stupidly and disastrously to have it crushed trying to cross the river Somme. The kingdom fell into great peril. The route to Paris was opened and the Parisians began packing their bags.

However, Coligny, at a thousand to one, held out in Saint-Quentin, and his stout resistance gave Henri time to call Guise back from Italy and to conscript an army from among his nobles. Meanwhile, anxious to seek an alliance with the Lutheran princes of Germany, Henri gave in to their request, and moderated (without altogether suspending them) his executions of the reformers. The Huguenots were not fooled by this semi-clemency. They knew that, once the war was over, the executions would start up immediately no matter how great their contributions to the war effort. But their travails had deepened their thinking on the matter, and they were more acutely aware than the majority of their countrymen that there was a difference between king and kingdom. They might hate the king, despise his cruelty and long for his death, yet the kingdom must be defended at all costs against foreign tyranny.

Périgord was fifteen to twenty days' ride from Paris, and many, even the most noble, loathed the idea of leaving their splendid chateaux—especially given the risks to their possessions engendered by a long absence—to seek, so far away to the north, wounds and suffering. Others, however, younger and poor as beggars in their dilapidated manor houses, followed their aspirations to adventure, glory, booty and joyful raping in the sacked villages.

Out of resentment against François I, who had banished his father, Bertrand de Fontenac, then twenty-seven years old, let it be known that his health was too delicate to permit him to follow Henri's call to arms. But few noble Huguenots—including those who barely hid their affiliation—avoided the call. Jean de Siorac, with the support of his beloved brother, and despite their mutual despair at the idea of this first separation in twenty-one years, made up his mind to arm himself for war and to set out with Cabusse, Marsal and Coulondre. Sauveterre, whose old injury kept him at Mespech, agreed in his brother's absence to take over command of the household, and the defence of their lands.

3

I WAS SIX YEARS OLD when my father left Mespech for the war. On the eve of his departure, as night fell in the courtyard of the chateau, the three soldiers loaded the wagon they would take with them. As long as it was merely oats for the horses, flour, salt, cured pork and nuts that were being stowed, we children could be content just to watch. But when they brought out the arms and cuirasses, our interest was sparked.

"What's that helmet with blinders?" asked my elder brother François.

"A burgonet," answered Cabusse.

"And this helmet with raised sides?"

"A morion."

Of the three soldiers, as I have mentioned, Cabusse was the only talker. But there were two reasons for this: Coulondre Iron-arm was economical in everything, even his words; Cockeyed Marsal stuttered.

"And what's that?" I demanded.

"Little idiot," said François, "that's a coat of chain mail."

"And that?" asked my half-brother Samson.

"A cuirass," answered François.

"Not at all," corrected Cabusse. "It's a corselet. It only protects the torso and the back."

"Cabusse," I said, "will the corselet protect you from being shot at?"

"A... a... a... las," said Marsal, looking at me sadly through crossed eyes.

"My little men," said Cabusse, "if I tell you all the names of the firearms, will you then be off to bed?" We all looked at each other, vexed by this manoeuvre; then François, always on his best behaviour, replied with great importance:

"Agreed, Cabusse."

"Well then," continued Cabusse, "this…"

"Is an arquebus," said François.

"Fuse or flint?" asked Cabusse, smoothing his moustache.

"Flint."

"No, Monsieur," corrected Cabusse, "fuse. But the fuse is missing. Here's a pistol. This is a small arquebus. Its advantage is that you can shoot it with one hand. Here's a pistolette—a small pistol. This is a gun you hold against your chest rather than your shoulder."

"These are proud weapons!" I exclaimed. "They'll kill lots of enemies."

"The enemy's got the same ones," replied Coulondre. He seemed, as usual, quite lugubrious, unlike Cabusse, who whistled as he worked, quite cheerful, it appeared, at the thought of leaving home and cutting loose.

Barberine called us all within, soldiers included, and, with Samson and me at the head of the pack, we raced to the great hall, where my father and Sauveterre were standing, backs to the fireplace, looking very serious. My mother sat at the far end of the table, between her chambermaid, Cathau, and Barberine, who held my two-year-old sister in her arms. Between these two groups, the three soldiers took their places and, opposite them, my two cousins from Taniès and the stonecutter Jonas, the three of whom would be staying to man the defence of Mespech during my father's absence.

To my father's right stood a little man dressed all in black save for an enormous white ruff that seemed to make his head smaller, like that of a plucked bird, his thin, arched, beak-like nose emphasizing this avian comparison and his jet-black, round eyes fixed on my father. This man stood absolutely silent, and since he gave us no command, we children slipped as best we could into the spaces left by the adults at the table: François on Sauveterre's right, Samson on Jonas's left and I on my father's right.

François and Geoffroy de Caumont finally arrived and, a few minutes later, Faujanet, who had tethered their horses after lowering the drawbridges for them. The Brethren and the new arrivals embraced each other with a gravity that made a deep impression on me. I noticed that Geoffroy de Caumont was content to wave to his cousin Isabelle from across the room rather than going around the table to greet her.

"Maître Ricou," said Jean de Siorac, addressing the little bird-beaked notary, "since we are dealing with a matter of the utmost importance requiring the presence of François and Geoffroy de Caumont, my wife Isabelle, my children, my cousins and all my servants, I took the liberty of troubling you to come all the way to Mespech, and I promise to have my men accompany you back to Sarlat." He paused to glance around at the assembled group. "Maître Ricou," he continued, "will read you the codicil that Sauveterre and I have decided to add to our act of brotherhood. Each of you should pay close attention to this reading, for any one of you may at some future date be required to testify as to its contents. Maître Ricou, please proceed."

Ricou pulled a scroll from his pocket, unfurled it, and though he read it slowly and distinctly, I couldn't understand a word of it at the time. As I read it today I remember that the only thing that struck me then was that my father might be killed in the war, a thought that had not yet occurred to me and that overwhelmed me.

If such an event occurred, Maître Ricou informed us, Monsieur de Sauveterre, Écuyer, agreed to consider Isabelle de Siorac as his own sister and to provide her with food and hearth for the rest of her days. He was also to provide for François, Pierre, Samson and Catherine, whom he would consider to be his own children. On coming of age, François de Siorac would join Sauveterre as lords of Mespech although the latter would continue to assume the management and defence of the household until his death. An appropriate sum of money would be given to each of his younger sons, Pierre de Siorac and Samson de Siorac, as they came of age, so that they might carry out their studies at Montpellier: Pierre in medicine and Samson in law. On her wedding day, Catherine was to receive the same fields, woods and quarry which Isabelle de Caumont had brought in dowry to Mespech. If Monsieur de Sauveterre were to die before the four children had reached majority, the Caumont cousins would become co-tutors with Isabelle.

Having finished his reading, Maître Ricou invited all present to pose any questions they might have, and my mother asked in a trembling voice whether the fact of naming Samson in the codicil was sufficient to legitimize his birth. "No," answered the notary, "in order for Samson to be legitimized, a special request would have to be addressed to the king, and in the present case, the child is merely recognized, which," he emphasized, "in no way undermines the inheritor of the estate." My father listened to this explanation without so much as a word, a sign or a look in my mother's direction.

François de Caumont asked if it might be possible to specify the "appropriate sum of money" which would be allotted to Pierre and Samson for their studies. Sauveterre proposed 3,000 livres for each, to be inflated or deflated according to the current price of grain, a proposal that was immediately accepted by my father and co-signed by Ricou.

Geoffroy de Caumont wished to know why, at the age of six, Pierre de Siorac was already destined to the study of medicine and Samson to the law. My father replied with a smile that, as younger brothers, we would need a serious profession in order to make our way in life; that he had already been struck by the interest I showed in sick people he had attended, and by all the questions I asked on this subject. As for Samson, he had a precise and practical turn of mind, which, my father felt, would lead him to an interest in the law. He added that, of course, he might be mistaken about all of this, but that, in any case, each of his younger sons should receive the prescribed sum whatever subject he wished to pursue in order to gain an honourable situation in life. François de Caumont requested that this consideration be added to the codicil, which was done. The act was then signed by Sauveterre, Siorac, Isabelle de Siorac, François and Geoffroy de Caumont, the two Siorac cousins, and Cabusse as well, who was the only one of our people who could sign his name, which he did with a great flourish.

After many compliments, the notary withdrew. Marsal and Coulondre were to accompany him back to Sarlat, armed to the teeth, for the roads had again become dangerous, and it was rumoured that a large band of Gypsies had been pillaging outlying farms near Belvès and even attacking some of the chateaux. As for François and Geoffroy de Caumont, they were to spend the night at Mespech, and set out the next morning with my father towards Périgueux, where a great assembly of nobles was being gathered for the march to Paris.

Once Ricou had left, my father announced in a sombre and sonorous voice, "My friends, in view of the perils we are going to meet in the north in our defence of the kingdom and of the dangers that those who remain here may have to confront, I ask that we all commend each other to the grace and mercy of God in a short prayer recited together." Whereupon, with a grave voice but without the bombast or any of the mechanical quality that our priest always adopts, without mumbling or stumbling over words, but pronouncing each of them in a sincere tone as if each one were new to him, Jean de Siorac recited the Our Father, and we all began to pray along with him, including the children.

Night had fallen and the hall was lit only by the two oil lamps on the table. I was astonished by this Our Father, recited so slowly, with such force and fervour. And believing that my father was going to be killed in battle, just as the horrible notary had said repeatedly while reading his document, a shiver went down my spine and tears streamed down my cheeks. Certainly I loved my mother and adored Barberine, who had suckled me and raised me and Samson—much more than my elder brother—and my little sister Catherine. But no one at Mespech seemed more admirable, stronger, more knowledge-able in all things, wiser, more able and indestructible than Jean de Siorac. I loved everything about him, his clear eyes, his eloquence, and especially the way he stood so straight and tall, head held high, the scar on his cheek adding to his majesty.

As the prayer came to an end, my tears continued to flow unre-mittingly and I didn't even try to wipe my eyes. Then an incident occurred which broke the solemnity of the scene and shook me to the core. In the silence following the prayer, Isabelle de Siorac sud-denly announced with her usual petulance, "My dear husband, I would like to add to the paternoster a little prayer intended for your special protection." And she immediately began the Ave Maria.

Had lightning struck the middle of the great hall of Mespech, it could not have produced a more terrifying effect. Sauveterre and Siorac stood silent, still as statues, fists clenched behind their backs, teeth gritted, staring icily at Isabelle. Geoffroy directed an equally furious look at his cousin, and his elder brother, who was also a reformer, though not so passionate as the others, seemed intensely embarrassed. Cathau, Barberine, little Hélix and I recited the Ave Maria along with Isabelle. Samson, who had never been prey to the influence of my mother and who was consequently ignorant of this prayer, said not a word. As for François, after reciting the opening words, he stopped short as soon as he saw my father's face. I resented his cowardice and continued reciting to the bitter end, convinced that my mother was wrong to have so antagonized my father, yet little inclined to abandon her, for I could see her chin trembling as she braved the terrible stares from all sides. As for my cousins and the soldiers, all remained immobile, their eyes glued to the floor, utterly silent, looking as if they wished they were a thousand leagues away.

"My friends," said my father when she had finished, his face pale, his teeth clenched, but his speech calm enough, "you may withdraw into your chambers for the night, I must take leave of my wife."

He warmly embraced François and Geoffroy de Caumont, who were the first to retire, followed by Sauveterre, who escorted them, limping, to their rooms. My cousins and the soldiers were next, and with them went François, who was no longer treated as a child and had his own room. Cathau and Barberine were slowest to withdraw, gathering the children in their skirts. Once the door to the great hall was closed, I noticed that they lingered in the kitchen, seeming to busy themselves there and imposing the strictest silence on all of us.

Their delay was rewarded, for, after a long silence, we could hear my father say: "Madame, you might have avoided offending me in front of my friends and my children, and this on the eve of my departure for the war unsure that you will ever see me again."

There was another silence, broken by my mother's trembling and tearful voice:

"My dear husband, I did not think to brook your anger in reciting a prayer of the Catholic religion in which we were married."

Here we could hear sobs as my father replied: "My friend, it is too late for tears." But his tone was considerably softened, and Barberine later told Cathau that if my mother had persevered in her tears and silence, everything might have turned out for the best. Instead, my mother added,

"Truly I did not mean any harm. I only wanted to bring you the protection of the Virgin."

"Is Christ not enough for you?" cried my father angrily. "Why do you need the intercession of your little gods and goddesses? Have you no sense, woman? There's nothing but pagan superstition, stinking idolatry and pestiferous ignorance of God's Word in your worship. I've explained this to you a thousand times, Madame, and since you have the good fortune to know how to read, why do you refuse to seek the Word of God as it is given in the Holy Scriptures, rather than relying blindly on the tales of your priests?"

At this point, little Hélix gave my arm a terrible pinch and I responded with an elbow, which missed its mark and hit a kettle, knocking it with a great crash to the kitchen floor. The door of the great hall flew open and my father's head appeared, flushed crimson, his eyes ablaze, and he thundered, "What are you doing in here? To bed! To bed! Or every last one of you'll get the whip, boys and girls alike, young and old, no matter what your condition!" Barberine gave a shriek, and, seizing her lamp, disappeared into the stairwell, all of us on her heels, panting with terror.

Cathau, the lithe chambermaid Cabusse had taken such a fancy to, slept in the little room adjoining my mother's bedroom, and she took a hasty leave of Barberine on the first landing, her eyes and lips full of the commentary they would share the next morning but must now sleep on. Our nurse, lamp in hand, shepherded her little troop into the room in the west tower where she slept in a bed whose great size was commensurate with her own. Catherine's bed was next to hers, little Hélix's on the other side, but shoved against the wall to allow passage between them, while Samson and I shared a bed on the far side of the fireplace. In the frigid winter weather, we lit a great blaze at nightfall against the terrible glacial draughts blowing through the machicolations pierced in the walls, which, during an attack, permitted rocks, hot pitch or boiling water to be hurled on any attackers, but which now allowed the humidity of the moats to infiltrate our beds.

Barberine placed the oil lamp on the night table and came to tuck us into our beds with the care, caresses and kisses with which she always dosed these rites, her deep, lyrical voice finding sweet words for each one of us (including Samson, though she'd never suckled him), calling little Hélix "My big rascal! Little devil! Sweet sorceress!"; Catherine "My little golden écu! My pearl of God!"; Samson "My little fox cub! My curly little St John!"; and me "My sweet! Dear heart! My little rooster!" These are only examples of her nicknames for us, for she imagined new ones every night, each one perfectly fitting the person and the occasion, never calling one of us by a name she'd used for another on another night, which, I'm sure, would have wounded us no end.

Catherine and Samson fell asleep during this rite, but not little Hélix, who, leaning on one elbow, and behind Barberine's spacious back, made her last faces at me. I did not doze off either, but only pretended to do so, and, turning on my side, one eye closed, seemingly the innocent angel, I watched Barberine undress, while her gigantic shadow, projected by the lamp onto the curved tower wall, made its final preparations for sleep.

I now understand that Barberine was not as colossal as I'd believed at the age of six. She was, however, a large woman with luxuriant black hair, a round face, large mouth, round and robust neck, wide shoulders, huge bosom with firm and abundant white breasts from which I had drunk life, and which now dazzled me in the lamplight as, sighing, she unlaced the red bodice which imprisoned them. And they seemed to swell, impatient for liberation, as Barberine undid with her large fingers the last knots holding the lacing firmly in place. Finally they made their appearance, milky and round, fabulously enlarged by the shadow on the wall, as if the tower itself had become a huge breast which would come to rest on our cheeks during the night. Barberine carefully folded her red halter and her corset, and then her skirt, her apron and finally her green velvet petticoat, striped with three red bands, one at the waist, a second around her thigh and the third at the hem. Then she pulled on an ample white sleeveless nightgown, cut very low so that her liberated bosom could undulate freely. As her body came to rest on her woollen mattress she sighed with sleepy content. I had only this brief moment to ask a question or make a request, since only seconds later the lamp would be extinguished and she with it, sinking into a sleep so deep that ten arquebuses firing simultaneously in the tower room would not have stirred her.

I slipped out of bed and ran over to hers to curl up and snuggle in her arms.

"And who is this pretty little mouse?" asked Barberine in her low sing-song voice, squeezing me tight. "What could it want?"

"Barberine, why did my mother make my father so angry?"

"Because she was upset herself," said Barberine, who never lied.

"Upset about what?"

"Because the notary called Samson 'Samson de Siorac'."

"Isn't that his name, then?" I asked astonished.

"Now it is, yes."

"And what was it before?"

"He didn't have a name."

I couldn't believe my ears.

"But he's my brother!"

"Of course!" replied Barberine. "And a handsome, strong and honest lad he is, like a shiny new coin. It would have been a great pity not to name him Siorac and God bless him!" And, between her teeth, "And the Virgin Mary, too. Go on, my little mouse, back to your hole. I'm dousing the lamp."

And even before I could get back to my bed, she blew out the lamp, so that I "lost my way" in the dark and found myself in little Hélix's bed, who, all ears, was wide awake and whose arms encircled me with astonishing force.

It's true that she was already ten years old and I don't know why we called her little Hélix, for she was no longer little, far from it and almost completely formed already.

"Aha, I've got you!" she whispered. "And now that I've got you, I'm going to eat you right up like a she-devil."

"S'not true!" I hissed. "I don't believe you, you don't have teeth like a wolf."

"What about this?" she said, rolling me over on my back and putting her full weight on me. "Me," she continued half-scolding, half-laughing, trying to nibble my ear, "I always begin with the ears, because they're the best morsels, like the coxcomb or the artichoke heart! But after the ears, I eat everything else, bit by bit, right down to the bones."

"Not true, I tell you, and you're crushing me! Get off me! Or I'll call Barberine!"

"My mother's asleep," she laughed shamelessly. "So, my little mouse, you've met your cat. Keep still or you'll feel my claws."

"If you're a cat," I answered bravely, "tomorrow I'll take my father's sword and cut you in two, from the guzzle to the zatch!"

"Fie then!" cajoled little Hélix. "No bragging little mouse! Listen once and for all: if you don't sleep in my bed I'll eat you all up."

I answered neither yea nor nay, so astonished was I to find her at once so plump and so strong, gave up the struggle and fell asleep in her arms. At daybreak, however, she woke me with a violent pinch and, pretending to be angry at finding me in her bed, sent me off to my own with dispatch.

My father's departure deprived us as well of Cabusse, who, among other duties, was our cook. He enjoyed an easy familiarity with Cathau and Barberine. Neither one, however, tolerated his advances for fear of being sent away, though Cathau would have been hard pressed to resist if the master's eye hadn't kept her in line, for she found herself attracted to Cabusse's formidable moustache, his great size, his coaxing ways and his Gascon accent. Alas, now, when she came down of a morning to fetch hot milk for her mistress, Cabusse would no longer be there to say in his warm voice, "Greetings, my sweet! How fare you this day? And how could you not fare well, fresh as you are, with cheeks as red as apples and lips like cherries! How you make the kitchen shine just by comin' in! They say 'A lass who's pale seeks her male,' but I don't believe it! It's just the other way round! Whoever saw a turnip fall in love?"

But even Cabusse, as hardy a soldier as they come, spoke in a whisper to Cathau, so fearful was he of being heard by the captains.

To replace Cabusse as cook, they tried Barberine, but Barberine, who had nourished so many children in the natural way, turned out to have no culinary talent whatsoever for nourishing grown-ups. So Sauveterre called on la Maligou, wife of the man who had had such trouble guarding Mespech against the evil schemes of Fontenac. La Maligou came and stayed. As voluminous as Barberine, she lacked our nursemaid's strength, and possessed not the least grain of common sense or reason in her great ruffled head, being all vanity and chatter, as credulous and superstitious as they come, genuflecting twenty times a day, crossing her fingers to conjure fate, throwing salt over her shoulder and in front of her pot (which she somehow cooked to perfection), always careful to draw a circle with her finger on the kitchen floor behind her to prevent the Devil from whipping up her skirts and cowling her while she was bent over her fire.

She brought with her daughter, named Suzon, but later we turned to calling her "Little Sissy", a name which stuck. At the time of her arrival she was a little devil of three years, with the skin of a Saracen, thin and graceful as a blade, her close-set eyes liquid and malicious enough to damn you, yet of a good heart all the same. At six, already tall for my age, I carried her on my shoulders, leaving Catherine to pout on her little chair, her two blonde braids encircling her scowling face, while little Hélix wrestled with her barely contained fury, for no one dared lay a finger on Little Sissy, since la Maligou had a sharp eye and a fast hand.

Her mother made a great mystery of the birth of this girl, whom she elevated in importance over all her other children, husband, father, mother and grandparents—with endless fussing, signs of the cross, and frequent pinches of salt thrown in the fire (a practice which, with salt so expensive, Sauveterre was quick to condemn). But, of course, unable to hold her tongue, she revealed that secret at least once a month, with murmurs, expressions of the greatest confidence, and a mixture of hidden pride and contrition. Little Sissy was not, alas! (this "alas!" was so hypocritical!) her husband Maligou's daughter, but was the daughter of a Gypsy who had taken her by force one night four years previously. La Maligou claimed that this Gypsy captain's armed band had pillaged their house, demanding all the cured meat hanging from their rafters, and threatened to burn their entire field of wheat, cast spells on the cows and cut down their vines. At the mention of the vines, Maligou gave in immediately. But once they had the meat, the Gypsy captain, a tall handsome brute who looked like a prince, put his evil eye on la Maligou and, drawing a cross on her breast with his thumb and another on her stomach, he said in his half-Catalan, half-Provençal patois, "I'll return for you tonight in the barn when the owl hoots. If you aren't there, I'll burn your body with the fires of hell from your womb to your lungs till the end of time."

And indeed, as midnight sounded, hearing the hooting of the owl (her husband sleeping drunk as a log beside her to forget the loss of his salamis), la Maligou, shuddering as she slipped on her clogs, went, against her will, to the barn, where in the inky darkness of the night the Gypsy captain threw her into the hay and had his way with her no less than fifteen times. "But there was no sin on my hands," la Maligou was quick to add, "because I was forced by magic to do it." So often was this story told that no one at Mespech or any of the surrounding villages (except perhaps for a few virgins who grew dreamy at its telling) was the least moved by it. Whenever he heard it, my father always laughed to split his sides, and I realized only later why he found it so amusing.

Among the new arrivals at Mespech were my cousins Benoît and Michel Siorac, sons of my Uncle Raymond, who had perished in the plague at Taniès. It was a great blessing for my cousins to live in the chateau. The curate of Marcuays, whose parish included the towns of Sireil and Taniès, had forbidden burning the corpses under threat of eternal damnation and so everyone feared another outbreak of the epidemic from the bad vapours from the earth of Taniès where the pestiferous lay buried.

Benoît and Michel were twins, and no two peas ever looked more alike in the same pod. They were merry lads in their thirties who spoke little and were secretly unhappy that neither knew which was the elder, since their mother and midwife had passed away and no one in Taniès could tell them which of them had been born first. Neither could lay claim to their small domain, and consequently neither could take a wife since the domain could support only one family.

La Maligou always said, out of their earshot, that they were fools not to take one woman to the altar before a priest, since no woman could ever tell them apart and thus there could be no sin where there was no knowledge of sin. In this way, the twins could have shared the pleasures of a wife without having the expenses of two families.

But these ideas would have seemed sacrilegious to the pious brothers. They were so dependent on each other that they simply accepted their celibacy and their coexistence. Indeed, if one were alone, he would search about, asking everyone anxiously, "Where is Michel?" By which we could recognize that it was Benoît who was speaking. Otherwise there was no way: they were the same size, the same breadth of shoulder, had the same black curly hair, same features, same way of sitting, sniffing the wind, spitting, breaking bread or supping soup.

Sauveterre had a blue ribbon sewn on Michel's shirt collar, and a red one on Benoît's, but since they slept together, their clothes thrown pell-mell onto the bed, Michel might easily slip on Benoît's shirt by mistake in the morning, so it was of no use. As pious as they were, the Siorac brothers were not terribly clever and should one of us, meeting one of the twins in the courtyard, ask "Which one are you?" the twin in question would invariably reply, "I'm the brother of the other one."

Jonas, our stonecutter, was unhappy to have to leave his cave to come to the defence of Mespech. He bit his nails worrying about his beautiful cut stones lying at night alone in their quarry. But for all that, the new company changed him for the better, especially the women, whom the poor hermit devoured with his eyes at the dinner table every night, most of all Barberine, whose abundance and milky complexion caught his fancy. With our three departed soldiers, the two Siorac twins and Faujanet, Jonas made the seventh bachelor, not counting all the young men of the neighbouring towns who were unable to marry since they possessed no house to lodge a family nor lands to nourish one. It was a great shame that so many of the girls of our countryside had to enter convents for lack of an earthly husband. I make these observations at an age where I myself, though born into a well-to-do family, am but the second-born and am unable to marry the woman who has enchanted me since I have no means of supporting her. Sadly, filthy lucre seems to dominate everything, even the sweetness of life.

Sauveterre became quite bilious at the news that an armed band of Gypsies were roaming the countryside around Belvès, taking advantage of the absence of the nobility and their men at arms to besiege the chateaux. For the strongest chateau is only as strong as its defenders, and these were too often too few or too cowardly, since the call to arms to save the kingdom had skimmed off the cream of the soldiery from our region.

The Gypsies were not a people who dreamt only of blood and carnage. If victorious, they raped the women, to be sure, but did not kill them afterwards. It was rumoured that they never touched children either, but seemed to love them so much that they often stole young ones if they found them beautiful. Before attacking, they would always enter into negotiations with the chateau or the farm and, in return for a pledge of neutrality, would carry off arms, silver and provisions. But it sometimes happened that, after receiving a ransom, they would break their word and attack anyway. It was said that they castrated the men they killed, which was very much an affront to our own customs, although I have seen it done by our soldiers—both Huguenots and Catholics—during the great civil wars of the kingdom.

The Gypsies were armed with makeshift weapons but were fearsome nonetheless, for they often attacked at night, silent as snakes, nimble as cats, quickly scaled walls thought to be unassailable, and were already within the walls by the time the alarm was sounded.

At Mespech there was now only one captain, Sauveterre, and a single soldier, Faujanet. Jonas was, to be sure, a sure shot with his longbow, but the Siorac brothers had to be taught how to shoot an arquebus. Even the women were taught soldiery, at least my mother, Cathau and Barberine were, for la Maligou, faced with the task, made such a fuss and cried so shrilly that Sauveterre sent her quickly back to her pots and pans. My mother also put up some resistance, but of another sort, claiming that it was beneath the honour of a noblewoman to touch firearms. To which a glowering Sauveterre crustily replied: "Madame, if Mespech is taken what will become of your honour then?" At this Isabelle shuddered, paled and gave in.

François was also given lessons in marksmanship. Samson and I bit our knuckles with rage, for our elder brother immediately put on unbearable airs with us. But Sauveterre found a use for us younger brothers. He had us make piles of large stones every three toises along the catwalks, and, wearing helmets much too big for our little heads, we were instructed to run back and forth along the ramparts brandishing pikes to give the impression of great numbers at the approach of the enemy. Little Hélix even got a helmet and a pick, but these were soon confiscated, so dangerous did this weapon seem in her hands. If ladders were raised against our walls, we were instructed to put aside our pikes and valiantly to hurl the stones from the battlements onto the heads of our assailants.

That autumn, the grain had been harvested and the grapes picked, and as soon as the ploughing was done, the livestock was brought in from the pastures despite the good weather, to keep them, and the cowherds, from exposure to the roving bands. We also avoided trips to Sarlat, to neighbouring chateaux or even to our villages, so wary were we of the roads where the Gypsies had become masters of the ambush.

Sauveterre ordered that a brief reconnaissance be made outside the walls at dawn each day, and after sundown each evening. He entrusted these little patrols to the Siorac twins, and, before opening the gates, had their horses' hooves trussed with rags to muffle their approach. The twins were great hunters and we knew we could count on them for detecting the least trace of man or beast on the roads and in the surrounding woods.

From the ramparts of Mespech, we could easily spy the fortified bell tower of the church of Marcuays and, off to the right, on a more distant hill, the imposing facade of the Château de Fontenac. Overcoming his repugnance, Sauveterre wrote to Bertrand de Fontenac a courteous letter in which he proposed that our two chateaux, being so close, should each give aid if the other were attacked by the Gypsies. But the wolf cub, showing his fangs for the first time, refused this proposition flat out: Fontenac had no need of help nor wished to be obliged to give it to anyone, least of all those who had banished his father.

As for the other neighbouring castleries, Campagnac, Puymartin, Laussel and Commarques, their forces were even more impoverished than ours. Nor could we expect any help from Sarlat, deprived of its archers and royal troops: the consuls had hastily organized a town militia which was barely capable of defending its walls, being few in number and unused to battle.

Sauveterre, never one to mask the truth, especially when it was unpleasant, repeated to us every night after prayers that we must not rely on the moat surrounding us, nor on our walls, our towers, our ramparts or our drawbridges, and that we had little hope of victory if the Gypsies attacked us. It was on hearing this that, for the first time in my young life, I began to think about death.

Mespech had withdrawn into itself as if it were midwinter, despite the beautiful autumn season, the clear October sun beginning to turn the leaves of the chestnut trees. It was a pity to think that we were sequestered in Mespech as if in a prison, the three drawbridges raised even during the day, my father and the three soldiers in danger of being killed in the war which weighed so heavily against France, and we ourselves, far from the battlefields of the north, in the greatest peril.

I was too young in 1554 to have retained any memory of the plague in Taniès other than the happy arrival of Samson, with his curly hair, his clear eyes, his strength and his exquisite manners. But ever since Ricou, the notary, had talked about the possible death of my father, and while Sauveterre, doubtless wishing to sharpen the courage of his little band, would not let a night go by without evoking the massacre that would attend the fall of Mespech, I believed we were all fated to die.

The twins, Jonas, and Faujanet took turns standing guard on the battlement walk, anxiously scanning the horizon. Thanks to our service as rock suppliers to the battlement walk, Samson and I were the only children allowed up there, a privilege we valued greatly since from there we had a marvellous view of the surrounding villages and hillsides. Breathless, our backs breaking from our labours, our hands rough from hefting the fieldstone, we would look out over the ploughed fields and the woods. As the sun set over Périgord, giving a sweet serenity to everything, the thought of death, which had so lately come to me, returned with a force it had never before had.

"Samson," I said, "when you die, do you go to heaven?"

"God willing," replied Samson.

"But on earth, everything continues?"

"Yes, of course," Samson said.

"Life goes on in Taniès, Marcuays? And Mespech? And the la Feuillade woods? And the marauders' field?"

"Yes," announced Samson firmly. "Everything goes on just the same."

"But we," I stammered, a lump in my throat, "we won't be here to see it."

"No," said Samson.

"But, Samson, how is that possible?" Tears streamed down my cheeks, I grabbed his hand and squeezed with all my strength.

The day after I had discovered that the earth would continue to be just as beautiful when I was no longer there, a rider bearing letters from the north for the chateaux whose lords fought for the king brought us a missive from my father. It was addressed to Jean de Sauveterre, and my mother seemed reluctant to take it when, his face beaming with joy, Sauveterre handed it to her after perusing its contents. But since he was called outside at that moment, he placed the letter on the table of the great hall and left. Seeing this, my mother approached almost in spite of herself, reached out a hesitating hand, as if both attracted and repulsed by the letter, and ended up by seizing it and retiring immediately to a window seat, at a discreet distance from Barberine and her children. She skimmed most of the letter rapidly, until she got to the end, which she read much more slowly, with sighs and tears.

Sauveterre, returning at this moment, went up to her and said quietly and with an unusual gentleness: "Well, my cousin, you see your husband is concerned about your health and your children."

"But the letter is not addressed to me," replied my mother with a half-angry, half-plaintive tone, her blue eyes brimming with tears.

"That's as it should be, since it's a matter of wars and campaigns. But the last part proves that Jean has thoughts only for you."

"And for you as well, Monsieur," answered my mother with an effort at generosity evidently much appreciated by Sauveterre, for he seized her two hands in his and pressed them.

"Am I not his brother," he said with a voice at once vibrant and veiled, "devoted to his person, his wife and his children to my dying day?"

This "to my dying day" resonated through me painfully, for I naively believed that our deaths were now literally imminent. I little realized then that people who use this expression are usually quite alive and consider their own deaths a possibility so remote that they can speak of it without anguish.

That evening after dinner and common prayer led by Sauveterre (and to which my mother and perhaps others among us felt it necessary to make secret additions in the privacy of their chambers), Sauveterre addressed us all, and particularly the children, regarding the affairs of the kingdom, and reporting the good news that my father had sent.

By his account, François de Guise had succeeded in extracting his troops from the Italian campaign, which had been but a series of errors, and had reached Saint-Germain on 6th October. Henri II had immediately named him lieutenant general of the kingdom and placed him at the head of an army, swelled by Swiss mercenaries (for the most part paid for by the burghers of Paris) and by the many nobles who had hurried there with their soldiers from all the provinces of France, which now numbered some 50,000 men eager for battle.

Guise apparently feared that all this ardour would burn itself out right there before reaching its true object. But a redoubtable adversary was beginning to undo the army of Felipe II of Spain: lack of money. "It may seem astonishing," wrote Jean de Siorac, "that a sovereign as methodical and painstaking as Felipe II should have undertaken such a great campaign without assuring himself of the financial means to carry it out." And yet that is exactly what was happening. Unable to pay his soldiers, Felipe's able general, Emmanuel-Philibert de Savoie, was cashiering his army. And Guise, instead of meeting the awesome legions, which had crushed Montmorency before Saint-Quentin, encountered only absence.

The French court now remembered that we were also at war with Mary Tudor and, though they had done little to support their Spanish allies with reinforcements or subsidies, our English neighbours offered at least one major advantage over the Spanish: they were quite close at hand. For 200 years, England had occupied Calais. Jean de Siorac was careful to avoid mentioning Calais by name in his letter, and yet by certain allusions which only his brother could interpret he implied that it was to that city that Guise would direct his blow and attempt to undo the knot of this war.

At this point in his presentation, Sauveterre paused to send Faujanet to fetch Jonas, who was standing guard on the ramparts, because he wanted everyone to hear what he was about to say. Then he ordered la Maligou to light both of the pewter five-stemmed candelabra.

"Both at once?" asked la Maligou hesitantly.

"Both at once, and all the candles as well," replied Sauveterre firmly.

This was a surprising answer, given how close a watch Sauveterre kept on expenses. La Maligou, rising to the occasion and, as always, prepared to see magic everywhere at work since the day the Gypsy had taken her by force, lit each of the candles with an air of great pomp and mystery. Already overjoyed at the news that our father was alive, the rest of us were filled with admiration at the unheard-of luxury of such an illumination—the two candelabra reflecting their light in the polished walnut surface of the table. Sauveterre had ceremoniously seated us on either side of him, François and Isabelle on his right, myself, Samson and Catherine on his left; behind us in a second row, Cathau, Barberine and little Hélix, la Maligou carrying Little Sissy in her arms and, lastly, behind the women, the Siorac brothers, Jonas, who had just come back from his watch, his blunderbuss in his hand, and Faujanet, limping at his heels.

Sauveterre went to the armoire of the great hall and removed a long scroll, which he unrolled on the table, weighting each corner with a blunderbuss bullet that he pulled from his pockets. "This," announced Sauveterre, his black eyes shining beneath his bushy eyebrows and his voice straining to contain an emotion we could all feel, "is the kingdom of France."

There was a long silence, and la Maligou made the sign of the cross with a terrified air. "Sweet Jesus!" she moaned in a trembling voice. "That's strange magic indeed that can reduce such a great kingdom to a piece of paper scarce as long as our table!"

"Fiddlesticks!" retorted Jonas. "It doesn't fit on the paper. It's just a picture, like the master craftsmen give me to carve my stones from. It's a picture made all small."

"That's right," said Sauveterre, "and the kingdom of France is a very great kingdom. Even changing horses every day, it would take a rider more than thirty days to gallop from Marseilles" (and here he tapped the port on the map with his index finger) "to Calais" (he indicated Calais with the flat of his hand).

"Thirty days!" gasped Barberine. "In other words a whole month! God preserve the king of France who must watch over such a vast kingdom."

"But where is the diocese of Sarlat?" asked Isabelle de Siorac.

"Here's Sarlat," answered Sauveterre, who didn't care for the term "diocese".

"And the Dordogne?" said François to show that he was eldest.

Sauveterre followed with his index finger the sinuous line of the river.

"God keep me from his devils and his sorcerers," breathed la Maligou. "But this Dordogne doesn't flow."

"Silly fool!" cried Jonas. "Do you want to feel the snow on the mountains as well? The great waters of the seas? And the winds and squalls that buffet the kingdom?" He appeared to be quite indignant about la Maligou's superstitions and stupidities, yet all the while he was taking advantage of the crowd around the table to press up against Barberine a bit more than he should have, Sauveterre lacking eyes in the back of his head.

"What about Taniès?" one of the Siorac twins asked suddenly, though for the life of me I could not tell which one.

"Yes, where is Taniès?" repeated the brother of the other one.

"It is not marked on this map," Sauveterre announced patiently.

"And why not?" asked one of the Sioracs, clearly offended by this omission.

"Listen, my poor friends," broke in Faujanet, "I've travelled this country over during my ten years in the legion of Guyenne, and I can tell you that there are so many thousands of villages in the kingdom that they can't all fit on this map."

Sauveterre raised his hand: "Well said, Faujanet. I'll simply add that Périgord is but one of the provinces of France. And Sarlat is only one among dozens of cities in France." And he continued, "Here is Paris, the capital of the kingdom, where the king lives in his Louvre. And here to the north-west is a little sleeve of water, at its narrowest only two leagues wide, called La Manche. On the other side of La Manche lies Dover, which belongs to England. And on this side is Calais which used to belong to the kingdom of France."

Sauveterre tapped his hand on the map and said in a trembling voice: "The English took Calais from us in 1347, exactly 200 years ago."

"What evil men these English are," said Faujanet. "But I thought Joan of Arc kicked them out."

"Not from everywhere," replied Sauveterre. "They hung on to this little piece of France in the north country, like ticks on the ear of a dog."

"Two hundred years!" said François, able to do his sums, to be sure, but whose imagination was surpassed by a figure so much greater than the ten years of his life.

"I am fifty-two years old," announced Sauveterre. "Two hundred years is about four times my age."

I looked at Sauveterre with his greying beard, his scarred and wrinkled face and his hands covered by large blue veins. Four times the age of Uncle de Sauveterre was an immensity. "But if God didn't give us back Calais after all this time," argued la Maligou, "it's because God didn't want to."

"Silly imbecile!" rejoined Jonas, who in his indignation leant even more heavily on Barberine. "If God had wanted the English to have Calais, He would have put it on the other side of La Manche, next to Dover."

"Ay, that's true enough!" said Barberine, struck by the evidence of this reasoning, simultaneously aiming a kick at little Hélix, whom she caught in the act of pinching me. As for what was happening immediately behind her enormous backside, she seemed entirely oblivious.

"Did the English take Calais by treachery?" François asked.

"Not at all," said Sauveterre, "but by loyal combat after their stunning victory over our poor King Philippe VI at Crécy."

During the summer, Samson and I had memorized the interminable list of French kings and I was terrified for a moment that Sauveterre, who was in the habit of asking such questions, might examine me as to Philippe VI's succession. But instead he continued, "At Crécy, it was the English, the best archers the world has ever known, who earned the victory."

"Excuse me, Captain," broke in Jonas, appearing to be deeply wounded, "but it's the English bow and not the English archer that is the best. You see, the bow is made of a wood that grows only on their soil."

"Right you are, Jonas. And if there had been 2,000 like you at Crécy, the battle would have turned out differently."

"Thank you, Captain," murmured Jonas, blushing with pride at the thought of the exploits he might have accomplished at Crécy 200 years earlier.

"How was Calais taken?" asked François, who knew how much his uncle loved such questions. Like my father, and like so many Huguenot noblemen and burghers, Sauveterre had enormous respect for knowledge, which extended to teaching the servants how to read so that they would have access to the Scriptures.

"Calais," he explained, "was taken after a year of terrible hunger, the English fleet having blockaded the port and Philippe VI unable to reach them from the land side. They had eaten everything: dogs, cats, and even horses, to the point that the valiant captain of the defence, Jean de Vienne, feared that the poor citizens of Calais would be reduced to eating human flesh."

"Horrors!" cried Barberine, who, because she herself was so white and succulent, had always nourished a secret fear of being roasted during a siege. "It's a capital sin to eat the flesh of a Christian."

"Christian or not," returned Faujanet, "hunger brings the wolf out of the wood, and human or not, a starving man becomes a wolf. In my ten years of service in the Guyenne legion, I saw things I couldn't tell you about."

"And 'tis well," said Sauveterre, showing no impatience. "In these extreme conditions and with no help in sight, Jean de Vienne capitulated. He asked Edward III to allow the people to leave the garrison. 'Nay, nay!' replied Edward. 'They have killed too many of my good Englishmen. Every one of them must die!'"

"The wicked man!" said Barberine.

"Not at all," corrected Faujanet. "It was his right."

"A barbarous right," said Sauveterre. "And the proof is that the English barons begged him a thousand times to temper his hatred. Well, Edward finally agreed that the people and garrison should be spared, but on one condition: that six burghers of Calais should surrender to him barefoot, bareheaded and wearing a rope about their necks, bringing him the keys to the city. And on these men," said Sauveterre, his brow furrowing sadly, "Edward would take his vengeance."

"And the people of Calais had to choose those six men," Jonas recalled. "I'll wager that it was not an easy task. Ordinarily, the burghers of these cities are well fed, crimson-faced and cleave as much to their skins as they do to their purses."

"They chose themselves," said Sauveterre, who did not much like Jonas's way of speaking. "And the first to volunteer was the richest of them all. He was called Eustache de Saint-Pierre."

"So he already had a saint's name," said la Maligou, but Sauveterre gave her such an angry look that she fell silent. "His name has nothing to do with it," he said severely. "Eustache de Saint-Pierre was a good Christian, who despite his riches aspired to eternal happiness in the sight of God. And in volunteering for the rope, he said this:

'If I die to save this people, I have every hope of obtaining the grace and pardon of Our Lord.' Of course," added Sauveterre, "Eustache was mistaken in this hope, for grace is not given for works alone." (How many times had I heard this Calvinist credo from his lips or those of my father!) "But his thought was no less noble or pious, since he sacrificed his life for his people and his city."

"Did he die?" asked Barberine, tears streaming down her cheeks, with Cathau and my mother close to tears as well, I think. "My heart breaks to think of this poor man forced to go barefoot like a beggar, without so much as a hat or doublet…"

"But there were no doublets back then," said François, a remark that seemed to me both pedantic and heartless given the great peril Eustache had accepted.

"He did not die," explained Sauveterre. "Nor did his five companions, all honourable burghers and well off in goods, one of whom had two beautiful and gracious daughters to marry off."

"Alas!" said Cathau, who was sensitive enough, but tried to appear even more so and lisped a bit according to the custom. "Such poor girls who, instead of finding a husband, lost their father to the stake." Cathau had already been my mother's chambermaid at Caumont, and put on a few airs among us, finding our nobility scarcely ancient enough to suit her. She was a sweet girl nonetheless, with bright black eyes, rosy cheeks and full red lips. Her one thought was to marry Cabusse someday. Ever since he had left, she had wept day and night, constantly broke into sighs and wore out her bed at night with all her tossing and turning.

"But he was not hanged," repeated Sauveterre. "Neither Eustache nor any of the others. 'Cut off their heads!' ordered Edward III."

"Sweet Jesus," cried Barberine.

"Nor were they beheaded," said Sauveterre. "For the gentle queen of England, though very pregnant, threw herself at the king's

94

feet and said, 'Good sire, ever since I crossed the sea from Dover to Calais in great peril to join you, I have asked no favour of you. But today I ask you, for the love of Christ, to have mercy on these six men!' And the king, relenting, gave them over to her care and she treated them worthily."

The women all sighed with relief at these words. In truth, as I discovered later, Sauveterre had changed somewhat the queen's words, for in her plea to her king she had said "For the love of the son of Holy Mary", a version that in Sauveterre's Huguenot mind had become "For the love of Christ".

"Nevertheless," said Sauveterre, "all the Frenchmen of Calais, nobles, burghers and artisans, were dispossessed of their goods and ordered to leave the city within the hour. Edward III replaced them with as many Englishmen of various estates. And so it is that the English cuckoo, throwing out the French eggs, laid its own in our nest and made of it a haven for himself and his people for the next 210 years!" He broke off and frowned. "But I hear our dogs barking furiously. Jonas, go see what has upset them."

Jonas left the room with his usual giant's gait. A few minutes passed before we heard the sound of someone running, and Jonas burst into the great hall crying with a trembling voice,

"The Gypsies are attacking!"

4

T HESE GYPSIES, so feared throughout the countryside, were really beggars who had been chased out of Spain and who were dying of hunger by the roadsides. A clever leader, taking advantage of the hard times, had armed them and organized them into gangs. They had sprung up like scum on a wave, and were to disappear just as quickly once peace returned to the land, their bands cut to pieces and their captain sent trussed up to be burnt at the stake.

In his heart, the leader knew very well how things would eventually turn out, which had the effect of lending a mad audacity to his desperate acts.

Sauveterre had predicted that their attack would take place at night, and he had taken the precaution of reinforcing the enclosure around our moat with numerous bear traps, solid enough so that our three newly acquired mastiffs would not spring them as they patrolled the grounds day and night, bristling with such ferocity that even Faujanet had trouble getting near them at feeding time.

On each of Mespech's four walls, Sauveterre had ensconced torches in the joints of the stones near each crenellation. Instead of an immediate call to arms after Jonas's announcement, his first thought was to light each of these torches, which gave the chateau and the moat a fairy-tale quality that enchanted Samson and me.

But the torchlight also revealed that the Gypsies had already occupied our island. A menacing silence had succeeded the furious barking of the dogs, and as soon as the south facade of the chateau was illuminated the Gypsies took cover in the recesses of the sheds that sheltered our ploughs and harrows.

Sauveterre, still clad in his doublet, not having had time to put on a corselet or a helmet, distributed blunderbusses to everyone, including François and the women, and ordered our torches to be directed towards the interior of the sheds. But we were so much higher up that the torches left large zones of shadow and our shots merely ricocheted off the roofing stones. To get a better angle on our adversaries we would have had to occupy the little round tower joining the bridges between Mespech and the island, but this would have required lowering one of the drawbridges.

Sauveterre felt that we were too few to send a detachment out to this advance post, which, though originally conceived for our defence, ended up serving the advantage of neither adversary.

From the cover of the island sheds, our assailants rained continuous fire on our crenellations, but this tactic was so ineffective that it seemed destined more to divert us than to engage us in battle. Indeed Sauveterre suddenly realized that, having drawn our attention and our fire to the island, the Gypsies must be preparing a rearguard action, and sent Faujanet and Jonas to patrol the ramparts.

It was a good thing he did, for when they got to the north wall Jonas saw a Gypsy pull himself up through one of the crenellations with the agility of a cat and land on the stones of the battlement walk a scant eight toises away. Our stonecutter froze in his tracks, then, calmly bending his bow, sent an arrow through the invader's heart. Clutching his hands to his chest, the man fell without so much as a whimper. Jonas made a sign to Faujanet to stay where he was, and crept ahead on all fours. He found eight scaling hooks fixed in the crenellations and, peering down, saw the Gypsies climbing their ropes, oblivious to the torchlight, using their bare feet to scale the facade. Stunned by their mad courage, Jonas withdrew a few paces into the shadows and sent Faujanet to fetch Sauveterre.

The captain came running, followed by the Siorac brothers and Faujanet, arriving just as Jonas dropped a second Gypsy in his tracks, just as silently as the first. Sauveterre positioned his three men behind Jonas and whispered, "Let the stonecutter do his worst. Don't shoot until I give the order."

One more Gypsy was hit, and then a fourth emerged, who, hit in a less vital spot by Jonas's arrow, gave a piercing cry and pitched backwards into the moat. Sauveterre then heard a series of splashes indicating that the other assailants had abandoned their ropes. Stationing his men at each embrasure he ordered them to fire at anything that moved. He himself stuck his head far enough out to see that the Gypsies had made a raft. Those in the water quickly rallied the raft and, swimming behind it, disappeared into the darkness.

Since the torchlight barely carried as far as the other bank, we could but dimly make out a group of men in flight, who must have come up in support of the first group after pulling the raft across the moat with the tie rope. The idea of a raft was most ingenious, for a swimmer would never have been able to toss a grappling hook high enough, but a man standing would have easily had the balance and strength to accomplish this task.

Sauveterre examined the three men killed by Jonas. Each was dressed entirely in black, wore a heavy cutlass at his belt and a pistol under his hooded cape. They were dripping with water, which indicated that they must have swum over, pushing the raft, and that only the band's most experienced thrower must have stood on the raft to launch the grappling hooks.

Sauveterre realized his palms were dripping with sweat. Ten men, alighting on the north battlement walk without being seen, falling on Mespech's defenders from behind while they were firing at the island, would have massacred every last one of us.

The grappling hooks and ropes were removed, and, leaving Jonas and Faujanet to continue their rounds, Sauveterre and the twins rejoined the group of women. On the island, there was now some movement in the sheds, produced no doubt by the arrival of the fugitives from the north wall, but we couldn't see anyone and their firing had stopped. Sauveterre said nothing to the women and gave no orders to fire. And, as my mother asked him, a little nervously, what had happened, he replied quietly: "It's all over, I think, but the Gypsies will have to show themselves to get away."

No one on the ramparts was more disappointed than Samson and I were, for, even to us, it was becoming evident that we were not to have a chance to cast stones down on the heads of our assailants. I am ashamed to report that, as a result, we lost interest in the whole affair, and that our heads, weighted down by the heavy helmets Barberine had placed on them, fell onto our munitions. And on this bed, though hardly a soft one, sleep overtook us.

The ringing voice of Jonas woke us with a start. "Captain of the Gypsies!" he shouted. "Come out of your hiding place. Show yourselves! We'll do you no harm. Captain de Sauveterre wants to speak to you."

I opened my eyes with a start, and the moon blinded me. Its brightness, though nothing like broad daylight, would have been enough to read by. I stuck my nose into a crack in the crenellation and spied a tall, handsome fellow wearing neither helmet nor cuirass emerge from the shadow of one of our sheds and advance proudly as far as the large tether pole that the Brethren had set in the middle of the island.

"Monsieur," said Sauveterre, "your villainous attack on Mespech has failed. You have nothing to gain by pursuing it. To put an end to all of this, I offer you an honourable escape without being shot or pursued."

The Gypsy captain burst out laughing loudly enough to be heard on the ramparts. "As for pursuing us, Captain," he countered in a Provençal accent tainted with Catalan and carefully choosing his words, "you couldn't even if you wanted to. Your little garrison has only five men including yourself, four women and some children. They're hardly enough to cut a hundred well-armed men down to size!" Having launched this bon mot, the Gypsy burst out laughing. He had beautiful teeth that shone, even at this distance, in the extraordinary moonlight.

"Ah, but we can make you pay dearly for your retreat," parried Sauveterre roguishly.

"Not if we wait until the moon is down to withdraw! And even then," returned the Gypsy captain, "we still have a few tricks to play. We could, say, burn down your sheds on the island as we leave, and all your wagons and farm equipment along with them. And we could also burn the woods at Taniès as we go by, destroying those chestnut trees that make such fine barrels…"

At this point la Maligou, who had hurried to our sides with Little Sissy on her arm the moment the shooting stopped, whispered in reverential tones that the Gypsy captain below was the handsomest man she'd ever seen, and that if this stranger knew Mespech so well then it must be by magic or sorcery.

"My friend," replied Sauveterre with quiet fury, "I am astonished your cooking is so good. You don't have enough brains to boil an egg!" And he sent her back to her kitchen. Her buttocks trembling, she departed without a word, more dishevelled than ever, making many occult signs and crosses.

"Well then, Monsieur," said Sauveterre after a long silence. "What do you propose?"

"Five hundred livres to raise the siege of your chateau and leave the region with no damage to your forests, your buildings or your tenant farmers."

"That's a considerable sum."

"Come, come, Captain," said the Gypsy smiling. "You have three or four times that sum in your coffers! You had a good harvest this year, not to mention the sale of your barrels and cut stone from your quarry!"

Sensing any further talk would be useless, and that the Gypsy would not come down one sol, Sauveterre asked, "Suppose I pay you this ransom, what guarantee will you give me of your good faith?"

"My word," said the Gypsy with pride.

"You can't cook a roast with smoke," replied Sauveterre. "I can't eat promises."

The Gypsy laughed. "I shall leave you a hostage, then, whom you can return to me after forty-eight hours."

"Done," said Sauveterre. "On condition that you reveal who informed you about Mespech."

"Captain, nothing shall come of nothing! This information will cost you fifty livres more."

"You shall have them," agreed Sauveterre after a moment's reflection.

"As soon as I get the 550 livres," rejoined the Gypsy, "I'll tie our hostage to the tethering pole here and tell you what you want to know."

Another moment of silence elapsed before the Gypsy spoke up in a changed voice: "I'm missing three men. Do you have them?"

"Yes," said Sauveterre, "they were killed as they leapt onto our ramparts. I'll give them a Christian burial and not mutilate them as some do."

"But I don't mutilate anyone!" shouted the Gypsy with sudden heat. "It's the Moors in my band who do. When they kill a man they want to strip him not only of his happiness but of his manly honour."

"You can't have the second without the first," replied Sauveterre. "And your Moors don't piss any farther for having done it."

"Of course, but you're right," agreed the Gypsy. "And yet I've given up trying to change their minds."

"Tie up your hostage," concluded Sauveterre. "I'll fetch the money."

The jute sack containing the 550 livres must have weighed heavy on his heart as Sauveterre lowered it on a rope through the peephole in the tower commanding the entry to the island. It was swung in just such a way as to land on the other side of the spit of water that separated us from it. The Gypsy seized it, and counted out our good livres by the light of the moon. As young as I was, I was infuriated by the injustice of seeing Mespech thus ransomed.

"Well, Monsieur, what about that information?" asked Sauveterre.

"Captain," confided the Gypsy, "your good neighbour loves you dearly. He gave me 500 livres if I would attack Mespech, and promised 500 more if I succeeded! I was operating without much profit near Domme when his messenger caught up with me and told me everything about Mespech, its garrison, resources and the bear traps in the outer fortifications. So we laid out planks to get past the traps. But for your dogs, which no one told me about, Mespech would be ours."

"What happened to them?"

"They were so fierce we had to kill them."

Sauveterre paused a moment before answering. "I don't suppose you've ever met Monsieur de Fontenac?"

"Only his messenger. An Italian named Bassano. I am supposed to meet him at dawn at Flaquière."

"Where in Flaquière?"

"The big walnut tree at the crossroads."

"And will you meet him?"

"Not if you grant me another twenty-five livres."

"Ten," countered Sauveterre.

"Fie then!" said the Gypsy. "Monsieur, we're not going to haggle over this."

"What do you stand to lose if you don't go? Bassano will have no money on his person since you've failed."

"It's not so much what I shall lose," replied the Gypsy, "it's what you stand to gain by going in my place."

Sauveterre did not pursue the discussion, and the twenty-five livres were delivered to the Gypsy by the same system.

"You will find me faithful to my word," said the Gypsy. "And I trust you will abide by yours."

"Most assuredly. Where shall I send your hostage when the forty-eight hours have elapsed?"

"He'll know how to find us. I bid you adieu, Captain. I regret that the necessity of survival and feeding my band has constrained me to such villainy, for I am a good Christian and aspire as much as the next man to find grace after death in the hands of the Lord."

"Monsieur," answered Sauveterre, not without some effort, "no one can foretell the judgement of God. But if your salvation is so important to you, I hope that you may be saved."

Here Jonas began to grumble something, but Sauveterre cut him short with an unmistakable gesture and the Gypsy, dropping the bantering tone he'd adopted from the outset of the conversation, said simply, "Thank you, Captain. I shall remember your words."

The Gypsy and his band departed, as they had come, swimming to the far bank, holding their blunderbusses high over their heads. A while later we heard the sound of their horses' hooves and the creaking of the wagons that must have brought them to Mespech.

When, on Sauveterre's orders, Jonas went down to the island to untie and unhood the hostage (for they had cloaked him from head to toe), he had a happy surprise: he found himself face to face with a girl whose beauty outshone the moonlight. Her hair was brown, her black eyes ablaze, her lips full and her body lithe and vigorous to behold.

Having untied her, Jonas gazed down on her from his full height without a word, and the wench, raising her head defiantly, said, "Well, what are you waiting for? Go ahead and have your way with me. Isn't that the warrior's right?"

"It's not desire I lack," gasped Jonas, who, given his long period of celibacy in the quarry cave, was already much moved by the sight of her and struck even more by her effrontery. He added, squaring his Herculean shoulders, "Nor, so it seems, do you."

"I'll defend myself tooth and nail," snarled the wench, but with the air of someone who, after a long struggle, is prepared for defeat.

"You're not a virgin?!" asked Jonas. "Is such a thing possible living among those Gypsies?"

"It's not like you think! They have their laws and their rites. And by the Holy Virgin, I am a virgin."

"Don't blaspheme here, Gypsy woman," said Jonas, lowering his voice. "And least of all in the name of the Virgin! How old are you?"

"Fourteen."

"You're certainly old enough, then," sighed Jonas. "Well, we at Mespech have our laws and rites too. You have to say 'I do' in front of the priest—or the minister: all of which is farce and charlatanism if you ask me, given how clearly nature calls. But, what are you going to do? I didn't invent our customs. My pretty, if I took you now, the captain would send me away and I'd starve again. I'm sorry to miss this dance, pretty fox, but I must think about feeding this hulk: belly before ballet."

"Ah, so your captain is saving me for his own bed!" sneered the wench, with an undulation of her hips and a toss of her dark mane of hair.

"Don't believe it for a minute!" laughed Jonas good-naturedly. And more softly, "To the captain, all women are trickery and sure perdition of his soul. The captain's mind is on heaven and not such pretty knockers as we have here." So saying, he lightly touched each of her breasts with the tip of his finger. "But by God! He's wrong, for a prettier little weasel I never did see, Gypsy though you are."

"I'm not a Gypsy, I'm a Moor," corrected the wench with pride. "They call me Sarrazine. But I'm a Christian."

"Oh that's all well and good!" chuckled Jonas, but again careful to lower his voice. "When it comes to a roll in the hay, I'm not particular about someone's religion."

The tone of the conversation changed when Jonas brought his hostage into the great hall, where Sauveterre and the rest of us (all except Faujanet, who was left to guard the ramparts), were enjoying a repast of rye bread, salt pork and a jug of wine.

"Sarrazine," said Sauveterre drily, giving her the briefest of looks, for the emotion produced by this bright-eyed girl on Jonas and the twins could hardly have escaped his notice, "you will not be our prisoner long. I shall let you out of your cage tomorrow at dawn."

"I'll never find the Gypsy captain," moaned Sarrazine, "for he never told me where he was headed."

"Never told you?" cried Sauveterre half rising from his stool.

"No, Monsieur!" replied Sarrazine, shaking her pretty mane. "It was to gag my cries of rage that the captain hooded me. I already understood his scheme, you see, when he tied me to that pole. He just wanted to give me to new masters like a dog no one wants any more."

"And what had you done to deserve his wrath?" asked Sauveterre, examining her severely.

"I loved him too much," said Sarrazine, "and since he wanted none of me, I attacked him with a knife."

"A villainous action," commented Sauveterre. "Like the lust which begot it."

"Ah, Captain, you are right!" confessed Sarrazine, her head hanging, but her sweet breast palpitating enchantingly. "And I am so troubled by remorse that every day I pray to God to pardon me this hot-blooded nature He has bequeathed me." But a prayer so confected had absolutely no chance of meeting with Sauveterre's approval.

The awkward silence that followed was suddenly broken by my mother, who, anticipating Jean de Siorac's return to Mespech, shrieked vehemently, "What are we going to do with this shameless wench? She can't stay here!"

"We shall take counsel on this," said Sauveterre, who was not going to let a woman get the upper hand, even if she were the wife of his beloved brother. "The day is dawning," he added, "and I have another task ahead of me. Jonas," he continued, rising, "bring me my helmet and my corselet."

He was referring of course to his rendezvous with Bassano, which until that moment he had hesitated to meet, fearing some treachery of the Gypsy; but Sarrazine's story had removed his reservations. The Gypsy had pocketed Fontenac's 500 livres, the 575 livres at Mespech and, by a most amusing trick, had purged his band of a murderess. Having won at every gamble, why would he risk his ante? At this very moment, bantering and self-satisfied, he was far from Mespech in search of other prey.

Of his encounter with Bassano, Sauveterre gave no account, not even in his *Book of Reason*, and the Siorac brothers, who accompanied him, were as mute as ever.

About an hour after they left, one of the twins returned, requesting a strong rope, which led us to believe that a tree was going to
bear a hanged man. But which tree it was and how it transpired we
found out only very much later, and not from Sauveterre, but from
our father, in whom Sauveterre confided. From the few words that
escaped my father here and there over the years, we learnt a secret
that was meant to have gone to their graves with the Brethren.

I have no doubt in my mind that Sauveterre's intention was
to take Bassano alive, make a prisoner of him and use him to
bear witness against his master. But Bassano, as soon as he saw
Sauveterre in the early-morning light, rushed at him, sword drawn,
and before Sauveterre had time to unsheathe his own weapon,
Bassano bore him a blow that would have killed him had he not
been armoured with his corselet. When the Siorac brothers saw
this, they shot the assailant and laid him out cold at the feet of
the assailed.

As for the tree on which they hanged the cadaver, it turned out
to be the same used by the Fontenacs for their manorial "justice".
It was a hundred-year-old tree standing on a *pech*, no more than ten
toises from their chateau, almost under the manor lord's windows,
from which it was his custom, as it was of his ancestors before him,
to watch the spectacle of the many poor beggars who had been
condemned to the rope.

What Bertrand de Fontenac thought when he awoke to the sight
of his bloody messenger dangling from the branches of the justiciary
oak, no one knew, for he brought no complaint before any judge
and was entirely silent on the matter, having fully understood this
wordless language adopted to send the desired message from one
chateau to the other.

*

The glorious news of the capture of Calais by the Duc de Guise reached Sarlat at the end of January, but we had to wait three more months, until the first leaves of spring, before my father returned home safe and sound with his three soldiers.

I remember the exact date of his return—25th April 1558—since it fell on my seventh birthday and because the day before I'd had a major bone to pick with François de Siorac. François, as eldest, always put on great airs which he never had the courage or strength to defend, for, despite his eleven years, he was scarcely taller than I, and displayed an indifference to physical exercise that was far from engendering my respect. He must have sensed his weakness in this domain, for he avoided the vigorous exercises which Samson and I enjoyed, preferring more tranquil pursuits, such as fishing, which I had little taste for since it required such immobility. This was the subject of the dispute that erupted between us.

At Mespech, along with la Maligou, I was always the first one up in the morning, unable to keep to my bed once I was awake. I was quite surprised, then, one morning, while I swallowed my bowl of warm milk in the great hall, to see François emerge and, from the minute he entered, speak to me in an unbearably haughty tone. It was a habit he had adopted from my mother and one which must have been contagious, for Cathau copied it as well, but only when speaking to la Maligou. (With Barberine she wouldn't have dared.) "My brother, it is my intention to go fishing in the pond this morning. You will accompany me. You will carry my lines and buckets; you will tie the hooks to my lines and bait them."

I had so often, and so reluctantly, completed such disgusting tasks under his orders, hating the role of valet to which my elder brother reduced me, that this time I followed my instincts and replied firmly: "No, Monsieur my brother" (for it was thus that he requested I address him), "I shall not go."

"And why not, if you please?" snapped François, his eyebrow raised proudly over a menacing eye.

"Because I have no taste for fishing."

"It matters little whether you like it. You will do what you're told."

"Not a bit of it," I responded, looking him right in the eye. This bravado astonished him and he was some time regaining his composure.

"I am your elder brother," he said finally. "You owe me obedience."

"I owe obedience only to my father and Uncle de Sauveterre."

"And to our mother," added François.

"And to our mother," I concurred, feeling a bit guilty for having forgotten her and annoyed that François had noticed this omission.

"And to me," continued François.

"Not on your life."

"Are you forgetting that someday I shall be master of Mespech, and you but a little doctor in Sarlat?"

This wounded me deeply, but I held my temper and said as proudly as I could: "I shall be a great physician in a large city, like Paris, or Bordeaux, or Périgueux."

"Large or small," sneered François with the utmost scorn, "what will you be doing if not healing plague and smallpox victims?"

"I shall do as my father does, and does willingly, without recompense of any kind."

Here François must have felt on shaky ground, for he returned to his fishing project. "Never mind your clamourings. I require your service as your elder brother and you must obey."

"Monsieur my brother, I said no."

"In that case, I shall have to punish you."

I rose and walked towards him with determination.

"Or I shall have you punished, which amounts to the same thing," added François hastily.

I sensed his retreat and pressed my advantage, for I was outraged at the thought that this ninny would someday be lord of Mespech, as he loved to remind me. Besides, I resented the fact that he so frequently evoked my father's death, the thought of which, ever since Ricou's reading of the testament, had plunged me into the deepest apprehension.

"I despise your fishing," I hissed through gritted teeth. "It's sport for a villein, not a gentleman, who should prefer hunting, horse riding or arms."

"Arms!" laughed François. "I shot at the Gypsies on the island while you were snoring away on your pile of stones!"

"I was not snoring!" I cried indignantly.

"Oh yes you were!" returned François. "And at your side, this milking girl's son whom you've befriended."

"Samson is my brother."

"Your half-brother."

"In that case," I said, clenching my fists, "a half-brother is better than a whole brother."

"How dare you insult me!" cried François, beside himself. "How can you prefer him to me, your elder? Don't you know Samson is a filthy bastard who's not worth the dung I shit?"

My will had no part in what followed: I threw myself on François and hit him so hard he bled, and then, since instead of fighting back the coward turned tail, I gave him a good kick in the arse. He fled from the room, moaning and bleeding, thoroughly deprived of honour in my eyes. I heard him shouting, on the stairs to Sauveterre's apartments, that I had tried to kill him like Cain.

Yes, it was certainly a memorable day in the history of Mespech, when I beat up my elder brother! And the most earnest remonstrations could not undo my feat, neither whip, nor bread and water, nor my mother's tears, nor the furious looks of Sauveterre, nor even imprisonment for forty-eight hours in the north-east tower. I was locked in a bare room with only a broom for a companion, which I made great use of against the spiders, raging against them like a devil, so painful was the spanking administered by my uncle. But (except for my mother) all the women of the household were on my side and later Barberine, tears streaming down her plump cheeks, brought me a loaf of white bread, still warm from the oven, and a pitcher of water, which turned out to be milk. A few minutes later, I heard the key turning in the lock and looked up to see Samson—with his bright-red hair, his freckles and sky-blue eyes—place a pot of honey on the floor, smile at me and sneak away.

My sense of shame forbade me repeat to Sauveterre what François had said about Samson, but he learnt it from la Maligou, who had heard our fight from her scullery. Entering limping into my prison to confirm this report, he caught sight of the honey, which I was spreading on my bread, and frowned.

"What's that?" he enquired.

"Honey, Uncle," I replied, rising to greet him.

"I can see that. Who brought it to you?"

"I cannot tell you."

"But I know already," said Sauveterre. He also spied the milk, for nothing escaped his piercing, deep-set black eyes, but he didn't say a word about it. Instead, he made me repeat precisely what François had said about Samson. Then he frowned anew and said unhappily, "Those are the words of a stable boy, low, offensive and unworthy of a Christian. François will be punished. But that does not excuse your own unfortunate behaviour. My nephew, you have too much violence in your blood. At the least provocation, you charge in like a bull! These tendencies must be corrected."

He then left the room without ordering my milk or honey to be removed. And, as I found out later, he called Barberine and gave her a piece of his mind.

"I must have made a mistake," confessed Barberine all a tremble. "The two pots look so much alike!"

"Come, come, my poor Barberine, don't lie to me," shrugged Sauveterre. "Every woman thinks with her heart and you love Pierre as if he were your own!"

"Well, he is a bit of my own," whimpered Barberine.

"To be sure!" conceded Sauveterre, and continued, "What a lot of trouble it is raising children! And why do men have to get married? We pay too dearly for these transient pleasures. And now I have to put the whip to Samson, who is the most amiable of the lot! For that little François has a woman's tongue and Pierre is a violent child, quick to strike and proud as an earl."

"But he has a good heart," said Barberine.

"The heart is no excuse for the body."

And so Samson was whipped for stealing the pot of honey, which I deplored, but was delighted, as he was, when he was sent to the north-east tower as my companion in captivity, to suffer the same punishment. François was locked in the north-west tower for forty-eight hours of solitary confinement (since they didn't dare to put him in with us) but got no whipping since my fist and foot were deemed sufficient corporal correction. And thus it was that my father, returning happily from the war, found his hearth in great commotion and his three sons in jail.

I watched his tumultuous arrival one radiant morning from my tower window. After Jonas had lowered the three drawbridges, my father left Cockeyed Marsal and Coulondre Iron-arm on the island to unload the wagon, and rode into Mespech followed only by Cabusse. He galloped around the courtyard shouting triumphantly, then brought his horse to a halt in front of the main steps as my mother flew down them dressed in her most appealing low-cut gown, her blonde hair flying in the wind, looking for all the world just as my father had first seen her thirteen years before in the great hall of Castelnau.

My father leapt from his horse and, running to meet her, reached the stairs just as she tripped and fell flying into his arms, all tears and laughter, begging his forgiveness for having so angered him on the day of his departure.

"Shush, my sweet!" whispered my father. "Let's speak no more of these differences!" (But, alas! they would speak of them again, and many days running, before two years had passed.) My father added in a sonorous voice: "For now, let there be rejoicing in our halls, Baronne de Siorac!"

"Baronne!" gasped my mother. "Are you a baron, then?"

"Indeed I am! On the recommendation of the Duc de Guise, the king has just raised the castle of Mespech to a barony, a title I shall henceforth bear, and François after me!"

At this moment, the entire household rushed into the courtyard from every side with cries and exclamations, Faujanet from his cooper's shop, la Maligou from her scullery and the twins from the stables; and, clambering down the spiral staircase of her tower, preceded by little Hélix, dishevelled but eyes afire, Barberine burst upon the scene, her breasts spilling generously from her half-tied petticoat and Catherine, all flushed with excitement, hanging on her red-bordered green skirt.

"Sweet Jesus!" cried Barberine, for my father was not only her master but her hero. Finally, Sauveterre emerged, dressed entirely in black, but his deep-set eyes shining, and, forgetting his dignity, descended the final flight of steps sideways like a crab to speed his stiff-legged approach to my father's side. As soon as he caught sight of him, Jean de Siorac left Isabelle's side and rushed to embrace him.

"My brother! My brother!" stammered Sauveterre, very nearly speechless and rasping his unshaven cheek against the other's. "But what's this I hear? You're a baron?"

"That's nothing," my father whispered, "I've brought things back from Calais a good deal more substantial than a title. The English were well stocked…"

Freeing himself from Sauveterre's embrace, he tenderly kissed first Catherine, her cheeks more flushed than ever, her eyes made bluer by all this pink, and then, in succession, little Hélix, Barberine and even la Maligou, but not Cathau, to avoid upsetting my mother. Then, going to each of his men, looking him straight in the eye and patting him several times on the shoulder, he pronounced each of their names in a way he had of making the very name itself seem a great honour: "Ah, my Siorac cousins! So, dear old Faujanet! Ah, Jonas, old man!

"But where are my young ruffians?" he puzzled, looking around in amazement. "Why aren't they already here? Are they still lazing in their beds when their father has come home from the wars?"

My father conducted his tribunal with Sauveterre in their study, where on Sundays they supposedly heard Mass. My mother was not invited to join them, for they suspected that she was at once judge and interested party in this affair in which "son of a milking girl" may well have been a term François had picked up from his mother.

Each of his sons appeared before my father in turn. Samson was reproached for stealing, I for my violent behaviour and François for his insults. Yet of these three sermons, the only one my father deemed worthy of inclusion in the *Book of Reason*, for the edification of his readers and future generations at Mespech, was his harangue to his eldest.

"My son, you're not lacking in intelligence, and yet you've acted like an idiot and justice has dictated that your pride be wounded. Your right of succession is not based on equity, but on the necessity of not weakening our domain by splitting it up. It confers on you no other right. In humiliating Pierre and treating him like a servant, in making him ashamed of his future profession, you have heaped injustice on injustice.

"You now know the consequences of your actions. By speaking of Samson in the terms you used, you have deeply offended me. Think about this carefully. I will not tolerate such an offence again. The words you used should never pass your lips again if you value my affection. Samson's mother is dead. It is not your business to wonder who she may have been, but only to remember who Samson's father is, and to accord his son honour equal to your own. I ask you to remember this."

I suspect that the Baron de Mespech, in transcribing this sermon, somewhat modified it, for his speech was not normally so Latinate. But to me this document is precious, for it put an end to the subordination my elder brother attempted to impose on me, and openly accorded to Samson equality with his brothers. As for the "violence" with which I was reproached, even today I consider it to have been as justified and useful as the barber's knife that lances an infection to drain off the accumulated pus.

The triple punishment was lifted, not without a ceremony inspired by our captains' memories of the military proceedings employed to avoid a duel. We were all three brought together under their auspices and ordered to make our reciprocal apologies and express the love we each nourished for the others. I executed these orders only with the greatest difficulty, but François appeared to have none, so easily did he mould his character to whatever was expected of him. Each boy's honour restored, we then had to embrace each other rather in the manner of the wax seals that, on the last pages of treaties, ordinarily signify the end of hostilities. François had to kiss his younger brothers on each cheek and, from the evident grace with which he accomplished this task, his long compliant face brimming with compunction, you would have thought he was wholeheartedly repentant.

On that day, and many others during my seventh year, I listened with rapture to the stories told by my father and his three soldiers of the fall of Calais and of how we chased the English from our shores. It seemed as though this was a great advance in the fortunes of France, this seizure of a port that the English had made their own ever since the Hundred Years War, giving them the keys to the kingdom and enabling them to land their armies of invasion at will. For this reason, they thought of Calais as the most precious jewel in their crown and, after installing good English subjects within its walls, had so fortified it that they held it to be impregnable. They had even inscribed on its gates:

> *The French will take Calais*
> *When lead floats on water*
> *Like cork.*

This boast proves that all peoples resemble each other and that even the English speak like Gascons when bragging about their valour. At the age of seven I was astonished at the idea that "lead could float on water", greatly admiring my father for having taken part in this adventure, and happy indeed that the kingdom was whole again and in French hands, a circumstance that the Brethren never tired of exalting. I write this twenty-five years after the event, now grown up and of sound judgement, and yet my heart never fails to skip a beat when I hear the word "Calais". That this city should have become ours again after having so long been a symbol of foreign occupation, I count as the most important event in the history of the kingdom in the middle of the century.

Our neighbour, Pierre de Bourdeille, lord of Brantôme, who, though an abbot, was friendly with the Huguenots even after they occupied his abbey, told my father that the "inventor" of the battle plan for Calais was Admiral Gaspard de Coligny. It was he who had led the defence of Saint-Quentin, giving Henri II time to gather his armies to counter the Spanish invasion. I don't need to remind my reader that the admiral met his untimely end fourteen years later on the night of the atrocious St Bartholomew's massacre.

The Colignys—I mean the three brothers of this illustrious family, Odet (Cardinal de Châtillon), d'Andelot (major general of the infantry) and the admiral—were held in the greatest respect and esteem at Mespech because they were the first great lords of France to be converted to the reformed religion, encouraging many lesser nobles by their example, and giving the Huguenot party a head and a sword.

According to Brantôme, though he was merely repeating something he'd heard without naming his source, the admiral sent Monsieur de Briquemaut in disguise to spy on Calais during the Treaty of Vaucelles. Briquemaut made his report, enumerating the weaknesses of the defence, and from it the admiral drew up plans for attack, which he showed to the king. Many months later, when the war between Spain and France had broken out anew, the king recalled Briquemaut's project, and sent for it from Madame de Coligny (the admiral having been a prisoner of war in Spain since the fall of

Saint-Quentin). He passed the plans on to the Duc de Guise, who used them to great advantage.

If this story is true, it is extremely interesting, for it reveals that the future head of the Huguenot party and the future head of the Catholic party—the former accused of involvement in the assassination of the latter; in time the son of the latter would assassinate the former—were able to collaborate, even if from a distance, the one in his design of the attack, and the other by his brilliant execution of that design in the deliverance of Calais. Proof that the French can do great things for the conservation of the kingdom when they are united.

In my father's view, the weakness of the defence of Calais was based on the misconception the defenders had of the strength of their position. The city was almost entirely surrounded by water, on one side by the sea, and on the opposite side by the moats fed by the Hames river, on the third side by the swamps, and linked to terra firma by a single jetty defended by fortresses. In winter, these waters rose significantly, and the English, trusting in this natural obstacle, had gradually got into the habit of making a winter drawdown in the size of the garrison maintained at Calais. They relied, as well, on the assurance of prompt reinforcements from Dover, as well as on the Spanish army, which seemed so menacing to the French after the disaster at Saint-Quentin.

"Our success," my father began in that wonderful way he had of standing very straight, his legs spread, hands on his hips—not out of arrogance or disdain, but because his natural strength and bodily vigour were always evident, even at more relaxed moments—"our success was based on the absolute secrecy of our attack, on surprise and the enemy's utter disarray when he spied us under his walls, and on our extremely rapid execution, which eliminated any help the English might have received from Dover." And he added, "This secrecy, this element of surprise, this speed, we owe to the Duc de Guise."

"What's he like?" asked Isabelle, her golden locks shining in the afternoon sun, which traversed the arched windows of the great hall.

"You mean physically?"

"Yes," answered my mother, blushing.

"Well then," laughed my father, "he is tall and well built, and, when he's not wearing his cuirass, he dons a doublet and satin slippers, coloured bright-red in honour of a certain lady, on his shoulders a black velvet cape bordered with red, and on his head a cap, also of black velvet with a handsome red feather. Are you satisfied, My Lady?" he added, half joking, half in earnest.

"Yes, Monsieur," replied my mother in some confusion.

"In three days," continued my father, "Guise stormed the fortresses of Sainte-Agathe, Nieullay and Risbank, which guarded the jetty leading to Calais. He then ordered d'Andelot—and I'll tell you more about d'Andelot later," he noted, turning towards Sauveterre and giving him a most telling glance. "Guise, as I said, ordered d'Andelot to cut a trench to drain off the waters of the moat surrounding the city. This was not an easy task. Cabusse and Marsal can tell you; they were there. And if Coulondre was not, it's because his iron hook prevented him from handling a pick or shovel, which were as important to the taking of Calais as guns and cannon."

"And so we were!" rejoined Cabusse, after a glance at my father assured him that he was indeed free to speak. (And never was Cockeyed Marsal more rueful about his stutter than when he saw Cabusse enjoy such glory for his part in the affair.) "Indeed, there was quicksand and mire enough to muddy us right up to our moustaches!" (His audience appreciatively inspected his own impressive version.) "And for sure, we would have been swallowed up to our necks in this soup, had not Sénarpont—"

"The governor of Boulogne," explained my father.

"…distributed wattles to support us while we dug, while BANG! BOOM! the English shot at us from the ramparts, BOOM! BANG!"

"B… b… but don't f… forget the sc… scr… screens," put in Marsal, who always began his sentences with "but" even though it was such a difficult word for him.

"Ah yes, the screens," continued Cabusse. "They put up wicker shields that Sénarpont had had constructed, and were attached to posts set in the mud. The best part was that we could move them along with us as we made progress in our trench work. And there's more than one worthy that owes 'em his life," said Cabusse, with a glance at Cathau intended to show her that he included himself among these lucky heroes. "Anyway," he went on, "we finished the trenches at low tide so that all the fresh water drained straightaway into the sea. Then we were given orders to occupy the drained trench works and set up our cannon—"

"B… b… but at high t… t… tide," said Marsal.

"But at high tide," Cabusse continued, "we had to abandon our cannon, which luckily were anchored well in the muck, for the sea, rushing back into the trench ways, completely inundated them. And we had to get out of there fast, because the sea comes up like a storm. 'Sblood, I've never in all my life wallowed in more mud and icy water."

"Don't swear, Cabusse," cautioned Sauveterre.

"Begging your pardon, Captain," said Cabusse contritely, and then went on with his story, with large gestures and heated voice: "And at low tide, we had to come back and clean off the cannon and fire 'em while all the time the English gentlemen were popping off at us with their arquebuses!"

"Well, but we were firin' right back at 'em to blunt their aim," broke in Coulondre Iron-arm, who, though a man of few words, found enough of them to add, "I was one of our marksmen."

"'Tis true," confirmed my father.

"These cannon, now," said Cabusse, "were enormous." He stroked his moustache and, looking over at Cathau as if he were confusing his own virility with theirs, he added, "They were the highest calibre we had! All fifteen of 'em. And they made an infernal racket! Some said you could hear 'em in Dover!" He paused for effect, and then continued, his eyes ablaze, "It's our cannon that created the first breach in the citadel's walls and enabled our troops to storm Calais."

"Ah, but don't forget that *we* had to storm the city!" corrected my father with a smile, for he was very fond of Cabusse and looked with as much indulgence on his obvious faults as he esteemed his hidden virtues. He added nevertheless, "And as to that I can say, like Coulondre, 'I was there!' Guise decided to rush the breach that same evening at high tide, and he was the first to leap waist deep into the icy waters of the trenches where we had set up our cannon. He was followed by several hundred marksmen, d'Aumale and d'Elbeuf, his brothers, and a group of gentlemen volunteers, including," laughed my father, "myself. As wet and frozen as we were, we scaled the ramparts and forced the breach in a furious assault. It was a handsome rout, the Englishmen in the citadel quickly overcome by our numbers. The poor devils never had a chance. Except for a handful who escaped into the city, they all tasted our swords in the heat of combat.

"Once we were masters of the citadel, Guise left d'Aumale and d'Elbeuf in command there and then recrossed the moats, this time in water up to his neck, in order to direct the major part of our army. Those of us in the citadel, however, were cut off from the army for an entire night, until the tide went out, and were separated from a hostile city by a single gate!

"The governor of Calais, Lord Wentworth, decided to mount an attack straight off, despite the impending darkness, and drove us back into the trenches before help could arrive. He reinforced the gates of the citadel with four cannon brought from the streets of the city, and launched numerous attacks on our position but couldn't manage to dislodge us. When dawn brought low tide, Wentworth, realizing he'd lost half of his troops, decided to surrender. At his request, Guise granted all of the inhabitants of the city safe conduct, just as Edward III had done for the French two centuries earlier, when he had taken the city.

"D'Andelot immediately entered Calais with forty officers to contain our troops and prevent sack, bloodshed and rape."

"And the English reinforcements?" asked Sauveterre.

"They arrived, but too late. The city was already in our hands. Yes, it was the speed of the attack that did it! The whole thing was done so quickly that Calais was ours in a week."

Jean de Siorac reserved the rest of the story for his conversation with Sauveterre in the privacy of their study, and for his sons when we should be old enough to be interested in such things.

"I never saw such booty!" exclaimed Jean de Siorac, walking back and forth in the little study, while Sauveterre, whose leg was troubling him, sat quietly in the great armchair. "I'm not just talking about the munitions, but the incredible quantities of goods, of beautiful silver pieces, merchandise of all kinds, handsome furniture, Chinese silks, sheets, pewter, bronze, enough balls of English yarn to be worth 100,000 livres, and sheepskins worth 50,000! D'Andelot took the sheepskins as his share... the rest of the captains got large sums: Thermes, 10,000 écus. Sansac, 4,000, Bourdin and Sénarpont, 2,000..." He hesitated, and looked silently at Sauveterre with an impish air.

"And you, Jean?" asked Sauveterre.

"You and I," replied Siorac, "received 4,000 écus."

"Four thousand écus!" gasped Sauveterre, eyes lighting up. "Why, you must have done some exploit that you haven't told us about."

"Shh! Exploits come and go, but the money stays. We'll be able to realize our project of buying a mill in les Beunes."

"There aren't any for sale."

"We'll wait. And while we wait, we'll place this money with some honest Jew in Périgueux to give it a bit of fat."

A moment of silence followed, as heavy as the 4,000 écus, dropping one by one into the coffers of Mespech.

"The Lord continues to watch over us," said Sauveterre gravely, "and to multiply our wealth."

"Amen," said my father. He sat down facing Sauveterre and continued, "You may find it surprising that I asked for my discharge before the peace was signed. But first, you should know that peace is imminent. None of the parties has any interest in prolonging the war. But, more importantly, things have taken a new turn for us. Guise and his brother—"

"Which one?"

"The Cardinal de Lorraine… met Felipe II of Spain's minister, Granvelle, at Marcoing. During these talks, there was some discussion of peace but, sadly, a great deal more about the struggle against the heretics…"

"I would have sworn it."

"And Granvelle, who must have had spies in our army, denounced d'Andelot to Guise. Granvelle claimed that he had been preaching Calvinist doctrine in Brittany, had sent suspicious books to his brother Coligny, a captive of the Spanish, and even, during the Calais expedition, had failed to attend Mass. So what do you think Guise did?"

"He repeated the Spanish envoy's accusations against his own general to the king."

"You guessed the odious truth. The king immediately had d'Andelot arrested, and since the latter openly confessed his faith the king ordered him to be imprisoned in the Château de Melun. And so the king of France has imprisoned the most illustrious general of the French infantry at the enemy's suggestion! You couldn't imagine a more stupid, more tyrannical act."

"And yet it is good news, despite appearances to the contrary," said Sauveterre. "D'Andelot is a man of war, and a person of great stature in the kingdom. Admiral de Coligny as well. What's more, they are nephews of Montmorency on their mother's side. If d'Andelot can hold out and if Coligny converts, the king will have a hard time bringing them to trial and burning them at the stake. And if the king does not burn them, how shall he burn the others? We'll all have taken a huge step towards the freedom of conscience we've been demanding."

Siorac merely shrugged his shoulders, disgruntled. "Your hopes, my brother, seem to me excessive. You haven't accounted for the king's stupidity. He could easily decide not to burn d'Andelot and yet burn lesser noblemen. Logic has never troubled him before."

Sauveterre sighed, and his deep-set, dark eyes filled with sadness. From Siorac's reaction, he understood that his brother was not yet ready, despite d'Andelot's example, to make a public declaration for the reform. "Jean," he said quietly, "you are still too much of this world. You cannot give yourself to God without reservation."

"'Tis not true," replied Siorac. "I hold back only so as better to devote myself when the time comes. But too many lives depend on mine for me to run headlong to the stake. The important thing is not to die but to make our faith victorious."

Whereupon Sauveterre sighed again and, clenching his fists on the arms of his chair, fell silent.

"Do you realize…" said Siorac, and at this he rose and, going to the window, stood before it, gazing at the familiar yet nearly forgotten courtyard of Mespech with its well, catalpa tree and constant hustle and bustle. "You'll be delighted to learn that our soldiers also did very well. Especially Cabusse! Unable to pillage the city, they pillaged the English ships in the port. So Cabusse has brought home in his baggage a handsome booty: a good thousand écus."

"And what will he do with it?"

"Buy some land and marry. But he's not in a hurry."

"Ah but, on the contrary, there seems to be a great hurry! During your absence, we had to watch our chambermaid weep torrents of tears and sigh enough sighs to fan the flames of a forge!"

"Aha!" laughed my father. "I always suspected that that little fuse, for all the airs she puts on, needed only a flint to set her off!"

"We're already beyond the spark stage," said Sauveterre, "and well into the fire. I suppose you caught the tender glances they exchanged during our Gascon's epic tale. To tell the truth, this little filly is so in heat and ready for the stud that she may break down the stall to get at her stallion. Better marry them before we have to punish them."

"Well then, let's marry them with a feast," agreed my father.

"But Cabusse must first buy his land. Le Breuil is for sale."

"Le Breuil? Where is le Breuil? I know the name."

"It's a large farm on the road to Ayzies, just beyond our quarry. There are rocks everywhere, but there's a good spring, and the fields would be good for raising sheep. With thirty head, Cabusse and his wife could make a go of it, especially if we turn our flocks over to him for a percentage of their growth. As you know, our lambs aren't making us a sol: our current shepherd is eating our profits."

"But is Cabusse a good shepherd?"

"When he was young, he managed a transhumance of three to four hundred head all by himself."

"And what about the house?"

"The roof needs some work, but Jonas can see to that."

"Well then," said Siorac, "it's decided. But Isabelle isn't going to like it. She'll lose her chambermaid. What have you done with this Sarrazine you told me about?"

"I didn't keep her more than a week. I found a place for her. Isabelle doesn't want her at Mespech and with good reason. This wench has no shame whatsoever. She could tempt the Devil himself."

Siorac opened his mouth as if to speak, then, thinking better of it, fell silent, turned away and began tapping two fingers absentmindedly on the lead casing of the window.

5

W HEN CABUSSE BOUGHT the le Breuil farm, he hired Jonas to
replace the stones that had fallen from the roof. But he did not
stop there. Having noticed a crack which zigzagged through the stones
in the north facade, he concluded that the weight of the stone roof
was putting too much stress on a badly constructed wall, and instead
of simply repairing the crack, he got permission from the captains
to build a buttress which shored it up and gave it an appearance he
was very proud of. "Looks almost like a fortification," he boasted.

He basked in the pleasures of ownership, and every God-given
day that spring he would walk from one end of his land to the
other, enjoying its rolling hills, its spring and its woods, and grew a
little vain as he contemplated large acreage, oblivious all the while
to the outcrops of rock which everywhere prevented ploughing
or planting of fruit trees, or even much of a vegetable garden.
The woods, moreover, consisted only of groves of scrub pine so
pinched by the meagre soil that they would give but few logs for
the winter.

This poor soil was good only for grazing sheep, as the Brethren
had foreseen, otherwise they might themselves have purchased
it. But they were well pleased that Cabusse, liege and faithful
soldier that he was, had acquired it, for they would not have
wanted an untrustworthy neighbour so near to the precious
quarry and bordering so closely on the Fontenac lands.

Besides solving the problem of their sheep—which a series of incompetent shepherds had failed to make prosper—Cabusse's settlement at the le Breuil farm reassured us, since he could bring aid to Jonas, should the need arise. Thus, the le Breuil farm and the quarry, in addition to the profit that could be derived from them—the quarry's considerably greater than the farm's—had the advantage of establishing a kind of outpost at the edge of Fontenac, from which the only road coming from Ayzies to Mespech could be closely watched. Moreover—and we had the proof of this the day after their attack, from the fresh horse manure on the road—this was the route taken by the Gypsy band, and had Jonas been at the quarry and not up at the chateau with us, he would surely have been alarmed by the noise of their horses and wagons, and, using his shortcut to Mespech, would have been able to warn us.

His boots wet with the morning dew, hands behind his back, his moustache bristling, his ruddy face breathing in the joy of life and of ownership, Cabusse approached the house where Jonas was working away on the buttress, and said modestly, "Takes a while to make the rounds of my farm."

"You ought to know," scowled Jonas, with little grace, "you walk it every day." And he fell silent, full of bitter thoughts.

Cabusse turned away, puffing out his chest, and walked around his new house, admiring it afresh. "It's a pretty lodging," he said.

"It's not bad," admitted Jonas. "But it needs a sheepfold."

"Then I'll have one built."

"The captains will make you pay dearly for the stone."

"I can pay," replied Cabusse. "I have money enough left for it."

"There are only two rooms," said Jonas. "Pretty small for a family."

"I've thought of that," answered Cabusse stroking his moustache. "When Cathau gives me children, I'll make rooms up in the loft and build a little tower with a staircase to get up there."

"So, a tower is it?" sneered Jonas. "And why not a drawbridge? A portcullis? Or battlements?"

"You may laugh, stonecutter," said Cabusse. "But you can't tell me your buttress isn't a handsome piece of masonry. It makes my house into a kind of chateau."

"It will look good enough when it's finished," conceded Jonas, wiping the sweat streaming from his brow with his forearm. "Lend me a hand with this block of stone, Cabusse, instead of standing around playing the gentleman while others work."

"Ah, Jonas, you're jealous," replied his friend, giving him a hand. "And envy is an evil sin."

Together they fit the stone in place, but not without some difficulty, as strong as they were and Jonas being yet a head taller than Cabusse. When they had finished, they stood up, sweating and breathing hard.

"Weighs a ton," said Cabusse.

"It weighs a bit," agreed Jonas. "But in 300 years it'll still be here. And us, we'll be long dead."

"But meanwhile, you're still alive."

"This isn't living," countered Jonas. "At night alone in a cave with my goats and kids, all day alone with my stones, eating my heart out in solitude. Sure, I love 'em, these stones, but I can't take 'em in my arms. And I don't own a thing in this beautiful Périgord countryside other than the shirt on my back. Sure I envy you, Cabusse, sinful though it may be. If I'd fought the English at Calais instead of fighting the Gypsies at Mespech, I'd now have land, a house and a wife. Not that I covet your Cathau, mind you, for it's not for want of pretty lasses that a man goes without. Take Barberine for example; now if she weren't already married…" And, after a moment's reflexion, he added, "Or Sarrazine."

"So that's it!" crowed Cabusse. "To think I've never even seen this Sarrazine. They say she's a bitch in heat."

"And what maid of her age isn't?" growled Jonas, grabbing his hammer and administering a series of cautious and precise little taps to the stone that chipped away successive layers of thin fragments, gradually smoothing the surface until it looked as if it had been saw-hewn. He repeated, "And what maid of her age isn't?" And then, "So where's the evil? Who's offended? Only the one of the two Jeans who doesn't care for that sort of thing, not the one who does: which is why My Lady had the poor maid sent away. Which means I don't even have the pleasure of seeing her any more. Foxes like to watch chickens, you know, even when they can't catch 'em."

Cabusse said nothing, almost ashamed that he'd left his good companion so far behind, now that he was so well to do. For he loved Jonas, who was always sure to speak his mind, and was as eloquent as he himself was.

Jonas measured the right angle on the stone with his T-square, drew a line with a sharp point and cut into the other face of the stone, the sharp blows of his hammer keeping time with his words: "The long and the short of it," he said, "is money. With money you can do anything you wish. A beautiful baby with your wife" (here a hammer blow), "and meanwhile another with a pretty shepherd-ess." (Another hammer blow.) "And all that with no fear of being out of work, since you're the master, and you can't even give yourself the boot! And why are you the master? Money. And how do you earn money? With work? Not on your life! Work only enriches your master while you barely survive. But money, real silver to buy God's good earth, it's by pillaging that you come by it. Or commerce. But commerce, friend" (another blow of the hammer), "or lending grain at high interest, as these Lords of Mespech do" (again the hammer blow), "are just other kinds of plunder, just a bit gentler than the other. And now, Cabusse, thanks to what you came away with from the plunder of those English ships, and though pillaging's a sin, you're now practically a gentleman, with a wife to boot, and a house and fields and woods—and your manly pride to go with it. Come now, Cabusse, do I seem to be worth less than you?"

Cabusse resorted to his Gascon finesse and cleverness (which had so captivated Cathau) to smooth the asperities of this blunt question: "You're worth a good deal more than I, stonecutter," he confessed, putting on his most serious air and deepest voice, "for you've got a good trade and you put your heart into it. And except for some shepherding in my youth, I don't know how to do anything but kill people. Oh, I can do some cooking, maybe shoe a horse, a bit of farming and some handiwork like that, but none of that's a proper trade."

"Well, a hell of a lot of good it does me to have a trade," muttered Jonas, shrugging his powerful shoulders. "I'm always alone. Like a wolf that's lost its pack. There are days," he added, "when I'm ready to ask the Lord God to make a miracle and turn my she-goat into a woman, or, which would maybe be easier, to turn me into a billy goat."

"It's a good thing you told me," laughed Cabusse. "If I meet a huge hairy goat wandering about my place after I move in here, I'll tip my hat to him."

Jonas laughed with him, but with a laugh that mostly caught in his throat. He was overcome by the sudden realization that, come winter, when he was wrapped in his sheepskin, the wind whistling through his cave of a stormy night, Cabusse and his wife would be snuggled in a real bed just a stone's throw away in a cosy house,

Cabusse wrapped around his Cathau, all sweet and warm with her long hair...

When Cabusse moved out of Mespech, la Maligou took over as cook and the Brethren asked the Siorac brothers to move in. (In truth we needed only one more hand, but how could anyone separate the twins?) They gleefully accepted, preferring the security of the chateau to their little house, and still troubled by the memory of the plague at Taniès which had carried off their father. The two Jeans, as legally minded as ever, decided to have Ricou write up an agreement with their cousins. This document states that the Siorac cousins from Taniès would receive, in lieu of payment for their labours at Mespech, food and lodging, but no salary. However, they would be allotted seventy-five per cent of the revenues of their lands at Taniès, which would henceforth be managed by Mespech. And finally, if neither twin married, their property at their deaths would be deeded to the Brethren or their descendants.

I do not know if it was Sauveterre or Siorac who drew up these terms, but they seem to me heavily to favour the Brethren and dearly to tax the cousins for their desire for the security offered by Mespech's walls.

Cathau was at the door, preparing to leave Mespech to be married to Cabusse at the church in Marcuays, when la Maligou rushed up to her looking very serious indeed and handed her a broom handle through the doorway. "Ah, you're right," blushed Cathau, embarrassed, "I almost forgot! Thank you, Maligou!" And raising high her petticoats, Cathau straddled the broomstick. True, she displayed some things better kept hidden, but for the price of this minor affront to decency, she assured herself of twenty years of marital happiness. One was certainly worth the other, and even Cabusse understood this, as everyone gathered there applauded—all except Sauveterre, whose frown eloquently translated his impatience with superstition. Jean de Siorac, for his part, fell into a reverie on the *droit du seigneur*, a custom fast disappearing from the Périgord region.

At the church, the couple were married by the curate of Marcuays, popularly known as "Pincers"—for reasons I'll disclose later—in a ceremony conducted in the dialect of the region (mixed with French) and in accordance with the rituals of Périgord in use since 1509. Cabusse, standing in front of the choir dressed in his uniform of a legionary cavalryman but unarmed, his boots brightly polished, his moustache well trimmed, his military cap under his arm, turned towards Cathau, who stood in her veils a few steps away, and called out in a loud voice, "Catherine Délibie!"

"What is your pleasure?" responded Cathau, taking one step towards him.

"I give myself to you," intoned Cabusse in his most sonorous voice, "for your good and lawful husband and spouse by my word of honour here present before the Holy Mother Church."

Cathau came up beside Cabusse and then both turned towards the choir and Cathau, a full head shorter than Cabusse, spoke with a trembling voice, "And I receive you!"

Cabusse took several steps backwards and Cathau, overcoming her tears of joy, called in a loud voice, "Jéhan Cabusse!"

"What is your pleasure?" repeated Cabusse, taking a step forward.

"I give myself to you," recited Cathau in a clear voice, "for your good and lawful wife and spouse by my word of honour here present before the Holy Mother Church."

Cabusse came up beside Cathau and said gravely, "And I receive you."

The rings having been blessed by Pincers, an incident occurred that greatly moved Cabusse. As he took her hand to place the ring on her finger, Cathau suddenly clenched her finger to prevent him from slipping it into place. This was the sign that she intended to be mistress of her house and command her husband. "Cathau," cried Cabusse angrily, "la Maligou taught you this trick! May the Devil take her, by God!"

"Don't swear, Cabusse!" broke in Pincers.

"Excuse me, Father," replied Cabusse, but continued, "Come, come Cathau, no quarter! Give me your hand!"

"Nay nay!" cried Cathau.

"Then I'll straighten your finger myself." And so saying, he seized her hand, forcibly thrust the ring the length of her finger, braying, "I shall be your master!"

"And so you shall," announced Cathau, happy that Cabusse had overcome her resistance in the eyes of all assembled.

Pincers's altar boy brought a pitcher of wine and two glasses and, when they had each taken a sip, Pincers announced with his usual wink, "And now you may kiss each other!" Cabusse seized Cathau's pretty head in the crook of his arm and planted his large moustache on her lips.

"Amen!" proclaimed Pincers.

My mother was very upset to have lost Cathau, who had entered her service at the age of twelve. Her thirteen years of close personal attentions had not, of course, been without their storms, given my mother's haughty and querulous manner and Cathau's own quick tongue, square jaw and look fierce enough to brave any tempest. When they got going, there was tumult enough to shake the entire chateau, and my poor father would send Barberine scurrying to Isabelle bearing a note pleading, "Madame, if you must scold your chambermaid, do it without such shouting."

But it would have been easier to turn the Dordogne from its natural course than to calm my mother's fury when Cathau provoked her. "Shameless hussy!" screamed my mother. "Worthless bitch! You came from nowhere and back you'll go to tend your cows!"

"I was never a cowherd!" protested Cathau, profoundly insulted. "I was born at the Château des Milandes, same as you!"

"How dare you compare yourself to me, you filthy slut," shouted my mother. "Soon you'll be saying you're descended, like me, from Raoul de Castelnau, who fought gloriously in the Crusades!"

"But well I could be," retorted Cathau, her eyes ablaze. "They always said that your ageing grandfather had a weakness for my mother while she was your mother's chambermaid! If that's true, My Lady, then, like it or no, I might just be your aunt—even if I am younger than you are."

This perfidious remark never failed to exasperate my mother: "My aunt!" she shrieked with a contemptuous laugh. "A fine aunt you'd make! A hussy! An ingrate! A minx who can't even do my hair!"

"A minx, My Lady," objected Cathau drawing herself up straight, "but I am a virgin!" And knowing how to get under my mother's skin, she added, "And if you don't believe me, ask Monsieur de Siorac to examine me, for he's a doctor!"

"Me?" screeched my mother. "Get my husband to stick his finger where I wouldn't even put the tip of my cane?"

"Madame," said my father, pushing his way into Isabelle's apartment, his brow furled and looking very severe, "either get rid of your chambermaid this minute or get used to her. But for the love of heaven, cease this squabbling and this infernal noise, both of you! The entire household is in the courtyard laughing at your bickering. And as for me, I'm going deaf listening to your screams."

If my mother had been a little less infatuated with her noble lineage (for Raoul de Castelnau reappeared frequently on her tongue) she might have realized that, as an orphan who had found little affection in Madame de Caumont, she had become attached to Cathau like a little sister. But she refused to recognize such a tender feeling for such a "worthless maid", and, resenting her own love for her, put her down constantly, which Cathau, for her part, could not tolerate. She admired her mistress and imitated her in everything, even to the point of believing herself to be at least partially of noble birth. Which is why their quarrels had something of a comic air to them, for the threats of dismissal could never have been carried out, the intimate connection between these two women being much deeper than any purely official one.

This was never more evident than when Cathau left Mespech. There were tears, sighs and hugs without number, and my mother fell into despair and melancholy from which she took many months to recover, even though Cathau and her husband (and Jonas) ate at our table every Sunday and Isabelle went twice a week to see her chambermaid at the le Breuil farm.

The Brethren complained that the escort required for this trip, given the danger of the roads, took two men away from their work for an entire afternoon, a special hardship during the summer months when there was so much to be done on the land. However, since he worried about my mother's deep despondency, especially now that she was pregnant again, my father always gave in.

Cathau was replaced by Franchou, a cousin of the Sioracs on their mother's side, a beautiful girl copiously endowed and of a placid nature, with vacant cow's eyes that seemed endlessly to ruminate on a pastoral daydream. As chambermaid, she wasn't worth Cathau's salt, to be sure, and she heard about it often enough. But she was so humble and submissive that no quarrels could have been conceivable. "Yes, My Lady. Certainly, My Lady. As you wish, My Lady. Of course, how silly of me. Begging your pardon, My Lady. My Lady is quite right, I don't know how to do anything right! My Lady is so patient with me"—a phrase which brought tears of laughter to my father's eyes whenever he heard it.

A few weeks after my father's return from the war, Isabelle de Siorac conceived, and, on the very day she was certain of it, Barberine left Mespech to go make a child with her husband so that she could serve as wet nurse for the new baby. When you stop to think about it, wet-nursing is a strange trade indeed, since your pregnancies have to coincide with your mistress's. The rest of the time, separated from her husband, Barberine had to remain as chaste as Jonas in his cave, for it would have been disastrous for her to make milk at the wrong time or to be dry when it was needed.

I was saddened by Barberine's departure, and missed her evening kisses, her large warm breasts and the infinite tenderness she dispensed to all of us alike as we were tucked into bed. Little Hélix, whose reasonable looks and pretence of good behaviour in the presence of the two Jeans thoroughly fooled them, was appointed to care for us in the tower. The first evening Barberine was away, my mother took it upon herself to climb the winding staircase to our tower room, preceded by Franchou bearing an oil lamp, and to burst in among us in her finery and jewels, like a queen, leaning on her cane. ("Madame," kidded my father, "what need have you of a cane? You're twenty-seven years old and your legs are yet solid.") We were all in bed and little Hélix was preparing to blow out the candle. "Madame," I said quickly, "should we rise?"

"No no," the Baronne de Siorac replied graciously, "you may remain in bed. You too, Catherine." But since she named neither Samson nor little Hélix, both thought it best to get up and remain standing barefoot beside their beds, clad in their nightgowns, though my mother seemed to take no notice of them.

"My good son," said Isabelle, cocking her pretty head to one side, her right arm outstretched resting on her cane, "how are you?"

"I am well, Madame."

"Bring your lamp here, Franchou, silly bird!"

"Yes, Madame."

"Ah, you look well indeed, though the sun is beginning to ruin your complexion."

I found it odd that my mother needed lamplight to notice this since it was not as though she didn't see me by the light of day, even if only at mealtimes. "Catherine," she continued, moving to her bed, "how are you? Franchou, stupid cowherd! Bring the lamp!"

"Yes, Madame," stammered Franchou.

"Well, Catherine, I asked you a question."

"Yes, Madame," whimpered Catherine, more dead than alive. Whereupon my mother began pacing up and down in our room in all her beauty and grace, the tip of her cane ringing on the wooden floor, passing back and forth in front of Samson and little Hélix, paying little more attention to them than she did to Cathau, treating them all as if they were nothing more than "little turds" by the side of the road.

Upon reflection, I did not have to search very hard to find the source of my brother's unfortunate metaphor about Samson. "Well," said my mother, abandoning her royal silence, "I wish you goodnight, my son. And to you as well, Catherine."

"Thank you, Madame," I said.

And with some delay, Catherine, in her tiny voice, which, I know not why, made my heart ache, breathed, "Thank you, Madame." Having thus dispatched her duty, my mother gave a little blow of her cane to Franchou's backside, indicating that she should lead the way, and disappeared down the winding staircase, her skirt sweeping behind her majestically as she cursed the narrow passageway. No sooner was she was gone than little Hélix jumped up on Barberine's bed and began to dance a jig with grimaces and contortions that brought roars of laughter from Samson. I laughed as well, but Catherine burst into sobs and I had to get up and take her in my arms to comfort her.

The following evening, my mother, dissuaded from returning by the staircase which she claimed had nearly "broken her neck", delegated Franchou to visit us, lamp in hand, to ask if "her son and Mademoiselle Catherine were well".

"Yes, Franchou!" I laughed, for, behind her back, little Hélix was imitating my mother with her cane.

"In that case," said Franchou, her cow's eyes fixed on me with astonishment, "Madame your mother wishes you goodnight."

"Thank you, Franchou," I cried, now laughing uncontrollably, for had I not laughed I think I would have cried. No doubt, despite her pomp, my mother did love us. Today I am certain of it, however much I may have doubted it at the time. So many of my memories of her prove she was not hard-hearted—for example, her intervention with the Brethren to put an end to the punishment of the marauders. It was only her absurd idea of her rank and birthright that led her to put on such airs with her children. How different from my father, who, when he met Samson and me in the hallways of Mespech, would put out his arms to block our way, saying in a joyful voice, "Halt right there, you little clowns! There's a toll to pay!"

"What toll, father?"

"Three kisses each! And you must pay in advance. No arguments!" Whereupon I would throw myself into his arms and he would pick me up and apply three sonorous kisses to my cheeks. And the same for Samson. And after a little tap on our rears, off he went gaily on his way.

My mother found this behaviour common and much too bourgeois. She was likewise shocked by the profits that the two Jeans
derived from their commerce in cut stone, barrels and grain, and,
even more, by the austere economy with which they conducted the
household affairs of Mespech and the accounts that were kept of
everything. "One hundred pins, for Isabelle: five sols," noted my
father in his *Book of Reason*. "My cousin," said Sauveterre, a week
later as he picked up a pin in the courtyard, and limped, breathing
heavily, all the way to her chambers to return it to her: "Here, I
believe this belongs to you. Don't lose your pins, my cousin. They
are not cheap, you know."

I feel certain that it was not the winding staircase that discouraged
my mother from returning in person to bid us goodnight, but the
presence of Samson, who evoked so many painful memories, and
little Hélix as well, whom she detested ever since she had caught
my father's eye lingering too long on the girl's budding breasts. She
was not fooled, as the two Jeans were, by Hélix's "good behaviour".
And her instincts did not betray her: for little Hélix, in Barberine's
absence, had taken over Barberine's large bed where, once Franchou
had left and the lamp was extinguished, she commanded me to join
her. I obeyed, half contented, half disturbed. And, in that propitious
darkness and warmth of the bedding, we engaged in such pinching,
sucking and biting, all manner of cooings and "I'm on top, you're
underneath" or "I'll smother you and you smother me" and numerous other games, none of which was altogether innocent.

Isabelle de Siorac gave birth in February 1559 to a stillborn and
poor Barberine was left out of pocket for her expenses. She had a
big baby boy on her hands and, as she put it, "milk for sale". But
since good wet nurses, who were healthy, gentle and rich in milk,

were rare, she soon received an offer from a rich bourgeois from Sarlat whose perennially pregnant wife had just delivered. My mother was greatly alarmed: to let Barberine go was to risk losing her. What would happen when she herself was ready to have another baby? She persuaded the Brethren to keep Barberine at Mespech as governess of the children for a sol a day, with permission to take in and suckle the newborn from Sarlat. My mother even went so far as to offer to be godmother to the new baby, and, taking her role to heart, was often seen, even in public, cradling the child in her arms, "little turd" though he was and "low-born".

After such fear of losing Barberine, Catherine, Samson and I were overjoyed to submit once again to her reign from her great bed in the tower, even if it did mean sharing our space with a little bawler.

When she returned, she wore around her fat white neck a necklace that her grandmother and her mother (both nurses, Barberine being the third in the dynasty) had worn before her and which was said to favour a regular and abundant lactation. Made of simple black thread it stood out against the brilliant white of her skin and held three carved agates, the middle one in the shape of an elongated olive and the framing ones perfectly round. My father joked that it was an ancient symbol of male potency inherited from the pagans, but I understood only later what he meant by this. As for Barberine, she immediately crossed herself at these words and protested that she was a good Christian and her mother and grandmother before her. Nevertheless, alarmed by my father's jest, she could not rest until she had added a cross to the necklace, which took nothing away from its virtues, quite the contrary.

At the end of April 1559, the sad news of the disastrous Peace of Cateau-Cambrésis reached Mespech, plunging the two Jeans into fury and desolation. How many times since have I heard my father quote the strong words of Montluc on this subject: "In one hour and by a single stroke of the pen was everything surrendered; and our joyous past victories dirtied and blackened with three or four drops of ink."

Henri II had had but two thoughts: to make peace at any price in order to strike the Huguenots again, and to liberate Montmorency, who was a prisoner of the Spanish. In his short-sightedness, he ceded to Emmanuel-Philibert the territories of le Bugey, Bress and Savoy without a fight, and threw into the bargain the hand of Marguerite de France, the daughter of François I.

"Sire," said Monsieur de Vieilleville, the governor of the Île-de-France, "what worries me so deeply is that you have made such an immense gift to the lieutenant general of your natural and mortal enemy, the king of Spain, who, thanks to this reallocation, will now be able to march to the gates of Lyons, which was formerly almost in the middle of your kingdom and now lies at its very frontier." But nothing could change Henri's mind, and, except for Calais, everything was surrendered, even Piedmont. To seal this awful treaty, Felipe II, who had just lost his English queen, married Henri II's daughter, Élisabeth. By this marriage and that of his sister to the Duc de Savoie, yesterday's enemy was now our ally.

The king had rushed to make this peace only in order to turn his guns on those of his subjects who had a different way of praying to the Lord. The ink on the treaty was scarcely dry before he struck, and his first blow was to the head.

The Paris parliament had been in session since the end of April to establish a policy regarding the Protestants. Certain of the parliamentarians hoped to protect the reformers from further persecution, some because their hope for the independence of the kingdom made them hostile to the influence of the papacy and Spain, others because they themselves had been converted to the reform. However, on 10th June, the king entered the hall where the parliament was in session and ordered their deliberations to continue in his presence.

The counsellors refused to be intimidated. Viole and Du Faur demanded the suspension of all attacks against the reformers, and proposed the establishment of a council. Anne de Bourg, protesting the tortures, cried, "It is not a matter of little consequence to condemn those who, from the flames that devour their bodies, invoke the name of Jesus Christ."

Henri II was little open to ideas, much less to new ideas. He listened vacantly to these orators, then, rising abruptly, ordered their arrest. This was not only a coup d'état without precedent in the history of the parliament, but also proof that, henceforth, no one would be spared, no matter what his position or birth. In destroying the authority of this great body, with his own hands, the king buried the legality of the kingdom and established himself as head of the Inquisition. In his entourage, there was much discussion of a project, designed to end this heresy once and for all, that simply outlawed all reformers, a measure that would have allowed the populace at large to kill them with impunity, and, once dead, to strip them of their lands.

This news reached Mespech on 30th June. "You see where we would be today, my brother, if I had listened to you," my father said to Sauveterre. "I can name you ten lords of Périgord, not even counting Fontenac, who would be all too happy to band together to parcel out Mespech, if we had given them the least excuse."

"When you serve God and God alone," replied Sauveterre, "you must trust yourself to His Providence. Israel endured numberless persecutions, yet the Lord has always punished her enemies in the end."

At the very moment Sauveterre pronounced these words, Henri II, who only that morning had been the healthiest and jolliest man in all of France, lay dying in mortal agony, his left eye pierced by the tip of a lance during a jousting match.

For this joust, all the paving stones had been removed from the rue Saint-Antoine in front of the Hôtel des Tournelles, so that the horses could gallop on sand and the jousters' falls would be less of a shock. Henri II, as defending champion, was to ride three jousts, his opponents one each. An avid sportsman, Henri took enormous pains to prepare himself for this great event, for he attached a much greater honour to unhorsing his assailant in a joust than to preserving a province of his kingdom. And when his first adversary, Emmanuel-Philibert de Savoie—who had long since assumed this title though he possessed not a square inch of Savoyard territory— entered the Hôtel des Tournelles to present his respects to the king, Henri, already armed and helmeted, said gaily: "Now, my brother, press your knees hard into your saddle, for if I can, I shall empty your stirrups, without a care for our alliance."

He did not succeed, however, for each of the two adversaries broke his lance on his opponent's shield, and the duc, his lance in the dirt, seized his saddle-bow and swayed but did not fall from his horse. The judges gave the advantage to the king, but the second joust, run against the Duc de Guise, was ruled a draw, for neither man had flinched. In the third and final joust, the king was matched against the Comte de Montgomery, captain of the guards, a tall, rather stiff young man in the bloom of his twenties. He and the king came together in a terrible clash, each breaking his lance but without clear advantage to either side. At this the king was angry, and raising his visor cried that he wanted his revenge on Montgomery and requested a fourth joust.

This request so manifestly violated the rules of jousting (no defender may joust more than thrice) that it met with some opposition: nota-bly from Monsieur de Vieilleville, who had already entered the lists to run his three jousts as the next defender, and from Montgomery himself, who, as assailant, was entitled to but one joust and feared that the other assailants would cry foul play. But the king, raising his voice, refused to listen to reason, sent Vieilleville from the lists, and ordered Montgomery to return. Montgomery returned very much in spite of himself, and stiffer than ever.

The king's obstinacy had created a certain unease among the spectators, so much so that when the joust began, the trumpets and horns which had made such ear-splitting fanfare for the previous matches fell silent. This mortal silence was later esteemed to have been a deadly omen.

Everything happened very fast. Each assailant broke his lance, but rather than throwing his broken lance to the ground as he should have, Montgomery held on to it. And as his steed continued its headlong race towards the king after their initial shock, the broken lance struck the king's helmet, forcing open the visor and piercing his eye. The king dropped his shield, fell forward on his horse, but managed enough strength to hold on to the animal's neck as it galloped to the other end of the lists, where it was reined in by the royal attendants. "I am killed," moaned the king weakly as he fell into the arms of the grand squire.

He lived ten more days in the most atrocious agony. From Brussels, Felipe II sent Vésale, the famous surgeon, who, assisted by Ambroise Paré, probed the wound and attempted to extract the splinters of the lance. To attempt to understand the extent of the wound, the two great doctors had four heads of recently executed criminals brought from the Conciergerie, and had each struck violently with Montgomery's broken lance. But these macabre experiments shed no light on their problem.

The king regained consciousness on the fourth day, and ordered the marriages of his sister and daughter to his recent enemies to take place at once. Which was done, though in the general affliction and the sense of the king's impending death, the weddings without oboes or violins resembled nothing so much as a funeral cortège. Those who were present found themselves repeating the sinister prophecy of Nostradamus:

The young lion the old shall overcome
On bellicose field, in singular duel;
In golden cage his eyes all pierced and numb
By two wounds one; then die by death most cruel.

It was whispered that "the young lion" was of course Montgomery, and the "golden cage" the golden helmet of the king.

The king died two days after the princely marriages, on 10th July 1559. The story I have just reported reached Mespech on 25th July in a letter from Paris. I found a summary of this letter in the *Book of Reason* written by my father, along with Sauveterre's comments scribbled in the margins: "My brother, was I not right not to despair? By arresting Anne du Bourg and the counsellors of the parliament of Paris who hold our ideas, Henri II hoped to strike a blow to the head of the reform movement. And it is to his head, in turn, that God has struck a blow. The judgements of the Lord are a deep abyss, illumined at times by a great light. The tempest of persecution that has so overwhelmed the entire kingdom will be appeased by this clearly providential blow."

To which my father answered on the following day, 26th July: "This is hardly likely. Henri II will be succeeded by his son François II. He's but a child and is married to Guise's niece, Mary Stuart, who has bewitched him. Power will not change hands, nor will the persecutions cease." Jean de Siorac was not wrong: Henri II was scarcely in his tomb before Guise was master of the kingdom. Six months later, Anne du Bourg was burnt in public as a heretic.

In 1560 the haying was done late in the season at Mespech because the first part of July was rainy and windy and even included a couple of days well below freezing, resembling winter more than summer. Finally, on the 15th, the weather turned hot and dry and Siorac, having had all the scythes brought to him, cleaned away the grease which coated them and found them all shining and sharp—except for one, which had gone dull from overuse. He asked Faujanet—whom no one could equal in this task—to beat the blade sharp again, and Faujanet, placing it on a little anvil, spent the next two hours tapping it gently with precise hammer strokes whose regular rhythm was so captivating that I stopped for quite a while to watch.

We had sent word to our tenant farmers that we required their help, and, at daybreak the next morning, our hayers, Cabusse, Marsal (Coulondre being unable to scythe given his iron hook), Faujanet, Jonas, Michel and Benoît Siorac, Maligou, Fougerol (from Taniès), and Délibie from Flaquière all lined up at the edge of our field at Haut Pré, measuring their distance from each other to get just the right sweep.

Since Samson and I were going on our tenth year, we had got permission to get up that day while it was still black as pitch and to cut the nettles along the way with an old chipped scythe, each taking turns cutting and raking. François, for his part, joined the Brethren and Coulondre Iron-arm on horseback, patrolling the crest of the hill and the edge of the woods, an unloaded pistol in his holster and his fists clenched on his thigh. But as soon as the sun began to beat down, he grew tired of the jolting of his little black gelding, quit his guard duties and went back to the house. He didn't even return to eat with us in the shade of the great walnut tree at eleven o'clock since he didn't much like mixing with our servants and sensed that he was not much liked by them. For, besides his willingness to work, what our Périgordians appreciate in a lad are frank speaking, an easy laugh and a quick repartee, and they didn't like the moodiness of our eldest, having learnt to mistrust a man who is too quiet, like a dog who won't bark.

With the heavy rains of this rotten month of July, the nettles had greatly thrived both in size and number, so that Samson and I undertook a terrible massacre, putting them all to the sword and taking no prisoners. "Take that, villainous Englishman," swaggered Samson, "that will teach him to invade Calais instead of staying at home!" We killed thousands of such unfortunates, especially since they were rather poor at defending themselves, hanging their stinging leaves forlornly and offering their stalks to be scythed, where a mere stick would have sufficed.

"Hey there, my rascals!" shouted my father, half serious, half joking from atop his horse. "You're behind the times on the history of the kingdom. Don't you know the English are no longer our enemies now that they've surrendered Calais, and ever since Elizabeth succeeded Bloody Mary? Elizabeth's no papist, as I've already told you."

The hayers were lined up awaiting the signal from the captains to begin. Some stood shivering in the cold breeze of early dawn since they'd dressed lightly, anticipating the heat of the morning and the sweat to come. With their left hands caressing the little cup hanging at their sides where the whetstone bathed in water, they draped their right hands over the back of their blades, the scythe held in profile before them like the famous engravings of Death.

But all nine scythers seemed more content than sad. For as hard as was the task before them, it was still a feast day.

At Mespech we never held back on the food at haying time. And all nine had already filled their paunches at four that morning with a thick vegetable and pork soup followed by a copious cup of wine. Lined up at the edge of the field, they silently watched the grasses swaying in the breeze all the way down to the edge of the wood below. Great God, the meadow had surely taken advantage of the rain, the bitch: high, green, shining and thick as a woman's hair the grasses stretched out in such immensity that the scythers told themselves there was no way they could ever cut all of it, even with nine of them working from dawn to dusk. Better not to think too much about it, but remember that at eleven there'd be good rye bread, some salt pork and all the wine you could drink.

Below them, on the hayrick, they could spot the nine loaded arquebuses that the Brethren had provided so as to arm the hayers in the event of an attack. They were grateful to the captains for these precautions, and for their patrols on horseback while they worked, something not every master would do for his cutters, some preferring to leave their workers defenceless rather than get a sore arse from a day in the saddle.

When Jean de Siorac raised his arm to give the signal, Faujanet, who was at the far left of the line, stepped forward and cut into the edge of the field, making his blade whistle in manly fashion through the dew-covered grass, carrying the entire bladeful with his backstroke, leaving a regular swathe on his left. Jonas, next up, gave him a scythe's-length lead before he cut into the field in his turn, and his neighbour, Fougerol, waited a few strokes as well before beginning his swathe. The distance from scyther to scyther was thus maintained right to the last, who, by the time it was his turn, was eight toises behind the leader. Thus each one had a clear view of the field before him and so avoided both the risk of catching the point of his blade on the heel of the other's and the problem of leaving uncut grass between them.

As first man on the left, Faujanet was leader of the field, setting the rhythm for the others and indicating each halt to sharpen their blades by sounding two notes on a small horn he wore around his neck. The Brethren had chosen Faujanet for this, not because he was the best mower of the lot, but, quite the contrary, because he was an average cutter, neither too strong nor too fast, and consequently a man everyone could follow without upsetting the overall rhythm and pattern of the field.

Of course, Faujanet did not understand his responsibility in this way. My father noticed with a smile that haying time was his moment of power and glory, and to watch the dark little man's face as he seized his horn to blow his two notes (or three to start up again), you could see the pride he felt in his post. Moreover, he loved to hay. Certainly, the scythe was not a plaything in his hands the way it was for Jonas. For Faujanet, the work required an effort of back, arms, hips and his stubby legs, to keep his torso from pitching forward with the force of his swing. But he was able to pace his work with an eye to the long day to come. He was careful not to catch too much grass on his blade or to hurry his backswing. As soon as he felt fatigue setting in, he would sound two notes on his little trumpet, using the blade-sharpening time to catch his breath, passing the dampened whetstone back and forth across each face of the blade. The important thing was not to go fast, but to finish the job.

Faujanet also knew that starting early was like eating one's dessert first, since at dawn the dew-covered grass was tender and accommodating, but when the sun reached its height and burned off the dew, the grass would require more strength at the very moment the cutters would have less of it, drops of sweat running from their brows into their eyes, and down their backs between their shoulder blades. He well knew he would have to make more and longer pauses for sharpening, not because the blade required it (though the blade can never be too sharp) but because the cutters did.

To some degree his duties kept Faujanet from feeling his fatigue, but when it became too insistent, he would distract himself by listening to the "swish… swish" of the nine blades penetrating into the grass to cut it at ground level. Since they never swung exactly at the same moment, there was never an interval, but rather a series of "swish… swish… swish…" which overlapped. This was music to his ears, because it sang of an abundance of hay in the loft, of well-fed cows, but also because it sang of the world of men: you never saw a wench out 'neath the hot sun cutting for hours at a time. She might rake or pitch hay, but she'd never scythe. Or at most, she might be given an old chipped blade to cut nettles by the side of the road like the master's little rascals.

One can be small, bow-legged, dark-eyed and dark-skinned like Faujanet, but still have brains, and Faujanet knew how to judge the quality of his hay. Moreover, as a cooper he had a higher view of things than a peasant who is caught up in his gleanings. A peasant worries about everything, even abundance, and his favourite saying is: "Year of good hay, year without pay." Which meant that an abundance of grass portended a year of mediocre grain harvests. But thanks to his superior judgement, Faujanet knew that one couldn't entirely trust these proverbs, and he quietly preferred the version: "Year without hay, year without pay," as had been proved in 1557 when a terrible drought had ravaged Périgord for eight months, burning the grass, drying up wells and springs and reducing livestock and peasants to famine.

On the request of the consuls of Sarlat, the bishop had ordered prayers in all the churches of the diocese that year, and a great procession to the chapel of the Virgin between Daglan and Saint-Pompon, under a blistering sun, behind a cross, with chants from the Litany of the Saints. They had taken great care to omit no one from this prayer, afraid of vexing the forgotten saint and causing him to continue the drought. The priests had gone hoarse reciting secret Latin prayers known to be particularly effective against drought. The faithful had gone to confession en masse and had given alms with unusual liberality, especially given how poor they were then, yet, despite all these remedies, no rains had fallen, and with winter real misery had set in, and farmers had sold or butchered their starving livestock, small sharecroppers were ruined as owners mortgaged their land away, hundreds of day labourers were dismissed and, without work, turned to wandering the roads of France, begging or eating acorns and tree bark.

So Faujanet was happy that the grass under his scythe was high, thick and succulent, for this hay, if bad weather didn't rot it before it reached the lofts, meant fatted veal, beef and mutton, lots of milk, vigorous horses to pull the ploughs through the fallow land—in short wealth and happiness for the little people. The lords, like his masters at Mespech, always had vast reserves to keep them alive, and even profited from bad years, but the small farmers never had enough. If the Lord's heart hardened again towards the people of Sarlat as it had in 1557—though no one could ever understand why He had it in for the Périgordians, who were not visibly more sinful than others—and if He stopped the clouds from sending rain on the province, then the poor would quickly suffer the pain and hardship of hunger.

That winter there was no end to the talk in the countryside around Taniès, Sireil and Marcuays about the wolf that Jonas had tamed. I myself couldn't wait to see it, and Samson and I got permission from the Brethren to accompany Jonas to his cave one Sunday evening and to spend the whole night there.

Certainly it's not every day that you get to sleep in a cave, whose entrance is closed by a large rock, like the one the Cyclops Polyphemus slept in, and which has a hole in the domed roof over your head to let the smoke from the fire escape. And it's not an ordinary thing, when you're going on ten years old, to sleep beside a wild-eyed wolf with feral coat, along with a goat and kids that the wolf doesn't touch, not to mention the Herculean Jonas wrapped in his sheepskin, and in his own fur which is as thick as the wolf's.

But I'm getting ahead of myself. First we got to stay up late, sitting around the fire Jonas had built on a hearth of raised stones, whose flames did battle with the cold wind that came rushing through the circular hole in the vaulted roof until they vanquished this cold breeze from above, which retreated before the smoke and the current of warm air from below. La Maligou had provisioned us with a roast chicken, wrapped in a napkin and placed in a basket, and Samson and I each ate a leg, Jonas the two breasts, and the wolf—or rather she-wolf—the carcass. It was wonderful to hear her cracking the bones in her powerful jaw, stretched out in her wild coat between Jonas and me, her head slightly askew, her eyes half-closed in the voluptuousness of the moment. For dessert there were excellent walnuts, which Jonas broke like peas between his thumb and index finger and then shelled in a trice. Throwing the shells into the fire, he planted their meat in a fresh cheese offered by his goat, who also provided us with milk for our dinner, which we drank from a pitcher Jonas passed around, the wolf even getting her share in her own bowl. You should have seen her lapping up this foaming milk as if she were a cat, then licking her chops to catch every last drop.

"Jonas," said Samson, "isn't your wolf going to gobble up your goat someday?"

"Why would she do that?" asked Jonas. "My goat gives her milk same as to me."

"But does she know it's the goat who gives it?"

"Surely she does. Don't go thinking that animals are so dumb. I never milk my goat without having my wolf at my side, her tongue out and mouth wide open hoping for a warm stray drop from her teat. Of course she knows."

"But wolves like meat," I pointed out.

"So I give her enough from my hunting." Without getting up, Jonas reached out his long muscular arm, grabbed a bulging sack and pulled out three handfuls of chestnuts, which, given the size of his hands, made a handsome pile in front of him. A little to one side of the brightly burning fire, he made a small oven of hot coals into which he slipped the chestnuts. A wonderful odour filled the cave and brought back memories of our evenings at Mespech when the first bitter frosts had come on.

"Jonas," said Samson, "they say that your goat is going to turn into a wench someday and that you'll marry her."

"Who says so?"

"Cabusse."

"If God could only grant such things!" mused Jonas without so much as a smile. "For I could well use the company. But all things being equal, I'd just as soon it were the wolf that would change into a woman and not the goat."

"Why so?"

"Because my goat gives me milk and cheese, which a woman couldn't. And besides," he added, staring into the fire and speaking in a tone so serious that one would have thought the transformation was not only possible but quite imminent, "my she-wolf is a beauty. Lots of wenches would be proud to have her bright eyes and her thick hair."

So saying, he plunged his hands into her fur and caressed the animal, and the wolf, turning her head towards him, gave out a sigh and looked at him so lovingly that I really believed that a miracle was about to be performed right there beneath my eyes as I stuffed myself with roasted chestnuts.

"Jonas," said Samson, "how did you tame your wolf?"

"With patience and love. I found her in a foxhole that she'd enlarged, her eyes all feverish and so skinny that her ribs showed. She'd broken a paw, and to get away from her pack, who, as you know, always kill and eat their wounded, she had hidden away there. I brought her milk, then a bit of meat, and when she was strong enough to pull herself out of the den I put a hemp rope about her muzzle and splinted up her paw."

"So you can also set bones, Jonas?" I queried, looking at him with new respect.

"Yes I can. I learnt it from my great-uncle, who was considered by his village to be a bit of a sorcerer, but for good, not evil, so much so that even the village priest respected him. Oh, if only he were still alive!" he sighed, his words trailing off as he looked dreamily at his wolf.

And conversing thus, Samson and I gradually fell asleep on the mattress of chestnut leaves prepared by Jonas, three large sheepskins piled on top of us. It was so warm that, when I awoke at dawn with the fire gone out, my face was frozen but my body toasty. I was amazed, on opening my eyes, not to find myself in the tower room at Mespech, and I was about to close them again when they encountered two yellow eyes of a wild animal staring straight at them. My hair stood on end. It was the wolf.

"Jonas!" I cried.

"What is it?" asked Jonas, standing over me at what seemed a prodigious height.

"Your wolf is staring at me."

"Like a dog looks at a bishop," answered Jonas. "Go to sleep, Master Pierre. It's not time for the morning milking and the fire isn't lit yet."

I went back to sleep and dreamt that an old man with a dark, terrifying look was entering the cave. He was enormous, bigger even than Jonas, and, leaning towards him, pronounced some unintelligible words and made some strange signs over his head. Then Jonas's face turned into a muzzle and his great body was transformed into a wolf's. He got up, yawned, showing huge pointed white teeth and then, moving over to sit next to his she-wolf, licked his chops. He looked at me intensely but I couldn't tell whether it was with hatred or friendship.

Scarcely were we back at Mespech than Barberine, who had been waiting for us, came running out to meet us, her baby in her arms and little Hélix at her heels, making faces at us from behind her back. "Sweet Jesus, there you are! The baron and Monsieur de Sauveterre are in the library waiting for you with some very important news. But you can't go in there like that! You stink. Go and wash your face and comb your hair."

Which we did, changing our linen as well since Barberine complained that even after a bath we smelt "like goat, or wolf, or worse yet". While we were each slipping on a starched shirt that smelt of lavender, la Maligou came in to sniff us. "Oh, my poor dears!" she moaned. "I smell sulphur on you." (And she made the sign of the cross over our heads.) "It's just as I thought, that wolf is a sorceress who has taken the form of an animal to bewitch our stonecutter and lead him straight to hell."

"Be still, Maligou," corrected Barberine. "The captains don't hold with this kind of talk, especially around our young masters." (But it was easy to see that la Maligou's words had made a huge impression on her.)

"So tell me, Master Pierre," said la Maligou, turning towards me with a knowing air, "does Jonas love his wolf?"

"Oh, yes!" I said. "So much so that he wishes God would turn his wolf into a woman so he could marry her."

"Alas!" said la Maligou, her whole jelly-like body trembling with compassion. "It's just as I thought. Our poor stonecutter is all bewitched and fooled and caught in the snares of the seventy-seven demons of hell. It's not the Lord God who changes wolves into women, Master Pierre," she continued authoritatively, "it's the Devil. And when it happens, there won't be any church wedding, but shameful carryings-on hidden in a cave with a goat to witness it. Alas, poor Jonas! There was never a prettier man in Sarlat. So tall, so strong and so hairy! But as they say: lust and lechery are the road to hell."

"You ought to know well enough," rejoined Barberine, much displeased by this talk, "you who sinned fourteen times in your barn with the Gypsy captain!"

"Fifteen," sighed la Maligou, making the sign of the cross. "But I never sinned. You know very well I was forced. At least the first time. As for the rest I gave myself up to the will of God."

The Brethren were waiting for us in the library in the company of an old man clothed entirely in black, and whose white hair, pale visage, broad shoulders and majestic bearing seemed to us the Moses of our Bible. I later learnt that his name was Raymond Duroy and that he was a minister of the reformed religion at Sarlat, though of course celebrating his services clandestinely. Sauveterre, also dressed in black, was seated with Raymond Duroy, both looking very grave and austere. But my father, dressed in green (which was my mother's colour), paced up and down, stopped in front of the window, pivoted on his heels, walked behind Sauveterre's armchair, seizing the back with both hands, then moved away again, returning to the window, his expression not so much grave as tense. Obviously unable to remain in place for one minute, and, in his usual way, with his brisk step, his perfect bearing, his rapid movements, and his elegant gestures, at times placing his hands on his hips in his favourite position, he swelled out his powerful chest, lifted his chin, and turned his head from one side to the other with an impatient air.

"Well, my little rascals!" he exclaimed as we entered, his face suddenly brightening but resisting the temptation to pick us up in his arms and give us his usual kiss. "Have you seen the wolf? Is it beautiful? Are you satisfied?"

"Yes, we are," I replied, a bit reticently after what I had just heard from la Maligou.

"Well then," said my father, who was quite intent ever since my famous quarrel with François that peace should reign among his sons, "greet your brother and be seated."

I stepped forward and now saw François, the back of whose chair had hidden him from view until now, and who was sitting opposite the Brethren and Raymond Duroy, cross-legged, looking very serious, the very image of virtue. I greeted him, and leaning towards us, he did me the honour of kissing me on each cheek, and did the same for Samson.

"My sons," continued my father, solemnly mastering his feelings, "we have some news of great import to share with you, as well as a grave decision Sauveterre and I have taken." He paused before continuing: "This is the news: François II died on 5th December of an infection in his ear. He had scarcely reigned a year and a half. He was only sixteen when he died." Here he stopped and looked at the Reverend Duroy as if expecting some commentary, and the minister, his hands resting on the arms of the chair, raising his long white beard and pale face towards us, said in a grave voice while remaining perfectly still:

"God has intervened in this! He has struck down the father in his eye and the son in his ear. The former because he would not look at the truths of the Reformation. The latter because he would not listen to them."

"As a consequence," said my father, "the Guise family has been banished from power. And the time was never so ripe as now for our cause throughout the kingdom. Two royal princes have taken sides with us: Anthoine de Bourbon, the king of Navarre, and his brother the Prince de Condé, whom Guise had imprisoned, but whom Queen Catherine, the regent, Charles IX being still a minor, has set free. Coligny has been reinstated with full powers. He is once again admiral of France, and d'Andelot again the major general of the infantry. Ten bishops of the realm have come out on our side, and among them the bishop of Périgueux. Michel de L'Hospital, the chancellor named by Queen Catherine, secretly favours our cause, and the regent herself, it seems, is inclined towards the Reformation. In truth," he continued with a rapid smile, "she is a wolf, but, like Jonas's, is becoming a sheep." He paused. "Here in Périgord the four Caumont brothers, whose power derives from the impregnable Château de Castelnau, have long since embraced the cause, and the Baron de Biron, captain of the companies of the king in the seneschalty of Sarlat, would not move against us even if ordered to. The proof is that when there was a riot at the beginning of December in Sarlat because the populace was upset that the Reverend Duroy here had buried a reformist, Monsieur Delpeyrat, under the lantern of the dead with neither priests nor torches, Biron refused to lend the bishop of Sarlat the support of his men at arms."

My father fell silent again, then said gravely, pronouncing each of his words clearly and emphatically: "Sauveterre and I have decided, after much reflection, that the moment has come to cease hearing Mass and openly to declare our faith. My sons," he added, coming to a halt in front of us, his hands on his hips and glancing at each one of us in turn with an impatient and severe look, "how does this sit with you? Speak! Will you follow your father?"

"I will espouse my father's faith right willingly and with all my heart," said François, somewhat too hastily, I felt.

"I am already of the faith," said Samson in a quiet voice. "I know no other."

Since I alone said nothing, my father threw me an imperious look and said curtly, "And you, Pierre?"

I replied, my heart pounding, "I was raised by my mother, by your agreement, in the Catholic religion. But I am only ten years old. I am still very ignorant. Grant me that, before I follow you, I may be given instruction in the reformed religion." My father's eyes blazed: "I will not be satisfied with a dilatory reply!" he snapped. "Beware, Pierre, lest this delay in following me be inspired by the Devil!…"

The Reverend Raymond Duroy raised his hand and, turning his noble and austere face towards my father, said in a grave voice: "Only on a resistant ground can a solid faith be built. Not everything can be imputed to the Evil One. If Pierre wishes to be instructed into the truths of our faith, I will accept the task of teaching him."

Still shaken by this sudden anger of my father—who was in everything my model and my hero—I stared at the Reverend Duroy. I was grateful to him for his unexpected help, but the more I observed his athletic build, his venerable white beard and his high forehead denoting wisdom and knowledge, the more diminished I felt in his presence. His deep dark eyes shone from his pale yet vigorous countenance and his stare was so intense that I could hardly look him in the eye. Then and there I told myself that I had about as much chance resisting this formidable champion of the new faith as I would wrestling barehanded with Jonas.

6

I T DIDN'T TAKE the Reverend Duroy a week to convert me. He even spent much of this time in other activities, for he was a man of untiring energy, always riding through the countryside preaching the Word among the people.

Even before he opened his mouth, I felt he had won the battle: I had already long since figured out that the Mass at Mespech was for women and servants. The Catholic cult seemed to consist of Father Pincers, an ignorant lecherous drunk, insistently posing scabrous questions about sexuality which always left me confused. I also equated Catholicism with the miscreants who had burnt Anne du Bourg and, before him, a long list of martyrs whose names were cited with veneration by the Brethren. I admired no one more than my father and Uncle de Sauveterre, and, through them, I had already adopted the cause of the persecuted Huguenots long before I embraced their faith.

And yet, I did not embrace that faith without some reticence, for I had some reservations I knew I must stifle to avoid worse quarrels with my father. For example, I could not grasp the difference between salvation by grace rather than by works, and, from my own simplistic viewpoint, my mother's religion was much more satisfying on this point. Moreover, I was much attached to the idea of Purgatory, which I found to be a most useful institution, where, in my repentance, I would have gladly accepted a short stay to wash away my sins, and in particular my games with little Hélix. I was even more attached to the Virgin Mary, whom I confusedly identified with Barberine, with her warm bosom, her sweet face and her consoling arms. In my humble and puerile opinion, there seemed to be only men to love in this new religion. And what I felt then, I still believe in some way. Even putting idolatry and images aside, no Creator can escape some resemblance to man. Isn't it a pity that nothing womanly is made holy, not even her maternal function?

My father had made his sons keep the secret of the Brethren's decision until such a time as I should be converted, and so during the week occupied by my conversion, my mother, the Siorac twins and all the servants were blissfully ignorant that Mespech was going to transfer to the reformers' camp, and all of them along with it. My father decided to speak to Isabelle de Siorac alone and so summoned her with Franchou to his chambers on the evening of Sunday, 22nd December. He had thought to take advantage of the presence among us of Jonas, Cathau and Cabusse to undertake a mass conversion of our household after dinner that evening.

The two candelabra (which had not seen service since the evening Sauveterre informed us of the fall of Calais to the English in 1347) were, on Jean de Siorac's orders, lit by la Maligou in order to emphasize the solemnity of the moment, or perhaps to symbolize the light that the Brethren hoped to bring to the servants. At the far end of the brightly polished table sat the Baron de Siorac, Monsieur de Sauveterre and the Reverend Duroy, whose white hair was illuminated from behind by the dancing firelight, which seemed to make a halo around his venerable head.

Along each side of the table, our servants (all except Franchou, whose service to her mistress was required in her chambers) took their places according to their priority in the household: from the head of the table (where the minister and the Brethren sat) to the far end where the women sat, were seated first the sons, then Catherine (six years old at the time), then the Siorac twins (because they were related to us), Cabusse and his wife (because they were landowners at le Breuil), the two soldiers (because of their length of service), Jonas and Faujanet (who, as more recent recruits, came after them), and finally Barberine, la Maligou, Franchou (when she finally arrived), little Hélix carrying our nurse's baby Annet in her arms, and lastly Little Sissy, who was the same age as my sister Catherine but as brown-skinned and dark-haired as Catherine was blonde.

Our household was not without some inkling that something was afoot, first because the Brethren's religious opinions had long been known to them, even if, for prudence's sake, nothing had ever been said of this outside the walls of Mespech, and secondly because they knew very well who Raymond Duroy was, ever since the tumult that had followed the burial of a Huguenot under the lantern of the dead at Sarlat had made him famous throughout our regions. But they could hardly have suspected the commitment that was to be demanded of them, believing perhaps naively that Catholic servants could continue in the service of a Huguenot master.

In this my father was quick to disabuse them. Sitting, standing, coming and going before them, stopping, crossing his arms, putting his hands on his hips, he spoke in his rapid and urgent manner, a bit rambling and lacking logical order, so passionate was he. Yet gradually the implications of his speech became clear: Sauveterre, the baron and his three sons, François, Pierre and Samson de Siorac, intended to declare publicly their adherence to the reformed religion, and they expected their relatives (meaning the Siorac twins), their friends (meaning Cabusse and Cathau) and their servants to follow their lead: first because this path was God's way, long obscured by the papists, but now revealed again by the reformers; next because, in these troubled times, it would be difficult for the Brethren to trust anyone who did not share their faith, fearing that such a one might, sooner or later, under the influence of a confessor, be led to betray Mespech to its enemies. Certainly my father did not say straight out that he would dismiss anyone who did not convert to the reformed Church, but that was the obvious conclusion to draw from his words, and I could see from the astonishment and terror of our household that this was what they understood.

When I think back on this scene today, it makes me uneasy. For the Baron de Siorac was doing at Mespech exactly what he so strongly reproached Henri II for having done in his kingdom: demanding that his subjects embrace his own religion. The difference is that he lacked the power to send them to the stake. At the very least, however, he could deprive them of their daily bread and banish them from his domain, a sanction which was of no little consequence given the vast number of beggars who roamed homeless and starving throughout the countryside. At a time when the Roman Church tyrannized the kingdom, the idea of religious freedom had certainly shown some progress of late. But that liberty was all too often claimed as a privilege of the upper classes, or, at the very least, of the rich burghers in the towns. It did not extend to the people, still entirely governed and constrained by feudal ties—the same people over whom the Roman Church maintained its sway by its pomp, its processions, its rich and lustrous ceremonies, and its appeal to popular superstition.

Having said his piece, my father sat down. Such was the terror of our household at the idea of being thrown out of Mespech like a snail from its shell, and thrust unarmed, naked and hungry onto the highways of the world, that their eyes bulged in fear from their sockets, and their dry tongues stuck to their palates unable to utter a syllable.

Considering each of them in turn, Sauveterre measured the degree of their terror and sensed a happy outcome in it. For he loved the servants of Mespech enough to desire salvation for each and every one of them. Moreover, to dismiss anyone because of obstinate adherence to papist abominations would have broken his heart, not so much because of the famine to which such a one would have been reduced, but because of the risk of damnation he would have to face after his death.

He said, as calmly as my father had spoken passionately, "The Reverend Duroy will now instruct you in the differences between the Roman cult and ours." Raymond Duroy did not rise, and when he spoke nothing moved in his countenance other than his dark eyes and his mouth, his body remaining as immobile as if cut in marble. He made not the slightest gesture, not even to raise his hands from the arms of his chair to emphasize a point. But out of this iciness came a great fire, especially when Duroy denounced the practice of simony and the corruption of the Catholic priests.

"These priests," he proclaimed, "have grown wealthy in the riches of this world and impoverished in spirit. They live among their earthly delights day and night. Their ministry is foul and spoilt with their greed. They refuse baptism without payment. They never bless a marriage without bleeding the poorest couples of their money. They never open the sepulchres to the dead except by charging for the grave. In sum, the priests have made a shopkeeper's commerce out of the administration of the sacraments. What's worse: through a great and terrible simony, they have bartered pardons and absolutions from sin! They sell indulgences! In this stinking rot of their corruption, it comes as no surprise that the Roman clergy has redirected to its own pleasures the tithes that princes and common men have offered for the poor and for the instruction of the people."

Here Duroy paused, and my father made a gesture inviting our people to speak, which they were quick to do, so much did they approve of Duroy's opening words.

"Miserly, for sure, they are," murmured Faujanet, who remembered having been rejected by the diocese of Sarlat when he went there begging for crumbs.

"And so greedy, they'd shave an egg," added Cabusse.

"I could tell you about a priest, and not far from here either, who, with his long rosary, has rustled a sol from more than one of his faithful."

"I kn… kn… know him too," confirmed Cockeyed Marsal.

Only Coulondre held his tongue, so much was silence his inveterate habit. But he was known to be little given to religion, not much taken with hearing Mass, and somewhat detached from the faith of his fathers because of his bitterness about losing an arm.

Cabusse was no more fervent than Coulondre, having a Gascon's irreverence for priests. Overwhelmed as he was with the riches of this world—the le Breuil farm, his sheep and Cathau—he was not much concerned with those of the next. We knew, by way of my mother's ex-chambermaid, what his prayers consisted of: in the morning as he stretched he would say, "Lord, your servant is getting up. Grant him a good day." And the evening prayer, between yawns, "Lord, your servant is going to bed. Give him a good night with his wife."

La Maligou and Barberine listened to all this without a word, being ashamed to speak in front of the men, but they exchanged a few whispered reflections and memories rehashed twenty times over concerning Pincers the priest—so named because some joker, passing by the presbytery and finding it empty, had thought to play a joke on the housekeeper by taking the pincers from beside the fireplace and placing them in her bed. But the joke had turned out to be on the priest since, while the pincers lay undiscovered in her bed, he railed for an entire month against his parishioners both in and out of the pulpit, believing himself the victim of theft.

"You're so right," said la Maligou. "A bigger lecher there never was. In confession and in the sacristy, he stares at the girls' tits and gropes their arses."

"And surely there's no mother's son in France," said Barberine, "who's a bigger drunkard. And for proof, at the funeral of poor old Petremol, just as they were lowering the body into the grave, and Pincers was mumbling his prayers for the dead, he saw Bellièvre, the smithy, in the front row of the mourners, and said to him in a loud and clear voice: 'Bellièvre, seeing you there reminds me that you still owe me a barrel of wine. Remember to bring it tomorrow. Your salvation depends on it!' After which, he went on with his prayers as if nothing had happened."

When silence had returned, the Reverend Duroy began a clear exposition and resume of the forty articles of the Calvinist confession of faith, as established by the synod of 1559. He spoke with a kind of tranquil certainty and had the art of making the most thorny subjects accessible to the people and to children of all ages. Even today I can remember the way he explained to us the Huguenots' interpretation of the Last Supper: "The Catholic priests," he announced gravely and with vibrant indignation, "maintain the presence of the real body and blood of our Saviour in the bread and wine of the Communion. But that cannot be, and to claim such a thing is foolishness and falsehood. You must understand that the body and blood of the Saviour nourish the soul in the way that bread and wine feed the body. To understand it any other way is an imposture. How could Jesus Christ be up in heaven and down here in the stomachs of those who take Communion? In truth, the body of Our Lord is as far from the bread and wine as the farthest pinnacle of heaven is from the earth."

To which, my father, raising his hand, added, "When Christ said, 'Drink, this is my blood,' and 'Eat, this is my body,' we must understand it as a parable, and not literally, the way the papists do." This idea—the ultimate blasphemy for a Roman priest—was well received by our audience who saw no malice in it and accepted it as common-sense truth. Nor was our household any more recalcitrant when the Reverend Duroy attacked the idea of the celibacy of priests. ("That's such hypocrisy," affirmed Jonas. "It's for sure that Pincers is a lot less chaste than me in my cave.") When Duroy talked about monastic vows, Cabusse pointed out with a chuckle that "monks are the lice of the people". And when he came to indulgences, Faujanet declared that "at that rate only the rich will be saved". On the subject of private confession, Barberine agreed that all they were doing was "letting Pincers in on the family secrets".

On the other hand, Duroy's attack on the cult of the Virgin and the saints was met with great astonishment and heavy resistance. He conducted his assault, in consequence, with the utmost tact and prudence: "According to the Scriptures," he said, "Christ is the only mediator between God and man. Therefore, you must not pray to the Virgin or the saints to intercede with Christ, nor make a cult of any of them. We must respect the saints as so many heroes of the faith, but we refuse to worship them. In the same way, we honour Mary as the mother of Christ, but we refuse to worship her. The Word of God in his Holy Scripture is clear and indubitable. The only intercessor with God is Christ. Whoever strays from this rule falls into idolatry. The cult of Mary and the saints is only an abuse and a trick of Satan."

These words were received with great emotion by our people—both men and women—and from their frightened silence, and the way they rolled their eyes and bit their lips, you could see that Duroy's words had collided with a centuries-old tradition. There was not a household in all of Sarlat that had not dedicated some corner to a niche where a statue of the Virgin stood, requiring a genuflection and a whispered "Hail Mary" of every passer-by. Every village of any importance had its saint, and the fountain of its saint, and proclaimed the miracles of that saint, to whom prayers were directed more fervent even than those directed to Jesus Christ, for He was a distant figure, like the king in the Louvre, or a lord in his chateau.

When my father, who knew these customs well, noticed the tumultuous silence provoked by Duroy's words, he tried to drain this abscess by taking a lighthearted rather than an angry tone: "Speak up, my good friends. Speak your minds openly. We won't punish you for it." But our "good friends" kept quiet, terrified at the thought of contradicting the Reverend Duroy, whose pale face, deeply set features, long white beard and immobility seemed too much like the saints in the stained-glass windows at church. "Come, come," said my father, becoming impatient, "don't be ashamed! Speak out, good people! Tell us your feelings. I command you!"

Everyone looked at each other and finally their looks converged on Barberine as if to ask her to serve as their spokeswoman, given her secure position at Mespech as wet nurse to the Siorac children— both those present and those yet to be born. After some hesitation Barberine expressed her strong feelings on the matter: "My Lord," she began, going pink from the roots of her hair right to her emerging and abundant breasts, "may I have your leave to speak before the men do?"

"You may, my dear Barberine," replied my father, who grew tender just looking at all that pink colour—all the more so since she hardly seemed to pose much of a threat. And he added, "You know how much we all love you."

"And well I thank you, My Lord," shuddered Barberine, her breast swelling out of adoration for my father. "Surely I am but a woman, and a most ignorant woman at that, seeing our two masters and the Reverend Duroy and the Siorac twins and our soldiers who have travelled the world over and Jonas and Faujanet who are such experts in their trades, and 'tis only by great courage on my part even to open my mouth in the presence of these gentlemen. I don't know nothing but how to give my milk like a poor cow in the stable. But touching on the Virgin Mary, whom, if it please my masters, I love and worship, I get to thinking this way: we pray to Jesus to intercede with God, am I not right, My Lord?"

"This is true, Barberine."

"Then," she continued, "if we ask the Son to placate the Father, why not ask the Mother to placate the Son?"

There was a silence, and I suspect my father realized he had underestimated Barberine, for he looked ill at ease and tried to hide his embarrassment with a little laugh. But the ever vigilant Duroy leapt to his defence:

"No doubt," he said in his gravest voice, "it is so in human affairs. But here we are dealing with God. And not just any son, but Jesus Christ—who is our Saviour. And since our Saviour is Christ and not his mother Mary, it is to Him we must pray for intercession with the Father, and not to her. Mary bore Christ, just like Barberine gives her milk: it is an act of nature and not an act of creation. The Creator is the Father. And the Saviour is the Son. Pray to the Father and pray to the Son, but do not pray to any other than these and the Holy Spirit, for you would be guilty of idolatry and pagan superstition."

This was so clearly and forcefully stated, and in a tone of such utter tranquillity and such absolute certainty, that one would have thought the venerable Duroy had consented to put off his own celestial rewards for a few months in order to correct a few misunderstood truths for those of us here below. And yet, as impressed as our people were, they all resisted, and, strange to say, their resistance abandoned the Virgin Mary (who was, after all, only a woman) to take up positions behind the saints—who were so numerous and so obviously beneficial (or, in some cases, harmful) that it seemed difficult if not impossible to deny their constant intervention in peoples' lives.

Here again, the men refused to speak, and looked to Barberine as if they wanted to hide behind that ample green skirt lined with red stripes. The wet nurse, however, shook her head defiantly, refusing to open her mouth twice in defiance of her masters. So the men perforce fell back on la Maligou, although she was hardly the most effective ambassadress they could have found, given her penchant for excessive superstition—even for their taste. But he who has no horse for ploughing must content himself with an ass, and this ass needed no carrot to coax it. More dishevelled than any gorgon or maenad, at the first sign of invitation, she threw herself into the breach and mounted the assault.

"May I speak, My Lord?"

"Certainly, my dear Maligou," said my father, trying to repress a smile.

"Ah, My Lord!" exclaimed la Maligou with a great sigh and rolling her dark eyes. "I would be terrified and horrified if we stopped praying to the saints at Mespech, for there are some pretty malicious ones in Périgord, especially here in the north. And what maladies we will see rain down on our chateau, on our people, on our livestock, on our harvests!"

"What?" retorted my father, raising his eyebrows and feigning surprise. "Have I lost my senses? Do the saints of Périgord bring evil?"

"And bitter evil it is, My Lord!" answered la Maligou with a terrible grimace. "St Siméon of Ligueux brings the worst of all. St Eutropius makes men infirm. St Paul of Agonac visits sickness and fear on children. St Avit afflicts your limbs with rheumatism. And the saint of Sarazac twists the legs of babes in their cradles."

"But these are real demons, your saints, my poor Maligou," laughed my father.

"No, My Lord, not at all," rejoined la Maligou. "And if you want the blessed water of a saint to heal you, you must throw sols in his fountain."

"Such miserly saints!" said my father with a smile. "And what are they doing up there in Paradise with all this money?"

"I know not. But the sols don't stay in the fountains very long."

"I thought not," mused my father.

"To give you an example," continued la Maligou, "poor Petremol, who died two years ago—"

"On 1st January," broke in Barberine.

"Right, on 1st January. Well, as you know, St Avit had twisted him and knotted him up with terrible rheumatisms for two years. And a month before he died, he went to St Avit, had a Mass said to the saint, and right there in the middle of winter, stripped naked as a baby, rubbed his whole body with the icy water of the saint and was cured."

"So he was cured!" replied my father. "Cured so well that a month later he died of pneumonia."

"Ah, but he was cured of the rheumatisms, My Lord."

"To be sure, where he has gone, I grant you, he no longer suffers from rheumatism. So St Avit gives rheumatisms and takes them away. This is wonderful!"

"Is it not right that he should undo what he has done, My Lord?" asked la Maligou. "Likewise the saint of Sarazac twists up the legs of infants, but can also straighten them again."

"For a Mass and a few sols."

"Well, but also you have to rub them with the water of his fountain."

"Which is the same water as our well," said my father. "My friends," he continued, rising, and taking a more serious tack, "you have now heard la Maligou. And what man, on hearing this poor hen, would not admire the ingeniousness of the priests in exploiting the credulity of the poor people? And so, instead of honouring the saints for the Christian virtues exemplified in their lives, they make them into little gods and demons just like the pagan ones. For the Romans also had their saints. In their lakes there were naiads who aided their fishing, and instead of loose change, they threw them vases, bracelets and flowers." My father paused and glared severely at la Maligou. "Oh, Maligou," he said, "we could write a fat book full of all your beliefs which have no other existence than in the folds of your small mind... Including your claim that Little Sissy is the daughter of a Gypsy, which is untrue."

La Maligou's mouth fell open at this unexpected piece of news, and Little Sissy opened wide her beautiful almond-shaped black liquid eyes and gazed at my father, but said nothing.

"It is wicked heresy," continued my father heatedly, "to attribute to our saints the power of healing. It is stinking idolatry to make idols of them and to worship them. There is only one God and He alone can heal soul and body. And it is to Him and to Him alone that you must pray."

La Maligou, still stung by my father's statement about Little Sissy's birth (for her rape by the Gypsy captain in the barn was the glory and crowning jewel of her life), sat tight-lipped, her eyes cast down and her thick greasy body hunched over.

Now that she had fallen silent, no one dared utter a peep. In truth, I do not believe that my father succeeded, in these few short minutes, in rooting out heresy and superstitious beliefs. But our people were too accustomed to obeying religious authority not to give way to that of my father, Sauveterre and Duroy, all learned and serious men who read books and knew things—especially my father, who was a great doctor and who cared for the common people without charging them a sol.

"Well then," said my father. "You have heard enough to know which abuses and errors we intend to correct. Will you follow your masters in the reformed religion?"

As no one wanted to be first to reply, a prolonged silence followed, and the longer it continued the more thoroughly embarrassed the Brethren became. Luckily, Annet, whom little Hélix was cradling in her arms and who had been quiet until that moment, suddenly burst out crying to wake the dead. Little Hélix passed him to Barberine who, unlacing her red bodice, brought out a large, firm and sumptuous breast, which the little bawler quickly latched onto. His little hands clutching her white flesh, he closed his eyes and quieted down into his happy lot. This was a spectacle which normally I could not get enough of, and I noticed that I was not alone in this pleasure: Barberine's swollen, snow-white breast attracted everyone's attention, even my father's, who smiled as he gazed at it. Only Sauveterre and the Reverend Duroy averted their eyes and conversed quietly with each other. Now that I was a strapping lad I would have blushed to catch myself dreaming of taking the suckling babe's place at Barberine's breast, and yet I could almost taste the sweet warm milk flow into my throat, and I envied little Annet his freedom to caress that beautiful round, full breast; for I had discovered this pleasure during my intimate nights with little Hélix, whose advantages unfortunately could not be compared to her mother's.

Reflecting back on this moment, I felt quite confused to have evoked such sins in my own mind before such an assembly, a thing I had never yet managed to do in confession to Father Pincers, fearing that he would tell my mother, who would put an end to the sleeping arrangements that made them possible. Thank God, now that I was a Huguenot I would not have to go to confession any more, which lifted an immense weight from my chest, so abject was my fear of my sessions with the insatiably curious Pincers.

I am certain that none among those assembled dared think that the scene of Barberine nursing her baby could have served as a model for a statue of the Virgin Mary and infant Jesus, but that's exactly what was going through my head, however Huguenot I had become. But I didn't breathe a word of it, for I wouldn't have wanted to vex my father, who, waiting patiently for the nursing to end to rephrase his solemn question, said to Barberine, half joking, half serious: "My dear Barberine, I am sorely tempted to take away your agate necklace just to prove to you that it has no effect on your milk."

"Ah, My Lord," wailed Barberine, who in the face of this threat felt her milk practically recede towards its source, "you wouldn't do that to me! You'd dry me right up! And my little Annet would waste away!"

"No, no," laughed my father, "I won't do it, my poor woman. Keep your agates, they're so pretty on your white skin!" (Here Sauveterre frowned, of course.) "And who knows whether your imagination wouldn't be enough, with the agates gone, to dry up your milk! A good nurse shouldn't be vexed, anyone can tell you that."

As he spoke, little Annet suddenly let go his prey, and, satiated, fell asleep. Barberine placed him back in little Hélix's arms and her breast back in her blouse, which seemed to have the effect of casting a pall over the assembly.

"Well, my good people," said my father, restoring the gravity of the situation, "back to business. Who among you will stand for the reform? Speak, Michel Siorac!"

"I will," said Michel and Benoît Siorac in one voice.

"Cabusse?"

"I will!"

"Coulondre?"

"I will!"

"Marsal?"

"I will!"

"Jonas?"

"I will!"

"Faujanet?"

"I will!"

My father then turned to the women, whose "I wills" were spoken with much less assurance—at least those of Barberine, Cathau and la Maligou, for in the eyes of little Hélix (thirteen and a half) and Little Sissy (six) it was only a good joke on Pincers.

Little Sissy having declared her faith, my father realized that he had not asked Catherine, who, as his daughter, should have come first, even before the Siorac twins. Catherine had noticed this omission and, believing herself banished from her father's love, pale and her blue eyes brimming with tears, she hung her head, her golden locks hanging mournfully about her cheeks. "Well Catherine, my girl," said my father with a big smile, "I seem to have forgotten you. But you heard my question: will you embrace the reformed religion of your father?"

"I will," sobbed Catherine in a trembling voice, and burst into tears.

My father, who was not unaware that these tears had something to do with my mother, grew sombre, and, getting up, said abruptly: "Barberine, it's bedtime for these children. They've been kept up too late."

As Barberine rose to gather up her brood, Coulondre opened his mouth like a fish. That usually meant that he was about to speak: an activity so unusual for him that it required a good deal of preparation, for from his open mouth no sound was emitted at first. Yet no one was fooled: Coulondre was going to speak his mind, an event so rare that all eyes turned to him. Despite the orders she'd received, Barberine made not a move.

Coulondre had placed his arm—or rather his iron hook—on the table to ease the burden on his shoulder. At forty his hair was already turning white, and his entire face, long as Lent, seemed to be turned downward: the corners of his eyes, of his mouth, the tilt of his nose. He had a way of closing his eyes during dinner which scarcely inspired conversation from his neighbours. Added to which, no one would have been much interested in hearing his opinion. For whenever Coulondre chose to emit real words instead of his usual grunts, it was to voice sad and calamitous thoughts. On the eve of my father's departure for the war, as Cabusse was showing us the firearms, I remember that when I cried, "These are proud weapons! They'll kill lots of enemies," Coulondre had merely said, "The enemy's got the same ones," with a look and a tone that implied that not one of them, my father included, would survive the conflict.

Such were Coulondre's tendencies and talents: he stripped the future bare of any vestige of hope. So at Mespech not only the servants but even the Brethren had ended up fearing Coulondre's least words, for they were always sulphurous vapours, heartbreaking observations, crushing truths—so immense was his instinct for sniffing out and revealing the worst side of things.

"My Lord," he rasped with the voice of the taciturn, "I would like to ask a question."

"Ask away, my brave Coulondre," said my father with his usual good humour, tempered now with a touch of uneasiness, a feeling we all shared faced with the prospect of this great mute's speech.

"My Lord," continued Coulondre, "will we continue to celebrate saints' days at Mespech as we used to?"

We all looked at each other and, as my father hesitated, Sauveterre interjected drily: "There's no reason to celebrate saints' days any more since in the reformed religion we don't worship the saints."

"I thought as much," mumbled Coulondre in a funereal voice, and he closed his eyes.

Everyone stared at him and a mournful silence fell over the table. There was such consternation among our people and such astonishment that they no longer knew—dare I say—which saint to turn to. It had just dawned on them that in one short evening they had lost fifty holidays a year.

It was on the afternoon of Monday 23rd December (as reported *in extenso* in the *Book of Reason*) that Baron de Siorac, Monsieur de Sauveterre, the Reverend Duroy and the four Caumont brothers, the eldest of whom, François, was the lord of Milandes and of Castelnau, convened in my father's library to instruct the Baronne de Siorac in the ways of the reformed religion and to invite her conversion. As good captains, Siorac and Sauveterre had wrapped up a successful campaign in their conversion of Mespech. With that same brilliant tactical sense Guise had shown at Calais, they had vanquished one by one each of the strongholds defending the city before bringing their entire forces to bear on the citadel itself. But if they had hoped to benefit from the same effect of surprise that Guise had enjoyed, they were sadly mistaken. For, through Franchou, whom Barberine had kept hourly informed of the conversion's progress within our walls, Isabelle knew exactly how her husband, her sons, her daughter, the Siorac twins, Cabusse and Cathau and all the servants, men and women alike, had been won over.

Isolated and as though surrounded on all sides by the "heresy", Isabelle wasn't about to let herself be taken—quite the contrary. With her pride as stiffened and reddened as a cockscomb, she appeared in the library in all her finery, superbly decked out, her beautiful golden locks adorned with her set of ancestral pearls (my father certainly too chary of the Brethren's resources to think of wasting them on such frivolity). And it was she who attacked before my father could even open his mouth: "Messieurs," she said in a declamatory tone, "why are so many of you gathered here? Are you in league against me? Are you my judges? Do you plan to torture me when you have done here? Is it for this that you have convoked my four cousins? Seven men against one unfortunate woman, and she attended by no one! Do you feel strong enough to defeat me?"

"Madame," said my father, greatly taken aback by her hardy overture, "your speech lacks reason or justification. No one here wishes your demise, quite the contrary. We all wish, from the bottom of our hearts, that you will be saved. If you see your cousins gathered here, it is because they are all that remain of your illustrious family, and having for some time now embraced the reformed religion, they desired to be a witness to our call to join our ranks. As for Monsieur Duroy, whom you see here—"

"I do not know this knave," said my mother in her most disdainful manner, "nor will I listen to him."

"Knave, Madame?" gasped my father with a start. "Monsieur Duroy is the minister of our religion, a man of passing knowledge and rare virtue. You owe him your respect."

"Monsieur my husband," replied Isabelle, "I owe my respect to the priests and prelates of the Holy Church in which I was raised, along with all of my ancestors, as well as the king of France, Charles IX, our sovereign lord, to whom I dedicate my allegiance to my dying breath. As for your pestiferous heretics, I want nothing to do with them!"

This was spoken with such forceful disdain that it reduced them all to silence. Sauveterre, Duroy and the Caumonts appeared to be turned to stone. As for my father, he rose and took several steps across the room, his fists clenched, drunk with inarticulate rage. "Isabelle," he said, turning to her, his voice muted by anger, "take care! All of us are, as you put it, 'pestiferous heretics', and if you wish to have nothing to do with us, we must understand that you are renouncing your entire family."

At this rejoinder, Isabelle realized that she had gone too far, and fell silent, yet remained standing stiffly, head held high, her manner bespeaking her rebellious intent. Nevertheless, her silence allowed my father to regain control of his feelings, to sit down and resume the conversation, though with a voice strained by the effort of controlling his anger: "Madame, I bid you sit down beside me in this chair and listen to what the Reverend Duroy is going to tell you about our religion."

"No, Monsieur, I shall remain standing," replied Isabelle in a softer yet equally resolute tone. "I shall not heed these dangerous novelties which you yourselves and your friends are trying to insinuate into the faith of our fathers!"

"But my cousin," said Sauveterre indignantly, "it is precisely in this that you are mortally mistaken, and your error is based only on your wilful ignorance. This 'novelty' is not on our side, for we are but trying to rediscover the pure and clear source of Christianity, which the Roman Church has covered with mud, soiling it with customs, idolatries, monstrosities and, as you call them, novelties. Our hope lies in adhering strictly to the Word of God as it is revealed to us in the Old and New Testaments. That is the pure source, from which any, provided he can read, may drink."

"And cast for himself his own little religion, according to the feeble lights of his own good sense," retorted Isabelle sarcastically. "No, my cousin, the Church rightly considers as a pestilential invention this translation your Huguenots have made of the Old and New Testaments into a vulgar tongue, spreading them, as you have done, among gentlemen, burghers and the common people, at the risk of corrupting the precepts of the Christian religion from top to bottom."

"What?" cried my father. "It is we who corrupt the Christian religion? When all we want is to reclaim the original purity of its source in offering the world the Word of God! This Word which your prelates and your Pope have nearly snuffed out beneath their interpretations, superstitions and extravagances!"

"Monsieur," replied Isabelle, "do not speak this way of the Holy Father or I shall withdraw immediately."

"Madame," said the Reverend Duroy in his soft bass voice, "if you wished to practise Christian humility, you would seek the Word of God not from the mouths of men, but from His own, in His Holy Scriptures. And you would not then call the Pope 'the Holy Father'."

"And why not, if you please?" sniffed my mother, affecting disdain, yet struck by the venerable appearance of the minister.

"Because Christ said in Matthew 23: 'Do not call any man your father, for you have but one father and He is in heaven.'"

It would have been a gross misjudgement of my mother to expect that she should be overwhelmed, or even shaken by such an objection.

"My own humility," she said, raising her head, "consists in not trusting to the weakness of my own lights, in not interpreting according to my own whim the holy canon, but to rely for such interpretation on the Church Fathers and holy prelates who, for centuries, have defined our dogmas and our rites."

"And," rejoined the minister, "multiplied falsehoods, corrupted and twisted the Holy Word and made cheap commerce of the rites."

"Monsieur, I shall not listen to you," said Isabelle.

"It suits you ill to speak, then, of humility, Madame!" said my father vehemently. "You who from the outset of this interview have opposed your family and your husband with a diabolical pride; you have ears yet hear not the truth, and eyes but see it not; you whom

I love and for whom I've prayed—more than a thousand times, oft on bended knee, on nights when the unbearable thought of your damnation kept me fast awake—to but read, to consent to read just once the Old and New Testaments."

This "whom I love" caused a terrible pallor in Isabelle and she vacillated more at that than at any other moment of the discussion. Yet she recovered herself almost immediately and said with utter finality: "I read my Catholic missal, and the hours of the Blessed Virgin, for these books are permitted me. But I shall read neither the Old nor the New Testament, for the Church forbids it of me. And I hold firmly to the belief that outside the Church there is no salvation."

"What are you saying, Madame?" cried my father, paling in his turn. And, turning to the minister, he said, his voice choked with grief. "Did you hear this blasphemy?"

"Alas," said Duroy, "it is a rare abomination to substitute the Roman Church for Christ and to make of it an idol. Madame, say rather, outside of Christ there is no salvation."

Isabelle, as yet unbowed by my father's anger, seemed deeply moved, not by Duroy's remark, but rather by the evident pain her own words had caused her husband. She fell silent, and there seemed to be a momentary truce among all combatants, as if each were regaining his breath and were trying to recover from the many blows given and received.

Geoffroy de Caumont, in his turn, took up the argument. The most zealous of the four Caumont brothers, he was prior of Brive and abbot of Uzerche, Vigeais and Clairac. But in becoming Huguenot, he had not abandoned his offices and benefits, converting his flock and his monks by high-handed rather than gentler means. In stature, he was a man of average height, with rather fierce eyes and dark skin and hair.

"My cousin," he said gruffly, "you, for whom all tradition is holy, you would do well to follow the other women in our family and obey your husband. You dishonour the Caumont family with your obstinacy. You're more hardheaded, my cousin, than the stubbornest goat, and you should be careful lest your wilfulness disgust your husband and cause him to repudiate you."

"Even if my husband were to send me away," replied Isabelle, her voice trembling, "I am too confident of your own friendship for me to fear that you should reject me."

"Not so, Madame!" frowned Geoffroy de Caumont. "Not so! Neither my brothers, François and Jean, nor your other relatives and friends would have anything to do with you, and there would be no haven for you in the entire length and breadth of our province."

Isabelle valiantly faced this blow, stating in a strong voice: "Monsieur, if you forsake me, the Church will not forsake me. And I prefer to be the most wretched person in the world than to leave the Church for men."

"Idolatress!" cried my father, torn between anger and grief. "The Church, always the Church! And God, Madame, what make you of Him?"

"For me," said Isabelle, "the Church and God are one and the same."

A troubled silence followed these words, and then Geoffroy de Caumont burst out furiously, "Madame, having a husband, a brother, sons and your entire family converted to the reformed religion, you must understand that by remaining a papist you repudiate all the natural and sacred ties that bind you to your family. And that by all of these you will be henceforth seen not as a spouse, but as the whore of the Baron de Siorac!"

"That's as may be," replied Isabelle, drawing herself to her full height, "but then, Monsieur, if I am a whore then you must be a whoremonger, for God knows you arranged this marriage."

Geoffroy de Caumont paled, and my father, for whom the words "repudiate" and "whore" caused as much pain as they did for Isabelle, rose and said in a curt but courteous voice: "Madame, this interview has tired you. We shall bring it to a close. And with your permission, I shall accompany you to your apartment."

"I shall go alone," said Isabelle. With tears in her eyes, but unvanquished and unbowed, she turned on her heels and left the room with a majestic sweep of her full dress.

As Isabelle remained anchored and unshakable in the faith of her fathers, and refused any compromise, the dispute between her and my father continued over the months and years that followed. It raged, in fact, from 23rd December 1560 until 15th April 1563, shaking Mespech to its very foundations. The ferment of discord, verging at times on hatred, that this furious quarrel raised in our ordered and peaceful community, not only drove a wedge between husband and wife, but plagued the servants, upset the children and at times even—especially in the matter of whether to dismiss Franchou or not—divided the Brethren.

Despite her grand airs, querulousness and the frequent blows of her cane, Isabelle knew how to win over her chambermaids, and Franchou, after Cathau, had rapidly developed an almost devotional affection for her. This explains why the Brethren and the Reverend Duroy, expecting an easy conversion of the servants after the mistress, were dismayed to encounter a stone wall. From the outset, crossing her big red arms over her large breasts, Franchou flatly swore by the Virgin and by all the saints that she wanted none of the wickedness that had caused her mistress such tears; that she loved Madame, and she intended to live and die in her mistress's religion. Neither carrot nor stick could dislodge her from this position.

My father was most distressed to discover the poor chambermaid so hardheaded, but in his heart he was secretly moved by the great love she bore her mistress, and once Franchou had left the room, Sauveterre's rough proposal to get rid of her at once ended up by rubbing him the wrong way. In a haughty and abrupt tone, he replied that it would be cruel to deprive Isabelle of her chambermaid at a moment when she felt so isolated at Mespech, and, moreover, the matter of Isabelle's servants fell solely under his own jurisdiction. Having said this, he turned and left the room, leaving Sauveterre deeply hurt by his tone, his look and his words.

And so it was that onto the larger quarrel was grafted a smaller one between the two brothers, as thorny for one as for the other, and which lasted a full month. Seconded by the Reverend Duroy, Sauveterre redoubled his attack. They argued that Franchou was a deplorable example to all the other servants, particularly Barberine and la Maligou, still much attached to the papist superstitions and likely to be inspired by their mistress's rebellion. This bad apple would spoil the entire basketful, and create a female clan at Mespech more or less openly supportive of Isabelle, one which would not be without influence on the children and the male servants. What's more, if they had to rely on Isabelle's discernment and discretion in her dealings with Pincers, the latter would be in an excellent position to pump all kinds of information out of the naive Franchou and pass it on to the bishop of Sarlat who would thus be weekly informed about everything that was going on at Mespech.

This reasoning finally persuaded my father, but lacking the heart to throw Franchou out (all the more so since, innocently enough in his own mind, he had a weakness for her), he found her a position with a Huguenot lady in Sarlat who treated her very well, won her over and within a month had converted her. My father was so happy with this outcome that he never went to Sarlat without paying a visit to our former chambermaid, bringing her some little gift and, in his playful way, patting her large red arms and giving her two big kisses on her fresh cheeks. All of this he did innocently and publicly, often in my presence, yet it surprised me for he never would have acted this way at Mespech.

My mother, however, seeing Franchou depart so quickly after Cathau, was plunged into black despair and was filled with bitter resentment towards my father. She kept after him from dawn to dusk, and often late into the night, with such biting recriminations that my father avoided her altogether, fleeing from room to room as though ten devils were at his heels.

"You were right, Jean," he confided to Sauveterre in his *Book of Reason*, "her breast blinded me to her cross, and now I have my own cross to bear for it."

Things got even worse when the Brethren decided to replace Franchou with Toinon, a girl from Taniès whom Duroy had converted. Scarcely had my mother learnt that a heretic had been placed in her service than she conceived a hatred for her and began to persecute her, showering her with insults, calling her "wench", "stupid hen", "lazy fool", "bitch", "whore", "bawd", "little turd", and worse yet. I even witnessed with my own eyes once, when Toinon was holding up her mirror for her preening, that my mother pricked her arm with a pin deep enough to draw blood simply because she moved the glass. After a month of such treatment, of being whipped, beaten, insulted and pricked, poor Toinon packed her bags in tears and left us.

"Madame," scolded my father, "if you insist on playing the child, instead of a chambermaid I shall hire a governess."

And so Mespech witnessed the arrival of a mountain of a woman, Huguenot to the core, with a moustache and broad shoulders, severe and tight-lipped, two heads taller than my mother, who received insults with a calm indifference. For two weeks my mother hesitated to slap her, so far did her broad face seem beyond her reach. But finally, one fine summer morning, in my mother's chambers the battle was engaged.

"Alazaïs," ordered Isabelle, "put this table over there."

Without a word, Alazaïs lifted the heavy piece and placed it where my mother had told her to.

"On second thoughts," said Isabelle, "that's not the right place. Put it over here."

Alazaïs obeyed.

"No, that's not right either. Put it over in this corner."

Alazaïs complied, but when my mother immediately ordered another move, she said in her rude voice: "Madame, that's enough wickedness. A fig for your games. The table will stay where it is."

"You riff-raff!" cried my mother beside herself. "How dare you speak to me like that!" And grabbing hold of her cane, she raised it to strike her. But Alazaïs, without budging an inch, seized the cane, tore it from Isabelle's hands, broke it in two over her knee and threw the pieces out a window overlooking the moat. For more than a month, the servants would secretly enjoy the sight of the two sticks floating in the water.

Isabelle gave such a roar that my father came running. When he opened the door of her chambers, he saw her, pale and dishevelled, eyes ablaze, rushing at Alazaïs with a small knife in her hand. But the robust chambermaid, without retreating one step, seized her wrist on the fly and twisted it, causing the weapon to fall and embed itself in the floorboards, from which my father immediately pulled it.

"Monsieur," howled my mother, "if this horrible bawd is not out of here within the hour, 'tis I who will be gone."

"Sit down, Madame," said my father in a tone that brooked no response, "and cease this shouting. If you've come to the point of assassinating our servants then perhaps you should leave. For you may be certain that, had you had the misfortune to kill your chambermaid, I would hand you over to the judges in Sarlat to spend the rest of your days languishing in jail."

"Oh, my lord, I can see well enough that you don't love me any more!" sobbed Isabelle, tears streaming from her eyes and wringing her hands with despair.

"Unfortunately, I do!" confessed my father slipping into a chair with such a tired and chagrined air that it caused Isabelle more trouble than any amount of reproaches could have. He added with a sigh, "Alas, if I did not love you so much I would not tolerate your antics one minute longer."

"Am I so mad, then, my poor Jean?" said my mother, throwing herself at his knees.

"Mad enough to tie up," sighed my father, who had never been able to resist my mother's beauty, her tears or her conniving ways. And on this occasion, he was so touched to see her kneeling thus submissive at his feet that he clutched her to him and kissed her on the lips.

Seeing this, Alazaïs raised her eyebrows, left the room and, with her heavy musketeer's gait, went searching for Sauveterre in his tower. "Monsieur," she said in her rough voice, "I think I must leave Mespech."

"And wherefore, my poor creature?" asked Sauveterre.

"I can see that the baron is bewitched by his papist. She just tried to kill me and three minutes later he coddles her and licks her face."

Alazaïs did not leave Mespech, and the spell cast on my father lasted only long enough for Isabelle to conceive. Whereupon, Barberine had to depart to get herself another child from her husband, and little Hélix again became mistress of the tower and the children, which made our secret nocturnal delights all the easier.

The episode of the dagger and the subsequent reconciliation were but a calm in the long quarrel between Isabelle and my father, after which the storm raged again day and night. For Isabelle was scarcely pregnant before she declared openly and brazenly that the child would be baptized according to the rites of her Church, as my father had promised her before their marriage. It was oil on the fire, which flamed up again right to heaven, not without great chagrin on each side. My father, given his great love for Isabelle, despaired at the thought that in persevering in her papist idolatry, she was consigning herself and his future son to eternal damnation.

I confess that in my tenderest youth and no less so now that I am grown, I do not see things this way. Raised as I was between two religions, and forced to choose between them by no little amount of pressure, I cannot hate the one I abandoned, cannot abominate its "errors" as much as my father did, nor can I believe that those who follow them in good faith are damned to hell, my poor mother least of all. But few people, men or women, in those times found such tolerance in themselves, as what follows will all too clearly show. For the cruel disagreement which split Mespech was but a feeble and tiny reflection of the disputes that raged at that time throughout the entire kingdom between Catholics and Huguenots, causing such passions, such tumult and, finally, such frightful civil wars that the fortunes of France were all but buried.

7

As a young man, Étienne de La Boétie, son of the police lieutenant who had helped the Brethren to acquire Mespech, had been named counsellor to the parliament in Bordeaux in recognition of his great talents. Each time he visited Michel de Montaigne, his "intimate brother and immutable friend" at his chateau, he went on to Sarlat to rest for two or three days in the house where he was born, or, if the season permitted, at the little manor house that he owned about a league from the town. On his return he never failed to stop off at Mespech.

I read in my father's *Book of Reason* that Étienne dined with the Brethren on 16th December 1561. As chance would have it, he encountered Isabelle's cousin, Geoffroy de Caumont, as confirmed a Huguenot, as I have said, as she was an unswerving Catholic. What is interesting in this chance encounter between the two men is that the regent, knowing the great reputation and wisdom of Étienne de La Boétie, had just named him counsellor to Monsieur de Burie, the lieutenant general of Guyenne (alas not the only person occupying this function). Burie had his hands full in these troubled times, attempting to accommodate or reconcile all the king's subjects. The meal, taken in the presence of our servants, was civil enough, but after dinner these gentlemen retired, as was the custom, to the privacy of my father's library, where a great fire was burning and where the conversation took a different turn, Étienne de La Boétie evoking the troubles that had broken out between Catholics and reformers in the Agenais, Quercy and Périgord regions. This conversation was transcribed verbatim the next day in my father's *Book of Reason*, so taken was he by La Boétie's effortless and eloquent wisdom, a grain whose meatiness was equal to the beauty of the wheat field that bore it. What a pity that death has since robbed us of this youth whose genius could have laid claim to the highest offices of the land, and offered so much through his wisdom and moderation.

It soon appeared that La Boétie had serious warnings not only for the Brethren but especially for Geoffroy de Caumont. Étienne's bright eyes and smile lit up his rather plain features, and his plainness was altogether forgotten the minute he opened his mouth to speak.

"'Tis a misfortune," he said with a smile, "that men do not easily accept others' beliefs. As soon as Catherine de' Medici and Michel de L'Hospital put an end to the persecutions which plagued you, the Reformation gathered strength, especially in the south. But your Huguenot brothers have matched gains in strength with an increase in intolerance. In Agen, as you know, they attacked the church of Sainte-Foy, broke crosses and altarpieces, destroyed relics and icons, burned the holy ornaments and the missals and converted the church into a temple barring entry to any Catholic priest. They did the same at Issigeac and in many other towns."

"The fact is," growled Geoffroy de Caumont, frowning, "that we cannot permit the papists' idolatrous cult of these relics, crosses and statues—a practice entirely contrary, as you know, Monsieur de La Boétie, to the Word of God."

"Quite the contrary, Monsieur Abbot of Clairac," replied La Boétie with gentle irony. "You must permit it, for the simple reason that you want the Catholics to accept your denuded temples. The iconoclasm of the reformers, besides their occasional destruction of masterpieces of art, offends the consciences of many good subjects of the king who rightly consider that they are entitled to the same rights as yourselves in this kingdom."

"If these same 'good subjects', as you say, had the king's ear," said Caumont, "they'd send us all right to the stake. We've already seen it happen under Henri II and François II."

"Guise and his followers were in command then," said La Boétie, "but with the regency of the queen mother, times have changed indeed. And do you believe," he added with a smile, "I'd burn you, Monsieur de Caumont, if it were in my power?"

"Ah, Monsieur de La Boétie," laughed my father, "you are an exceptional Catholic, and, like your good friend Michel de Montaigne, unusually tolerant and open to many things. You are a faithful servant of the king and yet when you were younger, you wrote a powerful declaration against absolute power. And you are a very particular kind of papist. You may go to Mass, but you are anti-Roman in spirit, hostile to icons, to relics, to indulgences, and a friend of the profound reforms within the Church. It was your insistence on the spirit of conciliation at Agen and Issigeac that convinced Monsieur de Burie to share the churches part-time between Catholics and reformers. No mean feat!"

"But, alas, one that had little lasting effect," said Caumont. "Despite your own moderation, Monsieur de La Boétie, and even your sympathies for our cause, you were not able to prevent the massacre of thirty of our people scarcely a month ago at the Orioles temple in Cahors. And is not the death of a man infinitely more deplorable than the destruction of statues, relics and crosses?"

"Indeed," agreed La Boétie, "but don't forget that an investigation is under way in Cahors. The queen mother has sent two commissioners for this purpose. And was it not a mortal sin, Monsieur de Caumont, that your own people committed in killing the old Baron de Fumel in his chateau?"

"But I was not there and had nothing to do with it!" snapped Caumont, flushing with anger. "And surely you are aware that the Baron de Fumel provoked his Protestant subjects by outlawing reformed services in his domains."

"There are so many rumours!" exclaimed La Boétie. "Why, Monsieur de Montluc, who as you know shares with Monsieur de Burie the supervision of Guyenne, even claims that you yourself, Caumont, secretly support the Huguenot sedition in the Agenais and Périgord regions."

Geoffroy de Caumont leapt to his feet, knocking his chair over backwards. "And who is this Montluc?" he cried, instinctively grasping the handle of his sword. "A creature of François de Guise! A man who believes in neither God nor the Devil, and who serves only his own interests while claiming to serve the king. And isn't it true, Monsieur de La Boétie, that he is about to welcome Felipe II's Spanish infantry?"

"'Tis so, alas," confirmed La Boétie, "all the more reason for prudence on your part."

"I beseech you, Caumont," said my father, "pick up your chair and pray be seated. La Boétie is our friend and seeks only to give you good and timely advice."

There was a long silence. Caumont sat down again, sombre and tight-lipped. La Boétie looked solemnly at him, shook his head and said after some thought: "Monsieur de Caumont, please do not take what I am about to tell you badly, but your family goes too far. Your brother-in-law, the Baron de Biron, is said to have given asylum to seditious Huguenots. Your elder brother François has transformed the church in Milandes into a reformed temple and thereby deprived his Catholic subjects of their place of worship. Montluc has reported all this to Catherine de' Medici, who was much displeased by this usurpation, as she was by the death of Fumel, whom she will publicly mourn. Since the regent is already much alarmed by these tumultuous events, it would be unwise, Caumont, to give her the impression that our Huguenots of Guyenne are a seditious lot and dream of rebelling against the king's laws."

Caumont, obviously irritated, opened his mouth to speak, but thought better of it, and as he persisted in his silence, La Boétie said amicably but firmly: "Alas, My Lord, I know all too well that the Roman Church is horribly corrupted by infinite abuses. I do not doubt your sincere desire for reform. But what can you hope to gain through force? Repression. Montluc has the means to do it. By nature he is inclined to bloodshed. And Monsieur de Burie will not be able to restrain him for ever. What's worse, the Protestants' position in Guyenne is morally weak: they demand from the king freedom for their cult, while, in areas under their control, they themselves offer none to those who share the king's beliefs." La Boétie paused, and then added in the most pressing tone, "I beseech you, Caumont, do not fall into such extremism. Be not so harsh or so violent. Make your peace with the Catholics. Don't go off on your own. You can see the extreme desolation and the dismemberment of the state such a spirit of partisanship has brought to the kingdom. If these disastrous tumults to continue, I fear the worst."

To this urgent speech, Caumont made no response, but instead sat stiffly in his chair, his eyes fixed angrily on the floor, maintaining a sullen silence. La Boétie changed the subject, complimenting the Brethren on the evident prosperity of Mespech, and after several minutes of such banter traded disconsolate looks with Siorac and Sauveterre and took his leave.

Here I must say a few words about the massacre of the Protestants at the Orioles temple in Cahors. Although there were more victims than at the massacre of Vassy, the latter is better known to the French for reasons that we shall see later on. But the tumultuous events at Cahors set the tone for what was to happen several months later at Vassy, and in so many other places where the murder of Protestants in the first months of 1562 served as a prelude to the frightful civil wars which ravaged the kingdom of France right up until the crowning of Henri IV.

In the year 1561, on 16th November, the Calvinists of Cahors were assembled for religious services in the Orioles temple, belonging to Raymond de Gontaut, lord of Cabrerets. It was a particularly mild day for that time of year, and the windows of the temple were wide open. As the reformers were singing the Psalms of David, a great crowd of people in a burial procession, led by Soubirou, the curate of Notre-Dame, passed under the windows, loudly chanting the funeral service.

Although the Psalms of David and the priests' canticles celebrated the same God, Catholics and Protestants alike felt insulted by this juxtaposition. The reformers, not to be outdone, sang louder. The Catholics did likewise. From street and windows, insults were soon exchanged; insults gave way to threats and threats to blows. The populace, rushing en masse to the scene, and goaded by some of the more fanatical Catholics, broke down the doors to the Orioles temple, and rushing on the "heretics" assembled there to "hear the word of the Devil" massacred thirty of their number.

As for the murder of the Baron de Fumel, it was a revolt conceived by his subjects under the guise of religion. So great was their hatred of their old master that, having stormed the chateau, they tore off his clothes and whipped him to death—and not content with his death, they filled his inert body with a rain of bullets and dagger wounds, everyone seeking a share of this savagery until the butcher of Libos went so far as to cut off his head with his knife.

The wise counsel offered to Geoffroy de Caumont by Étienne de La Boétie on the subject of such tumultuous bloodletting was not lost on the Brethren. But then it is also true that this counsel was in keeping with their own inclinations. My father was then fifty-six years old, Sauveterre sixty-one, and being both of a mind to preserve the wealth they had so arduously acquired, neither sought to jeopardize it through any excess. And so they never touched the church at Marcuays, nor even the chapel at Mespech, but left intact its crosses and statue of the Virgin (much admired by my father, for it was of painted wood and quite naively sculpted). Better yet, not wishing to run the risk of having my mother escorted on Sundays to the church in Marcuays by two Huguenot soldiers, which undoubtedly would have provoked some reaction by the more fanatical Catholics, they continued to pay five sols a month to Pincers to come and say Mass at the chateau for the sole benefit of my mother, who, dressed to the hilt in all her Sunday finery, went alone to the chapel, standing stiffly in proud meditation, holding in her hand as an emblem her Roman missal, without ever opening it.

After Mass, the Brethren invited Pincers to have a drink in my father's study and made pleasant conversation about the weather and the crops. Pincers, whose great nose protruded with a violent red glow, miser, thief and drunkard that he was, nevertheless was not entirely lacking in finesse. He appreciated the weighty advantage, in these troubled times so full of danger for priests, of maintaining good relations with the Huguenot lords of the domain, and downplayed the question of heresy in his sermons, never permitting the slightest attack, public or private, direct or veiled, against Mespech. And so, in this ocean of tumults that the kingdom had become, peace reigned in Taniès, Sireil and Marcuays. And when later the Huguenots gained control of Montignac and tried to force their iconoclastic beliefs on the church at Taniès, Siorac, his soldiers at his heels, nearly killed his horse getting to the church in order to dissuade them.

But there was danger in this very moderation, as we shall see—moderates in both camps being despised by extremists on either side.

Throughout this period, an underground papist idolatry continued to flourish at Mespech, especially among the women, under the cover of lip-service Huguenotry. I discovered all this through strange circumstances, bedded as I was with little Hélix in Barberine's enormous bed, now that she had gone off home for reasons I've already explained. In the middle of one very dark night, little Hélix began shivering so much she nearly shook the bed.

"What's the matter?" I asked, half-asleep. "Are you trembling?"

"Yes," she confessed, "I can't help it."

"Why not?" No answer. "Are you feverish?" I gasped, pulling away.

"No," she answered in a voice suffocated with fear. "But I think it's a great sin we are committing. Every night the Devil comes over us, and it's all your fault."

"My fault, silly!" I said, fully awake now. "How so? And who started it?"

"I did," she admitted ruefully, "but you make me sink into temptation, being such a cute little rascal."

"You should have resisted."

"And how could I, a poor peasant girl and you the son of the baron?"

"You must be joking, you vixen!" I said, irritated. "Son of a baron I may be, but it wasn't long ago that you were pinching my backside black and blue. And as for you know what, you taught me everything I know."

"But now I'm all repentant," she said, sobbing and crying hot tears.

I made sure her tears were real (knowing her to be so mischievous and the night being so dark) by drawing my finger under her eyes and finding it all wet. I was greatly moved by her chagrin, feeling as I did such deep friendship for her beyond the obvious attraction of our nocturnal games. "Hélix," I said, "if this is how you feel, then we should stop altogether."

"Oh no! No! No!" she cried. "Especially now that you're going on eleven and getting to be a man, thank God!" And seizing my head passionately between her two thin little arms, she thrust it between her sweet breasts, which doubly reduced me to silence given that I was now effectively gagged and because I loved my gagging, despite my raw youth.

But she soon released me and started again to cry and tremble. "Oh I'm done for, my pretty little man," she wept, her tears dropping on my chest, "when I think every day that I am going to burn in hell and horrible devils will skewer me in the flames with their pitchforks, now on this side, now on the other, so that I'll be baked evenly all over, poor little Hélix, who loves God and Holy Jesus so much!"

"But no one can foretell who will be damned," I said, more secure in my Huguenot theology than she was in hers.

"Oh yes they do!" she sobbed, blind to such nuances. "I know I'll burn. I can already feel it in my bones. Oh if only I were as old as you, then I could claim, like la Maligou did, that as a poor serving girl I was forced to submit to my lord's feudal rights. Then it wouldn't be my fault and there'd be no sin."

"And a nice lie that would be, Hélix! If you've forgotten all the tricks you started with, I'm going to make you remember them."

"Oh no! I won't listen, you rascal! Go away!" she said, pushing me away. "You enchanted me with your pretty golden hair which makes you look like a golden écu! But it's all trickery and false appearances. You're the Devil incarnate!"

"I am not and you know it!" I spouted. "Here is the Devil!" I said, touching the various parts of her body. "And if you dare repeat that I am the Devil, I'll go sleep in Samson's bed and you'll never see me in yours again."

"Oh no, no no!" she whined, immediately seizing me in her arms and squeezing me to her violently. "Don't go away, I beg you, Pierre de Siorac! Or I'd be so unhappy I'd throw myself off the tower into the moat." This threat did not move me. I'd too often heard my mother say it, and there wasn't a woman in Mespech who didn't go around repeating it after her. And yet I consoled little Hélix and gradually her tears ceased along with her sobs. And I thought her aslumber again, when she said in a piteous voice: "The truth is I'm too small for such a great sin."

"But what can you do," I reasoned naively, "since you don't want to give it up?" (Nor, in truth did I.)

"I know!" she cried, sitting up suddenly in the bed. "We'll both go and pray to the Holy Virgin to intercede for us with the Divine Child!"

"Pray to Mary?" I gasped indignantly. "But that would be pure idolatry! And for sure we'd be damned then!"

"For sure not! My mother secretly prays to her every day, and la Maligou and Little Sissy as well. And so do I!"

"What are you telling me?"

"The truth. La Maligou has set up a little altar to the Holy Virgin in the corner of the granary, with a beautiful image of Her and dried flowers. And it's there we go to pray one after another, kissing the feet of the image, and always someone to keep watch."

"Does my mother know?"

"Oh no! We don't dare tell her."

"Why not?"

"Because when she gets angry she can't hold her tongue."

"And when do you all do this?" I asked, utterly amazed.

"When the men have retired into the library for the evening."

Certainly the moment was well chosen. In the great hall during the evening, there was always such a lot of coming and going, with the women engaged in housework and the men sitting around the fire roasting chestnuts over the coals and occupied in lively and loud discussion in the absence of their masters, that it was easy to sneak away without arousing suspicion.

"I shan't pray to Mary," I said resolutely. "Neither here nor in the loft. But go ahead, if that's what you want."

"But if I do it alone, it won't help," protested little Hélix. "We have to pray together, since we've sinned together."

"And start in again together!" I thought to myself, half serious, half in jest, for I could sense the weakness of her reasoning. But, at her request, I promised to keep silent about their secret cult of Mary in our Huguenot stronghold. And I kept my promise, though not without a few pangs of conscience, my loyalty to my father pricking and stinging me. But I was too afraid that the Brethren would dismiss Barberine and little Hélix not to seal my lips on the matter.

Étienne de La Boétie had done well to warn Geoffroy de Caumont about Montluc, for after hesitating for some time between the Roman Church and our own, this man had ended up choosing Catholicism because of his desire to advance his own fortunes at court, his greed to fill his coffers and the frightful pleasure he took in spilling blood. Physically, he was a dry, bony man, with an emaciated face, high and prominent cheekbones, angry eyebrows and pinched lips. Hardly a fanatic, he killed men not for love of any cause, but for political ends, out of resentment and for fun.

It was at Saint-Mézard in the Agenais region that, in February

1562, he gave the first measure of his cruelty. There was a small uprising of Huguenots in that village against Sire de Rouillac who had tried to keep his reformed subjects from breaking the icons in the church of Saint-Mézard and from stealing the chalices (for in these affairs looting always played some part). But he paid dearly for this, for the people rose up and besieged his house. However, he was luckier than Fumel, and did not pay with his life, being rescued just in time by neighbouring noblemen. But great bitterness and angry words ensued on both sides, especially concerning a large stone cross in the cemetery which some of the Huguenots had broken.

Montluc swept down on Saint-Mézard with his troops at dawn on 20th February, but since none of his men knew the place all of the Huguenots were able to escape, with the exception of a man named Verdier, two other devils and a young, eighteen-year-old deacon, who were all seized. They were bound and taken to the cemetery where Montluc, followed by his executioner, brought them before the two consuls of Saint-Mézard and a nobleman of the town.

"Traitors," scowled Montluc, "is it true, as this gentleman and these two consuls claim, that when they told you the king would be displeased if you broke that cross, you answered, 'What king? We are the kings. Your king is a little kinglet of dung. We'll put sticks to him and teach him how to earn a living like other honest folk'?"

"Oh, Monsieur," said Verdier, "pity for a poor sinner."

"Miscreant," answered Montluc, "how dare you seek mercy from me when you have no respect for your king?" So saying, he pushed him rudely down onto the fragments of the cross, ordering his executioner: "Strike, villain!" Whereupon the man beheaded Verdier right there on the cross. Two others were strung up from the elm in the cemetery. Which left the deacon. Montluc demonstrated on his behalf a strange sort of mercy: given his youth, he got off with a mere whipping—which lasted only until he died beneath the blows. And it was thus that four of the king's subjects were summarily executed without arrest, judges or trial.

In Cahors, meanwhile, the two civil commissioners sent by the queen mother conducted their inquest on the massacre at the Orioles temple. They indicted fifteen Catholics, whom they sent to the stake. Montluc immediately hurried to Fumel, and, passing through Sainte-Livrade on his way, was brought six Huguenots, whom he strung up without lingering over them. But as he was joined at Fumel by Monsieur de Burie, he had to follow a few more formalities and sent for two counsellors of the seneschalty of Agen to judge Baron de Fumel's murderers. Which was done with great haste, and nineteen Huguenots were hanged.

From Fumel, Montluc travelled to Cahors to intimidate the two civil commissioners sent by the queen mother, who had been so bold as to imprison Monsieur de Vieule, the canon of Cahors, since they believed he had abetted the Orioles massacre. Scarcely had he arrived there than he confronted Geoffroy de Caumont, who had come to complain about him to Burie in the presence of a large assembly.

"Monsieur de Burie," said Caumont, "Monsieur de Montluc has falsely claimed that a minister preaching in my presence at Clairac offended the person of the king."

"I said as much, and it is no falsehood!" asserted Montluc, striding towards Caumont, his hand on his dagger and followed by fifteen of his gentlemen. "It is a great shame that you tolerated such words from your Huguenot preacher after all the benefits you have received from the king."

Caumont grew pale with fury and stood his ground: "I have said, and I repeat, that I was not present when this minister gave his sermon, and in any case I am not answerable to you." Whereupon Montluc took a step towards him, his dagger half drawn from its sheath. Caumont put hand to sword, but could not draw it, for

Montluc's men were on him in a trice and would have killed him had not Burie intervened to push him outside, saving his life.

"And I," shouted Montluc as Caumont was dragged over the threshold, "I have said, and I repeat, Abbot of Clairac, that you support the Huguenot sedition in Agen and Périgord and the king would be well advised to send you to the tower of Loches!…"

Once Caumont was out of the way, Montluc so terrified the civil commissioners by his insults and threats that they, too, fled from Cahors, leaving him lone judicial officer of the king, Burie no longer daring to oppose him.

The wind was indeed changing. The Duc de Guise (with the Church of France, the Pope and Felipe II of Spain behind him) quickly regained his absolute power. Of the whole cloud of forces now ready to descend on us, Montluc was but the willing and hostile instrument. The Brethren were well aware of this, and though they had had no part in the seditions of Périgord, they began to fortify Mespech.

The news from the north and from Paris was not slow to fan our fears. Accompanied by a large escort, Guise set out on 1st March for Paris from Joinville, where he had been visiting his mother. As it was Sunday and the morning well advanced, he stopped at Vassy to hear Mass. Never did a more brilliant assembly honour this humble church. The victor of Calais, superbly clad in his doublet and his scarlet satin shoes, wearing a red feather in his black velvet cap, was first to enter the nave, assuredly the most handsome and majestic of all the gentlemen in his retinue. He had other reasons too for holding his head so high at Vassy, for he considered himself lord of this city, since it belonged to his niece Mary Stuart.

But no sooner had he taken his seat in his golden chair in the choir than news was brought that some 500 reformers were celebrating their cult in a barn a mere stone's throw away. "What's this?" he cried petulantly. "Am I not practically at home here? And since Vassy is a closed city, even the Edict of January does not give these heretics the scandalous right they so presumptuously assume. So this is what their beautiful gospel is all about! They always want to exceed their powers! Let's go remind these reckless folk that as my subjects they're badly mistaken to believe that they can offend me so." So saying, he left the church with his retinue. Unfortunately, two of his impetuous gentlemen, going before him, entered the barn and provoked a tumult.

"Gentlemen," the Huguenots said politely, "please join us."

To which the young La Brousse replied, putting hand to sword, "'Sdeath! Let's kill 'em all!"

At this blasphemy, the Huguenots rose up and threw the intruders out and barricaded the doors. A few, however, were so ill advised as to mount a scaffolding above the door and hurl stones at the duc and his party when they arrived.

These were riddled with bullets; the doors were broken in and any who tried to escape over the roofs were shot like pigeons. When the duc finally put a stop to the carnage, twenty-four Huguenots lay dead, over a hundred others gravely wounded. The political role which the duc had lately assumed gave great weight to this event. He had formed a triumvirate with Montmorency and the Marshal de Saint-André over the head of the regent, whom they judged too indulgent of the reform. Their aim was the eradication of all heresy from the kingdom, and they were seconded in this goal by the frightful counsel of the Pope to the young Charles IX "to spare neither fire nor sword". And yet in Guise's mind this was all a bit abstract. A great warrior, he was not innately cruel. He thought himself, on the contrary, good, courteous and chivalric. At Metz and Calais, he had acted with great humanity towards his prisoners. At his death, he mentioned the Vassy massacre in his confession, but denied it was in any way premeditated.

My father, having served under him at Calais, liked and esteemed him, despite his Catholic zeal (which was not without its ambitious side), and always said that if the two sides had not quickly spoilt things at Vassy, the duc would likely have been content to reprimand his "subjects" for having broken the Edict of January, and let it go at that. In truth, my father claimed, events took François de Guise by surprise and their consequences quickly overwhelmed him.

In Cahors, the Orioles massacre had left many more dead than were counted at Vassy. But the man responsible was merely an old canon who had whipped up the zealots in the crowd. Both the canon and his zealots had been seized and executed for their excesses. But a lord more powerful than the king himself had presided over the carnage at Vassy. Guise had struck, and there was no one to call him to account, unless it was a prince like himself who was prepared for armed combat. Condé quickly understood his role, and began recruiting his soldiers.

Feeling that this incident did little for his reputation, Guise returned to Paris deeply troubled. The news of the massacre had preceded him and he was surprised to receive a hero's welcome in this city, which had been fanaticized by the priests. When the hero appeared in the city—his scarlet satin doublet set off against his black Spanish jennet—the Parisians, massed from all quarters, shouted "Vassy! Vassy!" as if Vassy had been the greatest of his victories. Maids and matrons pressed breathless from all sides, their hearts beating at the sight of the beautiful red archangel, the sword-bearer of the Church against the heretics.

Guise flew from triumph to triumph. At Guise's residence, the provost of the merchants was waiting, surrounded by his peers. He offered Guise 20,000 men and, more importantly, two million in gold—more than the rich burghers of Paris had offered Henri II to fight the Spaniards. These offerings were made, as the provost put it, "to pacify the kingdom", in other words to plunge it into the horror of a fratricidal war.

In less than a month, the conflagration lit at Vassy had spread throughout the kingdom. At Sens, on the occasion of a pilgrimage, a pious monk roused the mob against some Protestants, who were beaten, their throats cut and their bodies thrown in the Yonne river. At Tours, 200 Huguenots were bound, beaten and dragged into the Loire. At Angers, the Duc de Montpensier hanged, beheaded or burned every reformer he could lay his hands on. In a single afternoon at Gironde, Montluc, who had been waiting only for such examples from the north to unleash his fury, hanged seventy of our number in the marketplace of the town.

And everywhere the Protestants retaliated. They stormed the towns of Angers, Tours, Blois, Lyons and Orleans. As regent, Catherine de' Medici, now at Fontainebleau, watched as Charles IX's throne was rent asunder, unable or unwilling to take sides.

The triumvirs, at the head of a thousand knights, put an end to her indecision. They came and carried her off by force along with her son. Weeping with rage, Catherine de' Medici was obliged to take up quarters at the Louvre, prisoner of a fanatic people and now the figurehead of the Catholic party.

On 13th July 1562, the parliament of Paris formally outlawed the Protestants. Henceforth, throughout the kingdom, townspeople and field hands were allowed to arm themselves and set upon the reformers without fear of restraint, arrest or action of any kind by the police.

This permission, granted to one half of the kingdom to assassinate the other half, overwhelmed the Brethren. They feared the worst, especially now that Montluc had seized François de Caumont's chateau and set up a garrison there under Burie.

This done, Montluc headed to Clairac, and not finding Geoffroy de Caumont, whom he would gladly have humiliated, debated hanging all the apostate monks there but, greed overcoming religious zeal, he contented himself with demanding a ransom of 30,000 écus. Heading next to Périgord, he went to settle an old account, laying waste to the lands of the Baron de Biron, guilty in his eyes for having sheltered a group of seditious Huguenots. Montluc now commanded a troop of 30,000 Spanish infantrymen, and despite the regent's orders to join forces with Guise's army in Paris, he pleaded the necessity of pacifying Guyenne in order to resist obeying. Under Guise in Paris he would have been a nobody. Here in Guyenne he reigned alone, giving vent to his life's two greatest pleasures: hanging and filling his coffers.

When Montluc left the lieutenancy of Guyenne, he was richer by 300,000 livres. And as for the hanged men he'd left in his wake, he cynically justified his actions in his *Commentaries* with the caustic comment: "The necessities of war force us, against our better nature, to take no more account of the life of a man than of that of a chicken."

It is not as though our southern Huguenots did not represent a force to be reckoned with, even after they were outlawed. But led by untrained captains athirst for adventure, they were dispersed throughout the countryside in a thousand little actions which better represented the gods of vengeance and pillaging than that of Calvin.

We saw quite nearby a most unfortunate example of this. When our Huguenot neighbours at Montignac seized the chateau in their town, they hanged La Chilaudie, who defended it, then they stripped the church, including its tombs, and their leader Arnaud de Bord extorted a heavy tax on the terrorized Catholics of the place.

Montignac was but a few leagues from Taniès and Marcuays, so Pincers grew much alarmed at the rumours which, in early August, designated his churches and his own person as the next victims of Arnaud de Bord. He came humbly to share his fears with the Brethren.

"Good priest," said my father, "if you wish to avoid having your churches pillaged, clear them out yourself. Remove all the furniture, chandeliers, chalices, monstrances, sacred ornaments and the rest, and take them to the bishop of Sarlat."

"But will I ever see them again?" worried Pincers, lowering his eyes. "The bishop has very long teeth."

"In that case," smiled Jean de Siorac, "entrust them to the police lieutenant. La Porte is an honest gentleman."

"I scarcely have the means to transport them so far, nor to protect their journey."

"Mespech will provide wagons, horses and escort," said my father, an offer that somewhat displeased Sauveterre, even though he disapproved of Arnaud de Bord's excesses.

Pincers did as my father suggested, but scarcely had he completed this move than one of Arnaud de Bord's lieutenants arrived at Taniès with a few horsemen. Jean de Siorac hurried to meet him with his own soldiers. Batifol—the lieutenant in question—was outfitted for war with helmet and armour, and a fierce moustache to boot, thicker and stiffer even than Cabusse's. He broke out in the most violent rage when he discovered the empty church.

"There is fraud and trickery afoot, from what I'm told," he raged, putting on great airs, "and if 'tis true, then the curate of Marcuays and his accomplices shall pay for it."

"And do you count me among their number, my good Batifol?" asked Jean de Siorac, staring him coldly straight in the eye.

"Heavens no, My Lord, heavens no! And yet they tell me that

you provided wagons and horses to the priest to help him remove his goods from the church."

"They tell you the truth."

"Then you're but a half-Huguenot, My Lord," frowned Batifol, "since you protect papist churches."

"I protect its goods, not its faith. Mine, which is as good as your own, does not admit of pillaging and rapine between countrymen."

"May I repeat your words to Arnaud de Bord?" said Batifol, curling his moustache.

"You may and you must, Monsieur," replied my father, remounting his horse."

"Then your life hangs in the balance, My Lord," answered Batifol, mounting his own steed.

"Truly, Monsieur?" laughed my father. Batifol stared at my father with an air of false bravado, then turned tail and galloped off with his men. My father and his soldiers watched in silence as their troop rode away, and, on this occasion, Coulondre Iron-arm made one of his rare and lugubrious remarks: "That man smells of the noose," he said in a hoarse voice.

As this exchange between the Baron de Mespech and Batifol took place in public, it was not long before Pincers learnt of it from some peasants. He rushed to Mespech, his crimson face all gone pale, his great bulbous nose gone limp over lips that trembled so much he could hardly speak: "My Lords," he stammered, "the Montignac people can only dream of taking revenge on Mespech, but, alas, on me they can easily do it! Especially since Monseigneur the bishop forbids me from leaving my villages. Shall I wait in Marcuays to be hanged by the neck, like poor La Chilaudie?"

To this veiled appeal, Sauveterre, stony-faced as usual, replied not a word, and exchanged looks with my father, already deploring his younger brother's human foibles.

"Good Curate," said Jean de Siorac, "would you like to go into hiding for a while at the le Breuil farm with Cabusse?"

"'Tis hardly possible," replied Pincers, lowering his eyes to fix them on the end of his voluminous nose. "This Cabusse is a very jealous man. Even after his marriage he could not bear me to hear Cathau's confession."

This revelation came as no great surprise to my father, but it amused him all the same. He continued in a bemused tone, "Well then, what about Jonas's cave?"

"With that wolf in there?" cried Pincers, raising his eyes heavenward. "With that sorceress who has bedevilled him?"

"Curate, surely you do not believe this foolishness!" said Sauveterre, his eye gone dark and his tone dry as dust.

But Pincers would answer not a word and kept his eyes on the ground, for he did not wish to affront Sauveterre. As for my father, he too grew sombre, for he suspected Pincers, whether from superstition or partisanship, of having started rumours among his flock which had begun to ruin Jonas's reputation. He rose from his seat. "My friend, you will wish, no doubt, to pay your respects to Madame de Siorac before you withdraw."

Pincers went pale on hearing this dismissal, but did not entirely lose hope. He knew the influence Isabelle still enjoyed over my father, especially in her present condition.

And indeed, Pincers had scarcely crossed our three drawbridges before Isabelle had dispatched Alazaïs to the library to request Jean de Siorac's company in her chambers.

My father found Isabelle dolefully stretched out on the pillows of her bed, her belly already quite large and her breasts loosely displayed beneath a lace nightgown, and yet, despite her condition, all got up and decked out in her finery and baubles, her lips painted and her eyes lined, and her hair done up in curls by the hefty Alazaïs, whose offices were so often deemed frivolous by her mistress, and who had done her work with a Huguenot thoroughness—and even some tenderness for this poor obstinate papist, whom she nightly recommended in her prayers to God. And thus arranged in all her beauty, my mother lay there, as I so often saw her in the last days of her life in this transitory world which hastens us all on to our last judgement—her death so close at hand, though none of us, she least of all, suspected its approach. For she seemed still to be in the prime of her youth, with neither wrinkles, rheumatisms nor infirmities of any sort, beautiful and blonde in her finery, combed and sprayed with her perfumes, sensing all the love my father bore her, and secretly returning it a hundredfold, but restrained by the strictures of her pride.

"My dear," said my father with a joyful smile, "I am happy you've called me. You're looking so lovely and in such good health as your term approaches."

"May God grant, then, Monsieur," said Isabelle, already stiffening, "that you refrain from obstructing my wishes, since I am so near my hour that you might well spoil the unborn child."

"By my faith, lady!" said Jean de Siorac, laughing, "scarcely have I entered your chambers before you train your artillery on me! And what is this all about?"

"Monsieur…" said Isabelle. But she stopped in mid-sentence for she was somewhat afraid of my father, even in his gay moods, for he had a quick and violent temper.

"Let me say it for you," said Jean de Siorac, becoming serious. "You wish to shelter the curate of Marcuays for some time within our walls to save him from the gallows Montignac's band is preparing for him. Well, lady, let me set your mind at rest. I will grant your wish, but only under certain conditions: that he be considered your guest and not mine; that he refrain from appearing in the great hall or seeing our servants; that he sleep in Alazaïs's chambers, whom we shall lodge with la Maligou for the duration; and finally that he take his meals in your chambers and not below."

"Oh no, not that," cried my mother, raising her beautiful hands, so well preserved with ointments and creams, "it cannot be! His feet stink, and most horribly so! Even at Mass I am bothered and distracted from my prayers."

"Well then," answered my father, bursting into laughter, "the curate shall eat alone in his room and Alazaïs shall serve him."

But Alazaïs, present at this interview, drew herself up to her full height and flatly refused.

"With all respect, My Lord, I shall not serve the curate," she said in her deep voice. "It's not so much that he's a priest, but I cannot bear his drunkard's mug."

"Between his ugly mug and his smelly feet," laughed my father, "the poor devil will die of hunger! Well then, la Maligou will bring him his dinner!" he said, with a curt gesture meant to signal an end to the discussion and to dismiss Alazaïs. Then he sat down on the side of Isabelle's bed, took her hands and gazed adoringly at her in all her maternal splendour.

Following my father's orders, Pincers came to Mespech without baggage of any kind during the night, having told no one of his destination. He had been scarcely a fortnight within our walls when Monsieur Guillaume de La Porte arrived at the first drawbridge, accompanied by five men-at-arms, and requested to see the Brethren.

"Messieurs," said the magistrate gravely as soon as he was introduced, "there is a rumour running about Sarlat that you have kidnapped and sequestered the curate of Marcuays to prevent him from saying Mass."

"This is a rumour whose feet should be cut off, Lieutenant," replied my father, "so that it may be prevented from running madly about, besmirching our good name, even as we do our Christian duty for this poor priest by saving him from the gallows."

And leaving Sauveterre to explain things, he went to fetch Pincers, who confirmed everything with endless effusions of gratitude towards his hosts for all the goodness they had bestowed on him. He appeared in the most excellent form, glowing with portly splendour and health, his face reaching new shades of crimson, since la Maligou, who served him in his room, had plied him with extra wine and brought him the choicest cuts of meat.

As Jean de Siorac accompanied Monsieur de La Porte to the drawbridge, Catherine, who had been playing with her dolls near the well, ran up, her blonde braids flying behind her, and took my father's hand, but said not a word, having exhausted her entire store of courage in accosting him in this way.

"My Lord," said the police lieutenant, "I see that you are constructing a second wall around your moat. At such a moment, these new bulwarks are causing people's tongues to wag."

"They're wrong again, Lieutenant. Mespech's doors will always be open to the king…" (and he looked him straight in the eye) "and to the royal officers. But the Paris parliament has outlawed the reformers and I might have to defend myself against certain of my neighbours."

"Ah, you're worried about Fontenac," said La Porte, frowning, "and you're not wrong to do so. There's no worse little tyrant in our provinces, yet he is so well supported by the bishop and even at the court that I can do nothing about him. Do you realize that when someone in his family falls ill there's not a doctor in Sarlat that will dare to venture into his lair for fear of not getting out freely or even alive?"

My father returned from this conversation, holding Catherine's fresh little hand in his own, happy to see her so pretty and lively, but finding no words to tell her, so great was his love for her. As he took his first step into the courtyard, Alazaïs appeared before him, looking quite wild, a full head taller than he. She said in a most abrupt tone: "My Lord, I must speak wi' you about this excrement of a priest."

"Well?" Alazaïs glanced at Catherine, and leaning forward spoke a few words in my father's ear which caused him to start.

"Go back to your dolls, Catherine," he said in a curt voice, "and you, Alazaïs, send this bawd to my library immediately."

When la Maligou appeared in the library, all thighs, stomach and breasts (as my father put it), and mightily dishevelled, Jean de Siorac closed the door behind her and, after pacing in a circle around her, came to a halt in front of her, hands on his hips, and stared at her with his severest look: "Well, I have just received some interesting news! Every night you and the curate fornicate like rats in straw!"

As la Maligou began to shake her head in denial, Jean de Siorac raised his hand and said, almost in a shout, "Don't lie to me, Maligou, or I'll dismiss you within the hour!"

"Sweet Jesus!" moaned la Maligou naively. "But if I don't lie, you'll throw me out just the same!"

"So it's true!"

La Maligou began to shake all over.

"Alas, My Lord, I dared not resist: he talks so sweet!"

"But his actions stink! Are you not ashamed to carry on like a putrid whore, you a married woman, committing adultery, and especially with Pincers?"

"That's just it, My Lord, with a priest it's only half a sin! Especially if he absolves me afterwards!"

Jean de Siorac raised his arms heavenward. "No one can absolve you of a deadly sin, you hussy, excepting God who is in heaven."

"And so I pray him every night for the intercession of His Son," said la Maligou, lowering her eyes, for at the same instant she was promising the Virgin Mary to burn a candle in front of her image in the barn if my father, by some miracle, would not dismiss her.

"And what if Pincers gives you a bastard?"

"Oh, no need to worry about that," crooned la Maligou with her most sly and knowing look. "I know all the herbs and where to put them!"

"And what herbs are these?" asked my father, who was always curious about peasant customs.

"With all due respect, I cannot tell you," answered la Maligou. "The noblewoman who taught me them swore me to silence."

"You must tell me if you don't want to be sent away."

"My Lord," said Maligou, her eyes opening wide and her heart beating wildly, "if I tell you then you won't send me away?"

"You have my word on it," affirmed Jean de Siorac, who from the first had wisely decided to hush up the affair.

"Oh, thank you God and sweet Jesus!" chanted la Maligou, who, with her arms crossed over her belly and her eyes chastely lowered, whispered to herself a prayer of thanksgiving: "And thanks be to you especially, Virgin Mary, for this miracle which you have wrought, and for forgiving my sins. I thought that as women we could always come to an understanding. But thanks again for your sweetness, good Virgin, and you shall have your candle, and that's a promise, which only a wastrel would be fool enough to break."

After la Maligou had revealed her secret herbs and "where to put them", my father made her promise never to see Pincers again, day or night, from dawn to dusk, by candlelight or light of day, and never to brag of this fornication to any living soul. He then charged Coulondre Iron-arm to bring Pincers's meals to him, which Coulondre did without the priest's ever getting any information from him other than a few laconic and dire predictions about the end of the world.

Jean de Siorac was so discreet about the whole matter that he never said a word of it to Jean de Sauveterre until the priest was again outside our walls. "Oh Jean," Sauveterre reproached, "you have hidden something from me!"

"I had to. I was afraid of what you would do."

"And now that Pincers is gone, are you going to dismiss la Maligou?"

"Heavens no. I gave her my word. But most of all I don't want her going around bragging to the entire countryside about her exploits. No, my brother, let us close our eyes to her sins and keep them closed. What's more," he said with a grin, "there's not a pot nor a roast in Périgord that can touch hers."

It was not Montluc but instead the lord of Saint-Geniès, the king's governor in Périgord, who re-established the Catholic Church at Montignac. On 14th August his troops, armed with cannon, besieged Arnaud de Bord, who surrendered three days later with his partisans. On 11th September, after a vigorous trial, sixteen of them were hanged in the public square in Montignac, and among these sixteen poor Batifol, whose untimely end had been so lugubriously prophesied by Coulondre Iron-arm but two weeks before. As for Arnaud de Bord, he was not put to the torture until 18th October, though no one ever learnt the reasons for this cruel delay.

His future once again assured, Pincers had already been gone for two weeks when a certain Monsieur de L. (this is how he is designated in the *Book of Reason*) appeared at our gates one night accompanied by a small escort, and, despite the strict security measures at Mespech, he and his troop gained easy entry, for the Brethren seemed to be expecting them. His escort, though well fed and watered, was not allowed to mix with our servants, but was billeted in the barn where Alazaïs was alone sent to wait on them.

As for Monsieur de L., he took his meals alone in the library with the Brethren rather than in the great hall, served by François, Samson and me, all of us greatly excited by the mystery surrounding this character and bursting with pride to be invited by my father to remain in their company after the meal. François was then fifteen years old, Samson and I going on twelve already, and my father, doubtless deeming us old enough to participate in the defence of Mespech (for we were daily exercised in the use of the sword, the blunderbuss and the pike by our soldiers), admitted us, if we promised to remain quiet as carps, to this council at which the destiny of the barony was to be decided.

Monsieur de L., whom I watched with much curiosity, surprised me not a little. He had a larger ruff, a richer doublet and a less austere face than any of the other Huguenots we regularly hosted at Mespech. Moreover, he did not speak the *langue d'oc* as we did, but expressed himself in French, a language which I was certainly capable of understanding, but with an accent I had never heard before and which I afterwards learnt was Parisian. His face, sporting neither moustache nor beard of any kind, was like a stone polished by frequent rubbing with the other stones of the court, his gestures open and frank, his attitude gracious and, though his pointed manner of speech shocked me a bit at first, I soon realized that Monsieur de L. was a paragon of courtesy, prodigal in his salutations and compliments, and tending to use ten words where one would suffice. He wore his hair long, quite clean and well curled, despite the difficulties of travel on horseback; his gloves, which he wore throughout the conversation, captured my admiration: they were of a very fine, soft leather I'd never seen before in the Sarlat region.

"Messieurs," said Monsieur de L. after a long prologue of formalities, "you know my name, you know whom I serve as well as who sends me."

He seemed quite satisfied with this overture, which he must have used more than once before, for he recited it without hesitation and quite easily. At the same time, he took on an air of modest pride, as though he carried with him, though unworthy of it, the reflection of the majesty he represented.

"Come to the point of your embassy with us, if you please, Monsieur," said my father, whose tense expression and nervous hands indicated that he found this preamble a bit too long.

"Here it is," said Monsieur de L. "Our forces, as you know, are assembling at Gourdon under the leadership of Monsieur de La Rochefoucauld and of Monsieur de Duras. They are several thousands strong, though I cannot tell you the exact number, and intend to link up with the army of the Prince de Condé at Orleans. Duras is a warrior and commanded the legion of Guyenne. François de La Rochefoucauld has also proved himself in battle. But the prince thought that the Baron de Mespech, who has served so long and so well, might contribute the additional support of his valour and his experience."

I could see from my father's expression that he was not the least bit surprised by this proposal, and that, in fact, he had been expecting it, but was not in the least happy about it.

"Monsieur," he said with cold courtesy, "you serve the Vidame de Chartres, and accompanied him to England when he represented the Prince de Condé and Admiral de Coligny in negotiating the Treaty of Hampton Court with Queen Elizabeth."

"'Tis true," replied Monsieur de L., who, despite his easy manner, betrayed deep embarrassment at this reminder.

"It is said that for the price of her support to the Huguenots,

Queen Elizabeth exacted from our allies the surrender of le Havre, a token she would not give back to France once the war is over, except in return for Calais."

Monsieur de L.'s discomfort seemed to grow, and he appeared to pale considerably. "But surely you are not unaware, My Lord," he said in an somewhat shaky voice, "that according to the terms of the Treaty of Cateau-Cambrésis, France must return Calais to the English in 1567…"

"Or else, on that date, retain Calais indefinitely in exchange for 500,000 écus. And what king of France would ever prefer the solution I have just announced to the one you proposed?"

"But this is the solution that the Prince de Condé will most assuredly adopt, once the war is over."

"But he won't be able to!" cried my father heatedly. He rose and, pivoting around his chair, gripped the back with both hands. After some moments, his face contorted with grief and anger, he repeated, "He won't be able to! Since he has ceded le Havre as a token to Queen Elizabeth! And do you think she will give up le Havre for any sum of money, when her sole aim in lending us assistance was the return of Calais?"

After this outburst, my father sat down again, still trembling with indignation, and, though Sauveterre had not moved, I could see very well from his expression that he shared my father's sentiments about this deplorable bargain.

After a considerable pause, Monsieur de L. spoke in a quiet and flat voice, maintaining just enough dignity to impress my father: "I believe, My Lord, that when the Prince de Condé and Admiral de Coligny signed the Treaty of Hampton Court, they did not realize they had so gravely affected the future of Calais. They must have thought that the option of buying back the city remained open to them. Time was of the essence. The death knell of the reformers had been rung throughout the kingdom. But the prince and the admiral would think themselves most unhappy and unworthy if they had ever thought of reducing the kingdom."

"And yet they have mortgaged it!" claimed Sauveterre. "France waited 200 years to retake Calais from the English, and God knows how much blood and tears such an enterprise cost us. Ask the Baron de Mespech. He was there! And now, with a few strokes of the pen, the prince and the admiral have lost the city. And for what? For the help of 6,000 English troops, half of whom are slated to occupy le Havre! And 100,000 crowns of aid! A ridiculous contribution in view of what Elizabeth can expect in return! A piece of the kingdom of France and no insignificant piece either!"

Following this speech, there was a moment of silence, which Monsieur de L. broke with a grave voice: "Although present, I took no part in the negotiations at Hampton Court. I realized that the bleak necessities we faced allowed the English queen to strangle us, and that our conditions were disastrous, and that we had made a very bad bargain. But after all, a treaty is only a treaty… Condé and Coligny are fighting with their backs to the wall. Baron de Siorac, are you going to refuse them your aid when the stakes are nothing less than the survival of the true religion in the kingdom of France?"

My father rose once more and took several steps across the room, his face troubled and his hands clenched behind his back, while his sons and Sauveterre watched him anxiously. We were afraid that he would be unable to resist such a pressing appeal, and we could already see him armed and on horseback, leaving Mespech to rejoin Condé and Coligny in an uncertain, and in his eyes, illegitimate war.

"Monsieur," said Jean de Siorac finally, sitting down again and speaking calmly, "it would make me most unhappy to refuse you, for I would feel as though, in fact if not in spirit, I would be abandoning our cause. But if I accept, I would be equally distraught, for I would be taking up arms against my country and against my king. And so I must choose the former course. I will not join forces with the Prince de Condé. Please, Monsieur, I beg you, not another word. Anything you could say to me now, I have already told myself a hundred times over."

I looked at Samson, infinitely relieved, and although François, still as an icon, did not turn his head, he seemed to me to breathe a sigh of relief as well. Monsieur de L. did not press the point, but instead made a rather lengthy speech, asking his hosts for a monetary contribution for the maintenance of the troops Duras was gathering at Gourdon. The two brothers, after retiring to a small office off the library to discuss the matter, returned with the sum of a thousand écus —an enormous sacrifice for anyone who knew them well. Monsieur de L. counted the money as though it were a matter of a few sols without the least sign of surprise. This done, he wrote, in his florid style, a handsome receipt in the name of the Prince de Condé. After which he asked his escort to be alerted, and, with a thousand compliments, took his leave.

During the days that followed, my father seemed to lose his old sense of play, torn as he was between his two allegiances, the one to the true religion, the other to his king, or, as he put it, "to his nation". I learnt later that Condé himself, and even more so Coligny, had gone through the same agonies. They came out on the opposite side of this debate, and for this I certainly do not judge them. As for my father, it was the surrender of Calais that pushed him into the opposite camp, but not without a wound which took a long time to heal. A few years later, I heard Jean de Sauveterre remark that in a matter in which opposing duties came into play against each other, no matter what one chose, "one could only end up feeling he'd done the wrong thing".

*

One week after the brief appearance of Monsieur de L. at Mespech, my mother gave birth to a stillborn child and was stricken herself with a raging fever. My father did not leave her bedside, and slept each night in the little cabinet that had housed Pincers, requesting to have his meals brought up to his wife's chambers. Although he never appeared in the great hall, I knew that my mother's condition worsened daily by the long sad face of Alazaïs when she came to the kitchen to get meat for my father and warm milk for the invalid.

This situation had lasted for a week when my father summoned me to the little cabinet he now used for a bedroom. I found him seated, elbows on a little table and head in hands. He did not move when I entered, and, troubled by his immobility—he who was ordinarily so lively and outgoing—I remained standing before him, scarcely daring to breathe, and my heart full of apprehension at seeing him so entirely altered in his bearing. It was even worse when, feeling my presence, he withdrew his hands from his face revealing his eyes, from which tears streamed, one by one, down his unshaven cheeks. I couldn't believe my eyes and just stood staring at him, open-mouthed and stupid, my legs trembling beneath me, a terrible emptiness in my chest and my head swimming. The solid world I had known until now seemed to crumble and fall to pieces when I saw my hero crying.

"Pierre," said my father at length, in a feeble and scratchy voice, "your mother is dying and has asked to see you. I shall not follow you into her room. She wishes to see you alone."

When he rose his bearing and attitude suddenly appeared weak, bent and aged, and, worse still, unusually ill-kempt for someone normally so clean and well presented. This sight afflicted me almost more than the news I'd just heard. As if every movement had become unbearable, he gestured towards the door with but a slight wave of his hand, and walking past him, pale, sweating, my eyes cast down (so much did his weakness make me afraid and ashamed), I entered my mother's room.

My mother's strength calmed me, though even my young eyes could discern that death was written across her brow in her sunken orbits, hollow cheeks and feverish and bewildered eyes. But she was made up with all her usual colours, her hair curled with utmost care and her forehead haughty as usual.

"Sit down, Pierre," she whispered in a weak and hurried voice. "I have not much strength left nor much time. My mind is wandering and my head's in a cloud."

I sat down next to her on the little stool, where, I supposed, my father had spent many hours for the last week, eating his heart out watching her.

"Pierre," said Isabelle, "when I met Jean de Siorac, I was wearing a medallion of the Virgin around my neck. I want you to accept it from me and to wear it for the rest of your life, out of love for me."

I remained mute, stuck dumb by the gravity of what she dared ask of me.

"Pierre! Pierre!" she cried with feverish impatience, raising herself on the pillows. "I don't have much time left. Don't put off answering. Will you accept?"

"I accept," I said, "but shouldn't you give this present to my elder brother?"

"No," she hissed, falling back onto her pillow and closing her eyes. "François has no character. He wouldn't have worn it."

I saw her closed left hand advancing towards me and I seized it, opened it and found the medallion and its chain. "Put it on," she said, opening her eyes. I unbuttoned my doublet and obeyed, having, as I did, the impression of committing such a dastardly action against my father that I should never again, from this moment forward, examine my soul.

Isabelle blinked her poor hollow eyes, so feverish and already so bewildered, and she said in a faint voice, "I cannot see it. Is it around your neck?"

"Yes, it is."

"Will you wear it as I have told you?"

"Yes." She made a small, weak gesture, yet still imperious, to give me my leave, and as I was about to turn away, I saw her suddenly give me a look and a smile that were no longer those of a mother, but of a woman. The smile bathed her moribund face with tenderness and illuminated an unforgettable instant, as she said to me with an extraordinarily sweet but tenuous voice, already, it seemed, from the other world: "Adieu, Jean."

8

I SABELLE WAS BURIED, as she had requested, beneath the choir of the small chapel at Mespech. On the ochre stone slab that covered her coffin, Jonas undertook to engrave the following words dictated by my father:

ISABELLE, BARONESS OF SIORAC

1531–1562

Jonas wanted to make an engraving that would resist the erosion of time, and for two long weeks, wherever we were, we could hear the funereal sound of his hammer, striking his chisel. Jean de Siorac decided to leave the chapel exactly as it was when my mother heard Mass there. So its cross, its icons, its ornaments and its wooden statue of the Virgin remained. He ordered a double lock on the door and kept the key safely in his study. As for our reformed Church, it continued to meet as before in the common room.

My mother's death pained me but little, and it seemed to me that I should be more afflicted than I was—all the more so since I now realized that I had been her favourite son. But Isabelle had so little consented to know her children, and, despite her great love for them, she had loved them from such a distance that I never felt enough warmth from her to encourage my heart to reach out to meet hers. I faithfully wore her heretical medallion on my chest, hidden by my doublet, but it was only out of fidelity to my sworn word.

I would have felt truly heartbreaking grief only if I had lost Barberine for ever, but she was back again, distributing among her children her tender looks and sweet caresses along with the warblings of sweet nothings that she meted out each evening before blowing out her lamp. She now carried, nestled in her beautiful plump arms, a new nursling, Jacquou, whom my father had sworn to raise since she had borne him expressly to nurse Isabelle's child. And along with Jacquou, Annet now clung to her skirts, already a toddler, yet still continuing to nurse, as was the custom of the region.

Except for Barberine's return, there was little change in the household of Mespech after the death of Isabelle. Alazaïs was no longer needed as chambermaid, but our tall Huguenot shined with such rare virtues that the Brethren kept her on to work in the house and fields, and, if need be, for the defence of the chateau, the stout virgin worth any soldier's salt, having quickly learnt to handle a pike and a blunderbuss.

There came a day when, to our great relief, Jonas's chisel blows ceased, and our stonecutter emerged from the chapel, bent and covered with stone dust right up to his eyebrows, and asked my father to come see his engraving and tell him if it was satisfactory.

"'Tis beautiful work, Jonas," said Jean de Siorac, "but why did you engrave it so deeply?"

"The stone is handsome, but too soft, and it wears fast."

My father breathed a deep sigh.

"So you have done your best to preserve the memory of Isabelle de Siorac on this earth. But, my poor Jonas, it cannot last. In a few centuries, people will have so trodden on this stone that your beautiful work will be all effaced. And Isabelle will be nothing any more here below, not even a name."

At the time, Jonas found no answer to this; but sometime later while at the le Breuil farm, he said to Cabusse, "Nonetheless, Cabusse, in 200 years, they'll still be able to see my carving. And the passer-by who reads it will maybe say to himself, 'Thirty-one years old. She died so young, the poor lass.' And he'll feel a moment of compassion. And then I won't have done my work in vain and I'll be happy."

"And just where do you think you'll be at that moment?" asked Cabusse.

"Wherever I may be, I'll be happy."

Isabelle buried, my father, who had kept to his room throughout her illness, emerged into the light of day, blinking his red and swollen eyes and clothed from head to toe in black, and this tradition of mourning he maintained until his dying day. He immediately threw himself furiously into his work, and as for work, there was no lack of it.

The Brethren, as I have said, had undertaken to double the wooden enclosure surrounding the moat with a stone wall out of ladder-reach and surmounted by walkways with battlements. This second curtain was round in shape and built to connect up with a gatehouse, already constructed, a sort of large, square rustic tower two stories high, the ground floor of which contained a portcullis which defended a great oaken double door. This commanded a vaulted passage built directly under the tower. If the explosives of the enemy broke down these doors, they would encounter at the far end of the passageway an iron gate, which they might shake and twist, but they would only be able to do so by exposing themselves, caught as they would be in the weir of the vault, to fire from the arrow loops fixed on each side in the wall and stones hurled down on their heads from trapdoors.

As for the traps, which until then had been spread over the ground in the enclosure around the moat—a system not without its dangers for the stray cow or bull—they were collected into a circular area between the stone wall and the line of stakes. Anyone scaling and leaping from the wall would thus find himself caught up and badly injured by these.

It was thanks to Alazaïs that we recruited our nightwatchman, Escorgol, a cousin of hers, it turned out. He resembled her in size, but differed in his gaiety and his songs—but especially in a highly unusual feature: nearly blind in his youth, he had suddenly regained his full sight, without the aid of barber or doctor, at the age of thirty—a miracle which, as he said, had made him joyful and would keep him so for the rest of his days, since a man who has spent thirty years at the bottom of a well cannot but be happy to emerge into the light of day.

From his long sojourn in this twilight, Escorgol had, besides his good nature, gained a most precious quality for a nightwatchman: a remarkably acute sense of hearing. Sitting during the day in the common room with us, he could hear the sound of a horse's hooves on the Mespech road a full minute before the dogs outside in the enclosure.

Escorgol had bright brown eyes, a small nose and the lips of a good eater in a round, somewhat squashed face set in a completely bald head. Two enormous pointed ears emerged from this pumpkin, whose lobes shook when he laughed or spoke, which was often, for he was a greater joker and storyteller than any mother's son in the entire countryside.

So many cut or uncut stones were carted out of our quarry from le Breuil to Mespech during this period! And so many stones were carried or placed with the bare, chafed hands of adults and small children, men and women, each according to his or her strength! Everyone pitched in, except Coulondre, who, because of his iron arm, drove the carts, la Maligou, busy cooking her pots for everyone's paunch, and, of course, Barberine, who, besides Jacquou in her arms and Annet clinging to her skirts, still had Cathau's toddler to care for while Cathau vigorously lent a hand to Cabusse on the scaffolding.

To be sure, hands were not lacking. The Brethren had hired two journeymen stonecutters to help Jonas, who could not keep up with the demand, often filling the roles of both master builder on the walls and stonemason in the quarry. And when the wheat was harvested and the nuts were gathered, all of our tenant farmers arrived to lend a hand to the rest of our household: Faujanet, Marsal, the Siorac twins, Alazaïs (the equal of two men) and little Hélix (who wasn't worth a quarter of one, so preoccupied was she with watching them). Their lessons done, the baron's three rascals and the baron himself, throwing off their doublets, pitched in along with Sauveterre, despite his limp, and even Catherine and Little Sissy, who spent their time searching among the large blocks for flat chips that could be used as wedges between the stones as they were laid.

As the masters were so near at hand to their servants during this long project, and were drawn even closer by the work they did, everyone took advantage of the situation to deliver some message or other to them. In his discreet, indirect and Périgordian way, Jonas noted, as if in jest, that, as long as they were so engaged, they might as well build him a stone house over his cave while they were at it, so he wouldn't have to live out his life like a savage. My father did not greet this request ungenerously, and half joking, half in earnest, gave a half-promise that it should be done. But Sauveterre, already dismayed by the expense of the outer wall, turned a deaf ear to such talk.

In all, there were twenty-five mouths to feed every day and la Maligou, though basically happy to be doing her cooking outside and to see so many people, grumbled about the extra work, especially since Barberine was but little help, given that, the minute she took out one white breast to nurse Jacquou, Annet, as big as he was, immediately set to bawling to have the other, which she immediately granted him, sharing out her inexhaustible supply of milk like the she-wolf of Rome to Romulus and Remus. It was a pretty sight to see Barberine suckled on both sides by such avid little rascals.

I often paused in my work to watch them. I was moved to the depths of my entrails and a bit jealous to think that in the flower of her eighteenth year she had nursed me, just like these two, I who was now a strapping fellow, learning the martial arts, Latin and the history of the kingdom, as well as, from my father, the secrets of medicine.

Siorac and Sauveterre knew as well as anyone that, no matter how well fortified, Mespech could never resist a royal army furnished with cannon. They had said as much to the police lieutenant and would have the occasion to repeat it to Monsieur de Salis, the lieutenant general of Périgord, headquartered in Sarlat: as loyal subjects they would never close their doors to the king or to officers of the king.

But other perils were to be feared. Since the outlawing of the reformers by the Paris parliament, the dregs of the populace, feeling they now had the right to steal and to rape and kill their enemies, had crept out of hiding like woodlice out of a dead log. Brigands and highwaymen, fleecers and vagabonds, beggars and vagrants, emerging from the hovels where they'd been holed up and with religion as their pretext, committed the worst atrocities on the isolated houses of the Huguenots. To be sure, these bands had appeared thus far only in the northern regions of the kingdom, especially in the Anjou and Maine provinces, which they devastated, but with the progress of the civil war they might well descend southward towards Guyenne in search of adventure and new pillaging, where they would find no resistance from Montluc.

Yet we were confronted with dangers closer to hand, as Jean de Siorac had pointedly informed Guillaume de La Porte. Our neighbour, Bertrand de Fontenac, who resented us because of his father's banishment, had already provided the proof of his intentions by unleashing the Gypsies on us while my father was fighting under the walls of Calais. It was thus to be feared that, emboldened by the persecutions against us throughout the kingdom, he might again try some treachery against Mespech.

With our minds thus occupied by our fearsome neighbour, we completed work on our surrounding wall, and Escorgol was already installed on the walkway of the gatehouse when the Brethren received an unexpected visit from a messenger sent by the Baron de Fontenac. Siorac could hardly believe his eyes, nor Sauveterre his ears, when Siorac read the message out loud: the only daughter of the Baron de Fontenac, Diane, was suffering from a grave illness, which they feared to be life-threatening. Unfortunately, none of the doctors of Sarlat, Bergerac or Périgueux would consent to visit Diane at the Château de Fontenac.

"By my oath, they know the man too well!" observed Sauveterre.

As a consequence, the Baron de Fontenac beseeched the Baron de Siorac and Monsieur de Sauveterre, as good Christians, to pardon the differences which had arisen between their two families in the past…

"The 'differences'!" broke in Sauveterre. "That's a pretty way of putting it!

…and he humbly begged the Baron de Mespech to bring his medical knowledge to the aid of his daughter.

The two brothers stared at each other in disbelief.

"I am of the opinion we should flatly refuse," said Sauveterre. "Do we even know what she is suffering from, this Diane? It could be the plague. Some new cases have lately been discovered in the Sarlat region and it would be just like Fontenac to bring us this contagion!"

"Begging your pardon, but I believe we should accept," replied Siorac. "It seems to me the Christian and clever thing to do." He smiled and continued, "But of course only under certain conditions."

After a lengthy discussion, my father's opinion carried the day, and, within the hour, Siorac had composed a letter to the Baron de Fontenac. He noted that, although a graduate of the faculty of medicine of Montpellier, he was not a licensed physician and that there must undoubtedly be, in Sarlat, Bergerac and Périgueux, doctors more knowledgeable than he; that as yet he had only healed persons too sick to afford the care of these doctors; that he could not leave Mespech in such troubled times as these, much less visit his neighbour; but that if Fontenac wished to entrust Diane to his care, along with a chambermaid, he would attend her and lodge her on the first floor of the gatehouse of Mespech, whose south window looked towards the fortress of Fontenac; that he wanted it understood that he alone would decide on the care given to Diane for the entire length of her convalescence; and that during that time, neither Diane nor her chambermaid should receive visitors, either from Fontenac or any other party; that in the event of a tragic outcome of this illness, the Baron de Fontenac relieved the Baron de Mespech of any responsibility, and renounced in advance any recourse or legal proceedings against him; and that, finally, Diane and her chambermaid should be washed in hot water and deloused with the greatest care before leaving Fontenac.

I cannot explain this last, assuredly most bizarre, prescription except by reference to my father's maniacal horror of filth and certain pestiferous insects against which we waged a daily campaign at Mespech. Later, when I myself was staying at the court of Charles IX, I was often amused at the thought of how horrified my father would be to see one of the elegant and superbly dressed ladies in the king's entourage seize a louse from her hair and crush it between her delicate fingers without anyone around her seeming the least bit astonished.

In any case, Fontenac consented to everything, including the stipulation that a copy of the correspondence exchanged with my father on this occasion be copied by a court scribe and entrusted to the archives of the magistrate in Sarlat.

No one at Mespech, not even Escorgol, who lived downstairs from her in the gatehouse, was allowed to see Diane, who was described by my father as being fourteen years old and quite beautiful, with long black hair, large green eyes and very sweet and well behaved in the bargain, resembling in everything her mother and not at all the tiger she had for a father, a description which inflamed the imaginations of the three of us rascals of Mespech.

On the other hand, what Jean de Siorac kept from us was that he had recognized on Diane the marks of bubonic plague. Although the month of September was very mild that year, he ordered a great fire to be kept going night and day in the sickroom: he thought that the contagion of the plague could be spread by air and he wanted the air in the room purified by fire. For the same reason, he wore a mask over his mouth and nose when he approached Diane and, before leaving, he threw it in the flames of the hearth. Going directly to his library and avoiding all contact en route, he had two huge basins of hot water brought in, in which he bathed his entire body, believing in the virtue of heat against the contagion. He prescribed the same precautions for Toinette, Diane's chambermaid, and even for Escorgol, since he approached Toinette to bring her firewood and victuals. Never did poor Escorgol bathe so much in his entire life, and he complained bitterly about it, fearing that his skin would be worn out by it, or go soft on contact with the water.

My eminent professors of medicine at Montpellier made much mockery of this, when I later recounted these events, arguing that

water, even hot water, could have no effect on airborne contagion
since water and air are, by their very essences, incompatible. This
was doubtless infallibly reasoned. And yet no one at Mespech contracted the plague, not Toinette, or Escorgol, or my father. Perhaps
there was some good after all in all these "odd ways".

Diane was suffering from a raging fever and was very thin and
weak as her nurse at Fontenac had believed that a strict diet would
be good for her. My father, noticing that she urinated infrequently
and little, ordered milk to be given her whenever she asked for it,
and she drank up to two litres a day, spending all day shivering and
devoured by a prodigious thirst. On the sixth day, my father noticed
that a large bubo in her armpit was beginning to drain. He wrote
to Fontenac that his daughter was improving, since the sickness
seemed to be leaving her body, and that if the draining continued,
a complete recovery could be expected.

Two days after this letter, Mespech received a visit from a great
doctor in Sarlat, Anthoine de Lascaux, who, claiming he was sent by
the Baron de Fontenac, demanded to see the patient. And truly he
"saw" her and nothing more, for he never crossed the threshold of
her room. From this vantage point he pronounced that she looked
well enough, but that, to hasten her recovery, two pints of blood
must be drawn from her body every day.

"Bleed her!" exclaimed my father. "But why?"

Anthoine de Lascaux, who was a very handsome man, quite
portly and enormously sure of himself, smiled at the naivety of this
medical neophyte and hastened to enlighten him on the most recent
advances in medical science. "I see that frequent bleeding, as a cure,
hasn't reached these backwaters yet, My Lord. It is, however, the
sovereign cure for all ills, and the remedy of preference ever since
Leonardo Botallo, Charles IX's famous Italian physician, introduced
it to the French court."

"And what does this bleeding accomplish?"

"It releases the corrupted blood from the body of the patient. You are surely not unaware that the more bad water is skimmed out of a well the more good water will fill it. The same is true of blood and bleeding."

"Metaphor is not logic," replied my father after a moment of thought. "The well water is renewed by the spring that feeds it. But we do not know how blood is replenished."

"Blood engenders blood," said Lascaux with gravity.

"Perhaps, but not as fast. I witnessed during my military campaigns thousands of wounded who were greatly weakened by loss of blood, even though the wound was clean. And even when the wound was healed and closed, these same men remained greatly enfeebled for weeks afterwards."

Lascaux raised a magisterial hand: "Precisely because of the corrupted part of their blood. Their recovery would have been greatly hastened by drawing it out of their bodies."

My father reflected for a moment and answered: "If you believe that there is some 'corrupted' part, as you say, then you must also believe that there is some healthy part. Yet how do you know, when you are bleeding a person, that it is the corrupted part you are drawing out and not the healthy part?"

This seemed to embarrass Lascaux. But since he was sharp-witted enough, despite his bombast, he decided to turn the matter into a great joke: "Ah, My Lord, the authority of the greatest doctors in the kingdom is apparently nothing in your eyes! You're a great sceptic! You don't believe in bleeding any more than you do in the Virgin Mary, so you're a heretic in medicine as well as in religion…"

My father agreed to laugh at this flash of wit, and invited Lascaux to dinner and treated him hospitably. And Lascaux, on his return to Sarlat, wrote to Fontenac that the Baron de Mespech seemed well intentioned enough, but had a very odd conception of things. All in all, however, Lascaux confessed, the patient, whom he had been able to observe closely, gave every indication of an early cure. I found this letter from Lascaux among the archives of the Château de Fontenac, along with a note on the reverse side, from the baron, that he had sent fifty écus to the great doctor from Sarlat as a fee for his consultation.

As for other "consultations", there were none, for Jean de Siorac sent a firm but courteous letter to Fontenac reminding him of their agreement. Thus entrusted solely to the care of my father, Diane continued her long convalescence at Mespech, occasionally appearing at the windows of the gatehouse while we worked away below putting the finishing touches on the new bulwarks.

That September was sunny and so mild that occasionally, wrapped in a white fur cape, Diane would open the window and sit on the stone sill for hours watching our work with her large green eyes, the shadow of a smile playing at the corners of her still pale lips. I noticed that these appearances had a great effect on my eldest brother, to the point of riveting him to the spot, his eyes fixed and his hands hanging empty, not moving so much as an inch for minutes at a time. Who would have thought that this big dolt had so much blood in his veins, such a lively imagination and a heart capable of such tenderness? Diane certainly looked at all of us, and at no one in particular, but out of the corner of her green eye she couldn't have helped noticing François's confusion. And as he lowered his eyes and returned to his work, she would throw him, quick as a wink, a look, just one, and so rapid and quickly withdrawn that François was at great pains to see any encouragement in it. Such is the way of young women, it is said, when they are well bred.

But little Hélix, during our nights, displayed a more rustic style. "You're wicked, Pierre," she scolded as soon as the lamp was blown out, Barberine herself extinguished as well, deep in sleep. "You're always looking at that fancy floozy from the chateau. Your elder brother is already smitten and trapped, the poor fool! And does this tall skinny thing appeal to you too?"

"She's got a very pretty face," I said, to tease her.

"That's enough!" she retorted vehemently. "She's as pale as a turnip and her breasts are as small as my hands." So saying she jumped on me and, leaning forward, pushed her breasts in my eyes, "to stop them up", as she said.

Gossip was not lacking among our servants, especially in the kitchen and scullery where tongues wagged feverishly between la Maligou and Barberine. But in the library, between brother and brother, there was not a word, nor trace of a reference in the *Book of Reason*, nor the least allusion to François, who, taking his cue from this silence, looked the very image of despair.

On 1st October, the Brethren received an emissary sent by Monsieur de Duras, who was gathering the Huguenot troops from the south at Gourdon to lead them to Orleans to reinforce the Prince de Condé's army. This meeting took place in the Mespech library, and François, Samson and I were again present, since Jean de Siorac believed that it wasn't enough to have his rascals learn ancient history from Sauveterre: he felt we should learn the history of the kingdom as it was happening daily right before our eyes.

This emissary was named Verbelay, and he was far from possessing the self-assurance of the courtier, Monsieur de L. He seemed part soldier and part priest and as it happened he had left the latter profession for the former, having served as a novice at Cluny upon the recommendation of his brother, the bishop of le Puy. But when his habit produced a terrible rash on his young skin, he threw it in the nettles and, becoming a Huguenot, was overcome by a terrible itch to fight. He wore a rapier, a dagger, a pistol stuck in his belt and, above all this weaponry, two glowing black eyes, flattened hair and a large nose to smell out enemy blood. He was, moreover, truly courageous, as we were to learn later.

Verbelay began by thanking the Brethren for the thousand écus they had given to L., which L. had passed on to Duras. The gift had served to strengthen Duras's artillery, which at the time included but a set of culverins, by the addition of a huge cannon whose appearance gave renewed courage to the Huguenot soldiers at Gourdon. In keeping with their popular southern humour, they had giddily nicknamed it "Mass-chaser", baptizing it within the hour not with water but with Cahors wine, a few drops on the new bronze and the greater part in their gullets.

Mass-chaser was to have taken its first shots against the walls of Sarlat, which Duras wanted to take since it was directly on his way to Orleans, and he wanted the advice of the Baron de Mespech, who was renowned for having distinguished himself in a famous siege.

"At Calais," said my father, "it was a matter of chasing the English from the city. Our duty was clear. But here things are, in essence, more complex. For if it is true that it was a great crime to declare our reformers outlaws, it is likewise a crime to rise up against one's own sovereign and to take a city within his jurisdiction."

"I did not come, My Lord," said Verbelay, growing impatient, "to beg you to reconsider your decision. We are not seeking your armed intervention, but your counsel."

"Well, then, here's my counsel, since Monsieur de Duras does me the honour of requesting it thus," replied Jean de Siorac, somewhat piqued by his guest's tone. "If Duras's most direct route to Orleans is through Sarlat, I suggest that Duras make a detour and leave the city behind him."

"What?" gasped Verbelay, his black eyes shooting sparks. "Abandon this rich bishopric, when money is so lacking for our cause? And a city without a fortress, without a chateau, protected only by a simple wall, a few small towers and a tiny moat?! Why, from the surrounding hills we can look right down into the main square and see everyone's head and backside!"

Jean de Siorac made no reply, signifying that he had said everything he was going to say. And as the silence grew, Sauveterre, perhaps finding my father's response a bit too abrupt, continued: "Besides Mass-chaser, how many culverins do you have, Monsieur Verbelay?"

"Six."

"That's not many for a siege."

"But we are 12,000 strong. There are but 300 of them."

"Three hundred ensconced behind their walls," remarked Sauveterre, "and who will fight like tigers to defend their wives, their gold and their faith—whatever that faith," he added with a vague gesture. "Moreover Sarlat has learnt that Duras will attack. The consuls have abundantly stocked the city with provisions and munitions, and many good Catholic noblemen of the region have responded to their appeal: Fontanilles, Puymartin, Périgord, Claude des Martres, La Raymondie, all of these men have organized their forces into four companies which maintain a watch on the walls, bristling with blunderbusses, and, what's more, they are equipped with artillery which they've set up in the large tower of peace."

"Nevertheless, we'll take Sarlat!" said Verbelay resolutely.

"In ten days," replied my father. "Or rather you'll be able to take it in ten days if—and only if—before the ten days are out Burie, who is now in the Château des Milandes, and Montluc, at Agenais, don't fall on you from the rear. Monsieur Verbelay, I urge you to repeat what I have said to Duras. He might have taken Sarlat in twenty-four hours in a surprise attack. But your people have talked too much.

Sarlat is expecting you, and Burie and Montluc are forewarned and are preparing to throw up some obstacles in your path. Believe me the straightest, the surest and the fastest road to join forces with Condé at Orleans does not pass through Sarlat."

"I shall faithfully repeat these words, My Lord, and yours as well, Monsieur de Sauveterre," said Verbelay rising and taking his leave with as much brevity as politeness would allow. But his fiery eyes were ablaze and it was evident he was much displeased with the opinion he had to transmit.

From the window of our tower, Siorac and Sauveterre watched him mount his horse and speed away with his small escort. Sauveterre shook his head: "There's one excellent piece of advice that will go unheeded."

"I fear as much," replied my father, his fists on his hips and his head cocked. "If only Condé had offered me the command of the Gourdon army…"

"But it was yours for the asking…"

"No it wasn't!" said Siorac impatiently pacing back and forth. "They offered me what? To be Duras's lieutenant! But Duras is at best a good colonel of the infantry, wedded to routine, and short-sighted. He wants to claim an easy victory for his army by taking Sarlat. But he failed to pretend that he wouldn't attack, which is what Guise did so cleverly at Calais. He's lost any advantage surprise might have given him. He's not going to take Sarlat easily. He'll probably lose enough time under Sarlat's walls to be caught and cut to pieces by Montluc and his terrible Spanish infantrymen.

"No!" fumed my father, banging his right fist repeatedly on the table. "The first duty of Duras was to get his army out of this filthy wasps' nest in Périgord as fast as their horses could carry them, to escape by forced march from Montluc's claws and to lead his 12,000 men intact to Condé."

240

Seated, hands on my knees and, like my brothers, as quiet as a mouse, I listened to all this with admiration and yet some surprise, for I had just become aware that my father, Huguenot and loyalist that he was, might *perhaps* have rebelled against his king if he had been offered the commander-in-chief position at Gourdon. Jean de Siorac was thus quite right to say that the very question of duty in such troubled times was "in essence quite complex"… So it was, in any case, and only became more so when we learnt at Mespech that on the evening of 3rd October, Duras's army, having made its approach, had besieged Sarlat. It seemed from the Brethren's conversations on the matter that a Huguenot victory over a city to which they were attached by so many friendly ties plunged them into very mixed feelings indeed.

"Duras won't take Sarlat," said my father with a start when he heard the news.

"But Jean," observed Sauveterre, "you speak as though you wish the town wouldn't be taken."

"But do you yourself wish it?"

"I wish it," replied Sauveterre, without a trace of enthusiasm, "as a first success of our armies in an unjust war that has been imposed on us."

"But is this really a success?" asked my father, pacing back and forth impatiently. "Suppose Duras takes the city. What happens then? Our soldiers, who are, after all, soldiers like any others, will perform their usual exploits: sack, murder, rape of young women. They'll kill a few priests and ransom the very rich. They'll pillage and denude the churches. They'll exact tithes from the merchants. And after two days of such chaos, they'll leave Sarlat as firmly Catholic as when they arrived, and full of new reasons for taking revenge on the reformers. No, no, the fall of Sarlat accomplishes nothing. It's only in the north of the kingdom, between Condé and Guise, that any resolution will come."

"On the other hand," said Sauveterre, "if Duras fails at Sarlat, this failure will deflate the courage of our soldiers and provide a bad augury for what is to follow."

"Indeed, indeed!" agreed my father, his head bowed. "That's exactly what I keep telling myself. But imagine 12,000 soldiers let loose in a town the size of Sarlat, which counts but 5,000 inhabitants! My brother, is this what our gospel teaches?"

We learnt the following day that Duras had set up Mass-chaser and two culverins in the gardens of at the foot of the Pissevi hills, not far from the fountain of Boudouyssou. Firing began at eight that morning, and two hours later the opposing wall had been demolished, but Duras's battery had been so hastily installed, without earthworks to protect it, neither faggots nor gabions to cover it, that the harsh fire from the town had killed the master artilleryman, wounded the artilleryman and forced the rest of the crew to flee. Mass-chaser and the two culverins were thus abandoned in their garden, and any access to them prevented by an uninterrupted hail of bullets from the town walls. If the Sarlat townspeople had had enough troops for a sortie, the three artillery pieces would have been theirs. But they could not consider it and occupied themselves with reparations to the wall on that side.

At ten o'clock that evening, night having fallen, our troops sounded the alarm on all sides, with loud trumpet calls, beating of drums, strange shouts and much shooting and brandishing of ladders, and thanks to this diversion succeeded in removing Mass-chaser and the culverins from the Pissevi gardens and placing them in a more favourable position at the south-west corner of the town, on the Pechnabran hill, where they dominated the walls. There again, they broke down the defences. But Duras's assaults on 5th and 6th October were repulsed by the town. On the morning of the 6th, Duras, learning that Burie was moving to engage his forces, raised the siege, but not before burning all the outlying houses, the Cordeliers convent and the Château de Temniac.

He set out in great haste through Meyrals and Tayac in the direction of Périgueux, but never reached this city. On the 9th, Montluc caught him by surprise on the plains of Vergt and crushed his army. The carnage was terrible. The peasants joined in and 6,000 Huguenots were killed in the surrounding woods. No quarter was given. The remainder of Duras's Huguenots fled in disarray, and when Duras reached Orleans he had only 5,000 men, completely broken in strength, hope and valour. The three days he had wasted under the walls of Sarlat had cost the Huguenot party half an army and its first defeat of the war.

A week after the bloody defeat at Vergt, Samson, François and I were sitting in Escorgol's room in the gatehouse late one afternoon, listening to him weave one of his Provençal tales. But though our watchman told a good tale in a strong, sonorous *langue d'oc* accent (a bit different from our Périgordian tongue), I could see quite well that my elder brother was listening with but one ear, especially when a tripping little step could be heard above our heads, separated from us by a mere inch of chestnut ceiling which, in his hurry to finish, Faujanet had so roughly laid that you could see light through the planks. I cast a malicious glance at Samson, but innocent as he still was, putting his nights to the same use that Barberine did (I cannot think to whom, save the Devil, I owe such thanks that my guardian angels in the tower slept so soundly), Samson never took his eyes off Escorgol, all ears to his tale and his eyebrows knitting quizzically whenever some Provençal word bewildered him.

Beside the great fireplace—for on winter nights our watchman would need a good fire to keep him awake—a spiral stone staircase opened into the wall leading to the floor above, so twisted and narrow that the furniture destined for Diane and her chambermaid had to be hoisted through their window. Their fireplace was on the north side, set exactly above ours, the two flues joined before exiting through the stone roof. According to my father's orders, a blazing fire burned in the fireplace above us, and if you listened closely (as François was doing) you could hear the whistling and crackling of the burning logs.

The spiral staircase was separated from the first floor by two solid-oak doors furnished with heavy bolts, one on the first floor and one at our level, but the latter was now open, and we could see the first steps winding round the central stone pillar, well lit by a pretty little window just out of sight around the curve, so that all we could see of it was the light it shed on the handsome ochre steps that Jonas had cut. I remember that, sitting as I was, on a stool, leaning against the stone wall and listening to Escorgol, my eye, wandering about the room, often lingered on this shining, sweetly mysterious enclosure, where the steps wound around the pillar right up to the bolted oak door which enclosed our captive, whom we'd never seen except from afar at her window. As for me, I could enjoy the pleasures of my imagination in all this, but I could see it was a different story altogether for poor François, who, as little Hélix said, was already "smitten and trapped". With mournful eyes, and trembling lips, he stared fixedly at the luminous stairs set in the wall as if they were the forbidden entrance to the Garden of Eden.

Escorgol suddenly stopped and, closing his eyes, said, "What ho! I hear someone!" I jumped up and ran to the narrow window overlooking the machicolations and searched the dusty road curving away towards the les Beunes farm from the gatehouse. I could spy nothing, and, other than occasional birdsong, could hear nothing. Samson came up beside me and also lent an ear. Nevertheless

Escorgol, who had seized the blunderbuss beside his bed, closed his eyes again and then, immediately putting the weapon back in its place, said, "It's someone coming alone and barefoot." Having said this, he came up to the window to have a look for himself over our heads at the still empty road. François did not budge an inch, remaining seated in his chair lost not in his *thoughts*, but only in one.

At the far end of the road as it emerged from les Beunes, a head appeared, then a torso and finally the whole body. By her step there could be no doubt that it was a wench. As she approached I was struck by the fact that she had so much black hair that you could hardly see her eyes, yet she wore few clothes, her legs and her breasts half visible through her rags—robust and proud enough despite her poverty.

"What do you want, wench?" called Escorgol from the window, watching her with a half-excited, half-defiant air. "If you're begging, be on your way. Today we give no alms."

"I'm no beggar," said the girl boldly. "I've come to speak to Jonas the stonecutter for the masters of Mespech."

"Wait! I recognize you!" I cried leaning out the window. "You're Sarrazine, the girl the Gypsy captain left us as a hostage four years ago. Uncle de Sauveterre found you a place at la Volperie in Montignac."

"That's me, Sarrazine," she smiled, raising her head as if her name were some sort of title.

"If you know her," warned Escorgol, handing each of us a dagger, "go down and let her in the side door, but close it quickly once she's inside and triple bolt it. I'll remain here on watch."

I ran down the small spiral staircase on the opposite side of the fireplace from the one just described and which had the same dimensions, except that it was lit only from the arrow slits in the walls fixed there to enable us to kill any attackers who might have succeeded in breaking down our doors. Samson was at my heels, and as we threw back the three heavy bolts from the side door, he on the right and I on the left, we concealed our daggers behind our backs as my father had taught us to do. I set the chain, which allowed but a small opening of the door, and by this narrow aperture Sarrazine was able to squeeze in by crouching and turning sideways. Once she was through the doorway, I grabbed her roughly by the arm and, placing the point of my dagger at her throat, ordered her to keep still until Samson closed the door. This done, Samson seized her by the other arm and, turning her around, pointed his blade in her back and told her that I was going to search her. Which, returning my dagger to my belt, I did, at first quite carefully, inspecting the wicker basket she was carrying in her hand, and finding it empty. However, at the first frisk, realizing that the few clothes she wore (and these few quite full of holes) could hide no weapon, my search gained in thoroughness what it lost in roughness.

Sarrazine began to giggle and twist and shot me a saucy look from beneath her jet-black hair. "By my faith, young Master," she laughed with a raucous voice, "you've grown quite up in four years, I'll warrant, judging by the way you're inspecting me! Tell your red-headed brother not to poke my back so hard." And still laughing and struggling in our grip she announced, "I bear no other arms than those that make men's perdition."

"Ah but these you bear aplenty!" I rejoined, giving her a look that made her struggle even more.

"Sheathe your knife, Samson, and raise the portcullis," I said, holding Sarrazine by the arm, not out of any necessity but because her firm, cool flesh was so pleasing to my fingers and because I was so moved by the novelty of her arrival at a time when we were all so lugubriously shut up in Mespech by the troubles of the time and the decree that made us all outlaws. For there was no question of our being able to leave our walled enclosure, not even to go to Sarlat, where the most avid of the papists now held sway.

The portcullis was raised, then lowered. We gave a reassuring sign to Escorgol, who watched us enviously from his window—my brother François now being his sole audience, if he was listening at all. I did not hesitate long over whether to lead Sarrazine to Sauveterre or to Jean de Siorac, immediately deciding in favour of the latter, knowing what a sour face the older man would make at this wench and what pleasure she would bring my father. I also calculated that he would let us stay for his conversation with her. I then made sure that she was clean under her ragged garments and her dusty feet, that her hair was washed and her breath sweet-smelling so that she would in no way offend my father's sensitive nose.

I thus ushered the maid into my father's library and told him who she was. "Ah! Greetings Sarrazine! I've often heard news of you these last four years!" said Jean de Siorac rising to meet her, and enveloping the young woman with his blue-eyed gaze from which the sadness momentarily took flight. "And what brings you here?" he added with his old gaiety.

"To complain, My Lord," replied Sarrazine, making a deep curtsey, her ragged shirt falling open to her waist, a spectacle I did not miss a whit of, nor my father either, I suspect. And she added, lowering her eyes: "Your stonecutter, Jonas, has had his way with me."

"What's this?" gasped my father, pretending to frown. "But this is a capital crime! And demands the gallows! And where did this happen? On the road? By hill and dale?"

"In his cave," affirmed Sarrazine with a hypocritical wink.

"And what were you doing in his cave, my poor woman?" said Jean de Siorac.

"I came to see his wolf, hearing what a marvel it was that he'd tamed her."

"The marvel is," laughed my father, "that you walked five leagues barefoot from Montignac to Jonas's cave just to see this wolf. Did Jonas invite you there?"

"No, indeed, My Lord. I'd not laid eyes on him since he untied me from the pole where the Gypsy captain had left me. And yet when he saw me in his cave he was very nice to me."

"So I'll warrant," said my father.

"He gave me a drink of goat's milk, and since I was tired and his wolf was asleep he put my head on her flank and told me to pet her. Which I did. Then he stretched out beside me and I said, 'But you've also got beautiful fur on your chest, Jonas.' And with my other hand I caressed him. And with all that caressing of those two hides, with the wolf moaning sweetly beneath me and Jonas staring at me with his two eyes big as moons, after a while, by some strange magic, I found I was no longer a virgin."

A deep silence followed this recital, which set all three of us to dreaming, and even my innocent little brother Samson was blushing.

"I'm afraid I don't perceive the magic to this," said Jean de Siorac.

Sarrazine batted her lashes. "But he had his way with me."

"To some extent," mused my father. "Nonetheless, if you insist, I must exercise my seigniorial justice and send Jonas bound hand and foot to the gallows."

"Oh no, no, no!" cried Sarrazine passionately shaking her black mane. "This is no time to hang him, just when I want to marry him!"

"Now here's a wench without rancour!" laughed my father. "And what about Jonas?"

"He wishes it too, according to your Huguenot rites."

"But aren't you a Catholic?" asked my father, suddenly growing serious.

"I was raised in the faith of the Prophet Muhammad," explained Sarrazine simply. "But the Gypsies turned me into a Catholic. But from now on, I shall be of the religion of my husband."

"Which is to say that a husband is worth a Huguenot service. Well then, cheer up, Sarrazine," said Jean de Siorac. "You've not wasted your time going all that way from la Volperie to Jonas's cave!"

"Well, I've thought a lot about it these four years, and I've never seen a prettier or stronger man than Jonas in the whole countryside of Montignac."

My father burst out laughing. "Well, then it's as good as done, Sarrazine."

But she, ceasing her shaking and trembling for a moment, said gravely, "Not quite, My Lord." (And here she made a curtsey as deep as the first.) "I do not wish to live in a cave like a savage, with goats and a wolf. You must give Jonas permission to build a proper house over the cave."

"Ah, so that's it, you clever scamp!" laughed my father.

At that moment we heard Sauveterre's stumpy gait on the stair, then a knock on the door, and he appeared, frowning sourly as soon as he caught sight of Sarrazine. He immediately glanced apprehensively towards Jean de Siorac.

"Jean," said Siorac, repressing the gaiety that Sarrazine had brought into our ranks, "this is Sarrazine, the hostage that you found work for in la Volperie. She wants to marry Jonas according to our religion, on condition that he build her a house over his cave."

"A house!" exclaimed Sauveterre, scandalized, raising his eyes heavenward.

"Monsieur, you have everything you need for it and in abundance!" replied Sarrazine hotly and not without effrontery. "Stone for the roof and the walls, limestone and clay for mortar, chestnut trees for the beams and a stonemason to build it! And why should

Jonas, who serves you well and who fought for you bravely against the Gypsies, not have a house like a good Christian?"

"The wench has a well-oiled tongue, at least," said Sauveterre little pleased by her speech. He sat down with a sigh, but said no more, already guessing what Siorac was thinking. Indeed, the two brothers left off speaking for some moments in order to avoid a confrontation.

"Sarrazine, what is this wicker basket you're holding?" my father enquired, breaking the silence.

"A present I bring your household, My Lord," replied Sarrazine, bobbing a curtsey, but this time refraining from the full bow, knowing how much it would distress Sauveterre. "I made it with my own hands," she said proudly, "with willow shoots from the les Beunes farm which are plentiful down below the quarry."

"Let's see it," said Sauveterre, reaching out and taking the basket from her, which he examined carefully on each side, testing its construction and weaving. "This is very good work, Sarrazine," he continued, softening somewhat his tone. "You didn't waste your time with the Gypsies." He looked at her—certainly not in the way my father looked at her, but with a look reflecting his calculated meditation. "And do you know how to make a grape-gatherer's hod?"

"I've already made one," she replied with feigned feminine modesty, refraining from her usual bodily wiles for she could feel now that with Sauveterre things were beginning to go her way. "But," she added, "it takes more time and bigger willow shoots."

"So tell me," said Sauveterre coldly, "could you make four hods a month?"

"I think so."

Sauveterre glanced at my father and, in a single look, fell into agreement. "Well, then, we'll build you a house to lodge the both of you, Sarrazine, and you shall make us four grape hods a month.

You'll get no pay for the first year, but after that we'll give you two sols a hod."

"Three," corrected my father.

"Three," Sauveterre conceded, shrugging his shoulders with some vexation.

Sarrazine was overwhelmed and nearly jumped for joy when I walked her out to the main gate, reckoning twelve months' labour of fingers, arms and back a small price to pay for the joy of living in a house built by her husband—a construction that could only enrich the two masters' domain.

They were married, according to our Huguenot practice, two days later, since a longer wait was not feasible given that they already had carnal knowledge of each other. And straightaway afterwards, Sarrazine waded barefoot into the cold waters of the les Beunes river in search of willow shoots. And so it was that from that day on Mespech entered the business of selling wicker grape baskets, while the wine barrels made by Faujanet continued to sell at a brisk pace, an alliance which, if I may judge by the meticulous accounts kept by Sauveterre in the *Book of Reason*, turned a pretty penny.

The news of the defeat of our forces by Montluc at Vergt reached Guise while he was besieging the Huguenots at Rouen. That city was well defended by Montgomery, a tall, stiff young man for whom Catherine de' Medici had conceived a mortal hatred ever since his broken lance had pierced her beloved husband's eye during their jousting match. That the accident, now three years past, had happened completely by chance—Montgomery having run this last course at Henri's express demand and entirely in self-defence—in no way altered the passionate Italian's resentment. This little baby-faced cannonball of a woman with a carnivorous jaw had mastered the art of dissimulation from the many humiliations of her reign, which included Henri's preference for another woman. She could smile through those big wide eyes at her interlocutor even while she plotted his death, patiently biding her time, waiting for the right moment.

Montgomery's time had now arrived. The Huguenot would pay twice over: once for his revolt against Charles IX, and again for the broken lance he'd neglected to throw to the ground. Every day, the regent went down into the trenches, braving the cannonades and musket fire, and exhorted her troops by her heroic example.

Guise had intended to make his first strike against Orleans, but when Condé abandoned le Havre to Elizabeth of England by virtue of the fateful Treaty of Hampton Court, which had so outraged the Brethren, he hurried to lay siege to Rouen to head off any English disembarkation, which would have caused panic in Paris. He could not count on Elizabeth's lack of zeal in keeping her promises now that she had le Havre and could wait until the end of the war to exchange it for Calais.

The Catholic army felt victory within its grasp once it had taken Fort Sainte-Catherine, which dominated Rouen from the top of a bluff. This army was commanded in fact by Guise, though he belonged in principle to the triumvirate (Guise, Saint-André and the constable). Their ranks had lately swelled to four to include the king of Navarre, Anthoine de Bourbon. One of the first great lords besides Condé to have converted to the reform, Bourbon had a second time abjured his faith in return for a vague promise from Felipe II of Spain that he should regain Spanish Navarre, and once again heard Mass and worshipped the Virgin.

His wife, Jeanne d'Albret, scorned such recantations. She had remained in her little kingdom of Navarre, firm in her faith, disdaining the hypocrisies of the court. But Anthoine was a weak and flighty man who always believed the last person to bend his ear and followed the first skirt to catch his eye. "*Totus est venereus,*" wrote Calvin, who had never trusted him.

At Rouen, he tried to match the queen mother's bravery by his temerity in having his dinner table set directly behind a wall on which the Huguenots were firing. Having eaten his fill, and forgetting where he was, he stood up at the end of the meal and was immediately felled by enemy fire. Once the city was taken, he had himself carried through the streets by his soldiers on a litter to give himself the ultimate satisfaction of watching the massacre of the very Huguenots whom he had previously shared prayers with. That done, he immediately died as stupidly as he had lived, leaving behind a wife who was really the man of the family and a son who, luckily for the fortunes of France resembled his mother: the future Henri IV.

The sack of Rouen was the worst that can be imagined, but Catherine de' Medici did not enjoy the particular pleasure she had been anticipating: Montgomery escaped. He leapt into a boat and was taken downriver. Reaching the chain that the Catholics had stretched across the Seine at Caudebec, he promised his galley slaves their freedom if they could save him. The convicts set to shouting, pressed their oars and headed straight at the obstacle, which gave way. Montgomery was thus able to reach the sea and, ultimately the English coast. But destiny did not let him off so easily for she arranged a second meeting with Catherine de' Medici, two years later, this one ending in his death.

Seemingly, the fall of Rouen was but another jewel in Guise's crown, which, it was rumoured, he intended one day to substitute for Charles IX's. And yet, as he prepared to leave Rouen for Paris, the duc was exceedingly morose, for he had had to share the glory of this siege with three others: firstly with the constable, Montmorency, who during his service to three kings had grown older without growing wiser; secondly with Marshal de Saint-André, who, though younger than the constable, had no greater talent; and thirdly with the poor fool Anthoine, of whom it was rumoured he'd had himself shot on purpose so that he could be carried through the town like a dying hero.

In Paris, Guise was surprised to learn that the Huguenot army, reinforced by 3,000 horsemen and 4,000 German infantrymen, had taken Étampes, la Ferté-Alais, Dourdan and Montlhéry. Certainly these were no great victories: the Huguenots were merely prowling the countryside around the capital. The towns taken merely served as fodder and booty for the German troops clamouring for their soldier's pay. As that clamouring grew worse, Condé and Coligny decided to head for Normandy, attracted by the mirage of help and subsidy from Elizabeth of England. The Huguenots advanced westward, delayed by the heavy carts the German horsemen had loaded with their booty. The royal army rushed after them, and, despite their haste, were quickly at their heels. Coligny, fearing rearguard action by the royalists, convinced Condé to turn and face them. The spot was well chosen: Condé could deploy his horsemen on the Dreux plains.

Guise, positioned on the right flank of the royal army with his gentlemen and veteran bands of French soldiers, refused to give orders in this battle, little inclined to singe his hands again pulling chestnuts from the fire for others. Raised to his full height in the stirrups of his magnificent Spanish jennet, he commanded a full view of the entire theatre of battle, and watched without flinching as Condé and Coligny defeated the constable.

"Your Grace, the constable is being routed!"

"So I see," Guise replied.

"Your Grace, the constable is wounded!"

"So I see."

"Your Grace, the constable is taken!"

"So I see."

Entirely absorbed in cutting their enemy to pieces, the Huguenots were already crying victory when Coligny spied Guise and his men waiting on their right and cried, "I see a cloud there about to rain its fury on us."

A few moments later, Guise, judging his two adversaries to be exhausted, raised himself once again in his stirrups and cried: "Forward, my friends, the battle is ours!"

And with the Spanish infantrymen behind him, he routed the entire Protestant infantry. Condé was wounded in the hand and captured, and the Huguenots were put to flight. At four o'clock the battle appeared to be over.

At this point a force of 1,000 horsemen and 300 knights whom Coligny had succeeded in rallying fell on the victorious army's own right. They broke through the Catholic cavalry's lines but did not succeed in routing the battalion of French veterans armed with pikes. Coligny withdrew, but as everyone knew he was never so great as in defeat or retreat.

Guise did not dare pursue him too far. But he had succeeded beyond his wildest dreams in defeating enemies and rivals alike: the constable was taken and the Marshal de Saint-André dead. The triumvirate had been reduced henceforth to one. The beautiful red archangel of the Catholic Church had thus become the only support of the throne.

He wrote several letters to Catherine de' Medici filled with formulas of respect for herself and the king, detailing for her his stunning victory at Dreux. But this wasn't enough. A month later he came to Blois, breaking in on the queen mother as she was going in to dinner and requesting an audience immediately after the meal.

"Jesus! My cousin!" cried the queen mother, astonished but feigning to be more so than she was. "What are you asking of me? An audience? And for what purpose?"

"I wish, Madame," replied Guise, "to represent to the court everything I have done since my departure from Paris with your army."

"But my cousin, I am well aware of all you have done. You've told me everything in your letters."

"Madame," said Guise with cool aplomb, "I want to tell you personally and to present to you all the royal captains who so bravely fought for you at Dreux."

The queen mother acquiesced gracefully since she could hardly refuse. After dinner Guise reappeared before her dressed in crimson satin and surrounded by his captains like a king by his ministers. With a deep bow to the queen mother and Charles IX he began his epic adventure with a tale that appeared to be as naive as its purpose was calculated.

The queen mother listened, smiling with her large wide eyes and secretly gnashing her teeth inside her pretty plump cheeks. She realized Guise had found a way to win the battle of Dreux twice over: the first time on the battlefield and the second in its telling at the court.

Guise's harangue completed, the queen mother lavished on his officers a bevy of smiles, affectionate thanks and expressions of eternal gratitude. But she breathed a deep sigh of relief when Guise and his glorious soldiers had finally retired. She liked war little enough and ambitious generals even less. It was all too evident that Guise had grown too powerful and that, all told, the throne's sole support was shaking the throne a good deal more than he was sustaining it. As for the story of the exploits at Dreux, it stuck in her craw. The Florentine preferred to warfare her own particular brands of diplomacy: negotiation, royal marriage and political assassination.

Our friend, cousin and ally, François de Caumont, elder brother of Geoffroy the abbot, was present with the other courtiers at this harangue, as I later learnt from his servants. He had come to the court to complain about Montluc, who had seized his chateau at Milandes, had ransacked his brother's abbey and had devastated the fields of his brother-in-law, the Baron de Biron. The moment for such a complaint was clearly ill chosen, Guise being so popular. As the queen mother refused an audience since Guise was her guest, the eldest Caumont had the strange idea of addressing himself directly to God rather than his saints, and requested an audience with the duc himself. It was like putting his head in the lion's mouth.

Guise granted the audience, surrounded by his men, and with a royal and cold demeanour listened in silence as François de Caumont reviewed his grievances against Montluc. After which, raising his voice so all could hear, Guise said: "I am astonished you should demand justice from me. Your entire activity in your province accuses and condemns you. Admittedly, you have not openly raised your sword against the king, but you have aided and abetted the Huguenot rebellion. You have given shelter to the rebels in your houses and from them many blows have been directed against our people. Monsieur de Charry is witness to this, as are Hautefort and many other Catholic lords of your province. And so the only justice that could be meted out to you would be the very judgement you have demanded for Montluc, who is a good a faithful soldier and who has shed rivers of blood in the service of his king."

"Rivers of blood!" agreed François de Caumont. "Ah, to be sure, Your Grace, you speak the truth."

"Indeed, I do!" said Guise, rising angrily. "Montluc has shed more rivers of blood in the service of his king that you have dripped droplets from your sword and your three brothers' swords. And so

Montluc deserves great credit, and you very little. Heed my words well, Caumont, and change your ways while there is still time."

François de Caumont withdrew, fiercely embittered to be so humiliated in public. If he had been more prudent, he would have fled the court with all possible haste for his native Périgord. But Milandes lay heavy on his heart and he could not let go of the matter. Hearing that the duc had, later that evening, expressed regret for the severity he had shown Caumont, and since the duc was supposed to leave Blois the next morning to head for Orleans, which he intended to take from the Huguenots, Caumont offered to ride part of the way with him, and, in fact, the duc exchanged pleasantries with him as they rode stirrup to stirrup. After which, Caumont took his leave of the duc and returned to Blois. Scarcely had he gone a quarter of a league, however, before he met up with Edme de Hautefort, surrounded by a troop of captains, who angrily reproached him for allowing shots to be fired from his houses on Catholic partisans during the troubles in Périgueux. Caumont never had time to reply, for Hautefort drew his sword and, rushing at him, struck him a mortal blow on the head. This murder took place on 3rd or 4th February 1563, I'm not able to pinpoint it more precisely. And so great was the feeling against the Huguenots that his crime went unpunished and virtually unnoticed. This was, in Guise's own terms, but a drop of blood in the rivers that were yet to flow, for, on 5th February, Guise laid siege to Orleans.

He had already taken the outlying towns of Portereau and Tourelles. From the beginning of the siege, he would return every night to his lodgings at Saint-Mesmin, by means of a little boat which ferried him, his valet and their horses across the river. Once on the other side, they remounted and rode along the edge of a small patch of woods. On the 13th, the eve of Guise's planned assault on Orleans, a Huguenot fanatic, Poltrot de Méré, hidden in this thicket, fired three shots into the broad back of this man who had but two weeks previously harangued the queen mother. As he was wearing no cuirass, the bullets penetrated his right shoulder and Guise pitched forward in his saddle, but did not fall, saying, "I deserved this, but I don't think it's anything serious."

He died six days later. As for Poltrot de Méré, his shot fired, he galloped all night, but he lost his way and ended up at daybreak back at the scene of the crime and was immediately taken. Under torture, he confessed that Soubise and d'Aubeterre had put him up to it. He also named Admiral de Coligny, but retracted much of this and garbled his story terribly, right up until the time they drew and quartered him.

It was in vain that Coligny vehemently denied having had a hand in the murder and asked the queen mother to allow him to confront his accuser before the man was dispatched. The queen would hear none of it, and doubtless had her reasons. Nine years later, when she gave the order for Coligny's assassination, she made it appear as though the murder was attributable to the Guise family. Might we not imagine that she had a hand in the elimination of Guise and was happy to see that Coligny was accused of the murder?

"We cannot deny," wrote Coligny on learning the death of Guise, "the evident miracles of God," a sentence that the Florentine, who was not so naive, would never have pronounced. But the miracle of this death, whether she had a hand in it or not, changed her life, strengthened her power and solidified the throne of her son.

Guise was scarcely cold in his tomb before the queen mother began concessions to the Protestants. She ordered Montluc to desist from his devastation of Biron's lands and to return Milandes to the Caumont family. She played at compromise and at peace, but always in such a way as to pull as many chestnuts from the fire as possible for her own and her son's power. She was clever enough to open negotiations between the camps where Montmorency and Condé were held captive by the Huguenots and Catholics respectively. Each man desired his liberty of course, but the prince being the younger, more hot-blooded and impatient of the two (especially where women were concerned) conceded more than his party would have wanted.

The Edict of Amboise, which Montmorency signed in March 1563, abandoned some of the more liberal positions of the Edict of January, for it restricted the liberty of the Protestant cult to the houses of the lords "with their families and subjects" and for the reformed commoners it reduced the practice of their Church to one village in each district. Calvin severely criticized the vanity of this nobleman, who, provided that the members of his own caste were free to pray as they liked, cared little about the great mass of people in their villages on the land.

My father and Sauveterre (like all Huguenots of conscience) shared Calvin's indignation, but did not feel free to protest since they had not fought for their side. Of course, they were among those who benefitted "with their families and subjects" from the strictures of the Edict. What's more, the peace that resulted was immensely profitable to them, as I shall recount hereafter.

9

T HE EDICT of Amboise signed, the Protestants were no longer outlaws, since their existence and their rights were recognized by the treaty. This meant that we could again venture into our villages and that my father could go to Sarlat. Which he did, after having sent Diane de Fontenac back to her chateau all healed and vigorous again. He might have returned her thence a month earlier, but in the troubled times we had just lived through, and trusting Fontenac like a viper, he was happy enough to have this pawn at Mespech which protected him from any treason by our good neighbour.

Despite the fact that during her stay with us she never left the first floor of the gatehouse and none of us, save my father, ever saw her except at a distance, sitting in her window wrapped in her white furs and watching us with her green eyes, Diane's departure left us all feeling extraordinarily empty, as if a beloved poem had been for ever lost from memory. I won't elaborate on the woes of François, who did his best to hide his melancholy, which the Brethren did not even consent to notice.

Fontenac sent the Baron de Mespech a gracious letter of thanks with a present of 500 écus and a Spanish jennet. My father returned the money, but put the letter carefully away in safe keeping and kept the horse. It was a black pony, small enough in stature, but full of fire. I got to mount her for the first time on the day the Edict was proclaimed and my father rode to Sarlat on business, accompanied by Cockeyed Marsal, Faujanet, the Siorac brothers and his three rascals, all three outfitted with pistols in our saddle holsters and unsheathed swords hanging, tied to our right wrists. My father was less fearful of an ambush than of a popular demonstration at Sarlat, where the priests, even less happy with the Edict of Amboise than the Protestants, disgorged their hatred against us at Mass on every one of God's Sundays with a thousand insults.

However, the police lieutenant, Guillaume de La Porte, who had been notified of our coming, was waiting for my father at the la Lendrevie gate. He asked us to sheathe our swords, which we did, and, riding in front, stirrup to stirrup with my father, smiling and conversing all the while, he kept his eyes on the upper windows of the houses we passed, and crossed the entire town with us as far as the la Rigaudie gate. From there, closely watched by all the passers-by and many gawkers at their windows, the little troop turned on its heels and headed back towards the centre of town, passing in front of the episcopal mansion (where La Porte crossed himself and my father doffed his cap out of respect), arriving at length at the town hall, where my father was received on the steps by Monsieur de Salis, the lieutenant general of the Périgord region, and by the two consuls. All of this was accomplished without the least tumult or shouting, or hostilities of any kind from the populace, other than two or three nasty looks from the windows of some diehards who hated us purely out of religious zeal rather than out of any personal resentment.

In short, nothing happened and I was bitterly disappointed, for I was twelve years old and it was the first time I'd worn a gentlemen's sword, and though it was but a short sword I'd got a swollen head, and parading around on my Spanish jennet I thought I was invincible. Having dismounted and handed our horses over to our soldiers, we followed close behind my father, I on his right and Samson on his left. I walked along haughtily, my hand negligently draped over my sword hilt, looking to all sides with a hectoring air. At the end of the morning, my father paid his customary visit to Franchou, giving her a little present and speaking to her so long in private that I thought he would never leave off giving her kisses on both cheeks or tapping her comely arms, but at last he took his leave.

Although she was now Huguenot and married, neither le Breuil nor Mespech had altogether accepted Sarrazine and we had to keep working on getting the women to take her into their confidence given how scandalously different her eyes, her hair and especially her skin colour were. The first to take a clear position in her defence was Cabusse, because Cathau had refused her neighbourly duties, arguing that Sarrazine wasn't like other women.

"And how is she so unlike the others?" asked Cabusse in a terrible voice and pulling fiercely on his moustache. "Hasn't she got two tits like you and a hole to receive the male, and a belly to carry a wee babe? Maybe," he added with his usual Gascon tact, "she hasn't got your pretty looks, Cathau, and your housekeeping skills, but if my friend Jonas likes her as she is, why then the difference is only a matter of fur, like you see between dogs, some black, others brown or spotted and still others white as snow. It's not by the fur you can tell a good animal, but by its breeding." At bedtime, between la Maligou and Barberine, it was another story altogether. Since Isabelle's death, my father happily lingered among his servants at table of an evening rather than going right away to join Sauveterre in his library, where there was a warmer fire. But it was not that kind of warmth my father craved, but the ease and gaiety of his soldiers and the presence of women, of Barberine most of all. With her two kids, one clinging to her skirts and the other in its chestnut cradle on the floor beside her, which she rocked with her foot from time to time, she eventually suckled each one, which delighted us all, and my father more than anyone, he whose head was so close to his heart and his heart to his feelings. Moreover, those two, Annet and Jacquou, should have been suckled along with the two stillborn sons of Isabelle's, the second costing her her life. And as I have said, my father's wish was that they be raised at the chateau, not, of course, like my half-brother Samson, but rather like our cousins Siorac, somewhere between servant and relative. It was not exactly a blood brotherhood, but a milk brotherhood that joined us all together. Annet had, in fact, been the godson of Isabelle de Siorac. These kids were not covered with dirt like the urchins in our villages, with their heads full of lice, and, in the summer, flies in their eyes. They were, on the contrary, pink and chubby, their hair clean, given my father's insistence on cleanliness; so meticulous was he that he interrupted dinner to tell Faujanet at table, "Good fellow, your feet stink. Go wash them at the pump."

Despite the rocking Barberine kept up on Jacquou's cradle during the evening, he began to wail to burst your eardrums, which set Annet to crying in turn, which earned him boxed ears from his mother, for he'd had a good soup for dinner with goat cheese from Jonas, apple compote and even a bit of meat, which he had a taste for whether hungry or not. Leaning over, Barberine placed Jacquou in her lap, showering him with such tender cooings and murmurings that I nearly melted with envy. The nursling, quieted by these sweet murmurs, was passed to little Hélix, who carried on this lullaby as best she could while Barberine undid the laces of her bodice. This done, her eyes modestly lowered given the many men seated around her, yet for all that, with a certain air of pomp and pride, for she was quite conscious that she was plying her trade, and plying it well, Barberine gave her nurslings good plate and good soup, and to her onlookers a feast for the eyes. As always, her laces were knotted and the knots would not fit through the eyelets so she untied them one by one, without haste, with her large round fingers, thus prolonging our wait. "Barberine," said my father (but he said it every night), "you must remind me to bring you a new lace from Sarlat."

"Oh, this one does well enough, and they're so expensive," replied Barberine, untying the last knot. And this said, she drew out from her blouse with a firm hand and an easy gesture first her right and then her left breast, both so round and large and white that a great silence fell over the room so that all you could hear was the tiniest crackle of the fire and the gluttonous sucking of the two hungries.

Barberine got great relief from these double doses of her inexhaustible supply of milk, whose pressure between feedings caused her a thousand deaths, which is why Annet, now going on four, was still invited to these banquets, despite the inconvenience. "Ouch! Ouch!" moaned Barberine, both hands occupied with her charges. "Hélix, spank this little cheater, he's biting me." Hélix applied a firm hand to Annet's little bottom, who let off sucking for a moment to raise a howl, but quickly snapped up the teat again, this time careful not to bite. There was no doubt a bit of melancholy in my father's eye as he watched these two little rascals, so handsome and pink and strong, and Annet already a mischievous little tyke with his hands into everything just the way you'd expect, but not the two sons he had lost, who would be just their ages, with Isabelle still alive instead of enduring the tortures of hell. It is certain that damnation and salvation are in the hands of the Lord, and He alone judges our lives in His infinite wisdom, but for those who rejected Purgatory as we did, as but a detestable addition to God's Word, it was all but intolerable to imagine a beloved being plunged after death into eternal torment.

If my father was preoccupied with this thought—and he often was, since he made note of it in the *Book of Reason*—he must have quickly chased it away in order to enjoy the pleasures of the moment, for his eye began to twinkle as he listened to the conversation between la Maligou and Barberine that had been carried on in whispers all evening, but which, in the silence engendered by the suckling, caught everyone's ears.

"And what's more," Barberine was saying in that serene voice she got when she was suckling, "she's ugly enough to freeze the blood in your veins."

"Ah, and sure you're right there!" agreed la Maligou.

"And just who is so ugly?" interjected Jean de Siorac, raising an eyebrow.

"Sarrazine," replied Barberine, not without some embarrassment at being overheard.

"Sarrazine! Ugly!" laughed my father. "My poor Barberine, you're a pretty bad judge of women's beauty! You know that to be beautiful, a woman must have three features, like a horse: a good chest, good haunches and a beautiful mane. Now Sarrazine has these in abundance, the first two high and firm given her slender body, and as for her mane, in length, in thickness and in body, it's as good as the pony's that Fontenac sent me, whose mane is so beautiful when it's blowing in the wind."

"With all due respect, My Lord," said la Maligou, "there's the problem of the colour of her skin."

My father made a large gesture with his right hand. "The colour of her skin has nothing to do with it, my poor woman! Your Little Sissy has skin almost as dark as Sarrazine's, and she's still a pretty little wench who will break a few hearts."

At this, Little Sissy lowered her eyes, and little Hélix blushed with spite, while puffing out her chest to attract my father's notice.

"But that's because she's a Gypsy!" said la Maligou, looking at Little Sissy proudly.

"She's no more Gypsy than you are," my father laughed uproariously. "But on that subject," he added with a knowing air, "we'll hear no more tonight."

La Maligou broke the brief silence that followed this remark with a bitter reflection, as if to take her revenge on Sarrazine for the affront she had just received: "It's not so much that Sarrazine is ugly, My Lord, it's that she's the Devil's own daughter and a succubus."

"And how do you know this, Maligou?" asked my father frowning. "Did the Lord whisper it in your ear?"

"No, but there's proof enough, My Lord! First, Sarrazine came out of nowhere four years ago. You got her a place in la Volperie, and after three years she changes herself into a wounded she-wolf and gets taken in by Jonas in his cave."

"Ah yes, but she continued to work as a servant at la Volperie," countered my father, laughing. "Coulondre Iron-arm saw her there every week when he did his hauling there."

"She made herself double."

"Ah, really? How easy it all is! And which paw did the wolf break, Pierre? You saw her."

"The right rear one," I said, happy to play a role in this trial.

"And Sarrazine, at la Volperie, had her right leg broken?"

"Not in the least, My Lord," answered Coulondre. "She walked just like you and me."

"The Devil can do anything," said la Maligou.

"If this is true, then he's as powerful as God," said my father, changing his tone and immediately frowning angrily.

"Oh no! Oh no!" answered la Maligou, crossing herself, as pale and terrified as if the executioner were already fanning the flames around her. "If it please you to remember, My Lord, that I'm only a poor ignorant woman, and don't know the why and wherefore of things, and I can keep my peace if you think I've said too much."

"You haven't said enough, Maligou," replied my father, with his sternest expression. "I want the rest of your proofs."

"Oh they're not lacking, My Lord!" said la Maligou, regaining her colour a bit. "First of all, the she-wolf cast a spell on Jonas in his cave so that he'd fall in love with her and want her to change into a woman."

"That's foolishness," said my father.

But whether it was foolishness or not, I for one, who had heard Jonas, wasn't so sure. But I held my tongue, not wanting to add to the stonecutter's problems.

"And it was done!" cried la Maligou triumphantly. "The wolf was transformed into Sarrazine, and she married Jonas."

"If I understand this tissue of incredible silliness correctly," said my father, "the wolf, after changing herself into Sarrazine, continued nonetheless to be wolf, since wolf and woman lived together two full months on rather bad terms in Jonas's cave."

"Yes, but one day the wolf disappeared."

"Of course she disappeared, since she ended up eating one of Jonas's goats and fearing her master's anger ran away. And that's what you should do too, Maligou," added my father in a thunderous voice with glowering looks. "I'm telling you for the last time that if you have the misfortune to pursue such spiteful gossip in our villages, I'll send you away from Mespech and never set eyes on you again. Meanwhile, no one here, man or woman, who values my friendship, shall say or suffer to be said in their presence any of these wicked and damnable lies about Jonas and his wife, but shall hold them both, man and wife, as I do, in particular esteem. And as for you, Maligou, since you keep secrets with the Devil, ask him if he has made a double of you as well, so that while you tend our stove, he has made you a fat little shiny mouse in my loft who sometimes chews on papers I keep there that I don't need any more."

At this, la Maligou and Barberine exchanged a terrified look, for they wondered if my father wasn't letting them know that he had discovered in our stables the clandestine altar to Mary. But my father, having spoken, rose, sent the children off to bed, and after a brief goodnight to the two women, his face still marked with irritation, crossed the hall rapidly and disappeared up the staircase.

Despite famine and pestilence, which I shall recount later, 1563 was a bountiful year at Mespech. The Brethren were able to achieve a long cherished goal "and most excellent project" of purchasing a mill on the les Beunes river. Up until that time we had depended for grinding our grain on the mill at Campagnac, and though the lord of the place was friendly and his price reasonable enough, it still considerably augmented the cost of our flour. During the spring of 1563, however, there was an auction of Church properties at Sarlat, and the Brethren bought from the Franciscans the Gorenne mill for 3,567 écus.

It was a large and well-built mill housing three millstones: a white stone for wheat, a brown stone for rye, barley and millet, and a stone for walnut oil. Along with this mill they purchased some prime farmland in the ravine between Mespech and Taniès, fields laid out in long strips and snuggled between the hills of Mespech and those of the village. Along this valley ran the crushed-stone road leading west to Ayzies and east to the Château de Pelvézie.

These fields required long and arduous labour from all of our field hands, tenant farmers and migrant day workers alike. Section after section had to be drained of excess water, for they had become so swampy from years of good rain that in places we were up to our knees in mud. The Brethren effected drainage canals for the runoff all the way to the banks of the les Beunes river, where they built embankments to protect against high-water damage on both sides of the river. To solidify these embankments, they planted willow trees along each side. In so doing, they were planning for the distant future, for it would be many years before Sarrazine exhausted the supply of willow shoots, already plentiful on the hillsides two leagues away near Jonas's quarry. The spring of 1563 was so dry that this work near the les Beunes could be carried out without too many hitches, but this same drought played against us when it came time to build a road from the chateau to the mill on the north face of our hill in order to cart grains and flour back and forth. The hill was so abrupt that we had to construct this road in "s" curves. Felling the trees on this hill was no mean feat, and uprooting the stumps was even worse since the earth had grown hard as rock for lack of rain.

After this work was done, we had to find enough rock for paving. As for the mill in Gorenne, the Brethren were counting, as I have said, on a significant savings, but also on much profit, for the many small landowners in the neighbourhood came to the les Beunes mills when their grain was dry in the autumn—or even during the winter months if need arose—to have their milling done for a fee. The mill was so effective, indeed, that the Franciscans who sold it would have done well to run it themselves but, given the distance to the monastery, ended up letting it out to a farmer who ate up all the profits himself and was so miserly that he never repaired anything. For want of a nail, a roofing stone or a little work, this worthy had allowed an entire section of the roofing to cave in and ruin that corner of the building.

Mespech set to work to make the necessary repairs and it was promptly done, for we lacked neither the hands nor the means to do it. The choice of a carpenter posed another problem, for the Brethren had no wish, as they had done for their stonecutter, to have the Sarlat town crier recruit for them, trusting only men whose worth and mettle they already knew.

When the work was completed, the Brethren summoned Faujanet one evening to their library, and asked if he wanted to become miller at Gorenne, without giving up his work as cooper, which he could do just as well in the les Beunes, since milling was a seasonal and occasional job.

"For double work," added my father smiling, "double pay. And free flour for your bread. What's more, we'll find you a beautiful strong wench in the valley, who's of our religion and who will marry you, give you a hand at your work and bear you some rascals to provide for you later. It's not enough just to receive your daily bread, the bread of old age is kneaded in youth."

The dark little man whom my father had asked to be seated given his limp (which didn't slow his scything in the least) listened to these alluring proposals without batting an eye. As my father talked, Sauveterre nodding his assent, Faujanet's black eyes darted from one to the other, yet at every new enticement his look seemed to grow sadder. When my father had finished, he thanked him with dignity. "As for the job of miller, I believe I could do it, being quick with my hands and not too slow with my brain. And as for the extra work, despite my limp" (at this he looked at Sauveterre) "I'm not afraid of it, as my masters know. And my masters are generous in their offer to double my pay, but here at Mespech, having my hearth, my supper and my room and what I'm paid in addition I don't stand to gain all that much."

He paused, then continued as though ashamed, his eyes lowered. "As for the wench, I thank my masters kindly. But marriage, for a man who thinks a lot as I do, doesn't suit me, if I must say so. A wench who is sweet as honey on her wedding day grows a viper's tongue within the week. Woman is the opposite of a chestnut: all the soft parts are on the outside and the prickly part is underneath. I wouldn't trust one any more than a barrel without its hoops."

"But there's the matter of convenience," said my father.

"That's just it," replied Faujanet, shaking his head, "the convenience is short-lived and the worries are for ever. I'd prefer to be half-hanged than badly married."

"There are good marriages," argued my father, trying a new tack.

"Never saw one," Faujanet answered simply. At this Sauveterre could not repress a smile and my father fell silent; as Faujanet became silent as well, the silence grew.

"If I understand you rightly, my poor Faujanet," my father said finally, "our project doesn't really tempt you."

"I'm ashamed, after such honest propositions as you've made me, to refuse your offer," sighed Faujanet, "but going to live at Gorenne, even with the advantages you describe, would be like going to live at the gates of death for me. At Mespech, every one of God's evenings, I go to sleep peacefully on an island defended by high walls, a bunch of well-armed companions, and with two captains braver than any mother's son in France. But at Gorenne, the first band to pass by on the road from Ayzies to Pelvézie, seeing this pretty little mill by the light of the moon, will get the idea of stealing its grains and flour. And then there'll be twenty or thirty of 'em, breaking down my door, raping my wife and making lace out of my entrails. Or else, hiding their villainy behind a religious cause, they'll just roast me like a heretic with my own firewood."

"You are a veteran of the Guyenne legion," Sauveterre reminded him, "and you know how to defend yourself. And we would lend you blunderbusses."

"Even if you lent me ten," returned Faujanet, "they wouldn't be enough against thirty miscreants."

Siorac and Sauveterre exchanged looks, struck by this reasoning and realizing that they would doubtless hear it from others. Would the beautiful mill at les Beunes stand empty for lack of a miller?

The next evening, they summoned Marsal, but with more than his customary stammerings and cockeyed glances he displayed an equal repugnance at the idea of leaving Mespech to go to live at Gorenne, where he would feel, as he put it "as naked as a tortoise without her shell".

They had to face up to the evidence: our soldiers might be brave, but not enough to envisage a solitary combat in the les Beunes against the armed bands that were infesting the region. The Brethren had begun to despair when, forty-eight hours later, Coulondre Iron-arm asked to speak with them. That Coulondre should open his mouth was already an event, but that he should actually ask for an interview astounded the Brethren. They received him that evening, and as Coulondre began the proceedings with a protracted silence that risked outlasting their meeting, my father bid him take a seat on the stool in front of the fire.

Never had Coulondre's long Lenten face looked gloomier. His eyes, nose and mouth all seemed to fall earthward, and yet his brown eyes under those heavy eyebrows remained vigilant. "My Lord," he finally articulated, "why haven't you ever asked me to be your miller at Gorenne?"

"Begging your pardon, Coulondre," replied Sauveterre, "but do you think you'd be up to it with your iron arm?"

"Yes."

"And do you wish to do it?"

"Yes." And then he added: "But there are some conditions."

My father looked up, and Sauveterre answered drily: "Namely?"

"With the money I brought back from Calais, I've got enough to buy two sows. I'd need enough grain from Gorenne to feed them and their pigs."

"How many heads do you want to raise?" asked my father.

"Thirty or so." The two brothers traded looks.

"We'll have to see about this. Is that all?"

"No," Coulondre said. "I want fifteen per cent of the harvest from the les Beunes fields."

"Fifteen per cent of our les Beunes farms!" cried Sauveterre.

To this outburst, Coulondre made no reply. His face drawn and expressionless, he stared at the fire.

"We must think about it," said my father, But then he added thoughtfully: "But if you take fifteen per cent of our les Beunes fields and a part of our grain for your hogs, you won't need a salary."

"Oh, yes I will," Coulondre replied as sadly as ever, but with a gleam showing in the slit in his eyelids. "At least until the first of my pigs is sold."

"And is that all?" said Sauveterre haughtily.

Silence. Coulondre stared at the fire with the lugubrious air of a man who expects nothing of this life. "You'll have to look to my defence," he said, "and help me build an underground passage from the granary as far as the first thicket on the road to Mespech so that I can get word to you in case of an attack."

"A bell would be sufficient," said Sauveterre.

"No, Monsieur," replied Coulondre raising his iron hook with his good arm as if to relieve his shoulder of the weight. "A bell would also warn my attackers. They'd know that I was signalling you for help and could set an ambush for you on the way to the mill. With an underground passage, I could send my wife to warn you."

"Your wife?" said my father, sitting up in his chair. "Have you already chosen a wench?"

"Yes I have," Coulondre replied. "It's Jacotte from la Volperie. As you know, she's of our religion."

"But she's only fifteen!" said my father, raising his eyebrows.

"Old greybeard that I am, she's already agreed," answered Coulondre without blinking an eye.

"La Maligou is going to be talking about magic again," smiled my father.

"There is none," said Coulondre gravely. "Last spring, while returning in my wagon from la Volperie to Mespech, I saved Jacotte from four brigands who'd got her down at the bottom of a slope. Jacotte killed the first one with her knife. With my pistols, I killed two others before the fourth leapt on me. But I struck him down with a blow of my hook on his neck and then cut his throat with his own cutlass."

"And you said nothing of this exploit?" marvelled my father.

"Jacotte asked me to keep it quiet. You know how it is with rumours in the villages. People are quick to say that there was more to it than there was."

"Coulondre," said my father, "you've made an excellent choice. I know Jacotte to be a strong and valiant wench and one who will do well by you."

Another silence. Sauveterre, his black eyes ablaze, and his face ringed with wrinkles, said in a somewhat distant tone, tapping his two hands on the arms of his chair, "Well, our business is far from concluded! The baron and I must speak of all this."

To this Coulondre made no replay, but sat and stared at the fire.

"Coulondre," said Sauveterre, "if we build you an underground passage, would it not be a great temptation, if the attack were too severe, to abandon your post?"

A shadow of a smile crept over Coulondre's long and lugubrious visage: "Me? Abandon your grain? Your flour? And my hogs?"

It was a good response, but the Brethren had other worries in mind. For the first time in the life of Mespech, they were forced to discuss a contract that was not from the outset to their own advantage.

Their consultation on the matter lasted a full day, and it's a pity they did not report it in the *Book of Reason*. I would have enjoyed reading now, but at least I know the outcome of their palaver.

The next evening, the Brethren made a counter-offer to Coulondre. Would he consent to raising, in addition to his thirty pigs, an equal number for Mespech? "No," answered Coulondre. "Sixty is too many. Large stocks invite large epidemics. What's more there's not enough space at Gorenne for so many animals."

"If we give you fifteen per cent of the harvest of the les Beunes fields, you will have to cultivate them and we will deduct from your portion the cost of renting the cultivator, the plough and the horse."

"Thanking your masters for the rental," said Coulondre, "but from my savings I plan to buy a horse and farm implements."

"If we strike a deal with you on this, will you still contribute your days of work to Mespech like all our other tenants?"

"Yes," Coulondre agreed. "But only fifty a year."

"Why fifty?"

"In converting to the Huguenot faith," replied Coulondre, "I gave up fifty holidays a year which we used to dedicate to the saints. And if I give you fifty days more, that makes 100. With all due respect, that's enough. I need time for Gorenne."

Sauveterre frowned. "Do you regret becoming a Huguenot?"

"In no way," said Coulondre, ever lugubrious and respectful, his eyes fixed on the flames of the hearth.

When he had departed, Sauveterre declared angrily that they should chase Coulondre out of Mespech without further ado for his unbelievable insolence. "And furthermore," he added, his little black eyes blazing with fury, "he's a completely lukewarm convert."

"Like most of our household," smiled my father. "But at least he hasn't remained a papist at heart like some I could name." He paced back in forth in the room stiffly, hands on his hips. After a moment he continued, "And it's not so insolent to try to defend one's interests, just as we do."

"He's too interested in defending his own interests!"

"Just as he'll defend them at Gorenne! Our flour along with his pigs! Just as he defended Jacotte on the side of that slope, where the brigands had dragged her. With tooth and nail! By hook and by crook! And with the very insolence you reproach in him. Did you catch his clever remark about the bell alerting Mespech? This fellow is not light-headed or soft-willed."

"I still believe we should get rid of him," Sauveterre persisted, waving his right hand martially, his face twisted in anger.

"And I believe we should give him Gorenne!" laughed my father.

"What! Give him Gorenne! On his damnable terms?!"

"My brother, my brother!" said Jean de Siorac, coming up behind Sauveterre and placing his hands on his shoulders. "We have to give up a little to gain a little more."

The next morning, Sauveterre gave in. And so it was that, mercenary that he was, Coulondre became a tenant farmer, while in the hard times we were experiencing, many another small landowner was selling his property to the grain merchants in return for a few sols and cultivating it for them.

1563 was indeed a calamitous year in the Sarlat region. Just as six years previously, in 1557—the year Faujanet was always talking about, so terrified was he by God's awful anger and obstinate refusal to share the rain from His clouds—the drought was, in my twelfth year, unspeakably terrible.

Already the winter had been more cold than wet, and when March arrived the weather turned hot, almost like summer, and aside from a few showers, so weak they hardly dampened the ground, no rains fell from the heavens. The grass was even lucky to get a start on its brilliant green spring shoots, but it remained stubbly, like after the autumn grazing, and as early as May, with the hot sun blazing down every day, it began to yellow. The wheat got off to a bad start, its shoots tiny and scattered, the thin sheaves scarcely bending them, the harrowed ground cracking and splitting into fissures as if it were going to open up into hell, and, worst of all, our good rich and moist humus dried to dust and was carried off in swirls by the bitter north-west wind.

As early as July, the springs and wells dried up by the dozens, the ponds dropped dangerously low and the normally tumultuous current of les Beunes diminished to half its normal flow. The millers forbade anyone to draw their water, and the baronies in their turn outlawed any trench works or dams that would have siphoned off water from the mills downstream. Our neighbouring villages came to Mespech with vats on their wagons to beg water from our moat, enough to water their livestock, and at first we granted them permission, but soon we had to restrict such use to our own tenant farmers when we realized that our own spring had slowed to a trickle. Our well itself never went completely dry, but the level of the moat dropped a full five feet, which of course terrified us all, for according to the Brethren it hadn't even decreased that much in 1557.

Haying time arrived, but there was not enough grass anywhere to invite a scythe blade except down in the dales where the ground stayed fairly moist. But there we had to keep our eyes and ears open, for at night people came with sickles to cut what they could to give to their goats or their starving cattle. Our soldiers went to stand guard and quickly caught one of these miscreants, who, believing himself justly headed for the gallows, bemoaned not so much his own lot, but that of his widow and children. But the poor wretch was from Sireil and the Brethren were reluctant to hang a man from our own villages. It also turned out that he was a papist, and they were afraid people would believe religious zeal had prompted their actions. So they decided to look the other way and, after keeping him locked up in the tower for two nights, they released him against his promise to give us forty unpaid days of work in each of the next two years. The man gave us his word, and I can still see him at our table, sneaking half of what la Maligou served him into a sack for his wife and six children. His name was Pierre Petremol and he was the younger brother of the man who had cured himself of rheumatism—as well as life itself by diving into the fountain of St Avit in wintertime.

But the mercy of Mespech was not sufficient—any more than severity would have been—so great and pressing was the general need. Theft of our grasses continued. We had to hurry the haying in the dales and, as soon as the sheaves were ripe, do our harvest since, already, wandering beggars were devouring the standing wheatfields along the les Beunes river, stalks and all.

Escorgol had his hands full during this period, for there was a constant parade of shepherds and farmers, who arrived with tears in their eyes and their hands joined in prayer to beg a bit of grain for themselves and hay for their livestock. Loans were given against pledges of fields or future harvests, and since all, or almost all, of them were already in our debt—some paying us an annual percentage of their harvest—some went as far as selling us their land to pay for their bread. Others, unable to feed them, sold us their livestock, at prices favourable to us, for the price of cattle had dropped by half since the drought had so increased the number of sellers.

Thus, during every famine, Mespech increased its domain and multiplied its herds. My father was deeply troubled in his conscience. He said and oft repeated during this period that he would have felt fewer scruples selling our grain in Sarlat at the unheard of price of three livres a quart for wheat and fifty sols a quart for rye. But

Sauveterre preferred increasing our land to accumulating écus in our coffers, and would not give an inch on the matter.

"But what will happen to our villagers," protested Siorac, "who don't have any land to pledge or even to sell? Are we going to let them die of hunger?"

"Not at all. We'll lend them grain against the strength of their arms. They can repay us by workdays during the year. We won't have to spend so much for migrant workers when haying and harvest time comes, or for our road work."

My father lowered his head and stared at his boots, a sad frown furrowing his brow. "So," he said finally, "everything, even drought, brings us bread and honey, helps us to grow, brings us wealth. It seems to me, brother, that we prosper too much from the hardships of others."

"We are not responsible for the times," replied Sauveterre, "and remember, I beg you, Calvin's words: 'It is God's special grace when he brings us to understand what most profiteth our cause.'"

"True, true," answered my father. "But at this rate, the poor around us only get poorer and Mespech grows apace."

"I fail to see why this should cause us unhappiness or to whip ourselves in guilt," said Sauveterre. "Let us not take on the hypocrisy of the papists, who wear purple robes to preach the virtues of poverty. No, Jean, Calvin's teachings are most enlightening in this regard. That there are many poor and few rich is not due to chance. What each man possesses does not come to him by chance but by distribution from Him who is the sovereign Lord of us all."

"So I believe," my father agreed. And yet, after a few moments of meditation, he said in a quiet voice, "But why is my heart so troubled at this grace which is given to us, which often seems excessive?"

*

On 6th July, the Brethren received a message from Monsieur de La Porte. The police lieutenant informed them that the plague had broken out in Sarlat with great violence, and was taking 100 victims a day. To avoid the spread of the contagion in the whole seneschalty, he had ordered the consuls to close the town gates. But since the town had still to receive provisions, he requested that my father notify our farmhands that the markets would operate on the usual days, but outside the town walls in the la Lendrevie quarter. Thus, villagers could continue to bring eggs, butter, vegetables, cheeses and meat, but would not be allowed within the walls, all buying to be conducted by intermediary commissioners lodged in la Lendrevie who would deliver merchandise to their clients through windows established for this commerce.

Monsieur de La Porte asked if the Brethren would contribute to the town's supply by butchering and delivering a side of beef. "To tell the truth, the demand for meat is not what it was. All the nobility and rich bourgeois as well as the judges, the bishop and his curates have fled the town before the gates were closed and have sought refuge in their country houses. Nevertheless, there still remain two consuls, four surgeons, the royal officers and myself, who would prefer not to die of hunger in the awful peril we are in."

La Porte added in a postscript: "You will be distressed to learn that Madame de La Valade died of the plague on the 4th. Her body removed, her poor chambermaid Franchou, formerly Your Lady's servant, was quarantined in her mistress's house, the doors and windows boarded. A cruel practice of course, but strictly according to our rules and which I can do nothing to alter. Franchou receives her provisions by means of a basket which she lowers to the street on a rope from an attic window. She is subsisting only on public charity and at that not very well. The poor wench has nearly gone mad with fear, hunger and despair and spends her time crying, moaning and calling out, begging us to kill her rather than keep her prisoner in an infected house."

My father received this letter on the morning of 6th July, and it caused a most bitter exchange with Sauveterre. As the library window was open due to the unbearable heat, I could hear the echoes of their quarrel but could only guess at the reasons. However, I saw my father come down the steps a few minutes later looking quite tense and resolute, and tell the Siorac brothers to butcher a young bull we had just bought, to clean and quarter it and to load it on one of our carts.

The same afternoon, while François, Samson and I were engaged in our sabre lesson with Cabusse, who came every day from le Breuil to teach us, my father entered the fencing room with a worried look about him. "Good morning, Cabusse!" he said, attempting with some effort to adopt his usual lighthearted manner. "Good morning, my little rascals."

"Good day, My Lord," replied Cabusse saluting him with his sword and addressing him with a great display of finesse midway between respect and familiarity, as if he himself were almost a gentleman.

"And how is Cathau?"

"Rounding up nicely, My Lord," said Cabusse pulling on his impressive moustache with his left hand, his right leaning on his sword as if on a cane. He added with a large manly smile: "She's getting close to term. She's supposed to give birth at the end of July."

"The end of July! In this heat! The child will end up susceptible to colds."

"I fear it will be so," Cabusse agreed.

"And how is your neighbour, Jonas?" added my father.

"Oh Jonas! Jonas!" answered Cabusse with a sudden gust of Gascon poetry. "Since he's got Sarrazine and his house, he no longer whinnies after other oats, but, heart against heart, he's happy."

"Give him my greetings, and to your wife and his wife as well. And how are my boys doing?"

"Passably well," said Cabusse who was sparing in praise if not in words, being quite taken with his own eloquence. He continued: "Each has his faults and his virtues. Of the three, Master Samson is the best. He's got a wrist of iron. But, no offence to him," he added with a brusque sensitivity that appealed to my father, "but he's a little slow-witted. Master François there's got a quick and vigilant eye and he parries and defends well, but he's too careful and doesn't press his attack. Master Pierre, now, is all fury and onslaught, dreams of mortal wounds and charges like a little bull. But he doesn't keep his guard up. I could have killed him a hundred times over."

"Each of the three should teach the others his strengths," my father observed. "My rascals," he continued, suddenly turning serious, "the plague has broken out in Sarlat. I am going there tomorrow to take a side of beef to Monsieur de La Porte. Because of the contagion, I can't take any servants as an escort, only family members; the Siorac twins and one of you, if he is willing."

"Me," I gasped, still sweating and out of breath from the assault I'd just mounted on Cabusse. "Since I'm going to become a doctor, it's time I started to get used to sickness."

"Take me," said Samson as soon as I'd spoken.

"Me," added François with a moment's delay.

"No, not you," said Siorac. "I can't expose my eldest son to such a risk. But I'll take Pierre and Samson, since I have their consent. Good day Cabusse! Good day, boys. I'm proud of you. Bravery doesn't show only when you've got a sword in your hand." Whereupon, his eyes shining with emotion, he turned on his heels in his own brusque way and left.

That evening, my father told Samson and me to go up to the north-east tower room after dinner, where we'd been sent on my sixth birthday after I'd hit François. But it had been quite transformed in the last twenty-four hours: the walls were whitewashed, the floorboards washed with vinegar, and despite the terrible summer heat, a great fire blazed in the fireplace smelling of aromatics: gum benjamin, lavender and rosemary. I also saw two beds, separated by the entire width of the room, which indicated that Samson and I were not to sleep in the same bed as we usually did. And on a stool beside each bed were laid out our travelling clothes, smelling of the same herbs that were burning in the fireplace.

Against the wall, I spied the short swords that we were allowed to bear only outside the walls of Mespech. My heart leapt on seeing them. I unsheathed mine and practised wild blows to the right and to the left, cutting to pieces the plague and its terrible hired assassins, which evoked howls of laughter from Samson, though not at my expense, for mockery was completely unknown to his pure soul. After a good laugh with him, I blew out the lamp and fell asleep like a sack, without the least apprehension, but full of pride to be accompanying my father in such a hazardous journey and excited by the prospect of seeing and learning new things which bore on my future estate.

My father woke us at daybreak the next morning, bringing us each a bowl of warm milk with his own hands, along with a well-buttered piece of fresh wheat bread and a thick slice of salt pork.

He urged us to eat up, and while we sat on our beds on opposite sides of the room, heartily working our jaws, my father put his foot on the stool and said with great seriousness: "Pierre, and you too Samson, you must know that God never does anything that is not good and right, and thus has His secret reasons for sending us the plague. Yet, God acts only through natural agents, and against these agents it is meet and right to defend ourselves, either by taking precautions against them or by fighting them when they come."

He stood up straight, hands on hips, and continued in a clipped and clear voice: "You should know, my sons, that the plague's contagion reaches man through corrupted air which surrounds the infected person, his bed linen, his furniture, his house and the streets he has passed through. Some doctors claim that this pestiferous air enters us through a putrid vapour. Others, that there are tiny venomous creatures, so small that the eye cannot see them, and which penetrate our mouths, noses, ears and the pores of our skin, laying eggs in our blood and spoiling it. This is why it is important, first of all to eat well…"

"Why so?" I asked, my mouth full and astonished that what I took to be a pleasure was actually a remedy.

"Because the noble parts of the body, to which the venom attaches itself, can only defend themselves if they are fortified. For if the veins and arteries are not filled with new food, they can be more easily entered by the venom, which, finding empty space, gets a hold of the noble body parts, principally the heart, the chest and the genitals. Secondly… But you've finished eating. Stand up quickly, Pierre, and take off your shirt."

Which I did, not a little surprised. My father took from the ground a large saucepan of vinegar he'd brought and, dipping his finger in it, rubbed it on my temples, armpits, chest, groin and genitals. "This," he explained, "will preserve your body from infection."

"How?" I asked.

"Vinegar…" he began, going over to rub some on Samson in his corner. "But what a strong, well-built lad this is! It's a marvel to see how well put together he is at his age!" He stopped short and, turning his head quickly, shot me a piercing look as if he were afraid he'd offended me with this praise of my brother. But in truth I'd not given it a thought, so fascinated was I by his talk, my eyes and ears riveted on him.

"Vinegar, you were saying, father?" I reminded.

"Ah yes! Vinegar, you should know, is cold and dry in its essence. Now cold and dry are qualities wholly repugnant to putrefaction. Which is why we preserve herbs and onions in vinegar, which is consequently opposed to venom and keeps the body from corruption."

This said, my father came back over to me and strung a sachet around my neck, which he rubbed on my chest. He did the same for Samson.

"This sachet contains an aromatic powder which will preserve your heart. Get dressed, Pierre, and you too, Samson. It's time to be going."

When he saw we were dressed, he took two little sacks from his pocket, gave me the first and Samson the second. "This you must hang from your belts. They're cloves, a very costly herb which you must chew constantly while in Sarlat and other infected places. As you chew, the strong and healthy odour of the cloves will fill all the empty cavities of your mouth and nose and so the pestiferous vapours cannot find any place to gain a foothold in you and will be repulsed into the air outside your body."

I watched and listened to my father in a kind of beatific admiration of his immense knowledge, dumbfounded to learn in so short a time so many secrets about contagion. But, in fact, he had been speaking to me every day about this for the last week, and it was amazing how much I already knew.

"And finally, my knights errant," said Jean de Siorac, "here are your helmets: a little gauze mask, dipped in vinegar, which each of you will wear over your nose and mouth once outside Mespech. Well then, my rascals," he continued, coming to a halt in front of us with his hands on his hips, "you are now armed for warfare against the plague! So let's be on our way. May God guide us! And may the Lord protect us! In your saddlebags you will each find two loaded pistols, which will aid you but little against the plague but will protect you, peradventure, from the evils of men."

In the courtyard of Mespech, our servants had gathered, their eyes wide, all standing still as statues, to watch us take our leave as if they would never see us again except wrapped in shrouds and lowered into the grave. Sauveterre, doing his crab walk down the stairs from his tower, came to embrace my father with great feeling, and whispered in his ear with a husky voice, divided between anguish and fury, "This is madness! Madness! Madness!" And my father, perhaps attempting to cover these words, said in a very loud voice that when we returned Escorgol was to sound the warning bell, and that no one should approach us. At our arrival, great fires should be kindled in all the fireplaces, and vats of water set to boil in sufficient quantity for us to bathe and wash our clothes. Outside the walls, in front of the gatehouse, the Siorac brothers were waiting for us, already aboard the wagon loaded with the side of beef, both quite pale and their lips trembling. My father, turning slightly and raising his eyes, made a parting gesture with his gloved hand to Escorgol, at his watch behind the arrow loop above, watching us go with tears in his eyes, a detail that troubled me deeply, though no more so than the silent adieu of our servants in the courtyard. So it was that I began to have a better idea of the perils we were throwing ourselves into.

The cart set off with a lurch, and my father, urging his dapple-grey gelding up beside the dray horses, silently contemplated for a while the Siorac twins' anguish. "My cousins," he said, "I worry about you, seeing you so prey to your imaginations, which hold such sway over us. You're trembling! You believe you're already dead! But you must realize that, beset with apprehension or fear, the blood recedes from the heart, leaving it empty and allowing the contagious venom to gain easy entry. And so those who are afraid of dying actually make great strides towards death."

"It's not so much death I fear," said one of the twins (and when he named Michel, we knew it was Benoît), "but that Michel might die and I survive him."

"I'm troubled by the same thought," echoed Michel.

"Well, then, you may rest easy," counselled my father. "You are twins and your humours are so alike that the contagion will not strike one without striking the other. And so you will die together, or you will survive together, but you won't be separated."

"Lord be praised!" exclaimed Benoît with a sigh of relief. "My noble cousin, you have taken a great load off my heart."

"Mine too," echoed Michel.

From this minute on, the colour returned to their cheeks, their faces regained their composure and they made no more complaints save about having, as we all did, to wear gloves and masks in such stifling heat. It's true, that in addition to their gloves and masks, they were armed with chain mail and helmets, which didn't help their comfort, sweat streaming down their faces, even though it was still early in the day and the sun was scarcely risen. Each had a blunderbuss resting on his knees, the cannon turned to the outside of the path.

Two leagues from Sarlat, at a place called les Presses, we caught sight below us on the road, as it wound down the hill to the right, the body of a naked man, stretched out, his legs spread, on the parched yellow grass of the field. He was about a dozen toises below us and though the wind was at our backs, the stench he exuded was over-powering. "My cousins," said my father, "go on without stopping. You, too, Samson. Wait for us at the bottom of the hill." Benoît whipped the dray horses, and they set off at a gallop, followed by Samson on his white horse. My black jennet and the big dapple-grey gelding, wanting to join them, put up a struggle when we tried to bring them to a halt, but after a few whinnies, turns and wheels, they calmed down and stood quietly, their legs trembling slightly on the hillside above the corpse.

"Pierre," said my father. "This unfortunate bears all the signs of the plague I've described to you. Can you name them?"

"Yes, of course," I answered, my throat knotted and almost failing, so terrible a blow did the odour and view of this hideous cadaver strike in my heart. "This large abscess stretching the skin under his right armpit is a bubo. The black pustules on his stomach are gangrene. And the multicoloured blisters on his chest—reds, blues and violets—are called purpura."

"Very good," my father commended, pretending not to notice my unease. "Also notice that the skin is yellowed and soft, and livid in colour, the eyelids are black and the face contracted." And he added: "'Whoever dies, dies in pain,' said Villon, 'but a plague victim more than anyone.'"

"How does that man come to be lying here," I asked, "and not in his bed?"

"The sickness begins with a burning fever, a great faintness of heart, a swelling of the abdomen, a terrible nausea and a constant and fetid dysentery. After several hours of this, the victim experiences a terrible headache which makes him crazy and drives him deliriously out of his house and forces him to run until he drops exhausted."

"And so he fell there, without help, without friends, naked as the day he was born, and he died."

"He wasn't naked. Some passing beggars have stripped him. They will die and be ravaged in their turn. The clothes and underclothes of the dead man will be passed alas from hand to hand, killing all those who touch them. This is how the infection reaches into the farthest recesses of the countryside. My son," added my father, suddenly changing his tone, "do you see that crow sitting insolently on the top of that chestnut tree? Shoot him, please!"

Quite surprised by this command, but uttering not a word, I took out one of my pistols from its saddle holster, loaded it, took aim and fired. The bird fell, tearing the already yellowing leaves from the drought-stricken branches in its descent. I reloaded my pistol, a little astonished to have wasted a bullet on such a target.

"Would it have eaten the corpse?" I asked.

"No, no. Crows never feed on the flesh of pestiferous bodies. They're much too clever. Let's be on our way!" And my father spurred his gelding down the winding road, and when I had caught up to him and was riding side by side, at a walk, he said: "Ambroise Paré, the king's surgeon, a very good man, and, like ourselves, of the reformed religion, recounted that, the first time he saw a plague victim, he raised the sheet to examine him and the fetid stench exuding from the buboes and gangrene so overpowered him that he lost consciousness and fell into a faint. Well, Monsieur my son," smiled my father, "you have already surpassed the great Ambroise Paré, if not in knowledge at least in sangfroid. When you shot that crow, your hand wasn't trembling in the slightest."

Whereupon he spurred on his steed, leaving me delighted and comforted by his great praise, for, to tell the truth, the sight of this plague victim had struck me with unspeakable horror.

A little before la Lendrevie, as he rode along on his gelding in front of the wagon (with Samson and me bringing up the rear) my father raised his gloved hand to signal a halt. Then, turning in his saddle, he called, "We'll stay well clear of this awful procession," indicating three wagonloads of bodies coming from the town as they turned to our right into a large field where ditches dug in the clay gaped open under the leaden sun.

On the driver's seat of each of these wagons was sitting a man clothed in a cassock of white linen and wearing a monk's cowl. Each had a long hook fashioned of wood on his knees. When the first wagon made its turn a few toises ahead of us, I could see that the dead were naked and thrown pell-mell on top of each other. Even from this distance and with the wind at our backs, the stench was powerful.

"Is that a new cemetery?" I asked in astonishment.

"No, no. But during a plague it is illegal to bury the dead near churches so as not to infect the holy ground. So they put them in the first available place and in trenches."

"What are the gravediggers' hooks for?"

"They aren't gravediggers. The gravediggers all died in the first days of the epidemic. These hooded fellows are crows—so named because of their hooks with which they snag their dead to avoid getting too close to them."

"They stick them into their flesh?" I asked, horrified. "That's a barbarous custom."

"Yes, indeed, but if it weren't allowed, no one would do the work. The city recruits them for fabulous pay."

"How is it that the crows themselves don't die?"

"They do die. That's why they're paid so well."

At this point, the crow driving the third wagon stopped just as he was making his turn into the field. Through the slits in his cowl, he stared at my father, and then, suddenly dropping his reins, he raised his right arm in greeting. "Good day, My Lord!" he cried with a strong and joyful voice.

"Good day, friend! So you know me?"

"Indeed, and despite your mask. I recognized you from your dapple gelding and your build. I worked for you last spring building the road from Mespech to your mill at les Beunes."

"And what have you been doing since?"

"Alas, I've been mostly out of work, starving for three months and nearly at death's door."

"Mespech wouldn't have refused you bread and soup."

"But how could I get there to beg them? My poor legs can't even carry me any more. The plague saved me, God be praised! Now I eat my fill."

"How much does the town pay you as a crow?"

"My Lord, it's amazing! Twenty livres a month and I've already earned ten. The other ten at the end of July, if I'm still above ground and not under it." He laughed and crossed himself. "But I'm not complaining," he continued happily. "It's a great feast, after all I've been through, being rich, filling my paunch every day with meat and Cahors wine, and even sporting with the wanton wenches in la Lendrevie! God forgive me but I was chaste for too long!"

"Do you have wife or children?"

"No! I could never afford 'em."

"Well, then, friend, I wish you prosperity and a long life!"

"Prosperity I've got. But as for a long life, I don't believe in it," laughed the crow. "But every day that comes along is a boon as long as my stomach stays full."

Whereupon, whipping his team vigorously, he drove the wagon on into the field.

"Isn't it amazing that he's so happy?" I mused as I watched him go.

My father shook his head. "Poor folk have a kind of brutal and careless courage they get from their condition. Surely they need it more than others do, for it's not true as some have said that the plague strikes rich and poor alike. At the first sign of the plague your rich bourgeois can afford to apply Galen's precept, 'Go quickly, stay far away and come back slowly.' But the poor are stuck where there's infection, with no means of escape and no place to go. And because of the filth fate has bestowed on them, undernourished, all thrown on top of each other, the malady wipes them all out."

Having arrived at the la Lendrevie gate, my father called to the watchman and asked him to alert the commissionaires that we were bringing meat for Monsieur de La Porte and the consuls. Then, asking the Siorac twins to wait for us, he rode on into the middle of la Lendrevie with Samson and me. To purify the air, great resinous fires burned on the pavement at every crossroads, making the terrible heat of the sun even more unbearable. Not a soul was in the street, save for the invisible ones of the dead. And though there were always droves of them in Sarlat, not a dog, a cat or a pigeon. They'd been slaughtered en masse as potential carriers at the outset of the epidemic. Here and there I noticed more than one boarded window, from which you could hear the moans of the sequestered. Their doorways were draped with a black crêpe ribbon, indicating that it was a mortal offence to go in or out, or even approach.

My father drew rein on a square or rather a little squarelet, at the far end of which stood an old corbelled dwelling. I knew it well and realized then and there that the side of beef destined for La Porte and the consuls was not the only goal of our expedition.

Although armed for war, Jean de Siorac dismounted easily from his horse in his usual way, ordered Samson and me to do the same and to tether our steeds to the iron rings in the paving stones. This we did. We were then about a dozen steps from the infected house. My father, casting a quick glance around us to be sure he wouldn't be seen, crossed this distance and pulled on a basket hanging by a rope from the attic window. I heard the tinkle of a bell, and a head appeared in the dormer window. It was Franchou, her face drawn but good colour in her cheeks.

"Sweet Jesus!" she cried leaning halfway out the window, revealing two beautiful breasts barely contained in her bodice. "It's you, My Lord! You haven't abandoned your servant!"

"Shhh, Franchou! They'll hear us! Are you sick?"

"Only from fear and hunger. But otherwise I'm well. Since my mistress's death I haven't left this lodging."

"I'm going to get you out. Do you think you can climb out of that window? You're not a slim girl!"

"Of course!" Franchou replied. "I've got flesh enough, especially on my backside. But I'll wriggle through as best I can. Fat mice have to get out of their holes."

"Very good, I'll go and fetch what we need."

And leaving Samson to stand guard over the horses, my father led me through some neighbouring streets, searching in courtyards and sheds for a ladder. When he found one, which took some time because we needed one long enough to reach the attic window, we each took an end, and sweating heavily (for it was quite heavy and the heat overpowering) we came back to the house, greatly troubled by loud cries coming from that place.

"What's this commotion?" frowned my father, quickening his pace. When we burst into the little square in front of Madame de La Valade's house, we dropped the ladder in astonishment. Samson, whirling his white horse, pistol in hand, was holding at bay a band of thirty or so beggars, armed with pikes, cutlasses, scythes and iron bars, and two even carried blunderbusses. They surrounded him and our two tethered horses, yelling and growling, though no one had yet dared strike the first blow. Samson had not fired either (as I might have in his place). His angelic face betrayed neither fear nor anger and, with his reddish-blond hair flaming in the sun, he stared at this mob with his blue eyes wide in surprise, and repeated with his charming lisp, "Whath thith? Whath thith?"

"What's this?" scolded my father in echo. "What do these people want? Be brave, Pierre and have at them!" So saying, and unsheathing his sword—I behind him brandishing my own—he strode into the crowd, distributing blows with the flat of his sabre, careful not to wound anyone, and opened a path to the horses, untied them, threw me the reins and leapt into his saddle. "Turn your horses' backs to the wall so they can't get behind us," he whispered to me. And turning his gelding, which made some space around us, he backed him towards the La Valade house. My black jennet wasn't as well trained, but I eventually got myself into position on his right with Samson on his left.

At this point, with our reins on the pommels of our saddles, all three of us held our pistols in both hands with our swords dangling at the ready from our right wrists. My father would have attacked straightaway had he had a couple of his veteran soldiers instead of his two sons at his sides. But he didn't want to risk the lives of his rascals in a street fight. He preferred to talk his way out, all the more so since the populace, though armed, seemed more weak and hungry than truly menacing. "So, my friends!" he cried, rising in his stirrups, in a stentorian yet gay and military voice. "What's all this fuss? Is this the way you greet visitors to la Lendrevie? Why are you rushing at us like this?"

"To kill you, Baron, you and your two sons!" shouted a large fat man standing at the front of the crowd, whom I recognized by his bulging black eyes, his clothing, his fat paunch and the large knife in his belt as Forcalquier, the butcher of la Lendrevie.

"These are nasty spiteful words!" laughed my father, all the while scanning the crowd and especially the two armed with blunderbusses with a vigilant eye. "Kill me, Maître Forcalquier! You want to try what the English couldn't do! But supposing you try, those I don't kill by my hand will die by the rope for this murder!"

"And who'll hang 'em?" rasped Forcalquier. "La Porte?" (Hoots from the crowd greeted this name.) "That little turd of a police lieutenant is barricaded in his house! He's scarcely got enough soldiers to guard his doors. And if he had enough to catch us, who'd judge us? The Présidial judges? They've fled!" (The jeers increased.) "Baron, figure it out for yourself. There are no more royal officers, bourgeois, judges or lords here. We're the masters now."

"And you're the leader?"

"I am. I, Forcalquier have named myself Baron de La Lendrevie, and high commissioner of justice in these parts. You shall die, then. And your lads with you. Thus has my justice decided the case." To this affront there was much laughter and applause, but if Forcalquier appeared resolute, those around him seemed to be much more inclined to enjoy his insolent threats than to enact them.

My father, feeling this mood in the crowd, continued his role in this dangerous game without changing tone: "Butcher-baron of la Lendrevie," he said, reprising the tone of heady humour that had prevailed, "you're very quick in your work, for never did judge render so hasty a decision! But pray, what may be the motive for your judgement: for what crimes are we to be punished?"

"For having approached an infected house and tried to remove the wench closed up in it. That's a capital crime as you know quite well."

"But this wench is healthy, I guarantee it and I'm a doctor! Her only malady is hunger!"

"We're sick with hunger too!" cried a strident voice from the crowd, and this cry was immediately echoed from all corners of the square in a chant that was fed by lamentation and protest.

"All right, Baron! Enough talk!" shouted Forcalquier. "You hear my subjects! You must die!"

So saying, he pulled his knife from his great belt. Whether this man was brave or simply foolhardy, I cannot tell, for the cannon of one of my father's pistols was trained directly at his heart. But my father did not fire. "Take care, Master Forcalquier!" he counselled gravely. "After the plague, you'll be questioned, you and your subjects, about this commotion!"

"After the plague!" cried Forcalquier. "There won't be an 'after the plague'!" he pronounced with a great sweeping gesture of his knife as if he were beheading every person in the town. "I have it on divine authority," he added, his bulging black eyes fixed on my father's face. "The Virgin Mary appeared to me in a dream and told me, on the faith of her divine Son, that there won't be man, woman nor child who survives the epidemic in la Lendrevie. Baron, you'll be preceding us by a very little bit into the kingdom of death. The plague isn't going to spare anyone here, Heaven has told me." And he gave a quick slash with his knife in the air. "We're all going to die!" he cried, raising his voice.

"All! All!" cried the crowd in a lugubrious echo.

And I could see by my father's expression that he was beginning to fear the worst from these desperate peasants. And yet, when he spoke again, it was with the same jocular and friendly tone: "Good people, if we must die, what will my death profit you?"

"We can eat your horses!" cried one.

"So, my good friends," my father answered with admirable repartee, "now I understand you and am reassured. It's not wickedness that drives you, but hunger! And if that's how it is, then I propose a ransom for our lives and for the freedom of this poor wench: a beautiful fresh side of beef slaughtered just yesterday! I said," he continued, raising himself in his stirrups, "a beautiful fresh side of beef! My son Pierre will go and fetch it at the town gates. Fresh meat, my friends! You're going to eat meat!"

I immediately spurred my black jennet through the crowd and valiantly took off like an arrow. The Siorac brothers were preparing to sell the last quarter of beef at the town's meat counter when I got there. Shouting and waving, I told them to leave off and to follow me. And soon, the wagon lumbered after me with an infernal racket onto the square where my father was still holding sway over the crowd and preventing Forcalquier from getting a word in.

Sweat dripping from his forehead and his eyes, my father heaved a great sigh of relief seeing us arrive, all the more since the Siorac twins, armed for battle, their blunderbusses at the ready, scattered the crowd to either side—though not Forcalquier, who stood his ground, open-mouthed but still clenching his knife.

Immediately reholstering his pistols in his belt and leaping directly from his horse to the wagon without touching foot to ground, my father—I cannot imagine where he found the superhuman strength to do this—raised the entire quarter of beef over his head, and standing thus, his feverish eyes on the crowd, shouted: "Hey there, Butcher-baron of la Lendrevie, cut up this portion for you and your subjects!"

And suddenly, from up there on the wagon, he hurled the slab of beef with all his might right down in the butcher's face. So struck, Forcalquier staggered and fell backwards, hitting his head on the paving stones, and lay there unconscious. In a flash, the entire pack of beggars swarmed over him, dropping their arms and rushing like mad dogs at the meat, tearing it to pieces, some with their knives and others with their very teeth.

My father, seeing them occupied thus, leant the ladder against the infected house, and Franchou edged out of the window, feet first, then ankles, and thighs, but alas, being too wide in the middle, she stuck fast in the window frame at mid buttocks. "Ah, my sweet!" cried my father, "you're too much of a good thing! Push, I beg you, push! Our lives depend on it!"

Twisting, trembling and pushing as hard as she could, Franchou, making plaintive little cries and a rosary's worth of Sweet Jesuses, finally squeezed through, slid more than she climbed down the ladder and fell into my father's arms, who, brandishing her as he had brandished the slab of beef, literally tossed her onto the bed of the cart.

In the wink of an eye, he leapt into his saddle and, all of us giving spur, whip and voice and shouting wild cries in our relief to get away, we galloped our five horses out of the square, their shoes raising a hail of sparks on the cursed paving stones of the town.

10

THE MOST PAINFUL PART of the trip to Sarlat for Samson and me was not the adventure in la Lendrevie, but the twenty days of quarantine that we had to spend in the north-east tower upon our return to Mespech. Michel and Benoît Siorac were no better pleased by their enforced reclusion in the room beneath ours. Through the spaces between the floorboards we could hear them take turns—but could never tell which one was talking since they sounded just alike—complaining the whole day long. And long it was: this period was punctuated only by the three meals brought each day by Escorgol. At least these were hearty enough, since my father wanted to fortify our veins and arteries against the entry of the fatal vapours.

My father had chosen Escorgol as messenger since he had survived the plague two years earlier in Nîmes. He had reason to believe that, having once triumphed over the venom, his body would chase it away again if attacked. Having received this assignment—as well as that of maintaining a hearty fire in each of our fireplaces—Escorgol was relieved of his duties as watchman at the gatehouse and replaced there by my father, who spent the term of his quarantine on the ground floor and Franchou hers on the first. It was my father who decided on this distribution, and I note from a brief but bitter allusion in the *Book of Reason* that Sauveterre would, had he been consulted, have made a different arrangement.

From the second day of our captivity onwards, Uncle de Sauveterre, fearing the effects of laziness, had us brought our Titus Livius and Latin dictionaries, as well as *The History of Our Kings* (which he had copied for us by hand), with instructions to translate one page of the first and to learn two pages of the second each day. Lastly, we were brought the Bible, with orders to read marked passages out loud thrice daily.

In his written instructions, Sauveterre exacted from me a promise not to help Samson with his Latin, but, in my written reply, I respectfully declined to make such a promise, since, as I argued, if Samson were deprived of Sauveterre's usual help, he ought at least to have mine, without which he might quickly become despondent, since he took his studies so much to heart. And, after some reflection, Sauveterre consented on condition that I underline those passages I'd helped him with. Not that Samson was so bad in Latin, but he was weak in French, and it was precisely into French and not into *langue d'oc* that we had to translate our Latin. I was pretty fluent in the language of the north, since, while she was alive, my mother exhibited the elegant affectation of speaking only in French when addressing me or my father, who, for his part, also resorted to this tongue when talking about medicine. But poor Samson had had none of these advantages and was the sorrier for it.

I made other written requests to Sauveterre that met with varied responses: 1. "May I ask Escorgol to bring us two swords and two breastplates?"—"Granted. But take care in your enthusiasm not to poke his eyes out." 2. "May I send Escorgol to fetch my cup-and-ball game?"—"Refused. You are no longer of an age, my nephew, to be wasting your time on such frivolous enjoyments." 3. "May I correspond with my father about the plague?"—"Granted." 4. "May I write to Catherine and to little Hélix?"—"Refused. You have nothing to say to these girls of the least consequence, either for them or for yourself."

This was hardly my view of things, nor little Hélix's, as the short note she succeeded in slipping under our bolted door one morning proved so well:

Dere Pier, I gav a notte for u to that wikid portur, butt he gav it to Soveterre who redit and putt it in the fire and ordurd Alazai to whipped me. Ha! mye pur reer! Butt thas nothing. Dere pier, mye thauts are about u all da longe and it mayks me very saad. Hélix.

I too, locked away in the north-east tower, had "thauts about little Hélix all da longe", especially in the evening, when I'd blown out my lamp, and was alone in my bed with no one to snuggle up against. How sweet was my sleep after we'd tired ourselves out with our little games and I could rest my head on her sweet breasts, my left arm under her waist and my right leg draped between hers. Alas, poor little Hélix, where are you as I write this? In hell, or in Paradise? Even today I cannot think it such a great sin to have enjoyed such happiness, peace and quiet in your silky arms, nor such an iniquity that you fluttered around me with your happy chirping to entice me into your nest.

The room where we were sequestered was quite large, airy and wonderfully aromatic, for it served as our apple cellar with all our apples set out on screens, wrinkled, rumpled and shrivelled like a baby's skin, but not rotten, though it was already July. Added to their delicious smell was the odour of the aromatics which burned day and night in the fireplace along with resins, which crackled in the flames. With this fire inside and the fire of the July sun outside, we toasted in an oven despite the open windows. It was even worse during our fencing practice, our torsos sweltering under the heavy breastplates. Our swordplay done, our sabres in place against the wall and our armour removed, we threw ourselves naked on our beds, panting, gasping for breath, our bodies bathed in sweat.

"Sweat," wrote my father in answer to my anxious questions about prevention of the plague, "is one of the best remedies against contagion. That's why Gilbert Erouard, a medical doctor at Montpellier (I hope, my son, that someday you shall study under him, for he is a very wise man), recommends the pestiferous to swallow a large glass of pickled anchovies every morning. This strong drink provokes abundant sweating and can produce a cure. Also, according to Erouard, salt—which we use as you know to preserve pork—consumes the unspeakable putrefactions that the venom introduces into the sick person's body.

"Some doctors greatly value scorpion oil. They marinate 100 scorpions in a litre of walnut oil and administer this remedy, mixed with an equal amount of white wine. The drug provokes violent vomiting and thus, according to these doctors, attracts the venom and succeeds in evacuating it.

"I am not sure what to think of so brutal a cure," wrote my father, "since the plague victim shows a great inclination to vomit anyway, and I do not see the need to add to it.

"I cannot see what advantage is to be gained by purging him, since he suffers already from a continual dysentery. Also, in my view, bleeding can only further debilitate the patient, when he is still so weak. And the same would be true of dieting.

"I have seen surgeons—oh what an ignorant race of men!—cauterize plague victims' buboes with red-hot irons, and others attempt to cut them away with knives. But those practices are as barbarous as they are useless. The bubo needs to drain without any intervention other than removing the pus, for if it evacuates it's a sign that the venom seeks issue from the body. We must therefore allow it to egress.

"I administered theriacal water to Diane de Fontenac, which I'd confected from a number of different herbs and spices crushed in white wine: angelica, myrtle, scabious, juniper, saffron and cloves. I limited my care to this sole remedy, all the while making sure to feed the patient, to have her drink plenteously, and to keep her clean. I also worked to keep her fever down, and minimize her fears of death with words of hope. All else is prayer."

This letter, which I've kept along with all the others my father wrote me, is proof enough, if such proof were lacking, that my father was, as Monsieur de Lascaux (who, great doctor though he was, had fled Sarlat at the first alarms of the plague) put it, "a heretic in medicine as in religion". For, other than the theriacal water, he seemed to place no trust in the majority of the most celebrated remedies for the plague, including the pickled anchovies and the scorpion oil, which, years later, I still heard discussed by the doctors at Montpellier.

Oh, how slowly the time dragged by for me during my quarantine! Every day seemed a month—a month of very long days... And how great my languor and mournful indolence would have been—despite Titus Livius, the Bible and our kings—if I hadn't had Samson's company. What a godsend he was! To live twenty days, nay twenty times twenty-four hours, locked in close quarters with your brother, without the slightest cloud, nor the least hint of a quarrel or squabble, and end up loving him even more than before (if that's possible), shows of what pure metal this brother was made, for, as for me, I know all too well of what imperfect stuff I am devised.

I've already described him, no doubt, but I want to recall his portrait once again: Samson was, first of all, handsome, of such a beauty to light up the darkness; his hair was strawberry blond, capping his robust appearance; his eyes of an azure blue; his skin as pale as his features were harmonious. I do not even speak of his face nor of his body, which were to become with the years worthy of a statue in their virile symmetry. But his great beauty, his grace and his infinite charms were but the outward and visible symbols of the soul that inhabited this envelope.

Cabusse claimed that Samson was a numskull because he was slow to parry a blow and slow to force his advantage. Cabusse was wrong: it was scarcely a deficiency of mind, but rather an excess of virtue. Samson loved his fellow adversary so much that he couldn't believe he could be wounded by him, nor wish to wound him in return. Wickedness, even that which we feign in sport, was unintelligible to him. I have thousands upon thousands of proofs of it. And the ultimate proof is this image, which I'll always remember, of Samson on his white horse, face to face with the mob in la Lendrevie, his wide blue eyes fixed in amazement on the furious crowd, repeating with his customary lisp, "Whath thith? Whath thith?"

Even with the most generous people on earth, there comes a time when egotism raises its ugly head. But this moment never came with Samson. Without ever a second thought, nor any attempt to turn things to his own advantage, Samson always thought of others first. He wept when my mother died. And yet, for his whole life, my mother never said a word to him, nor ever looked his way. How did he manage to love her, and what could he have seen in her—he who was invisible to her? I cannot guess. For he spoke little, inept at expressing the love he carried within. But of this immeasurable love which shone on all of us like the sun, he gave me yet another, most touching, proof during our quarantine, as I shall have occasion to relate further on.

My father took advantage of the leisure hours of his quarantine to address a letter to Monsieur de La Porte, recounting the commotion at la Lendrevie. He had it brought thither by Escorgol with orders to hand this sealed missive to La Porte's soldiers at the end of a long stick, split at one end. Escorgol was also to collect the money due us for the slabs of beef we had sold them, but there again his orders were quite strict: the coins which we suspected of carrying the infection since they'd passed through so many hands at Sarlat were to be handed over in a pipkin filled with vinegar. Guillaume de La Porte had his response brought to Mespech by a messenger two days later, but to this man my father spoke only through a mask soaked in vinegar and from a window of the gatehouse, accepting the letter he was carrying by means of a long stick similar to the one Escorgol had used. Having thrown aromatics on his fire, my father disinfected the letter by holding it over the beneficent steam emanating from the fireplace. Then he opened it, but wore gloves for this purpose, and read it holding it as far from his face as possible. He later recounted these precautions, holding them up as exemplary.

The police lieutenant wrote that he was not unaware of Forcalquier's villainies, but, just as Forcalquier himself had said, La Porte had only enough soldiers to guard the town gates. He lost one or two each day, and though he was willing to pay handsomely, he could find no replacements. Worse, the survivors would scarcely obey his orders, so sure were they of dying just like Forcalquier's mob. In truth, anarchy reigned, and corrupted the people like leprosy. One of the two consuls (though I shall not disclose which one), having lost a chambermaid to the plague and having himself been threatened with being boarded up in his own house, had fled during the night of 9th July, paying off the soldiers standing guard at one of the town gates. La Porte never did discover which one, but even if he had, he never could have punished the corrupted man, for he no longer possessed the means to do so. The executioner and his aides had died, along with the two jailers in the city prison.

Things had got so bad that, far from being punished, those who had been locked up were now set free, since they could be neither imprisoned nor fed, since municipal revenues were drying up and the city's expenses exorbitant. Besides the crows and the soldiers, the first receiving twenty and the second twenty-five livres a month, wages had to be paid to the disinfectors, who collected thirty livres a house to go in and burn flowers of sulphur inside. The four surgeons who had agreed to stay in Sarlat each received 200 livres a month. And their aides had also to be paid, along with the guides who preceded them into the infected houses, a torch of flaming wax in hand to chase away the venom.

The remaining consul and Monsieur de La Porte asked the Brethren if they would consent to loan the city 2,000 livres at fifteen per cent for a year, offering as security some land purchased from Temniac by the city when the Church properties were being auctioned off. La Porte stressed that the security had a value much greater than the amount of the loan but that the consul and he had made the arrangement fearing that the city would never be able to repay the monies, threatened as it was with extinction by the loss of all its inhabitants. Already, in the terrible plague of 1521, Sarlat had lost 3,500 of its 5,000 inhabitants. If the epidemic raged at this same rate for another few months, death would ravish everyone.

My father told me that when he read this despairing letter, he had wept and immediately sent a note to Sauveterre urging him to agree to the loan. Which Sauveterre, equally troubled by the letter, had done within the hour, though not without remarking that the security offered was of but little interest to Mespech, being situated much too far from the chateau to be farmed except by renting it out, which ate up all the profits, as his brother well knew.

My father wrote to Samson and me every day since, in his own idleness, he'd obtained permission from Sauveterre to correct our Latin translations, which he did to perfection, his own French being more refined and more elegant than his brother's. To these corrections, he would add on my copy excellent lessons on the treatment and cure of blunderbuss wounds, according to Ambroise Paré's book, as well as knowledge he himself had obtained during his nine years in the Norman legion. Later I learnt that he had also received permission to correct Catherine's, little Hélix's and Little Sissy's lessons, which were normally handed to Alazaïs, whom the Brethren had promoted to this task when my mother died.

The care given to the education of the girls at Mespech might cause some surprise, yet mistresses and servingwomen alike had to learn to read, in order to gain access to the Bible for themselves and later for their sons and daughters. Religion, the Brethren reasoned, had to be transmitted like language itself, justly called the mother tongue, passing from mother to baby from the tenderest age. Thus, Little Sissy and little Hélix, thanks to our Huguenot zeal, knew more at their age than many young Catholic noblewomen, who could scarcely sign their names. It is true that Alazaïs, having her own system of spelling, passed it on to her students, but my father took no notice of this imperfection, replying with laughter to Sauveterre, who had criticized it, that Catherine de' Medici could write no more correctly than little Hélix, though she was queen of France.

Three days before the end of our quarantine, I received a second letter from little Hélix, dusted with the same flour as the first, my correspondent having "thauts about me all da longe". But I was angered to learn that tongues were wagging in the kitchen between la Maligou and Barberine about Franchou. I hesitated to inform my father of these scullery rumours, but knew that I couldn't manage it without appearing to be involved in such matters or else betraying Hélix. So I said nothing, not even to Samson, about this second letter and immediately threw it in the fire.

As the end of my quarantine approached, I excitedly fixed my heart on the morning when I would be able to leave this room where

Samson and I had been sequestered for three long weeks. And yet when that day dawned for me, it brought nothing but sadness and heartbreak.

It had been agreed in letters exchanged with my father to wait for freedom until he himself came to deliver us. While we waited for the heavy key to turn in the lock of our great wooden door, Samson and I had decided on one last fencing match, which we fought, nearly suffocating under our breastplates. Once these were unlaced and removed, our swords in their scabbards, we each threw ourselves on our beds, naked as the day we were born.

Then, hearing the long awaited grinding of the lock, I sat up on my bed and saw my father come in all smiles and eyes flashing happily. Samson and I both got up and ran to him from our respective corners, happily anticipating the fulsome abandon of his welcoming hug. But suddenly my father stared at me, grew deathly pale and, changing without warning from the liveliest joy to a cold anger, he cried in a terrible voice: "My son, have you become an idolater?"

"Me, an idolater?" I stammered, confused by the shock of this incredible accusation and brought up short in my rush to meet him, whilst Samson, too, froze in his tracks, his wide-eyed look fixed on my father and me.

"Isn't that a medallion of the Virgin Mary you're wearing around your neck?" asked my father, pointing a trembling finger at it, his eyes blazing.

"You know it well," I choked. "It is my mother's medallion."

"So what?" screamed my father violently, taking a step towards me as if to rip it from my neck. "Never mind where you got it. Or who you got it from! You're wearing the damnable thing!"

"Monsieur my father," I said, collecting myself and speaking more firmly, for I was deeply wounded by his "So what?", "my mother gave it to me on her deathbed and made me promise to wear it all my life."

"And you promised!"

"She was dying. What else could I do?"

"Tell me about it!" cried my father, his eyes bulging out. "Tell me about it at once! I would have released you from this monstrous promise! Instead of which, you preferred to hide it from me like a thief, and wear this idol stealthily, betraying your faith!"

"I've betrayed nothing, and I've stolen nothing!" I replied, my anger getting the better of me now, and drawn up like a cock I stared outraged at my father.

"Yes you have! You've stolen my tenderness, which, from this day forth you no longer deserve, having hidden your stinking idolatry from me all these months!"

"But I'm not an idolater!" I shouted, my eyes ablaze, nearly defying him, so indignant was I at his injustice. "I never pray to Mary! I pray to Christ or the Lord without any intercession whatever from Mary or the saints! This medallion's no idol for me! It's an object sacred to the memory of my mother."

"No object is sacred!" answered my father with vehemence and a violent gesture of his hand. "To believe the contrary is precisely idolatry! No, Monsieur," he continued loudly, "however much you twist your logic, you cannot claim to wear this medallion innocently, if only because you could not have misunderstood your mother's purpose in giving it to you. At your birth she named you Pierre, and you know very well why! Nor can you be ignorant of the reason she gave you this medallion!"

"No, I'm well aware of her purpose," I said defiantly and heatedly, "but that doesn't mean I'm corrupted by it. Being named Pierre doesn't make me a papist. And this medallion hasn't changed my faith."

"You may think so," sneered my father, "but the Devil has more than one way of insinuating his poison into your heart, and more than one mask for approaching you, including the mask of filial love."

"Monsieur my father," I answered, "I cannot believe that the Devil can have any place in a mother's love for her son, nor a son's for his mother."

"It must be so!" raged my father with such ferocious resentment that I was frozen to the spot. And he repeated: "It must be so since he counselled you to hide from me that you were wearing this thing. When I woke you on the 7th to go to Sarlat, you were naked as now and yet you were not wearing this idol. Where was it?"

"Under my mattress. I don't wear it at night, it hangs too heavy on me."

"It hangs too heavy on you, indeed, from dissimulation, from ruse and deception! Untie it from your neck and give it to me!"

At this, Samson took a step forward, and joining his two hands, looked into my father's angry eyes and begged with a sweet, entreating tone: "Oh no! I beg you, my father!"

It was so out of character for Samson, always so discreet and modest, to intervene in a quarrel he was not involved in, that my father stared at him for a full second, his eyebrows raised in surprise at this "Oh no!" Then his face grew dark again and I thought for a minute that he was going to unleash his anger on Samson, but he turned again to me, his eyes full of wrath, and said in a clipped tone: "Well! I gave you an order!"

I knew in that instant that my whole life, or, what amounts to the same thing, the idea I had of myself, was going to be made or undone by my response. I stiffened and speaking coldly, but with a strange assurance: "Monsieur my father, it cannot be. I made an oath to my mother. I cannot break this oath."

"I will dispense you from it!" he cried, beside himself with rage.

"But you don't have the power," I replied. "Only my mother would, if she were living."

"What? You defy me!" cried my father. "You dare to oppose me!" He stared at me as if he were about to hurl himself at me, but thinking better of it, began pacing rapidly about the room, biting his lips, his eyes ablaze, cheeks and forehead scarlet. "Monsieur," he said, positioning himself in front of me, hands on hips and his chin jutting out, "either you give me this medallion as I've ordered you, or else I shall within the hour cut you off from my family like a gangrened limb and throw you out of Mespech."

I felt myself grow pale. Sweat streamed down my back and my legs began to shake as if an abyss had opened up before me. I could likewise not coax a single strangled word from my lips.

"Well?" my father said.

"Monsieur my father," I said finally, tearing my words one by one from the knot in my throat, and barely controlling my anger, "I am in despair to have to displease you. But I cannot without dishonour do what you ask of me, and rather than do it, I'd rather be driven away, even if unjustly."

"Well then, you shall, Monsieur!" replied my father in a leaden voice. And he added, shouting, "With an oath which I *too* shall keep, never to see you again!"

A long silence followed these words. The world fell away before my eyes and it seemed as though I'd ceased to exist. There I stood before my father, stiff as a block of stone, deprived of speech and very nearly of feeling, though I fumed with a terrible anger.

It was at this point that Samson intervened a second time. Although I recall this as through a mist, it seemed to me that tears were streaming down his cheeks, which surprised me since my father and I, though each animated by a like anger, were dry-eyed, whatever the inner feelings that may have tormented us. Samson, on the other hand, was weeping. Meanwhile, without ever deviating from his usual sweetness, nor seeming to take sides, he flew to my defence. Coming up close to me, he placed his left arm on my shoulder, and his upturned face had the effect of a great light shining in the darkness. He lisped simply, "Pierre, I'll not abandon you. If you leave, I'll come with you."

Lightning from Sinai striking at my father's feet could not have produced a greater effect. He stared at Samson as if he were trying to summon up against him all the fury which tore at his heart, but Samson wept, not for himself, but for me and for my father, sensing all the ravages this great quarrel had made between us. And my father, who had managed to hate me for daring to defy him, was unable, try though he might, to harden himself to Samson or even to look at him angrily or utter a single word against him. Feeling his powerlessness, trembling with rage and half-crazed, as I was, with grief, he decided his only course of action was turn on his heels and storm out of the room. He was so blinded by his emotions that he crashed into the door frame and left the door gaping behind him.

I fell into Samson's arms and, suddenly letting go, cried hot and bitter tears against his cheek, and shook with great sobs I was powerless to control. I was ashamed to be thirteen, only two years from adulthood, yet weeping like a baby. After a moment, Samson pulled away from me and counselled me gently but firmly to get dressed. My duty, he argued, before leaving Mespech for ever, was to ask my father to pardon me for this fidelity to my mother which had led me to defy him. This advice seemed good to me for I was sorry to have stood up so firmly against my father, even if in my heart I believed I was right. I dressed, strapped on my short sword as proof of my intention to leave Mespech, and with a firm step that belied the heartbeats that shook my ribs from within, my head swimming in confusion from the shock I'd suffered, I headed for the library. But, as I neared the door, I was brought up short by the sound of a violent argument concerning me coming from within. And as I hesitated, not knowing whether to knock or withdraw, daring neither to break in on this new quarrel nor withdraw and risk not having the courage to return, I listened, stunned and mute, my breath cut short, to the words which flew in rage between my father and Sauveterre.

"There are," cried Sauveterre in a violent and accusatory tone I'd never heard him use before, "there are greater sins than wearing a medallion to the Virgin around your neck!"

"And just what do you mean!" replied my father, furious.

"Just what I say!" stormed Sauveterre. "And you understand me perfectly! You go from folly to folly, my brother, I'm telling you exactly what I think. And first among them was to risk the lives of your younger sons and your cousins in that harebrained expedition to a plague-infested town!"

"We had to deliver that side of beef, you know," protested my father.

"And carry off Franchou! Do you think it was an accident that La Porte went on about the maid in his first letter to you? He knew all too well how to set his mirrors to catch his lark. Beef for him! Franchou for you!"

"My brother, I demand you retract these damnable words!" cried my father. "There is nothing between that poor wench and me! I only did my duty as a Christian to her!"

"So, find her a position somewhere! And far away! At la Volperie, for example, where, having lost Sarrazine and Jacotte, they need somebody!"

"No. Franchou will be Catherine's chambermaid. We won't discuss it any further. I've decided once and for all."

"Oh marvellous! We already have la Maligou, Barberine, Alazaïs and Hélix and Little Sissy, which makes five servingwomen in all and now we need a sixth!?" As chambermaid for Catherine who's not even ten years old!? A pretty light assignment, *if* it's the only one!"

"My brother, this is too much!"

"I'll say it's too much!" Sauveterre fairly shouted. "For while Mespech is enriching itself with a superfluous servant, it's losing one of your sons, whom you've decided to throw to the mercy of bad weather, famine and plague, since it's true evil begets evil. Oh, my brother! Let me tell you," he went on, more in grief than in anger, "you give your love to those you shouldn't and withhold it from those who deserve it!"

A long silence followed these words, which was broken by my father's hushed voice: "But why did Pierre have to defy me so and prefer his mother to me?"

"Am I dreaming?" cried Sauveterre. "Pierre prefer his mother to you! His only thought was to keep his word and preserve his honour. Don't you know you're his hero, that there's no one in the world he loves or admires more? That he models himself after you in all things—which, frankly, scares me given how you carry on!"

"Go easy on me, brother! Easy! Don't judge me!" said my father roughly yet much softer than his earlier tone. "I haven't decided anything yet. I have a deep aversion to this medallion as you know. It has been my life's cross."

"And isn't it now Pierre's? And do you think he wears it lightly?"

Hearing this, I knew I was saved. And, strange to say, as soon as I had this feeling, my conscience, which until then had raised no objections to my eavesdropping, suddenly pricked me sharply and I withdrew on tiptoe and went to find Samson in our tower room. I told him the whole story.

"What?" he gasped, eyes opening wide. "You eavesdropped?"

"Yes I did," I said, pacing about the room and shrugging impatiently. "I had to! It was about me!"

But Samson seemed greatly troubled by this news, and realizing that he blamed me for it, I suddenly understood with secret pleasure that Samson was my Sauveterre. I went up to him, kissed him on both cheeks and said in a rough but cordial tone: "Go easy on me, brother!"

At this very instant, the real Sauveterre entered our tower room, dressed in black and wearing his high Huguenot ruff. He closed the door carefully behind him, and looked at me thoughtfully out of his black eyes, set so deep in their sockets that their very depth gave them a penetrating quality. "My nephew," he said finally, "take off your sword. Your father would be unhappy to see you wearing it at your side. You forget that it is to be worn only outside our walls."

I could have kissed him, I think, for having so eloquently tendered me the olive branch. But he was so ceremonious and correct, speaking French rather than Périgordian, that I didn't dare. "My nephew," he began anew, as if this conclusion to the whole matter were the most natural thing in the world, "as punishment for defying your father, you shall compose twenty Latin verses in which you present your deepest and most sincere apologies to the Baron de Mespech for having preferred the duty due to the deceased to that owed to a father."

"I shall not fail to do so, my uncle," I responded with immense relief, "and in the very terms you have prescribed, and which so faithfully render the truth of my dilemma."

So saying, I bowed, and though his face showed scarcely any sign of it, I could tell that Sauveterre was satisfied both by my words and by my reverence.

"Must I also," asked Samson piteously, his eyes betraying his fear, "compose twenty Latin verses?"

Sauveterre smiled. "For you, Samson, the baron will accept a note of apology." He raised a finger. "Provided it's written in French and in good French."

"It shall be done," sighed Samson.

"Take your time, my nephews," said Sauveterre with a penetrating look in which we could detect a small glow of irony mixed with affection. "To help your composition along, you shall be locked in this room until tomorrow afternoon, and so as not to burden your reflection, you will be served bread and water only."

Whereupon he made a parting nod, to which we each responded with a deep bow. And limping away, his powerful shoulders squared, his carriage straight as a board and his demeanour almost jaunty, he left and bolted the door behind him.

And so our quarantine was prolonged by forty-eight hours, and when finally we emerged from our tower room, our Latin and French excuses duly composed, our father proclaimed the peace and his pardon with an embrace. But a notable change had taken place at Mespech during our incarceration: Catherine was now installed in my mother's rooms and Franchou, her chambermaid, slept in the adjoining cabinet—which also happened to adjoin my father's room. If, as my father had protested to Sauveterre—and I'd heard it with my own ears—there was nothing "between this poor wench and himself", he was putting temptation directly in his path. All the more so since Franchou was overcome with infinite gratitude for his having so gallantly saved her from the claws of death. Whenever he entered the great common room, she had eyes only for him, and, like a needle to a magnet, hurried to take up her position behind him at table, rushing to fill his goblet almost before had he drained it—to the great displeasure of Barberine, who had always filled this office in the past.

I imagine that before the outbreak of the plague at Sarlat, Franchou must have awaited my father's visits to the La Valade household with baited breath, if one is to judge by her trembling welcome: "Oh, My Lord, welcome! My Lord, I'm so happy so see you!"

"Good day, my friend, and how goes it?"

"Should I tell Madame you're here?"

"No hurry, Franchou! I've a little present for you, a silver thimble so you won't prick your fingers sewing."

"Sweet Jesus! A thimble! Made of silver! My Lord, you're so good to me!" And good he was, certainly, and familiar as well, since, to thank her for her gratitude, he always gave her a big kiss on her fresh cheeks, patting her round arms affectionately while she blushed deeply, all hot and bothered by his attentions.

I couldn't argue with Uncle de Sauveterre about all this. It would have been better to place Franchou at la Volperie than in such convenient proximity, separated from the enemy by only a little door without even a bolt to secure it. For hers was visibly not a fortress, like Calais, that needed much assault, but rather one that would fall at the first sign of attack, the population running out to be sacked by the assailants.

While awaiting such an outcome, the rumours flew freely between kitchen and scullery, and our hens and chicks jealously cackled their discontent day in, day out, but never dared peck at Franchou directly, so naive, so stout and so well protected was she. Sauveterre, all sullen, never unclenched his teeth at table and never took his eyes off his plate. And, as in the days when he had to countenance my father's many loans to Jehanne, the words "I pray for you, Jean" reappeared in the *Book of Reason*, soon followed by a brotherly exchange of biblical quotations, some denouncing lust, others praising fecundity. In extremis, Sauveterre even fell back on poetry (though, to be sure, it was written by a king's sister), and cited with the clearest of intentions these beautiful ascetic lines from Marguerite d'Angoulême:

> *Much more I've loved my fragile body's ways*
> *For which I've laboured nights and days,*
> *Than I've adored my God and idol dear;*
> *Much more inclined to this soft flesh adhere,*
>   *Than to salvation.*

To which my father replied by missing the point, in a most peremptory tone: "My body is not soft, nor am I fragile." And, despairing of his cause, Sauveterre finally played his trump: "At your age, Jean! And at hers!" To which my father, but little troubled, responded with a Périgordian proverb: "What does it matter how old the ram if the ewe's in heat?"

Franchou was the daughter of Jacques Pauvret, well named since he was a poor tenant farmer on our lands, who lived in a dilapidated farmhouse in the valley. Franchou had subsisted on parsimonious grain, few loaves of bread in the hutch, meagre flames in the hearth and rags for clothes. She had known more slaps than kisses, constant terror from wolves and bands of armed beggars and, at the first sign of drought, a gnawing famine that reduced them to eating acorns. Of course, like all the other poor girls in her village, she was told by Pincers to be a good girl and stay at home. How could she be blamed for having little nostalgia for her youth as she dreamily sewed at our table, her thumb crowned by the silver thimble my father had given her? The baron's wench? What was so bad about that? Where was the shame? Little bastards who would eat their fill and perhaps, like Samson, end up with the glorious name of Siorac? Could she be reproached for settling for a life with board, bed and fire behind great walls which protected her from roving bands, hunger and even sickness, since, during the great pestilence, Mespech had fallen back on its immense reserves, so that even when the plague came to assault our mighty defences, it couldn't get in?

While, in his little kingdom, my father was wrestling with his conscience as to whether he should harvest this round, ripe and velvety peach, Catherine de' Medici, far away in her Louvre, lusted after another fruit.

Le Havre remained in English hands. During the civil war, our leaders, Condé and Coligny, had given this beautiful city to Elizabeth of England, in exchange for subsidies arranged at the Hampton Court treaty, with the promise of exchanging it for Calais once peace had returned. But Condé, reconciled with Catherine after the Edict of Amboise, now blushed to have signed this disadvantageous treaty that would have amputated Calais from France again after she'd so dearly won it. "This little prince so very pretty, here a laugh and there a ditty", had happily perjured himself, while Elizabeth fumed against the perfidious French who couldn't keep their word, Huguenots and papists alike. To pour oil on this fire, Catherine sent Monsieur d'Alluye to the English queen, who boasted a great deal and was marvellously impertinent, refusing to give up Calais and even daring to demand the return of le Havre. "I shall keep le Havre," sniffed Elizabeth haughtily "to make up for Calais which is rightly mine."

This was enough for Catherine de' Medici to rally behind her banner both Catholics and Protestants alike. We witnessed the heretofore unimaginable sight of Condé joining forces with the constable's army. The French had been cutting each other's throats in the name of religion and now were lining up side by side, armed and saddled, ready to rip another French city from the English invader's hands. Poor Elizabeth could not believe they would take from her what she held "by right". But she only barely held it at all, not having had time to fortify it properly. On 30th July 1563, Condé and the constable carried le Havre by storm.

Alas, though the reconciliation of the generals and their troops was quick and easy, peace was not so simple for the rest of the kingdom after the Edict of Amboise. Zealous priests and fanatical barons armed companies of brigands who ambushed reformers coming home from the wars. In areas of Huguenot strength the edict was equally ignored. The Protestant "captains", Clermont de Piles and La Rivière, stormed Mussidan and, only a short time later, effected a breach in the walls of Bergerac one night and sent into the town's streets a few men who sounded drums and trumpets. The garrison, believing the town taken, sought refuge in the citadel, which was then besieged, starved out and taken.

Even in Paris, peace had not truly returned. D'Andelot, restored to his rank of colonel of the infantry after the Edict of Amboise, saw his authority contested by a Catholic, Catherine de' Medici's favourite, Charry. Rumour had it as well that Charry was preparing a massacre of the Protestants to exact revenge for the assassination of the Duc de Guise. As this rumour spread and gained credence among our partisans, one of Coligny's officers, Chastelier-Portaut, attacked Charry as he was crossing the Saint-Michel bridge and drove his sword into his body, "twisting it twice round to enlarge the wound". Catherine de' Medici, as we shall see, was not to forget this wound, from which Charry died a short time later.

And so, for more than four years after the Edict of Amboise, there reigned throughout the kingdom a dangerous and violent state of affairs, not quite war yet not entirely peace. Our own family, tucked away in the Sarlat region, had displayed such fidelity to the Crown that we needed fear nothing from the king's officers. Due to the spread of the plague throughout the valley surrounding Sarlat, the royal power was so weakened that it could scarcely protect loyal subjects from attack by the wicked.

Towards the end of August we received heartbreaking news. Étienne de La Boétie had been travelling in the Périgord and Agenais countries, and unable to find lodging there because of the outbreak of the plague had returned home to Bordeaux in apparent good health. Indeed, on 8th August he had enjoyed a game of tennis with Monsieur des Cars, the king's lieutenant in Guyenne. But having got overheated and sweating abundantly, he complained of chills as he went to bed. The next morning he received a note from Michel de Montaigne inviting him to dinner, to which he replied that he was suffering from fever and unable to attend. Montaigne went post haste to see him and found him already quite changed. As La Boétie's lodgings were in the centre of Bordeaux, surrounded by infected houses, Montaigne succeeded in convincing him to leave within the hour and go as far as Germinian, a village between le Taillan and Saint-Aubin, but two leagues from the city. La Boétie obeyed, but, arriving at Germinian, became so ill that he could not continue the voyage. And it was in this chance site, surrounded by his relatives and friends who rushed to his side, that he died nine days later.

It seemed that La Boétie was not afflicted with the plague, for he presented none of the usual symptoms, but instead complained of dysentery and constant migraines. Moreover, he was unable to eat and visibly wasted away, his eyes hollowing and his skin paling every day. Fearing his disease to be contagious, he urged Montaigne not to remain in his presence except "in flashes", but Montaigne would hear none of it. He remained at his "immutable friend's" bed until his death.

La Boétie was entirely conscious of his impending death right to the end, and undertook to settle his affairs with remarkable sang-froid. Having lived a Catholic, he chose to end his life religiously, confessed and took Communion. He then dictated his last will and testament.

Montaigne has detailed his friend's stoicism. Some find Michel de Montaigne's version of this final agony somewhat too philosophical and long-winded. But I find this a captious and heartless judgement. During his lifetime La Boétie was wonderfully eloquent and it is to his great credit that he retained this touch of Roman greatness even in the jaws of death and prey to the most unspeakable agonies. There is, moreover, a passage of this funereal speech which, even when I was a grown man, made me weep, not so much for what he says as for what he implies. When he was ready to pass on to his final judgement, La Boétie confided to Montaigne the following sentiment: "If God gave me the choice of returning to life or ending my voyage now, I would be hard put to choose." Words which show how awful had been the road to death and how little he would have wished to travel that road a second time.

He died on 19th August 1563, not yet thirty-three years old. My father called him "a very unusual kind of Catholic". Like Michel de L'Hospital, La Boétie had always found the torture and imprisonment of the Protestants a senseless and harmful business. He had always hoped that the Roman Church could, through serious reforms of its "infinite abuses", "rehabilitate itself" enough to attract the return of the Protestants. On the other hand, he did not believe it possible to maintain two religions side by side in the kingdom, having observed the crimes each side had authorized against the other. "The passions aroused in each camp," he said, "are fed by the pernicious belief that the cause of each is so just… that every means of its advancement is justified."

Alas, he spoke the truth, but the Council of Trent, which was convoked as he was dying, hardly fulfilled his expectations for conciliation. The Pope flatly refused every reform proposed by the French bishops. My father noted on this subject in the *Book of Reason* that when La Boétie had warned Geoffroy de Caumont against too much partisanship, he had painted a sombre picture—still true today—of the "extreme desolation" into which the kingdom would most certainly be plunged by the struggle of the two religions. To which Sauveterre penned the following: "Let us remain vigilant. The embers of civil war are still burning and will soon flame up again."

Ever since Cabusse had gone to live at the le Breuil farm and Coulondre Iron-arm at the Gorenne mill, our Siorac cousins, having more licence to speak their minds than our servants, complained of overwork. His marvellous ears perked, Escorgol stood watch in the gatehouse. Faujanet quietly worked away in his shop, fashioning his barrels at his leisure. "Now when it comes to dressing the horses and cleaning out their stables, milking the cows, feeding the hogs, baking bread, carrying water, hoeing the vegetable garden, carting grain to the mill, gathering honey and capturing new swarms, clearing out draining ditches, harvesting walnuts and chestnuts, apples and other fruits, there are only three of us," grumbled Michel, "Cockeyed Marsal, Benoît and me, when five would barely suffice. Now, I'm not talking about the ploughing, haying, wheat and grape harvesting, where everybody lends a hand, but of the endless daily chores here. Three men just aren't enough, and if an armed band attacked Mespech like the Gypsies did that time there wouldn't be enough of us to station on the walls."

To these complaints, Sauveterre, who husbanded our reserves, turned a deaf ear. My father agreed with them, but could do nothing to gratify them since the plague had so ravaged the countryside that it was impossible to find anyone to hire. Yet fortune intervened in an unforgettable way.

I was in the habit, as I have said, of getting up very early, disdaining my bed once I was awake, and of going down to the common room at daybreak, before la Maligou had lit the fire and boiled the milk. In truth, I liked to be the one to rekindle the fire, blowing with all my lungs on the coals, turning them bright red before throwing on the kindling. Such was my employment on 29th August, enjoying the silence of the sleeping chateau and the early-morning birdsong, when I heard a faint noise in the larder, the cool room scarcely lit by an arrow slit on its north side, in which our many slabs of salted meat hung from the rafters. Thinking it must be our old tom stalking an errant mouse, I crept up on tiptoe to the door to watch his sport. What was my surprise when, instead of cat, rat or mouse, I spied a lad of about fifteen, clothed in rags and dripping wet, sitting on our stool, a ham hock on his knees, chewing one large slice whose ends protruded greedily from both sides of his mouth, and already sawing away with his trenchant knife on the next. I stood open-mouthed and mute on the sill, scarcely believing my eyes and wondering how this fellow had managed to scale our walls, when he suddenly raised his head and saw me. He leapt to his feet like a tennis ball from a racquet and, dropping the ham, rushed at me, knife in hand.

Cabusse had taught me how to parry such a treacherous attack. I gave him a kick in the stomach and, as he bent double from the blow, I applied a second to his face. The knife fell from his hands, but not the ham from his teeth, and he fell like a sack. Looking around me for something to tie him up with, I spied a rope and grappling hook next to the stool where he'd been perched. I bound his hands behind him and, dragging him unconscious into the common room,

I leant him against one of the legs of the heavy oak table and tied him fast.

This done, I sat down to catch my breath, dumb with astonishment. For, even with a rope and grappling hook, how could this lad have evaded Escorgol's acute ears, scaled the surrounding wall, crossed the trap-filled meadow without harm, flown over the three drawbridges, and despite the triple locks on the lodging doors found himself in our larder calmly chewing on a slab of salt pork? In came la Maligou, who, at the sight of the thief, stopped in her tracks. "What's this? What's this?" she stuttered.

"I don't know. I found him in the larder." La Maligou, her entire fat frame shaking, threw her arms heavenward and, clucking like a terrified hen chased by the fox, cried, "Lord God! Sweet Jesus! Holy Mary and St Joseph, protect me! The Devil's got loose in our lodgings. Or at least one of the seventy-seven demons of hell!" And, crossing herself, she ran to fetch our wooden salt cellar and began throwing pinches of salt around the thief.

"Silly goose!" I said, grabbing the box from her hands. "Throwing salt around like that! And invoking the Virgin! Shall I tell my father on you?"

"But it's the Devil himself!" she howled, crossing herself again and so agitated and all atremble that her bonnet fell down around her neck. At this instant, the thief opened his blurry eyes, and even before completely regaining his senses began chewing the piece of ham which had stuck, unconscious that he was, in his mouth. "It's the Devil!" howled la Maligou, retreating as though hell itself were opening up before her, and falling on her knees, her eyes turning in their sockets, her hands joined fervently, she shrieked: "Oh Holy Mother! As one woman to another, protect me from this demon!"

"That's enough, you ninny!" I commanded sternly. "That's not the Devil. Can't you see he's eating?"

"But the Devil eats, too, Master Pierre!" cried la Maligou, nearly forgetting her terror in her astonishment at my ignorance about Satan's ways. She pulled herself to her feet, saying, "The Evil One has the same needs as man only multiplied by seven. He boozes like a curate in his parish house, stuffs himself like a smithy, pisses like a cow, burps like a king and fornicates like a rat in straw."

"He fornicates?" I said, raising an eyebrow.

"Oh yes!" replied la Maligou. "He's got a shaft seven times the size of a man's, and on Sabbath nights from midnight to daybreak he mounts seven times seven witches without stopping."

"That would suit you, silly gossip!" I laughed. "You've got your quiver open to every arrow."

"Holy Mother of God, keep me from such evil thoughts!" answered la Maligou, lowering her eyes modestly. "And if such evil thoughts get the better of me, at least don't let it be my fault, but by force."

"Get on with you, you corpulent bawd!" I said. "Go tell my father about our unexpected visitor. No wait," I added, "on second thoughts, I'll go myself."

"Jesus!" howled la Maligou, all a-tremble like jelly. "I can't stay here alone with this frightful demon who can fly over our ramparts and pass through our walls!"

"Go then, and inform the écuyer. And I'll go tell my father. This devil won't go anywhere tied as he is." And yet, as I ran, I couldn't be sure, and, arriving breathless at my father's room, I knocked impatiently. No answer came. Astonished at this silence, I tried the doorknob, and partway opening the door, glanced around the room. I saw the bed unmade and the sheets all disarranged, but no Father! "The Devil," thought I. "One appears, the other disappears! That's strange!" Suspecting, however, that this devilishness was all too human, I quietly closed the door and then, knocking as loud as I could, I shouted, "Help! Father, come quickly!" I then rushed as fast as my legs would carry me back to the kitchen where my thief was still sitting, tied fast to the table leg, happily chewing his bit of ham, saliva dripping from both sides of his mouth. He certainly had a good appetite for one who was to hang from the end of our baronial gibbet within the hour. Sitting down opposite him, I watched him in silence and was filled with pity. For he was a handsome lad of about my age, neither brutal nor wild-eyed at all.

He seemed to experience some difficulty swallowing our ham, since it was very hard, dry and salty, and when he'd finally managed it with several great glottal efforts I went to fill him a bowl of milk, and putting it to his lips, gave him to drink, which he did quite avidly, looking at me all the while with his different-coloured eyes, one blue the other brown, which gave him a strange look to be sure, yet his aspect was also as sweet and affectionate as a dog's. I noticed that his head was covered with thick, short-cropped tawny hair.

The milk swallowed, he gave me a big, naive and friendly smile with his wide mouth full of white, pointed teeth, as though he'd already forgotten that he'd attacked me with a knife, and that I'd kicked him unconscious. As I stared at him, the common room was filling with our servants, all them quiet as mice and moving along the walls at a good distance from our visitor, their eyes wide and their breath short from excitement and curiosity. Faujanet, the Siorac twins and Marsal put up a good front, but the group of women and children were all huddled in the far corner shaking, Jacquou in Barberine's arms, Annet pulling at her skirt, and—shame on her for all her seventeen years—little Hélix cowering, not to mention Catherine, face white as snow between her braids, and Little Sissy moaning. La Maligou muttered strange prayers with many signs of the cross, grimaces, affectations and gestures over her bodice as if she were trying to defend it from all the infernal armies. Not a sign of Franchou. I noticed it immediately.

In came my elder brother François, in truth no paler or more distant than usual (that is, since Diane's departure), his long face pinched and proper and affecting not to see me—proof that he already knew I was the hero of the hour. Announced by the heavy tramp of her woodsman's gait, Alazaïs appeared shortly thereafter and, scorning the women's corner, went to join ranks with the Siorac brothers whom she towered over by a good six inches. From there, her arms crossed over her breasts, she watched the scene without batting an eye, fearing no mortal man in this transitory life, her eyes set on the Eternal.

Samson, of course, looked for me the minute he entered the room to make sure I was all right, his shining hair creating a halo around his head, then came over to me, took my hand and stared at the intruder. Having finished this inspection, incapable of fear or hatred, he smiled at our prisoner.

With Sauveterre limping at his heels, my father finally made his appearance, buttoning his doublet, holding himself very erect, and managing somehow to look both tired and dashing, though with a countenance nowhere near as angelic as Samson's. "Where did this fellow come from?" he asked, indicating our intruder in a lighthearted way that seemed hardly to question his presence within our walls.

Rising, I quickly gave a reasonably honest though not entirely complete account of things, omitting his attack on my person since I didn't want him charged outright. This omission was greatly appreciated by my poor captive, as I could see from his different-coloured eyes, so gratefully attached to mine.

While I spoke, my father gradually descended from the happy cloud on which he'd floated in, and by the time I'd finished he'd managed to get both feet on the ground, and found an appropriately concerned and sombre aspect. For if this young rascal could get over our walls, across our moats and through our defences into the heart of our lodgings, others could as well, which would be much more serious.

"So, you rascal," said my father, remaining a good distance from him, but for very different reasons than la Maligou's, "what's your name?"

"Miroul."

"And where are you from?"

"A hamlet named la Malonie, near Vergt."

"Ah," sighed my father with relief, "from the north!" (The part of Périgord that had not yet been touched by the plague.) "Did you pass through any infected towns?"

"No. I avoided all the towns and villages. I lived and slept in the woods."

"How did you become a thief?"

"On the 25th of last month, a band of armed brigands came by night and killed my family," said Miroul, his colourful eyes brimming with tears. "They cut my father's, mother's, brothers' and sisters' throats and raped all the women. I hid in a haystack in the barn, and as soon as the devils were drunk I took this grappling hook and a knife and fled."

"So you became a brigand in turn?"

"Not completely," explained Miroul raising his head proudly. "I don't take anything from the shepherds or the peasants. I only steal from the chateaux. And never the same one twice. And only for my food. Three nights ago it was Laussel. Night before last, Commarque. Last night, Fontenac. And tonight, Mespech."

"Fontenac?" asked my father intrigued. "You managed to get inside the Château de Fontenac?"

"It was child's play," replied Miroul. "Of the four, Mespech was the hardest to get inside."

"And how do you do it, Miroul?"

"I cover my feet with rags, and my grappling hook too, and I scale the walls just before dawn."

"Why so late?"

"That's the hour the watchmen always fall asleep, feeling night to be almost over."

"What about the dogs?"

"The dogs smell me, lick me and never bark."

"It would be miraculous, if true!"

"My Lord," said Miroul, drawing himself up indignantly, "misfortune has made me a thief but not a liar. If you wish, I can show you how I got in, from the bottom of your surrounding wall right to your larder."

Jean de Siorac contemplated him for a moment and then said coldly, whether in jest or not, I could not tell: "That would put you to a lot of trouble since we're going to hang you afterwards."

Miroul shook his head more out of sadness than fear. "I'm not afraid of the rope, since I have no love for the life I lead. Solitude by day and villainy by night. My hunger is the only thing that keeps me going. But I'm sore troubled by my conscience, knowing that the Lord hates all abomination, and that He is great and in His power sees everything."

At this biblical quotation, Sauveterre pricked up his ears. "Miroul, are you a Huguenot?"

"Indeed so, and my deceased family as well."

After a pause, my father said: "Well, then, Miroul, I want you to demonstrate your skills. Untie him, Pierre." And turning to our servants, he added, "Sauveterre, my sons and I will go alone to watch. The rest of you shall remain here and breakfast. Let no one peek outside."

Poor Escorgol was so devastated with chagrin after he appeared in his window to hear my father's brief account of the episode that he was unable to say a word. Normally a ready tongue, all the poor watchman could do was to stick his little fingers in his ears and turn them like tops. "Escorgol," said my father, "close your window, lie down on your mat and listen carefully. This rascal is going to try to repeat his exploit."

"As you wish, My Lord," murmured Escorgol, flushed with humiliation, his brush of hair, normally so proudly plumed, limply falling into his eyes.

On my father's command, the group divided in two. Sauveterre, François and Samson, each armed with a pistol in his belt, accompanied Miroul outside the walls. I remained inside the enclosure with my father and the three mastiffs named, like their unfortunate predecessors who had been killed by the Gypsies, Aeacus, Minos and Rhadamanthus, complicated mythological names that had been Périgordized by our servants into "Acha" (hatchet), "Minhard" (delicate mouth) and "Redamandard" (he who asks for seconds).

Noiselessly, muffled as it was in rags, the grappling hook landed on the top of the north rampart, at the farthest point from Escorgol's watchtower. Miroul soon appeared, pulling his cord behind him, unhitched his hook and, running noiselessly along the top of the wall, reached a point on the eastern side from which he could toss his hook to the branch of a walnut tree a few toises away. Gripping the cord with both hands, he swung out, flying over the entire area where the traps were set and landing at the foot of the tree. Again he extricated his hook, and as our three mastiffs rushed up he fell full length on the ground, lying quite still and offering his neck, which they sniffed along with his face and whole body, and then they left off growling, stopped bristling and began wagging their tails. Miroul raised one hand and all of a sudden the dogs were competing with each other for his caress. This trick lasted for a few minutes, first while Miroul was lying down, then crouched, then on his knees and finally standing, slowing all his movements and accompanying them with gentling sounds to each mastiff. With the dogs now quieted and even licking his hand, Miroul rewound his rope into a bandolier, which he slung over his shoulder, and headed for the moat. He slipped into the water, swam noiselessly over to our wash house and scaled one of its pillars with remarkable agility, slipping onto the roof in the twinkling of an eye and scampering up to its highest point.

Next came the hardest part of all. Looping his rope again, he tossed his grappling hook, aiming for one of the metal clips that Sauveterre had had placed at intervals in the wall, just before the Gypsies' attack, to hold the torches in place. This was a small target and Miroul had to make several throws before succeeding in anchoring his talon. And the climb was not without its dangers and difficulties. The sconce being set nearly half a toise from the nearest crenellation, he had to hang by one hand with his feet braced in the wall, in obvious peril of losing his balance and falling into the water, then undo the hook and toss it again to the top of the curtain. Again he hit his mark.

"Let's go and get the others," said my father. "Miroul is already inside the chateau. And other than the dogs, I'll warrant that Escorgol heard nothing."

"Father," I asked, trotting along by his side, my throat tight with worry, "after such an exploit, you're not going to hang him are you?"

My father's expression hardened. "I'm not overjoyed about it, but yes, I must."

"But think of the service he's rendered Mespech by pointing out the holes in our defences: the walnut tree, the wash house, the sconces for the torches, and the larder window."

"That's all quite true. And yet I must hang him. He's a thief."

"A very petty thief. It has cost you a mere slice of ham to learn Mespech's weaknesses."

"He could have killed you."

"But he didn't try," said I, troubled to have to repeat this lie even for a good cause. "What's more," I added, pricked by my conscience towards a sort of half-truth, "even if he had, who could blame him? A rat bites when he's cornered."

"Of course, I understand. But he will die. He's a thief."

"If I were fifteen, and my family had been slaughtered and I'd become an orphan without a sol, wouldn't I become a thief as well?"

"You, perhaps, but not Samson."

I noted, not without a tinge of secret pleasure, that my father didn't even think to mention François. I added: "Samson, all right, Samson's an angel. But on my sixth birthday he stole a pot of honey to nourish me. Observe, Father, the enormous difference in retribution: a lashing for a pot of honey, and the rope for a slice of ham."

"'Tis a pity," said my father coldly, "that you're to study medicine. You'd make an excellent lawyer."

"May I go on, anyway?"

"Miroul will be hanged. But you may continue."

"My father, are we going to hang a lad who's bold enough and agile enough to succeed in getting into the Château de Fontenac by night without striking a blow? Who can tell if one day we won't need such talents?"

Here I hit the bull's eye, I believe. Yet my father did not yet consent to admit it. Trying to sound as gruff as possible, he countered, "I don't know where you get your obstinacy. Maybe from your mother."

"No, Monsieur, begging your pardon, but from yourself. What's more, I resemble you a lot. Everyone says so."

Now my father knew this very well, but I knew he enjoyed hearing me say it.

"Now that's an excellent *captatio benevolentiae* if I ever heard one!" he said, happy though not taken in by this appeal to the jury's beneficence. "But we're nearly out of time. You must conclude." And indeed, at that very moment, we were passing over the third drawbridge.

"Monsieur my father," I urged, "I was the one who surprised the thief. I cornered him and I captured him. Is it not my right to ask you the favour of giving him to me for my service, as Cathau has Franchou for hers?" My father raised an eyebrow, stopped short in the middle of the drawbridge and threw me a searching glance—to which I responded with my most innocent look.

"*In cauda venenum!*" he laughed. "You've saved your poison for the last word. Really, Pierre, you're more malicious than a woman, cat and monkey all in one!"

I turned to face him: "Well, Father, what about Miroul?"

"We'll see."

I threw myself in his arms and, standing on tiptoe, gave him kisses on both cheeks, tears streaming down my own. He returned my embrace vigorously, then, pulling away, all smiles, a glint of sunshine in his eye—just as when he'd arisen that morning—he grabbed me by the arm and pulled me along, nearly at a run, towards the common room.

Our servants were at breakfast around the great table, but seemed quiet and withdrawn. Imagine their astonishment when my father and I went into the larder and returned with Miroul whom, only minutes previously, they'd seen accompanying us out the door. Their surprise was prodigious. La Maligou began crossing herself convulsively, but scarcely had her mouth opened for her customary ejaculations than my father closed it up tight.

"That's enough tittle-tattle, Maligou! There's no magic here, but wonderful skill and agility. I saw it as I see you before me. Pierre, go lock Miroul in the north-east tower. The écuyer and I shall discuss his fate."

And so they deliberated. And Miroul, whom my father gave to Samson and me, helped out with the daily work at the chateau, much to the Siorac twins' relief, and is, to this day, in our service, having followed Samson and me to Montpellier, where we went to study, and later to the royal court in Paris, and through many and various adventures, as you shall hear in good time.

11

From 29th august 1563—the date of Miroul's magical appearance in our larder—until 28th May 1566—the day Samson and I, with Miroul as our valet, left Mespech for Montpellier—three years flowed by during which I put aside childish things and became a man. Not that I didn't already believe I'd achieved manhood at twelve, since in my view I had all of its privileges, from the short sword that hung at my side to the use I made of my nights. But the truth is that manhood is like the horizon, always seeming to recede the closer you get to it. And so we must be thankful to parliament for having established fifteen as adulthood, an imaginary boundary to be sure, but reassuring enough as long as one didn't look too closely. And yet some never really leave off their childhood habits, no matter how many years separate them from their nursemaids. Several years after quitting Mespech, I had the most extraordinary good fortune to find myself in a game of tennis with our sovereign, Charles IX, at the very moment they informed him of the assassination of Admiral de Coligny. To my extreme astonishment, overwhelmed as I was by the news of this odious crime, I saw the king pout, petulantly hurl his racquet to the ground and whine in the most childish tone: "Why won't they ever leave me alone?" Rather than being terrified by such news, which boded so ill for peace in the kingdom, the king was merely annoyed at having to leave off his game. Charles IX was then twenty-two years old, and the blood of our people, in which, goaded on by his mother, he was to revel, dirtied rather than seasoned him.

As for me, I could not afford to tarry too long, even at twelve, at being young: I was a younger brother. I knew that I would never inherit anything from Mespech, neither chateau, nor the les Beunes farm, mill, hill or vale, nor yet rich farmland or green prairie—nothing, except perhaps a plot of land big enough for my grave when I died, and God knows how little space we take up when we've breathed our last. I would owe my fortune and my estate only to my own efforts, and I repeated this hard truth to myself every day as I recited my Latin, my kings, my Bible and my medicine, always trying to understand the world from the place I occupied in it.

I believed then as I believe today that there is no greater maturity than that gained by the mind's honest apprehension of what we accomplish and what we endure. Among the events, great and small, which occupied my life during these three years before my departure, there were two that inspired such reflection, such astonishment and—the second of these events especially—such melancholy, that I want to share my distress with my readers, so they will not feel so alone in their own misfortunes. For if joy is shared among loving hearts, suffering often imprisons you in yourself, cutting you off, as if mutilated, from the company of others.

It was not until May 1564 that the plague disappeared, as suddenly as it had broken out, and the seneschal, the bishop and the two consuls, who had fled the city, returned to Sarlat along with the Présidial judges, the rich merchants and the doctors. Of the four surgeons who had stayed to care for the diseased, but one had survived. This Lasbitz, as he was called, was owed 600 livres by the city, but since the municipal finances were in ruins due to the loss of two-thirds of its taxpayers, it seemed he'd never be paid.

Moreover, the revolt was at its height in the outskirts of the city. Forcalquier had not died as he himself had predicted, nor had fully half of his band—another false prophecy—who now, heavily armed, served this foolish and bloody butcher-baron in his pursuit of an endless series of excesses. And thus the town was besieged by a kind of ongoing peasant uprising which the royal officers could do little or nothing to combat, since not a single soldier had survived the plague and there weren't a hundred sols in the town treasury to raise an army of mercenaries.

In this extremity, the city consuls sent messages to the nobility throughout the Sarlat region, begging them to raise their own militias and come to purge Sarlat of these desperadoes. Pressed by the Catholic bishop, the consuls were at first inclined to address this appeal only to the Catholic noblemen in the region, but the seneschal and La Porte were quick to point out that it was not right to exclude the loyalist Huguenots from this plea since some had already come to the aid of the city with loans and provisions of meat. Their opinion prevailed, and an appeal was addressed on the Catholic side to Fontanilles, Puymartin, Périgord, Claude des Martres and La Raymondie, and on the Calvinist side to Armand de Gontaut Saint-Geniès, Foucaud de Saint-Astier, Geoffroy de Baynac, Jean de Foucauld and the Baron de Mespech.

Not everyone responded, as you might expect, but it is not my intention here to name those who stayed quietly at home and those who gave of themselves in this combat. As life flourished anew after the terrible fear of the plague, they had to be either quite brave or quite resolute to risk their lives in a street fight against an entrenched band of brigands with nothing to gain from such an affair but unhappiness or the glory of serving the city.

Mespech set a condition for its participation: that my father be given the command of the entire army of volunteers—a rank that was accepted without any haggling, so great was Jean de Siorac's reputation as a general.

I could have predicted it: my father insisted on a tactic of secrecy and surprise. To cover his plan, he got La Porte to distract Forcalquier with negotiations, including an offer of the very lucrative privilege of collecting a toll at the la Lendrevie gate. But Forcalquier wanted more. He now wore ruffles, a doublet and a feather in his cap, and held court among his beggars and whores, cutting the figure of a nobleman. In his madness, he demanded that the city request of the king that he be ennobled, and La Porte, greatly amused by the foolishness of this stuffed shirt, played his part to the hilt, leading our man through endless mischief, raising fine points such as: "Could the king ennoble Forcalquier without granting a fiefdom? What fiefdom could he be given without dispossessing its landholder? Which nobleman should be dispossessed?" "Some stinking heretic," was Forcalquier's noble reply, who doubtless recollected that my father had heaved a full ninety livres of beefsteak right in his face.

As La Porte lulled the butcher-baron with empty promises, my father secretly set the date, time and details of our attack. Everything was centralized at Mespech. For a day and a night Coulondre Iron-arm left his mill, Jonas his quarry and Cabusse the le Breuil farm. From within the chateau itself, he enlisted his three rascals, Miroul, the Siorac twins, Marsal and Escorgol, leaving only Sauveterre and Faujanet to guard the chateau, to whose number Alazaïs was added. (My father said laughingly, well out of his brother's earshot, that "of the three men, she was the most agile.")

It was only on the eve of the date he had secretly set that my father drew me aside after dinner and whispered to me that I should get to bed early, for he would awaken me the next morning at three o'clock. I went straight to bed, and once the lamp was out, joined little Hélix in hers. Cutting short our usual games to proceed right to their concluding moment, I made ready to leave her when she grabbed me and held me tight, whispering: "So, my Pierre! Tomorrow's the day!"

I thought about the secret that would no longer be hidden from her at three when my father came to wake Samson and me, yet I breathed not a word of it.

"Don't go getting yourself killed, my Pierre," little Hélix went on in a hushed voice, but without relaxing her embrace. "All the time you were quarantined in the north-east tower I had love-thoughts about you."

"Love-thoughts, or just thoughts?" I asked, to tease her.

"Both," she replied but without her usual punishing pinch. "Both, Pierre," she repeated in a sad and trembling voice. "And if these brigands were to kill you, I'd die within the month."

"And what a loss it'd be for Mespech to lose such a dawdler," I teased, for the thought of my death unsettled me and I did not wish to sentimentalize it with women's talk.

"Oh Pierre, don't laugh," she cried, wet tears moistening my cheek. "I love you with a great love, as it is written in books. When I pray to Lord Jesus, it's you I see in my mind."

"Then it's an idol you worship and not God."

"This I know not, but it's a great and beautiful love I have for you, greater than any woman ever knew in Christian lands."

So saying, she hugged me very tightly with both her plump little arms. I could feel that little Hélix was opening her heart to me and, overcome with tenderness, I left off teasing and said, with equal gravity, "I too love you, Hélix, with a good and faithful love, and I will never in my life let you be scorned, suffer hunger or cold, nor be clothed in rags. And though I'm but a younger brother, I shall provide as best I can for all your needs and comforts to the end of my days and yours. This I witness and swear before the Lord God, amen."

"Oh, Pierre," she said. "You're good like Lord Jesus, but it's only friendship that you bear me."

"Indeed!" I replied with a very male abruptness. "Isn't that already a great deal?" Little Hélix sighed deeply and, without another word, began crying softly on my cheek until it was so hot, so bitter and so wet that I pushed her gently away and whispered, "Let me go, now, sweet Hélix. I must get some sleep for tomorrow."

She released me and I gave her a quick kiss on the cheek and went to slip into my bed, where Samson was already deep in his innocent sleep. To tell the truth, I felt a pang in my heart for little Hélix, who gave so much when I returned so little. How many times since have I felt this same pang and wished I could have lied a little better to the poor dear about these love-thoughts she had for me and wanted so much for me to share with her. But alas, who can foretell the future? Man is a silly creature and believes that the iridescent and speckled bubble dancing in the air before him shall be his for ever.

After the commotion in la Lendrevie, my father, sparing no expense, had chain-mail corselets made to fit each of his sons, and so it was, armed for war and fully helmeted, that we three appeared at the great table. The night was still dark and the eleven soldiers from Mespech—twelve with my father—sat down to a thick broth, all serious, quiet and a bit pale, so unlike harvest and wine-making days, when we were up before dawn all laughing and clamouring, our paunches filling with wine, soup, salt pork and wheat bread, our hearts warming to the tasks of the rather festive day to come. But today's harvest would be human heads and its wine the blood of our enemies, in a feast which our guests attended in great danger of losing an arm or their life, for it was said that Forcalquier's band were a resolute lot, fighting as though none expected to survive sword or bullet, ever since that plague itself had spared them.

Sensing this morose mood around the table, my father rose at the conclusion of the meal and, after a short prayer by Sauveterre, bade all of us sit down again and said: "My good people, I see worry gnawing at your spirits, wondering what may befall you in la Lendrevie. But have faith in the Lord God: He alone decides if the sparrow will drop from its branch or no. This is why, though nothing is more certain than our death, nothing is less certain than the day we shall die. Wisdom lies, then, in placing our fate in the hands of the Great Judge, and in setting our minds at rest." He paused, and then continued in a more lively tone: "As for me, I predict a happy outcome to our project! First because of our numbers. We are twelve. At the Château de Campagnac, where we shall assemble, there are ten more. Nine soldiers will arrive from Puymartin. Add it up: that makes thirty-one in all. This is more than we need to destroy a band of twenty beggars whose only strength lies in the weakness of the unarmed burghers of Sarlat. They'll shake like leaves in the wind when they see you, for these are but smithies, weavers and tradesmen, little practised in the arts of war. What's more, of the three groups meeting at Campagnac—I'll say it here because it's true—ours from Mespech is the most awesome. Cabusse, Cockeyed Marsal, Coulondre Iron-arm," continued my father, making their names resonate in his mouth as if he were having them trumpeted by fame, "fought for years in the legion in Normandy and again with me at Calais. My good cousins Siorac helped me in the defeat of the brigands of Fontenac at Taniès. Jonas killed three Gypsies with his infallible bow when they attacked Mespech. My boys, whom you see here, braved the angry mob at la Lendrevie without batting an eyelash. Escorgol has admittedly not yet fought, but he's strong enough to kill a bull with his fist, good with a blunderbuss and as valiant as any Provençal. As for our Miroul—for he is ours now— I'm counting on using his marvellous agility and audacity in a way I

343

shan't yet reveal," he said with a knowing wrinkle of his brow, "but it will count for much in the success of our endeavours."

Looking around the table, which was for this occasion adorned with our two chandeliers all shining with candles, my father arrested his gaze on each one of us in a very deliberate way, then said in a loud and sonorous voice: "My lads, I've ordered la Maligou to draw our best wine and to roast half a dozen of our best chickens, so that we can replenish our strength at noon when the battle is done. Then everyone can tell the others of his exploits, whose fame, I assure you, will resound for a long time in our villages." Raising his voice even more, he said: "And now, Maligou, Barberine, Franchou, seconds on soup for everyone! Let's mix in some wine!"

Such a rousing speech was half the battle, for our hearts were fortified by the taste of our future glory. A manly banter could now be heard around the table. The women, who had been standing fearfully in the kitchen doorway, now ran forward to serve our warriors, whose faces shone and eyes glistened from the warmth of the wine broth. My father's able speech had stiffened our backs and squared our shoulders in our corselets, whose steel gleamed proudly in the candlelight.

For my part, I was enjoying my share of my father's praise for having, along with Samson, "braved the angry mob at la Lendrevie without batting an eyelash", and I maliciously thought that his "rascals" did not include my elder brother, François, since this was to be the first time he would face the cannon. This thought made the blood course in my veins all the more, since little Hélix had poured me a hefty portion of wine along with her tender glances, and the grog was now going a bit to my head. My chest inflated in my brand-new armour, I looked confidently around me, already in a hurry to be under way. Alas, I hardly imagined, caught up as I was in the intoxication of war in which my father's words had swept us all up, what my mood would be a few hours later, "at noon when the battle is done".

We reached Campagnac by trails we knew so well that we and our horses could have followed them blindfolded, but luckily the night was not so black, the moon appearing from time to time between clouds. The lord of Campagnac was in bed, prey to a high fever, but his men at least were at the ready. Now nearly tripled in strength, our band set out immediately for Sarlat, my father riding in the lead with Puymartin, a handsome Catholic nobleman who had taken part in the defence of Sarlat against Duras, not so much from religious zeal as from a desire to prevent the city from being pillaged. He admired my father greatly, and, galloping behind him, I heard him remarking what a pity it was that Mespech led such an austere and isolated life, instead of participating in the brilliant parties the Catholic nobility of Sarlat were forever putting on for each other in their chateaux.

Fearing the noise from our cartwheels and our horses' hooves, we dismounted about a quarter of a league from Sarlat, entrusting our steeds and our rings to three men, to whom we recommended extreme vigilance. We made the rest of our way on foot, the band dividing into little groups which travelled at twenty toises from each other. Cabusse, Marsal and Coulondre marched well ahead of the others as scouts, their shiny armour hidden under black cassocks and their feet wrapped in rags. They were able to penetrate la Lendrevie and made their rounds without encountering a single sentinel, a sure sign that the butcher-baron, lulled by his negotiations with La Porte, had relaxed his guard. Cabusse came back to report this news to my father who, along with Puymartin, whispered their exhortations for the success of the enterprise, and sent men to guard each of the streets leading away from Forcalquier's headquarters, to cut off the retreat of the scoundrels once they'd been flushed from their lair.

This lair consisted of a large house which had formerly belonged to an order of nuns who, contrary to the priests of the bishopric, had remained at Sarlat during the entire duration of the plague to bring religious comfort to those afflicted with the disease. Death had rewarded their marvellous devotion, sparing but two of their order, whom Forcalquier had shamelessly evicted in order to take possession of their convent, whose furnishings he coveted. Surrounded by all his knaves, as well as a group of trollops whom our crow had told us about, Forcalquier wallowed in drink, feasting and lechery, and a strange cult devoted to the Virgin, whom, he claimed, had spoken to him in a dream.

Day was just breaking when, with the town surrounded by these small outposts—Samson, François and I, commanding one of these in a very narrow street affording a good view of the convent—the larger part of our band quietly occupied an abandoned house opposite the butcher-baron's lair. Miroul then crept up, his grappling hook in hand and cord around his neck, and wound in a bandolier over his shoulder some cotton packets which, as I later learnt, contained flower of sulphur. To my great astonishment, after having studied the facade of the convent, he began scaling it, using his hands and feet but no grappling hook of any kind, looking like nothing so much as a fly moving up the side of a wall. Reaching the roofing tiles, he ran in zigzag up the very steep roof until he reached one of the chimneys, caught hold of it and took out one of his cotton packets. He then struck his flint and lit the bag containing the sulphur, fanned it into a flame with his breath, then tossed it down the chimney flue. He did the same with each of the other packets whose number corresponded precisely to the number of flues, proof that my father had previously sent someone to spy out the place. This done, Miroul came down from the roof with such speed as to leave us breathless, and as soon as he had landed on the paving stones ran over to join my brothers and me. My father had assigned him this post in view of his age, planning to shelter him from the bitterest part of the combat once his rooftop mission was accomplished. If my father had hoped to smoke the fox out of his lair with these sulphur packets, the results did not meet his expectations. For after a tense period of waiting, all the windows of the place were opened simultaneously and the cotton packets thrown burning into the street and the windows shut again before any of our men could fire on the openings. Indeed, my father's orders had been to refrain from firing into the windows and to shoot at the brigands as they fled the smoke-filled building.

And so, in a matter of seconds, my father's plan was destroyed, and the advantage of surprise eliminated. Now the wind, blowing the sulphurous vapours towards the place where the larger part of our troop was stationed, began to create a serious problem, since the abandoned house where they were hiding had neither windows nor vents. Luckily there were doors at the rear of the building, and my father ordered his men to withdraw through them. This was an orderly enough retreat, yet Forcalquier, who had been watching from one of the convent windows, decided to seize the advantage of this moment for a sudden sortie before my father could redeploy his troops.

Forcalquier's band, divided into three groups, burst from their lair, partially hidden from view by the sulphurous smoke, and, trying to flee the town, ran directly into the small outposts my father had established. And since the brigands outnumbered and were better armed than the men at these posts blocking their way, there followed a series of confused and savage street fights—exactly the eventuality my father had hoped most fervently to avoid. The noise of blunder-busses, the clash of swords and shouts of rage or pain broke out on all sides of the town. For François, Miroul, Samson and me, posted in a passage so narrow that three men couldn't walk it abreast, our situation became quickly critical when we spied seven men armed with pikes rush at us on a dead run.

"Let's hide in the doorways," whispered François, "and let them pass."

Whereas from Samson or Miroul this advice would have seemed reasonable enough, from my elder brother I could not accept it. "No indeed!" I hissed. "That would be too cowardly." And taking up a position in the middle of the street, I drew the two pistols I had in my belt, fired and brought down two men. Miroul, who had but one pistol, also fired and wounded his man. But François, stunned by my bravery, remained frozen to the spot and Samson did not budge either, surely not from fear but rather from his usual laconic manner. As for the four remaining bandits, they let out ferocious shouts at seeing their comrades fall, and, looking truly immense in the narrow street, they rushed at us brandishing their pikes. I saw François draw his sword and drew my own, but as Samson stood ever immobile, no doubt forgetting his, I leapt to his side and shouted in his ear, "Your sword, Samson, your sword!" He drew it, at last, but distracted by his slowness, I failed to see the terrible pike blow aimed at me by one of our assailants. The point was stopped by my armour, but the shock was so great that I rolled to the ground, just managing to hold on to my weapon. The man, who seemed to me gigantic, was suddenly standing over me, brandishing his pike and shouting, "I'm going to kill you, little rascal!"

I rolled to one side just as the pike was planted in the unpaved alleyway. The absence of paving stones saved me, for in the time it took the man to unearth his weapon I'd leapt to my feet and given him so vigorous a thrust that the point of my sword traversed his body and entered the greeny loam of the mud wall behind him. It seemed to me that the handle of my sword tore itself from my grasp, and I just stood there unable to move, staring at this poor wretch, whose lung was pierced, and who, as though nailed to the wall, stared back at me, blood beginning to flow from the corners of his lips. I picked up his pike, but no one seemed to require my help. I didn't see what happened, but learnt afterwards that François, meeting his enemy's blow with his sword, had suddenly remembered the pistol in his belt, drawn it with his left hand, cocked it and fired. Miroul, who had the advantage of being armed with a pike, had used it with such dexterity that he'd wounded his assailant, who lay nearby moaning piteously. Alone, Samson still fought on, bleeding from one arm. He was pressing his advantage, but his natural goodness prevented him from concluding his affair. His adversary, seeing this and observing that he was alone against the four of us, turned tail and fled as fast as his legs would carry him down the alley.

"Fire, Samson, fire!" I cried. But Samson looked at me astonished through his big blue eyes without even making a gesture to draw his pistol:

"Why thould I? He'th running away!"

I answered not a word. The thought had just crossed my mind that I must pull my sword from the body of my assailant, and this thought deeply horrified me. Staggering slightly, my armour dented and dirtied by the mire of the alleyway where I'd fallen and rolled, I returned to the man whom I'd pinned to the wall. His eyes were closed, but he held himself erect, his face all a grimace, yet emitting no sound whatsoever as the two rivulets of blood continued to flow from the corners of his mouth. However, as soon as he saw me, or rather as soon as he felt me take hold of my sword handle, he opened his eyes and staring at me said, in a hoarse and raspy voice: "If it please you, Monsieur, wipe the point of your sword before pulling it out of me. I wouldn't want the dirt of the wall to enter my body."

Though this man had tried to kill me, this supplication filled me with an inexplicable chagrin. Calling Samson, I told him to hold the wretch by the shoulders, and going behind him I pulled him away from the wall to disengage the point of my sword. Then taking the white scarf I was wearing about my neck, carefully cleaned the point, marvelling at the delicacy of this peasant, who, even if he weren't to die from his wound, would surely be hanged.

Then, standing in front of the man, I told Samson to hold him up and, seizing my sword by the blade, pulled it vigorously towards me. The man let out a piercing cry, and, despite Samson's help, went limp. I tried to hold him up with the flat of my hand, but he vomited out such a flood of blood on my hand and arm that I instinctively retreated at the feel of this hot, viscous liquid, and, despite Samson's efforts, he fell, large and heavy, to the ground. Lying there, he made not a peep, but kept his eyes fixed on me.

The only sounds we could hear now were, in the distance, from various points in the town, muffled blunderbuss shots. My father burst into the alleyway on the run, his blood-soaked sword in hand, followed by Cabusse and Coulondre. "Well, my rascals," he called as soon as he spied us, "everyone healthy and happy?" And as we were slow to respond, all four too stunned by this carnage to speak, he caught sight of the dents in my armour and the blood on my arm and scarf and cried out in an anguished voice that went straight to my heart: "My little rascal, are you wounded?"

"No, father, this is the blood of my adversary. I am all right, but Samson is wounded, I think."

"Ith jutht a thratch," lisped Samson.

Without a word, my father seized his dagger, split his sleeve open and looked at the cut. "A slash," he reported, "but not very deep. It'll heal within a fortnight. All the same, when we get back to the wagon I'll wash it and bind it. So," he continued, but not quite with his usual gaiety, "you did good work, my boys." We could manage no other response than a mournful silence, and my father said in a much-changed voice, "Alas, we've defeated them, but we paid more dearly for it than I'd wanted. Campagnac lost a man, Puymartin two and there are a few wounded as well."

At this very moment, Jonas appeared at the end of the alley, running towards us. "My Lord!" he cried, "One of our men is gravely wounded from an ambush."

My father paled and, sword in hand, set off at a run, his three sons at his heels. Opposite what had been the butcher-baron's hideout, the Mespech wagon was drawn up and stretched out on its bed, livid, his eyes shut, his corselet shredded and bloody, lay Cockeyed Marsal. My father leant over him and, as he tried to turn him so he could unlace the thongs of his corselet, Marsal opened his eyes and spoke in a weak voice, but for the first and last time in his life without any stutter whatsoever, a whole sentence which years later none of our servants could recall without a knot in their throat and tears in their eyes: "If it please you, My Lord, don't touch me—it's no good, I'm going to die."

So saying, Cockeyed Marsal opened his mouth three times, prey to a terrible convulsion, and expired.

"I'll go to look to the wounded," said my father, tears rolling down his cheeks.

Our troops reported ten wounded in all, three of them from Mespech: Samson, his arm cut by a pike; Cabusse, his scalp grazed by a bullet which pierced his helmet and caused him to bleed like a bull; and one of the Siorac twins, his cheek slashed by a sword. Having given each a drink of a few drops of brandy, my father cleaned their wounds and bound them, trying, despite his own heavy heart, to cheer them up with his banter. "And which one are you?" he asked Siorac.

"I'm the brother of the other one."

"I know. Michel or Benoît?"

"Michel."

"Well, then, Michel, you're going to have a nice scar on your left cheek, just like the late Duc de Guise and me. From now on, thanks to this mark, we'll be able to distinguish you from your brother."

"But I don't want to be distinguished from my brother," moaned Michel tearfully, and Benoît wrapped his arm around his shoulders to console him.

Handsome Puymartin came up with a sad gait and sadder mien, to ask my father if he could place his two dead soldiers on our wagon. The slain man from Campagnac was added as well, while my father was finishing his attentions to the wounded, Puymartin standing by watching him pensively. "Don't you find it strange, My Lord, that you're as good at healing men as giving them your sword?"

"There's a time for everything under this heaven," replied my father. "A time to kill and a time to heal."

"I don't know that proverb."

"Ecclesiastes, chapter three, verse three."

"Huguenot," smiled Puymartin, "do you have a biblical quotation ready for every act of your life?"

"Of course. Isn't that the Word of God?"

"Well then, find me one for my present troubles: I've lost two men just when haying and harvest times are coming."

"There is a time to rip and a time to sew."

"But how can I sew when thread and cloth are lacking? How can I recruit two labourers to replace these poor fellows when famine and plague have swept away so many men that there's not a healthy man left without work in the whole province?"

"I've got enough worries about this myself to bite my nails right off," agreed my father. "We were already too few at Mespech." I noticed nevertheless that he did not offer to help Puymartin with his haying and harvesting as he might have done for a fellow Huguenot.

Cabusse brought up the wagon to where my father was attending to the last of the wounded. Looking very heroic with a bloodstained bandage encircling his head, his eyes flashing and his moustache bristling, this man said to my father in the same semi- familiar, semi-respectful tone my father had adopted with him: "My Lord, Forcalquier, who is merely wounded, asks to speak to you in private."

"What does this miscreant want with me?"

"I don't know, but he's very insistent."

"I'm coming."

"Be careful, Mespech," warned Puymartin. "The scoundrel may have a weapon hidden on him."

"My boys will search him." I followed along behind him, quite intrigued, as did Samson, but I noticed that François, as though troubled or distracted by his reverie, had pretended not to hear my father, and had gone up to Puymartin. Since this man was Diane de Fontenac's cousin, I judged he intended to ask about her.

Forcalquier was seated, leaning against the wall of the La Valade house, covered with blood, apparently wounded in every part of his body but his vital organs. I leant over him, my pistol at his temple, and opened his doublet (for he was wearing no armour) and searched him, but found no knife. Moreover his arms hung limp at his sides. When I had finished, he fixed his bulging eyes on my father and said in a firm voice:

"My Lord, I've three requests to make of you."

"Speak, traitor," replied my father, looking coldly at him from a toise away.

"In this house I'm leaning against are hiding two monks whom I chased from their lodgings. My prayer is to have one of them brought to hear my confession."

"You're not yet at death's door, though not so far from it either."

"True enough, but that's the point of my third request. My second is this: that you keep your soldiers from pillaging my house and shop for the money they'd find there. This money was honestly earned while I was still an honest man. I want my widow and children to have it."

"Granted," said my father. "And what's your third request?"

"My Lord, what will you do with me now, except hand me over to La Porte, who will lock me up, see to my wounds and then torture me, have me judged by the Présidial court and condemn me to death. I'll be eviscerated alive, my shaft and balls will be cut off, then I'll be drawn and quartered by four horses, hanged, cut down, my four members lopped off along with my head. And all this will," he said with some irony, "not be done without a hint of cruelty."

"You're a fine one to talk of cruelty, you scoundrel!" said my father indignantly.

"Excuse me, My Lord, 'tis true I've killed people, but I never tortured anyone. The Holy Virgin forbade it."

"Did not she forbid you to take the lives of your fellow men?"

"No, she never did," responded the butcher-baron with tranquil aplomb. "And I'll tell this to the monk to mitigate my crimes."

"What are you getting at with all this nonsense?" cried my father impatiently. "And what do you want from me, you bloody fool?"

Forcalquier lowered his voice: "After my confession I want you to kill me with your dagger."

"Absolutely not!" my father answered.

"Yes, you will!" Forcalquier replied. His black eyes twinkling with cunning, he continued, "My Lord, the city hasn't got a sol in its treasury and already owes you 1,000 écus. It'll never be able to compensate you for the expenses, risk and losses this expedition has cost you. But I can."

"You?!"

"I've got a cache of 3,000 écus, stashed in the monk's lodgings in a place only I know about, and so cleverly hidden that you'd never find it in a hundred years without my help."

"I'll think about it," replied my father abruptly and turned away. Samson and I followed him back to the wagon practically on the run to keep up with his long steps. Taking Puymartin aside, he whispered to him: "What do you think of this strange business? Obviously I don't like the barbarous tortures inflicted by our authorities. I'm of a mind, however, to refuse."

"And I to accept," answered Puymartin. "What do I care about the torture of this rascal on the public square in Sarlat? It will amuse the populace and titillate a few girls, but won't put a sol in my coffers, which have withered quite empty in this drought. I'm not so rich as you, Huguenot."

"It's not so much that we're richer," smiled my father, "but we spend less. Nonetheless I find this bargain repugnant… If news of it gets around…"

"Who will know if the butcher's dead? Let's divide this cache in three unequal parts. Twelve hundred for you, 1,200 for me and 600 for Campagnac, since he didn't come and didn't take the same risks. Mespech, will you ever reap so much from one dagger thrust?"

My father held out for a while longer, but rather in the manner of one who wants to be convinced. In such a delicate matter his Huguenot conscience, unlike the Catholic one, needed to be converted by degrees.

"My rascals," he said to Samson and me, pulling us to one side and putting his arms around our shoulders, "you must be silent as tombstones. Our honour is at stake."

"Certainly," I said, though somewhat troubled that my father had used the word "honour" for such an occasion.

"For my part," Samson sighed, "I'm glad this poor rogue won't be tortured the way he described to us."

*

The cache revealed and our booty stashed in a safe place, my father called the two monks and requested their offices. While they confessed Forcalquier, he stood apart out of earshot but positioned so that he could observe the butcher-baron's face. When they had finished, my father approached the elder of the two monks: "My brother, this man appears to be happy, as if at the minute of his death he were going to be borne by angels right up to Paradise and sit on the right hand of Christ."

"And of the Holy Virgin," said the monk, not without a touch of malice, "to whom he dedicated a fervent cult during his lifetime."

"Yes, I know. But whence comes his certainty? If it is by works that man gains salvation, as your Church teaches, by what works has Forcalquier been judged if not by his murders?"

This white-haired, bright-eyed monk studied my father: "'Tis true. Forcalquier is poor in works, but he's rich in faith. And as you know, My Lord, grace works in mysterious and impenetrable ways."

"So I believe," replied my father.

And as he said nothing further, the monk added: "Is he going to die? He looks ruddy enough despite his wounds."

My father shrugged his shoulders. "Would it not be an act of charity to expedite these beggars to their deaths rather than save them for torture, the gallows and dismemberment?"

"Indeed so," said the monk glancing quickly at my father, "if charity is really your purpose."

"Charity is one of my purposes," answered my father with an overly literal truthfulness that left me wondering whether I admired it or not.

The second monk, who, until that moment, had stood by, his eyes lowered and his hands in his sleeves in a most modest posture, now looked up and said sweetly, "And what may your other purposes be, My Lord?"

My father put his hands on his hips and laughed outright: "So, my brothers! We Huguenots don't sanction hearing confession, didn't you know? So great is your talent that you were going straightaway to hear a confession of my sins right out of my mouth, as if I had any…"

Then, in a more lively military tone:

"My brothers, time presses. Continue your offices to the wounded. I must tell you as I take my leave that I admire the devotion that kept you in Sarlat during the plague. Here is an expression of my admiration," he added, placing several écus in the hand of the elder monk, "if you will take alms from a heretic."

"No doubt," said this worthy monk as he whisked the money into his cape, "our Holy Church considers you a heretic, but as for me, I will judge you here below by your works" (here he smiled) "and I prefer to believe, *charitably*" (again he smiled) "that you are but a Christian gone astray into a path other than mine, but that we'll meet at the end of the road."

"I accept this augury," my father said gravely. And having said goodbye, he went off, his arm on my shoulder. When we were safely out of earshot, I said softly to him: "These monks were inside the La Valade house when Forcalquier made his requests to you. Maybe they heard. Is that why you greased their palms?"

"That's *one of my purposes*," smiled my father. "The other is that they are genuinely poor, truly charitable and completely devoted, none of which is much honoured by the bishopric."

When he arrived at the square where our wagon stood (with its funerary cargo of the four dead), my father called Cabusse.

"As soon as our horses are brought up, Puymartin, I, my sons and Coulondre Iron-arm are going into the city to meet with the consuls, who, as you've noticed, still haven't dared come out of their doors. While we're gone, Cabusse, you are to command here.

357

Your first duty is to finish off all the wounded brigands, beginning with Forcalquier. This done, if Campagnac's and Puymartin's men want to have their way with the butcher-baron's whores, just close your eyes to these excesses. But make sure no one from Mespech joins them. I tell you this as a Huguenot, but also as a doctor. Some of these willing wenches are infected with the Naples pox, I could see it at first glance. I realize that when men have taken a life they seem to want to make one, which is the reason for all the rape when cities are conquered. But since you've got a beautiful and gracious wife, Cabusse, don't go poking around, as my late wife use to say, in places I wouldn't touch with the end of my cane."

"Amen," replied Cabusse, pulling on his moustache. "It shall be done, and *not* done, as you have ordered."

The consuls, who had gathered in the city hall with the seneschal and La Porte, complimented my father and Puymartin on such an admirable and bold enterprise, quickly adding, however, that as the city was financially ruined they could never adequately reward this brilliant action. Puymartin responded that the glory they'd won was enough, and my father, made a profound reverence but said nothing. La Porte enquired whether any prisoners had been taken.

"There are none," my father answered. "Our soldiers have dispatched every one of them."

"'Tis a pity," mused La Porte. "If we'd had a prisoner, just one, we might have put him on the rack and forced him to tell us where we could find the treasure that the butcher-baron accumulated from the tolls he exacted at the la Lendrevie gate."

Somewhat troubled by this speech, I glanced at my father, but he remained impassive.

"How is it," La Porte continued, "that there's not a single survivor from this entire heinous gang?"

My father still remained silent but Puymartin said, frowning:

"Because of our losses, our soldiers were greatly embittered against these brigands."

"I see," said La Porte, obviously dissatisfied.

And yet he too complimented us generously, though not so effusively as the seneschal, who, as the highest officer of the city, spoke last, assuring us that he would write to the governor of Périgord and that the governor would write to the king. After which, he embraced both my father and Puymartin, and François and Samson, but he forgot to embrace me, doubtless because I was so filthy and bloody. He was a tall gentleman, entirely clad in pale-blue satin topped by a large, exceptionally white ruff, an exquisitely trimmed beard and curly clean hair. He was so pulverized with perfume that with every gesture—and he made many—he fairly embalmed the entire group.

The two consuls spoke in Périgordian dialect, sprinkled here and there with a few French words; La Porte, as becomes a royal officer, used a French somewhat mongrelized with provincial expressions. But the seneschal, as Monsieur de L. had, spoke pure Parisian French, in a high voice, his articulation short and pinched, his mouth opening scarcely wider than the slot in a church alms box.

As Puymartin and my father were leaving the hall, the populace, who had been waiting outside, pressed up around them with shouts of acclaim. My father, all smiles, leapt nimbly into his saddle, followed by his sons and Puymartin and Coulondre Iron-arm, who with his one arm had held our horses' reins during the meeting inside and responded not one single word to the peasants around him who were clamouring for an account of the battle. Throughout Sarlat there was great joy and relief at the realization that the butcher-baron could no longer tyrannize the city, and all the more so since many young rogues within the town had threatened to join up with him and daily made insults and jokes on the townspeople like lackeys and pages at carnival time.

Making our way through this crowd, our little troop reached the la Lendrevie gate, but just as we were passing under it, my father noticed a man who was weeping as he drove by on a little cart drawn by a red donkey. Telling Puymartin to continue on without him, my father retraced his steps, the rest of us at his heels. The red donkey stopped when it saw its way blocked by our horses, and my father said, "Good day, friend! How goes it? Not well, if I'm to judge by your tears. What's your name?"

"Petremol."

"I knew a Petremol from Marcuays who tried to cure his rheumatism by bathing in the ice-cold waters of the fountain of St Avit."

"That was my cousin."

"And I knew another Petremol from Sireil, whom I almost hanged last year for stealing a sack full of hay from my fields."

"He's also my cousin."

"Well, then, Petremol, I feel like I know you because I know your cousins. And where might you be headed with your cartful of skins and pulled by your red donkey? Don't you know the Norman saying, 'As treacherous as a red donkey'?"

"The only traitor I know," Petremol wept, "is my own destiny, which oppresses me, and not this good beast who only wants to do my bidding. If you'd hanged my Sireil cousin last year, My Lord, I'd envy him. For I know you as well."

"You have a very heavy heart, Petremol, and yet you're not poor as far as I can tell, for you've got a donkey, a cart and lots of skins, as well as your trade, for you're a tanner or harness-maker if I'm not mistaken."

"I'm both at once," Petremol replied, "and for the last year I've been working my trade for your cousin Geoffroy de Caumont in his Château des Milandes. But alas, with the plague ended, I'm heading back to my home at Montignac where my wife and children were

carried off by the disease, and my house was burnt by the consuls
to disinfect the place."

"Then they owe you damages."

"Which I'll never collect, since the city's ruined. But what do my
lodgings matter when there's nobody to put in them, no wife, nor
any of my four beautiful children not yet ten years old, as pretty as
this fellow," he said pointing to Samson, who by this time was also
in tears over this story. And, indeed, on second glance, Petremol, his
hair as red as his donkey's, was a handsome enough fellow, despite
his defeated manner, his unkempt beard and the suffering that lined
his face.

"And where are you headed now?" my father asked.

"To hang myself, if it weren't for my donkey who loves me and
leads me where he will. He's the one led me here, for he had a
mate here once. But at Sarlat, just as at Montignac, no one needs a
harness-maker any more, since all the horses got eaten during the
plague. And my donkey can't find his mate: she must have been
eaten as well."

"Well then, Petremol, tell your noble donkey to bring you to
Mespech. We've got horses that are very much alive, an abundance
of pelts that need tanning, saddles to make and harnesses to repair,
and for you, if you like it, a hearth, a bowl and a bed, lots of company and even a jenny for your donkey."

And without pausing for acceptance or thanks, my father turned
bridle and rode away so quickly that I found myself at the rear of
the company, side by side with Coulondre, who looked at me and
cleared his throat as if he were going to say something. I was quite
surprised and, trotting along with him, looked at him apprehensively,
for I knew that he never opened his mouth without breaking your
heart. "So," he intoned finally in his most funereal voice, "we've
won again. One's left us and another's arrived. And this one, who's

worth his weight in gold, neither stutters nor is cross-eyed. God be praised."

Our women greeted us with wails and lamentation when we crossed the last drawbridge into Mespech, Marsal lying dead on the wagon. The Brethren ordered la Maligou and Alazaïs to remove his armour, clothes and boots and to wash his bloodstained body and wrap him in a shroud before laying him on a bed in the room of the north-east tower where the Siorac twins had been quarantined. As was the custom, the shutters were closed and an oil lamp lit. La Maligou, who had already dined, took the first watch. But the dead man was soon visited by Faujanet, who came to measure him for a coffin. Having an ear to fill with her gossip, la Maligou complained in a hushed voice that her masters' religion prevented her from placing a crucifix in the dead man's hand. "A lot of good that would do him now!" hissed Faujanet between clenched teeth, la Maligou's remark disturbing his own mourning.

For this was the second coffin he'd had to make since his arrival at Mespech (the first being for my mother). Greatly troubled inside, he began to wonder if, by virtue of the power of numbers, he wouldn't soon be making a third. "But don't you see? It's still the custom," whined la Maligou, who couldn't imagine how Cockeyed Marsal would ever get up to heaven without a crucifix in his hands.

"What's certain," said Faujanet, continuing his thoughts out loud as he took his second measurements of the body, "is that if I'm the third one to go, it won't be me who builds my coffin." Faujanet seemed suddenly calmed by his own reasoning, and pushing his idea a bit further, found it a reassurance for his own future; turning his attention to the dead man, he began to pity his fate. "Poor Marsal, who was alive only just this morning and had such a good appetite for his soup." He said "poor Marsal" and not "Cockeyed Marsal" out of reverence for the dead, whose closed eyelids would never open again.

"Poor Marsal," echoed la Maligou, "when I think how brave he was, how good a worker, how he was sober as Jesus and as little a womanizer (a fault in a living man and a virtue among the dead) as you could find. Our masters will bury him dry-eyed and puritanical like they did Madame, according to their new religion."

"When I think," continued Faujanet, "that poor Marsal not long ago refused flat out, as I did, to become miller down at les Beunes, because of the danger of being killed by roving bands of brigands. And here he is all stiff and cold, and Coulondre Iron-arm working at the mill, drinking his fill and every night leading his little Jacotte to the mounting blocks. Not that I envy him: I don't hold much with women, as you know, Maligou."

"Alas, there's no holy water either," moaned la Maligou, "which my masters says is idolatrous. But it's still the best thing to keep the seventy-seven demons of hell away from the deceased."

"If I didn't have a gammy leg," mused Faujanet, "instead of staying to guard the chateau with the écuyer and Alazaïs, my masters would have taken me to Sarlat, and I might be lying here, and not building your coffin, my poor Marsal. Which is proof," he whispered to the corpse, "that it's better to have a limp than be cockeyed."

All the while, in a room in the south-west tower, Barberine was busy washing away the filth and blood as I sat in a steaming tub, though I'd assured her I was now man enough to wash myself. "Not on your life, my little yellow beak, for who would wash your back?" I was too sad to resist further and gave myself over to the caresses and scrubs she lavished with those large hands, which rubbed good Mespech soap over my whole body. "Sweet Jesus," Barberine said admiringly, "look at these little rascals who've grown up right beside me and I didn't even notice it. This little Pierre whom I nursed when I was only eighteen, and now look at him! Thirteen and almost a man! Big shoulders, his chest's all filled out, his thighs as hard as iron and hair growing everywhere and prancing like a stallion."

"Alas," I moaned, "I don't much feel like prancing."

"All the same," said Barberine, "they tell me you did well in the battle, killing three of those rascals, two with bullets and a third with your sword."

"Yes, but the third one," I muttered, hanging my head, "I had to pull my sword out of him and he vomited blood all over me."

At this, Barberine sighed, but said nothing. She poured a vat of hot water over my head and shoulders to rinse me, told me to get out of the tub and stretch out on the bed, where she began to massage me with all the cares and tenderness she'd showered on me as a child, fondling and caressing me, and with her deep singing voice, spreading a litany of sweet nothings over me: "My sweet, my pretty little rooster, God's little pearl, my fresh little heart."

Fresh though it may have been, my heart was still heavy with lugubrious thoughts, and in such a flood of tenderness it couldn't contain itself any longer. I clung to Barberine and, burying my head in her beautiful breasts, burst into sobs. "There, there, my pretty!" calmed Barberine, leaning against the wall and cradling me in her bountiful arms.

But the more she cradled me with her arms and her coaxing, kissing my forehead, the more I gave in to my tears and a deep sadness. I would have gone on sobbing a lot longer had not little Hélix appeared at the door of the winding staircase—where my mother had once appeared in Barberine's absence to bid me goodnight—her black eyes flashing in anger.

"Monsieur Pierre," she broke in rudely, "My Lord is waiting on you for dinner."

I stood up, dried my tears, put on the clean clothes Barberine had laid out for me from the chest, and followed little Hélix down the winding staircase. At the last step, out of her mother's earshot, she turned, stared at me, her eyes blazing, and hissed in a low voice filled with fury:

"You big sissy, aren't you ashamed to be crying like a baby on the bosom of an old lady!"

"An old lady!" I replied indignantly. "What a way to speak of your mother! She's barely over thirty! And who gave you permission to call me a sissy!"

"I'll call you what I wish! Big sissy, if I wish. Coward, if I wish. Crybaby, if I wish!"

"Well," I answered hotly, "this is for all your kind wishes!" And I slapped her hard on both cheeks.

"Oh, my Pierre," she cried, less terrified by my blows than by the coldness of my stare.

"Your Pierre isn't yours any longer," I said haughtily, "and tonight I won't come you know where. Not tonight or any other night."

Whereupon I turned coldly away and walked briskly to the common room, distracted for the moment from my sombre thoughts by my quarrel with her.

All the combatants were seated around the table, but nothing could have been further from the warm feast which that very morning before daybreak my father had foreseen for us: "Everyone can tell the others of his exploits, whose fame, I assure you, will resound for a long time in our villages." Instead, everyone was eating, but no one made a sound, and not even the chickens roasted on the spit over a fire of vine branches, nor the selection of succulent meats, nor even Mespech's best vintage wine could loosen our tongues or lighten our spirits. For the deceased was still with us as he had been this morning, but now he lay in the north-east tower, a gaping hole in the middle of his body. Cabusse and Coulondre Iron-arm, who had known Cockeyed Marsal twenty-four years, since 1540 when he had entered the Norman legion as a captain, unabashedly wept as they ate, their noses in their plates. They hurried through their dinner, swallowing everything without tasting anything, and before the meal was over asked permission from the Brethren to withdraw, one to the le Breuil farm, the other to the les Beunes mill so they could reassure their wives. Permission was scarcely granted before Jonas requested the same: "Sarrazine is pregnant," he explained, "and is worried by my absence."

Those three having left, the mood was even darker than before. My father tried to get each of us to tell what he had done in the battle with the brigands in la Lendrevie. We obeyed him, but they were sad tales, since neither our hearts nor our pride were in it. During the conversation that followed my father's request, little Hélix, who was serving at table, but whom I'd avoided looking at even once, sidled up to me to fill my goblet and whispered in my ear:

"My Pierre, if you won't smile at me I'm going straightaway to throw myself down the well."

To which I replied in a whisper: "Silly flirt, you'll spoil our drinking water."

Still, I smiled at her, though only on one side of my face so that she'd know that I'd only halfway pardoned her.

My father, seeing our servants' dispiritedness, was too polite to insist further and hurried to finish his dinner, which, though conceived as a victory feast, resembled a wake—though no doubt had Marsal died of a sickness the guests would have been a good deal livelier (wine aiding, of course). But from their discomfort, their furtive glances, their persistent sadness, it was clear that what troubled them was that this death could have been avoided and that my father had advanced his own glory and secret fortune (but how could our servants have known of it?) at the expense of his servants.

At la Lendrevie, my father had explained to Cabusse that the raping that followed the fall of a city is due to the fact that when a man takes a life he wants to make another one. Besides the fact that little Hélix had secretly learnt from la Maligou about herbs and "where to put them", I didn't feel much like giving her anything at all that night but asking instead for tenderness and comfort in her sweet embrace. But she didn't see things my way, and by means of tickling and caresses finally got what she wanted, though only once. And when shortly afterwards she began again, I told her rudely to stop her carrying on and hold still, and if possible to keep silent, for my heart wasn't into such games.

"My Pierre," she asked (for she wasn't able to hold her tongue for very long), "what makes you so sad?"

"Everything about our expedition," I said, "from the beginning to the end."

"Marsal's death?"

"That too."

"Killing three men?"

"Yes. Especially the third, when I had to pull my sword from his body."

She wanted to continue, but I told her to stop her questions and her sneaky movements, and to leave me to myself. Which she did, but being unaccustomed to so much silence and immobility she went straight to sleep.

Her body felt sweet and warm in my arms and wholly mine as she slept. How could I ever have told her that what made such a knot in my throat wasn't Cockeyed Marsal, or my peasant stuck through and through, but rather the strange commerce between Forcalquier and my father, which made my hero seem less great?

12

ABOUT TWO MONTHS before our expedition against the butcher-baron in la Lendrevie, Catherine de' Medici and Charles IX had decided that, with peace now restored (though in fact it was only half restored), they would take an extraordinary tour on horseback of the entire kingdom. This cavalcade was to last two full years, during which the regent and the young sovereign were preceded and followed by their men at arms and accompanied by so many ministers and royal officers that it seemed as if they wanted to transport the entire Louvre palace with them. Such a procession greatly impressed their subjects, who, to be sure, had never before seen so much silk nor so much gold on so many of God's creatures. It also greatly disheartened them, for everywhere this magnificent company travelled they left behind neither meat nor egg nor grain of wheat, the valleys in their wake being so devastated that they looked like a forest after an infestation of may beetles.

In the midst of this travelling court, coloured like so many spring flowers in their bright clothes, were eighty maids of honour, chosen for their beauty, and making a radiant retinue around Catherine de' Medici. Strangely enough they were called the "flying angels". And yet however one might understand the word "flying", they lifted up nothing other than young men's hearts. And far from flying through the air like angels, they descended, when required, to the lowest favours with men in order to serve their mistress's designs.

They could flush out an evil intention, surprise a plot, bend a will. Secret agents, state spies, Machiavellis in petticoats, their tread was not so light as it was political, and they paid for confidences with their ravishing bodies, consenting to serve as the sumptuous means to ends only the queen mother could know. One of these "angels" visited the Prince de Condé in prison after the battle of Dreux and so blinded him with her dazzling charms that he signed without reading the unfortunate Edict of Amboise, which Calvin and Huguenots of conscience so bitterly reproached him for.

Our allies, after so much torture and murder, expected only the worst and always doubted appearances, wondering about the ultimate goal and secret purpose of this splendid cavalcade over the roads of France, especially given the terrible heat of 1564, the kingdom scarcely back on its feet, despite the charming ditty of Ronsard, for whom:

> *The Frenchman is like the green willow tree,*
> *The more it is cut the more we will see,*
> *Many new branches and greeny bright leaves*
> *Taking vigour from every new hurt that it grieves.*

Beautiful verses, though somewhat dishonest and flattering, France being still badly beset with mutilations from the civil war, from famine and from the plague. Yet despite this ruin and the thousands of corpses, who were swept out of the way just in time to let the queen mother pass, Catherine insisted on showing both the kingdom to Charles IX and the young king to the subjects over whom he held sway. Or perhaps, as she went from city to city lending an ear to the Huguenots here and to the Catholics there, hearing all their reciprocal complaints, her intention was to pacify her subjects by an outward show of equality.

It was all highly suspect. Not that there weren't any concessions to our cause. Charles IX occasionally scolded parliament and the governors for excluding Huguenots from affairs of state. He gave permission to the reformers in Bordeaux to refrain from decorating their houses for Catholic processions, and dispensed them in the courts of justice from swearing by St Anthony. And yet, as the royal cavalcade progressed from town to town, additional restrictions were tacked on to the Edict of Amboise, which was already bad enough. In June the king forbade reformed merchants from opening their shops on Catholic feast days. In that same month, he outlawed Huguenot religious services from anywhere the king happened to be. In August, he enjoined all judges from admitting to their chateaux any reformers other than their own vassals and servants.

The Brethren sought in vain any firm principle in the king's inconstancy, which seemed dictated merely by circumstance or personal pressures. The king, who was only fourteen, yet seemed more childish than his age, had no will other than the regent's. The niece of Pope Leo X, Catherine had inherited her uncle's high forehead, bulging eyes and deep scepticism. Foreign to religious passion and almost to faith itself, she neither hated nor loved the Reformation: it was but a pawn on the chessboard of France which she could play according to the moment or need, saving it or sacrificing it as she wished.

In mid June the Brethren found new reasons to grieve. A courier brought news that Calvin had died on 27th May in Geneva, worn out by his great work. The Reformation had changed the face of the world. Through his enlightened writing, his often improvised yet clear and carefully chosen words, by the firmness of his doctrine and the integrity of his character, by the ardent proselytizing which inspired his many letters, which touched so many people, by the democratic organization he had given to the churches, by the inspired pastors he had taken time off from his many duties to train, he had spread the reform from Geneva to Lausanne, on into France, England, Scotland, the Netherlands, Hungary and Palestine.

"Calvin is dead," wrote Sauveterre in the *Book of Reason*, "but his work will live on."

"I believe it will, too," added my father, "and yet our fiercest ordeals are yet to come. In this strange cavalcade of the regent and the king across the kingdom, I think I can detect a gathering of clouds which, sooner or later, are going to open up over our heads."

At the end of June, when the grass had grown tall in our fields and the summer heat threatened to dry it out too fast, my father sent me to the le Breuil farm and the quarry to seek Cabusse and Jonas to help with the haying the next day. I went alone on my black pony, Samson having sprained his ankle in a fall from his horse the day before. Not finding Jonas at his quarry, I set out to look for Cabusse, and caught sight of him, hair beginning to grow back where he'd been wounded, making a fence so that he wouldn't always be having to watch his flock of sheep.

"An expensive project," I laughed as I dismounted, leaving Accla to graze freely.

"Not so much expense really," answered Cabusse, pulling on his moustache, and happy for an excuse to pause in his work. "The fence posts come from my own woods. Anyway, I'm rich again since the baron gave me thirty écus for the expedition to Sarlat."

"Thirty écus! Were you the only one to get paid?"

"Oh no. The baron gave twenty écus to Jonas, twenty to Coulondre Iron-arm, twenty to Escorgol, twenty to Benoît and twenty-five to Michel, since Michel was wounded. But Michel said he wouldn't take more than his brother, and returned five écus."

"And you got thirty?"

"Five more than the others because I was wounded and five

because I was in command." After a moment of reflection, I said, "This booty has troubled my conscience. Where did it all come from if not from the purses of the people of Sarlat who had been paying tolls to the butcher-baron?"

"Well, but who liberated the people of Sarlat from the claws of this scoundrel? Booty is a right of war. And the liberation of Sarlat was well worth this little tax on the fat burghers who stayed quietly at home in bed while we were fighting."

"So that's how you see it, Cabusse?" I said astonished. "And what about killing all the wounded?"

"An act of mercy for those who were caught. If I'd been one of those good-for-nothings condemned to the worst tortures, I'd have paid to be killed."

And that's just what Forcalquier did, I thought. But I said nothing. Cathau had just appeared in the sun at the foot of the meadow, all fresh in a red petticoat bordered in blue, her bonnet perched on her head, her feet bare in the new grass and carrying a pretty little baby in her bare arms.

"Good day, Cathau!" I cried with a playfulness I'd learnt from my father, though I felt a pang in my heart, for she'd served for so long as the chambermaid to Isabelle de Siorac that I could never see her without thinking of my mother and the medallion I wore about my neck.

"Good day, Master Pierre!" she returned. And added eagerly, and not without a hint of malice: "What news of Mespech? I hear Franchou is quite pregnant."

"Who will ever keep a woman's tongue from wagging?" said Cabusse unhappily.

"Well it did seem to me," I confessed "that Franchou was indeed getting a bit stout. But as for the cause, I couldn't say. You'd have to ask my father, who is a doctor."

"Well said, Master Pierre!" laughed Cabusse, as Cathau turned away, confounded by my response. But she had also turned in order to nurse her baby, since, unlike Barberine, she wouldn't show her breast in public, Cabusse being too jealous.

"Anyway," I said, "our plan failed and we lost a man."

"Hey, Master Pierre," said Cabusse straightening up, a hand on his hip and the other stroking his moustache. "Plans in war are like thrusts in fencing. The best cogitated of 'em" (he favoured this word "cogitated" lately having learnt it from my father) "the best prepared and the best executed sometimes get parried."

"But Cockeyed Marsal is dead."

"He died in combat. It's the best death and comes quickly. It's a pity for us, but lucky for him never to know the sweat and suffering of a stinking sickbed."

"Hey! Don't talk about such things, Jéhan Cabusse!" said Cathau, turning slightly so that I just barely caught a glimpse of part of her breast. "Those are foolish and sorrowful words and they give me the shivers."

"If Master Pierre weren't here, I'd quickly change your shivers into frissons!" joked Cabusse with a laugh. "But I'm not interested in sorrow. And the baron did a worthy thing in telling Faujanet to make a coffin out of chestnut to bury his old soldier. That's a lot of expense for a servant when you think about it. I know many a gentlemen in the region who has buried his mercenaries right in the ground just sewn up in sacking."

"Thank God," I said modestly, "the Brethren are rich."

"But they've got their hearts in the right place as well," said Cabusse. "And remember what Calvin said: 'Gold and silver are worthy creatures when they are put to good use.'"

This quotation hardly surprised me since Cabusse had gone from a lukewarm Catholic to a fervent Huguenot, I mean deep down in the grain of his being, though he was still the same fun-loving, joking Gascon on the surface.

"Well, I must be on my way," I said. "Otherwise Accla will eat your whole field like a grasshopper in wheat."

"There's no lack of grass on my le Breuil farm," Cabusse proclaimed proudly.

"Here, Accla!" I called. But Accla, a few steps away, her reins tied to her withers, entirely absorbed in her feast, carefully selecting the sweetest and most savoury grasses, leaving the less appealing ones to the sheep who would come after, pretended not to hear me, her eyelids batting hypocritically over her oblique eyes.

"Accla, come here!" I called more sharply, striking my boot with my whip. Pulling out a last mouthful of grass with a sigh, Accla remembered her manners and, trotting over to us with her gracious and lofty gait, head held high, her mane well brushed, she came seeking caresses from each of us, making a friendly "pfffut" and even giving a little lick to the baby.

"She's a beauty," said Cabusse. "Did you ever see such a gorgeous horse come out of such a wicked place?"

"Master Pierre," Cathau said, "you should breed her. It's time."

"I know," I agreed, "leaping into the saddle. "The problem is finding a stallion of her same breed and colouring. Goodbye, Cathau. See you tomorrow, Cabusse!"

"See you tomorrow! At daybreak!"

Unlike the terrible drought of 1563, when Mespech had very nearly hanged Petremol's cousin for stealing grass from our fields, 1564 was a year of abundant hay, especially for those, like the Brethren, who were smart enough to cut it and get it in early, for there were heavy rains at the beginning of July, followed immediately by a stifling heatwave which dried the harvests to perfection but must have seriously inconvenienced—we often joked about this—all the precious courtesans dressed in silk who were travelling the highways and byways of France with the king.

During the haying, our Petremol, leaving off his saddle and harness work, proved he was a good field hand, taking just the right cuts with his scythe, moving through his swathe in a straight line, keeping the general rhythm set by the lead cutter and moving at the same pace as his neighbours. And when it came time to pause and sharpen the blades, he put aside his sorrows and got into the spirit of the day, catching on quickly to the jokes and responding in kind, brushing off cracks about the colour of his hair with easy laughter—the kind of laughter that relaxes a man and gives him the heart to attack his work without complaint. For men are a lot like women in their work: able to get pleasure from their tongues to compensate for the pains of their labour.

In the evening of the last day of haying, the Brethren retired early because of the many long days in the saddle riding watch over the hayers. Samson and I stayed up with the servants and tenant farmers as they sat around the big table, all the windows open wide to the summer evening, and two fingers of plum brandy in their cups. When la Maligou finally sat down among us with heavy sighs and a series of *"Aïma! Aïma!"* to indicate that, even if she hadn't been out haying like Alazaïs, she'd been slaving like the damned over our supper, she looked over at Petremol and said with utter seriousness: "My poor Petremol, hair redder than yours I've never laid eyes on."

Petremol, who thought it was another joke, just smiled and said, "Red hair I've got and so has my donkey, but a braver beast than him or me I've never laid eyes on either." The rest of us smiled at this, but not la Maligou.

"I'm not joking," she said gravely. "It's a great rarity for a man to have such red hair."

"Hey, Maligou!" called Cabusse, Cathau's head leaning on his shoulder and their baby asleep in her arms. "Don't go getting fooled! Petremol's no Gypsy captain!"

"And he hasn't got a magic wand!" Escorgol chimed in, always quick on the uptake. Everyone laughed, and Alazaïs, disgusted by this turn of the conversation, got up from table and left without a word to anyone, her neck stiff and her back straight. As soon as the door had closed behind her, Escorgol put in:

"My friends, now that we're alone, I've got a riddle for you! Cathau! Jacotte! Sarrazine! A riddle!" And he paused for effect. "What gets bigger when a woman's hands touch it?"

"Dirty old lecher!" said la Maligou.

"You're the lecher to think such dirty thoughts!" Escorgol replied. "Let's see, what gets bigger when women's hands touch it? It's a… It's a…" And since everyone was laughing but no one would venture a guess, Escorgol said triumphantly, "It's a distaff!"

Everyone laughed uproariously at this riddle, and Cabusse observed amiably, "That's a good jest our Provençal has brought us from his Provence. But, my friends, don't laugh too loudly or we'll wake the captains."

"You may wake one, but not the other, I'll wager," whispered Cathau.

"Peace, woman, hold your tongue!" snapped Cabusse. At this everyone lowered their eyes and there was not the least smile, except perhaps secretly.

"A distaff, a distaff!" said la Maligou, putting on airs. "You can't talk seriously with such men. Always hot in the kidneys and tight in the crotch!"

"Who are you to complain?" said Jonas, who still resented la Maligou for her evil gossip about his wife. "Sarrazine," he added, "since it seems you were a wolf, go bite this fat bawd on the arse and draw out some blood since she's got too much of it."

"*Aïma! Aïma!*" cried la Maligou, genuinely scared and pulling her fat body into a ball on her stool as she rolled her eyes. We all gave a great belly laugh at her terror, but none harder than Petremol, who got tears in his eyes, though perhaps from gratitude as much as hilarity, since he was working his trade again, surrounded by good and jolly companions who already accepted him as one of their own. Poor Petremol, who tried so hard not to think of his wife or his four little ones, save that at table he always sat next to Samson. Everyone knew very well why, of course, and Samson most of all, angel of mercy that he was, who always went out of his way to talk to him and even visited his tannery during the day to ask him about his work.

Cabusse, who always played the master in the absence of the Brethren, especially now that his house had a spiral staircase which gave it a lordly look, raised his hand and said: "Friends, let Maligou speak! She wants to tell us about the rarity of red hair."

"But redheads aren't so rare," objected Michel Siorac, whom we could now recognize by his scar, at least when he turned his head to the left.

"Samson's also got red hair," echoed Benoît.

"No, no!" cried la Maligou. "It's not the same at all! Samson's hair is copper-coloured. Petremol's is red like rust. For my purposes, Samson's no good to me!"

"And lucky he is!" joked Escorgol, and everyone laughed again. But Cabusse pulled at his moustache and said sternly: "All right everyone, let her speak!"

"Well, as you see," la Maligou went on, "from scratching myself so much, I've got red marks on my eyelids, caused by the smoke from my fire, being all day bent over the pot. Now the baron told me to wash my eyes with boiled water every night, but with all due respect, water doesn't do them any good. And since I know another remedy, I'd like to try it, if Petremol will accommodate me, seeing as he's a redhead."

Surprise and some laughter greeted this announcement, but Cabusse silenced them with a gesture.

"If it won't cost anything," said Petremol prudently, "either to my body, my modest savings, or my health, I'll do it."

"It won't cost you a sou," la Maligou assured him, "only a bit of your excrement, collected in the morning when it's freshly laid."

"Sweet Jesus!" Barberine gasped. "It's not possible you're going to stick shit in your eye?"

"'Cause at noon or at supper time it may fall out into the pot you're cooking," added Escorgol.

At this another round of laughter shook our bellies that even Cabusse couldn't silence, especially since he was laughing harder than the rest of us. When finally this hilarity began to calm down, la Maligou went on haughtily: "Ignorant barbarians that you are, you probably aren't aware that the excrement of a redhead is the best cure for redness in the eyes and problems of vision, as well as against the film that covers your eyes in old age."

"But," Petremol cautioned modestly, "you know my excrement stinks."

"Like all stools," replied la Maligou. "You don't think, you peon, that I'd apply it to my body just the way it comes out! No, you have to distil it, and since even when you've gathered its essence it smells, you've got to mix it with camphor and musk."

"Bless me," Petremol exclaimed, "if my shit is going to be distilled, and mixed with musk and camphor, then I'll give it all to you, Maligou, every single blessed day I make it!"

We laughed again, even louder, longer and more uproariously than before.

"Oh lord, I could die laughing, my stomach hurts so," cried Sarrazine. "Maligou, I won't sink my wolf's teeth into your arse, I'm so amazed at you! I forgive you!"

At this, Coulondre, who hadn't cracked a smile the entire evening, got up and, leaning his arms on the table, cleared his throat to speak. Of course, we all expected one of his lugubrious and icy remarks, but he contented himself with announcing that it was late, and that he didn't like leaving his mill for so long with only his dogs to guard it. Jonas and Cabusse also stood up, saying that it was a long way back to le Breuil, and so ended our haying night, which we remembered for a long time at Mespech and in our villages, we had laughed so much and so hard.

One night later, as we lay in the darkness of our tower, Barberine's lamp extinguished, her snores going full steam like a forge, little Hélix spurned our nightly games but lay quiet in my arms and said to me in a strangled voice as if she had a knot in her throat: "Pierre, I have a terrible ache in my head and such awful pain that I think I'm going to die."

"You don't die of a headache," I answered. "It's just too much meat and drink, whose vapours fill and muddle the stomach, and ascend through your veins and arteries to the brain."

"Oh, my Pierre," she moaned, "I know you're very learned, but this headache is a thousand times worse than any I've ever had. I'm afraid of dying, being so young and so full of my sins."

I reassured her again, and took her in my arms, where she cuddled but could not relax in the least, troubled by shudders and moans that were like to break my heart so evident was her pain. I am greatly ashamed to admit that, as worried as I was about her, I was the first to fall asleep, being so tired from the last several days in the saddle from dawn to dusk.

However, the next morning, Hélix was better, though still weak and quite pale. Her headache was benumbed, she said, but she complained that a veil would come over her eyes from time to time, making everything vague and misshapen, as though through a mist.

On 12th July, Franchou lay down alone and without a whimper bore a son whom she called David. My father sent for Ricou, the notary, and added to the will he'd drawn up before leaving for Calais a codicil stating that, upon coming of age, the boy would receive a settlement of 2,000 écus and that he should be named David de Siorac.

I don't know why the summer and autumn seemed to slip by so quickly that year, perhaps because we spent so much time debating the reasons for the royal cavalcade through the kingdom. Everyone at Mespech got into it, and Miroul most of all, having a mind as agile as his body. Moreover, he was learning fast under Alazaïs's rod—and I mean rod literally, for during her lessons she was armed with a stick which she employed, at the least error, to rap her students' knuckles.

"Poor Miroul," I would say when he entered the stables, "I can tell where you've been. Just look at your fingers."

"Oh, that's not the worst of it," Miroul would reply as he began brushing down Accla's right flank while I tended to her left. "The worst," he continued, looking at me over the pony's rump with his strangely coloured eyes, "is that she won't answer my questions."

"Well, ask me then."

"May, I, Master Pierre?"

"Of course," I replied, for I was trying to educate him, believing it to be my duty as a Huguenot.

"I'd like to know," Miroul said, "why Prince Henri de Navarre lives at the court of our king and not in his own kingdom with his mother."

"He's of our religion, like his mother Jeanne d'Albret, and since Navarre is so close to Spain, Jeanne is afraid that he would be educated by the Catholic king."

"But could he leave the court of the king of France if he wanted to?"

"Oh no! He's a guest of Charles IX, but also somewhat his hostage."

"But why is he held hostage?"

"He's a Bourbon. If Charles IX and his brothers died childless, Henri de Navarre could accede to the throne."

"A Huguenot, king of France?" Miroul's blue and brown eyes lit up with such deep joy that I thought I'd better temper it a bit.

"But Henri de Navarre is only eleven years old, Miroul, and it would be amazing if the three Valois princes were to die childless."

"Still," Miroul said.

At the end of November, Geoffroy de Caumont, whom we hadn't seen in a long time, came to see us from Milandes, full of stories about the meeting of the two queens, Jeanne d'Albret and Catherine de' Medici. Jeanne had been invited to join the royal cavalcade while in progress, in order to embrace her son and discuss with the king her grievances against Montluc.

"I was among the 300 knights who escorted Jeanne d'Albret on her departure from Pau on 2nd April," Caumont announced proudly. "The extraordinary thing is that the queen of Navarre has been travelling north, gracing our reformed churches with her favour and her wealth, while the queen mother and the king have been heading south making new laws against us… Did you know that in Limoges, where she is vicomtesse, Jeanne d'Albret forced the canons of Saint-Martial to carry the cathedra from the altar out onto the public square, where she sat for two hours, with the wind in her hair, gesticulating and preaching the reformed religion to the populace? Would you believe it? After she left, the canons took their revenge by spreading around a nasty lampoon they'd composed: 'Indoctrination's but a joke, / When the sermon's by a lady spoke.'"

"This is base verse and basely thought!" said my father.

"Of course," agreed Caumont. "By its poison do we know the snake."

"Have the consuls of Bergerac told you about the school that Antoine de Poynet wants to establish for our religion?" asked Sauveterre, who took this project much to heart.

"Yes indeed! And she is going to broach it to the king. You know, my cousin," added Caumont, his black eyes afire under his bushy eyebrows, "the best part of all was the meeting of these two retinues at Macon. Monsieur de Sauveterre," he continued, turning courteously to my uncle, "and you my cousin, I urge you to try to imagine the astonishment of the Florentine's eighty perfumed and gold-brocaded whores when the queen of Navarre appeared without a jewel, not one pearl, entirely dressed in black, surrounded by eight Huguenot ministers and followed by 300 Gascon horsemen, dressed in leather, not in silk, all booted and dirty, perfumed with garlic and sweat not musk. Well, my cousin, there's not one France but two! The northern one is rich, proud, powerful and spoilt rotten with vice. The southern one is worth twice as much as the other."

My father laughed at this joke, but Sauveterre gave a brief smile and said gravely: "There are not two Frances, Caumont, just one, and someday that one will, I hope, be Huguenot."

"Amen!" said Caumont.

"Did you see Henri de Navarre?" my father asked.

"Certainly, and more than once. And I was able to observe him at my leisure. He's a handsome little prince who though so young seemed to display all the qualities of a mature man. He knows very well who he is, and when he converses with his courtiers, he says exactly what he is supposed to."

"Ah," mused Sauveterre, "if only the court weren't such a den of corruption, I'd say that the dangers and intrigues surrounding him would sharpen his mind…"

"…and he's got a very lively one, Monsieur! As well as an easy manner of speaking, much courage mixed with great prudence, and a sharp eye which is a good judge of men."

Listening to these praises, I became a bit jealous of this prince, who, though only two years my senior, seemed so superior to me in so many things. At the same time, I was taking careful notes of Caumont's portrait of him so that I could repeat it all word for word to Miroul.

"May God dry up these Valois with sterility," said my father gravely, "as Christ did the ungrateful fig tree. And may the Crown of France land on Henri de Navarre's brow!"

"Would you believe it?" said Caumont, so moved by his enthusiasm that he got up from his chair and paced excitedly about the library. "The great Nostradamus has prophesied it!"

"Humph!" my father grumbled, raising an eyebrow. "A physician who makes prophecies!"

"And why not, if they are right?" cried Caumont. "Are you forgetting, my cousin, that Nostradamus predicted the fatal wounding of Henri II during his joust against Montgomery, right down to the last details?"

And Caumont straightaway began to recite the verses that all of France had repeated at that time: "The young lion the old shall overcome, / On bellicose field, in singular duel…" He got no further, for Sauveterre interrupted him: "We know those verses," he said, a little impatiently, "and don't doubt the marvellous clairvoyance of their author. Please, Caumont, go on."

"Listen," Caumont said. And in a loud voice, his eyes shining, he recited: "On the seventeenth day of the month of October 1564, the royal retinue was staying at Salon and Michel de Nostre-Dame most insistently requested Catherine de' Medici to allow him to observe Henri de Navarre alone and at his leisure. On the queen mother's order, he was taken to the prince's rooms where he found the prince naked, waiting to be clothed in his shirt. Nostradamus quietly ordered that he be left in this condition, wishing to observe him naked. Indeed, he watched him so long that Henri, not knowing who he was, wondered if he'd been kept naked because they were planning to whip him for some mischief or other."

The severe face of Caumont broke into a sympathetic smile here as he paused in his recitation. "Nostradamus," he continued, "finally withdrew without a word, and before taking his leave, stopping and looking at the prince's attendants said in a grave voice: '*This child will inherit everything.*'"

Caumont sat down again. My father and Sauveterre seemed to be cast in bronze, and for a full minute such a pall of grave meditation fell over the room that I hardly dared breathe, fearing the noise I might make. I saw out of the corner of my eye (for I didn't even dare turn my head) that Samson and François also appeared to be petrified. I don't know how long this silence, immobility and the furious beating of my heart went on, but I remember quite well that it was Sauveterre whose voice first broke in on our terrible hopes for a Huguenot king. He said in a voice so raspy that it seemed to be ripped from his entrails: "My brothers, let us pray."

And, bad leg and all, he steadied himself with a powerful hand on the back of his chair and lowered himself to his knees.

The haying of 1565 was as abundant as it was the previous year, but I stayed away from the festive dinner that followed, having no heart for the bawdy jokes since I was so troubled by little Hélix's health. In the year since she had been afflicted, her health had not really returned, indeed far from it. Her complexion had gradually worsened, leaving her face a pallid, sickly colour, and when she was struck from time to time with extreme pains and dizziness she would virtually go blind, lose all speech and almost all reason.

My father examined her repeatedly and, unable to make a diagnosis, called in Monsieur de Lascaux, despite the raised eyebrows of Sauveterre, who was against going to such expense over a serving girl. But my father persisted, feeling compassion for little Hélix, and even more so for Barberine, who was tormented with worry to see her daughter waste away month after month.

Monsieur de Lascaux came one Thursday in his carriage, accompanied by two aides, who seemed to serve no other function than to make him seem important. Learning that there was no fever, he had her undressed, and, with a mask over his face, felt her arms, legs and abdomen with his gloved hand. He asked Barberine if, during her infancy, she'd had smallpox, measles or mumps.

"No," Barberine answered, tears streaming down her fat cheeks, "she's never had any of 'em."

"I thought not," answered Monsieur de Lascaux. Then, withdrawing into the library with his aides, my father and me, he paced gravely back and forth, his head bowed under the weight of his heavy thoughts. However, when finally my father courteously asked if he'd like to sit down, he deigned to take a seat in one of the armchairs.

"Well, Monsieur de Lascaux, what do you think?" my father asked, impatient with this long silence.

"The case is perfectly clear," pontificated Monsieur de Lascaux. "The source of this malady is in the mass of bad corrupted blood that never got purified in this poor girl by smallpox, mumps, measles or any of the other outlets Nature has provided for this end. Now, this great mass of blood, growing ever more infected over the years since it was never purged, has ended up entering the entrails, the liver, the spleen, the viscera and other surrounding parts of the body. Thus, since everything has been perverted, the brain is also debilitated and has been filled with fumes, vapours and exhalations of venomous acrimony and acidity. This results in these terrible headaches and dizziness which you have observed, for the unhealthy vapours I mentioned have obscured, stifled and oppressed the sensitive nerves and meninges to the point where the animal spirit is unable to circulate and sight and language are weakened. In short, we have here a sympathetic epilepsy rather than an idiopathic one, since it's not coming from the brain itself, which is not prey to any corruption—"

"And yet that's where the pain is," observed my father.

"The pain," corrected Monsieur de Lascaux, obviously irritated at this interruption, "comes from the vitriolic vapours and exhalations which are ascending to the brain from all parts of the body."

After a moment my father said, "It is thus your opinion, Monsieur, that it's a case of epilepsy. And yet the patient has never fallen."

"She will," opined Monsieur de Lascaux.

"She displays neither stiffening nor convulsions nor any shortness of breath."

"She will," said Monsieur de Lascaux. There was a long and awkward silence.

"And what cure do you recommend?" Jean de Siorac asked.

"Frequent bleeding," replied Monsieur de Lascaux, rising and making a deep bow to my father, for he knew all too well how opposed my father was to this sovereign remedy. But my father did not say a word and, rising in his turn, he politely walked Monsieur de Lascaux out to his carriage, the two aides following at a distance, their arms drooped at their sides, their minds blank and mute as portraits.

"Well," Sauveterre said, limping into the courtyard after my father and keeping his voice low so the servants would not hear, "what did you get from this consultation?"

"Lots of straw and little grain. A nice speech. A fallacious diagnosis. And an imbecilic cure."

"Good money thrown away..."

"True enough! But I had to!" replied my father irritably, and, with me at his heels, he walked brusquely away towards the library.

"Father," I said, my throat in a knot, "what is your view of this sickness?"

My father looked at me, astonished at my emotion, but careful not to say anything about it, whatever he may have thought. "My son," he said, "the only remedy for ignorance is knowledge, not talk. Pedants, like the ravens on our tower, love to crow about things they know nothing about. But what is such vain crowing to us? We hunger for truth. If I could only open her skull without the poor thing dying, I could learn the cause of her suffering. What I do know is that the sickness is inside her head and only in her head, for the rest of her body is healthy and her vital functions still unimpaired."

"Father, is it possible it's the nerve alone that's disturbed?"

I asked this question in such a strangled voice that my father stared at me, then after he'd considered me for a moment, he said, unable to hide his feelings, "In truth, I fear it is some terrible damage to the meninges. Possibly an abscess."

"An abscess!" I cried. "But how could it ever drain since it's covered by the skull?"

"There's the rub," my father said. "You've put your finger on it."

"Is there no cure?" I asked, my voice trembling. My father shook his head.

"If it is what I think it is, then there is no remedy. All I will be able to do, when the poor girl's suffering gets unbearable, is to give her some opium."

I pretended that Cabusse was waiting for me in the fencing room, and, with a brief bow, I left as quickly as I could so that he wouldn't see my tears. In the corridor leading to the fencing room I ran into François, who was returning from his lesson and who, as he passed me, raised his head haughtily and, without looking at me or appearing to address me, uttered between his teeth: "What a lot of trouble for that little slut."

He was already past me, so I ran after him and, seizing his arm roughly, pulled him around to face me and, my eyes still brimming with tears, yet furious, I screamed: "What did you say, knave?"

"N-nothing," he replied, turning pale and casting an anxious look about him, for we were alone and entirely out of earshot in a long, dark and damp vaulted passageway, lit only by small barred windows overlooking the moat.

I repeated my question, shaking him with both hands, gnashing my teeth and burning with an overwhelming desire to strike him like iron on an anvil.

"I was merely talking to myself," he stammered, quite undone, realizing that in this lonely spot he could expect no help. I suddenly realized that, though we were the same size, and though he was not a weakling and was a good rider and swordsman, he'd never been able to get over the fear I had aroused in him when I'd beaten him up at the age of six. Fear and hatred existed side by side in him, one feeding on the other, both stewed to boiling point from such long resentment. It was clear I wouldn't be a frequent guest at Mespech when he was baron!

"My brother," I said with a menacing politeness, "did you not just now pronounce the word 'slut'?"

"No indeed!" he lied, his upper lip trembling.

"Well then, be very sure not to pronounce the word, lest you incur my wrath. And now, be on your way, Monsieur!" And as he set off without a word, I followed him silently for a few paces and then administered him a sudden kick in the arse. He spun around.

"But you've struck me!" he sputtered in indignation.

"No indeed!" I replied. "You didn't pronounce the word 'slut', and I didn't strike you. Let us leave it at this double mistake."

Camped in front of him, my chin raised and my hands on my hips, I glowered at him. He gave me a nasty look and I thought for a second that he was going to light into me, but his excessive prudence (a virtue he'd inherited neither from my father nor from Isabelle) kept him at bay. He preferred to bottle up his complaint and to store it carefully away in his great chest of bitterness rather than suddenly purge it in an explosion of rage. Without a word, ashen with barely contained fury, he turned on his heels, leaving me the shreds of his honour.

I realized how wise my father had been to forbid us to wear sword or dagger within the walls of Mespech, for François's vile insult had me beside myself with wrath and, had I possessed a weapon, I surely would have unsheathed it. After François had left, I thought about it a great deal. Master of the field, having vanquished and humiliated him, I was still uncontrollably angry, and I dreamt of blood and wounds to purge the insult he'd directed at my poor Hélix.

I leant against the wall of the arched passageway, and, when my mad fury had finally passed, I felt weak and unhappy, a knot gripping my throat, breath coming so short that I could hardly stand. And yet I did not cry, but contemplated my solitude stretching out before me as long and sad as this dark passageway and damp walls. For I was now sure that little Hélix would die slowly but surely right before my eyes over an unbearably long time.

The day after Monsieur de Lascaux's visit, as if to give the lie to this terrible unhappiness and to my father's hopeless diagnosis, little Hélix suddenly recovered her usual strength and gaiety, if not her colour. Though still of pallid and unhealthy complexion, her terrible headache seemed to have subsided along with the dizzy spells and troubled vision. Barberine, rejoicing in this improvement, broadcast throughout Mespech what a great and marvellous physician Monsieur de Lascaux was, since he'd completely cured her without administering any remedy other than touching various parts of her body with his black-gloved hands.

And seeing her health returning, I pardoned my elder brother François. Meeting him alone in the vaulted passageway that led to the fencing room, I stopped and presented him with a confused apology for having struck him. He listened coldly, and just as icily told me that he regretted the language he'd used, but that I must excuse him for his worry that I was stooping too low in my attachments. The apology was, of course, almost worse than the insult, but I accepted it without raising an eyebrow, saluted my brother and went on my way. I understood that François both despised and envied me for having preferred a close and vulgar affection to his noble and inaccessible love.

On 14th June, the very day Lascaux, followed by his two attendants, had made his grandiose consultation at Mespech, Catherine de' Medici and the king convened with their daughter and sister, Élisabeth de Valois, queen of Spain. At this meeting in Bayonne, arranged well in advance, Élisabeth was accompanied by the Duque de Alba, Felipe II's most trusted advisor.

Huguenots throughout the kingdom reacted tumultuously to the awful and threatening news of the Bayonne meeting, all the more so since it took place in secret, without a single Huguenot among the French, who were represented by the constable, Henri de Guise (the son of the assassinated duc), the Cardinal de Bourbon, Montpensier and Bourdillon, all zealous Catholics little inclined to conciliation.

Thus was the reason—or at least the ultimate goal—of the royal cavalcade across the entire length of France finally revealed: a meeting on the Spanish frontier between the French king and the avowed enemy of our faith.

This meeting had been requested, nay insistently beseeched, of Felipe II by Catherine de' Medici. A woman whose great energy vastly exceeded her wisdom, Catherine remained entirely wedded to her family interests, preferring them, when necessary, to the needs of the kingdom. Now it seemed that the "shop lady", as her enemies called her, was obsessed with the desire to make princely marriages for her children. She was ready to unite her most cherished son, Henri d'Orléans (the future Henri III) to Felipe II's recently widowed sister, Doña Juana, on condition that Felipe cede to his sister some part of his extensive empire as dowry. As for Catherine's daughter, Marguerite de Valois, then twelve years old, the queen mother sought the hand of Felipe's son, Don Carlos, though he was known throughout Spain as a "half-man", unable as yet "to prove his virility".

On 2nd August, a month after the Bayonne meetings, the principal Protestant lords of the Sarlat region, still greatly alarmed, met at Mespech. Armand de Gontaut Saint-Geniès, Foucaud de Saint-Astier, Geoffroy de Baynac, Jean de Foucauld and Geoffroy de Caumont arrived separately, under the cover of darkness and in the greatest secrecy. Our entire household had been sent off to bed and Escorgol had even been sent to the le Breuil farm on some business or other and replaced in the gatehouse by the utterly loyal Alazaïs.

François, Samson and I were permitted to attend this meeting, which took place in the library. I was deeply impressed by the sombre faces of these men who were normally so self-assured and confident of their fortunes, yet now seemed quite uneasy, wondering aloud if their fellow religionaries weren't going to pay dearly for the secret transactions between Felipe II and the Florentine. It was well known that Catherine had no heart and less conscience, and that Felipe had already drowned the Reformation in blood in his own kingdom and aspired only to exterminate it among his neighbours.

Of the five Protestant lords present (not counting the Brethren), Caumont and Saint-Geniès appeared to be the best informed, perhaps because they had spent the most time with the royal cavalcade and had successfully gleaned some information there. I noticed as well that everyone spoke with infinite circumspection, as if our very walls had ears, and used biblical code names which it took me a while to master: Catherine de' Medici became *Jezebel*; the Duque de Alba *Holofernes*; Henri de Navarre *David*; and Admiral de Coligny *Elijah*.

"I have it on good authority," Caumont began, "that David heard Holofernes telling some French lords in the conference room one day that they would have to 'get rid of five or six leaders' of our party."

"Did he name them?" asked my father.

"Yes. They included Elijah and his two brothers, d'Andelot and Odet de Châtillon as well as the prince himself. One of the Frenchmen pointed out to Holofernes that the mass of reformers should all be punished. To which Holofernes replied, clearly indicating Elijah: 'A good salmon is worth a hundred frogs.'"

"Have you any idea," my father asked, "what Holofernes wanted from Jezebel?"

"I think so," replied Saint-Geniès. "First of all, France's acceptance of the Council of Trent."

"But this doesn't depend entirely on Jezebel or even on her son," Geoffroy de Baynac argued, "but rather on parliament and also on the French Church, which is quite hostile, as everyone knows, to this council which has given the Pope extensive powers he'd never previously enjoyed over the French Church and the French king."

"And in the second place," continued Saint-Geniès, "Holofernes wants the revocation of the Edict of Amboise."

"Or what's left of it," mused Sauveterre bitterly, Jezebel having eaten away at it already for some time.

"And thirdly," said Saint-Geniès, "what Caumont just said: the death of the salmon and all other fish of the same size. After these assassinations, the frogs would be given three options: convert, go into exile or risk the stake. Either of the second choices would entail confiscation of all their property."

A lugubrious silence followed this announcement, during which each doubtless imagined the worst: being forced to leave for ever his beautiful chateau, his lands, his servants, his tenant farmers and his villages.

"And what was Jezebel's answer to all this?" asked my father.

"The shop lady was ready to do business," Saint-Geniès spat out bitterly. "In short: 'Give your sister and your son to my children and we'll give the knife to the Protestants.'"

"She'd sell us all!" cried my father. "And what did Holofernes say?"

"'This is not an honourable trade, Madame.'"

"As indeed it is not!" said Sauveterre.

"'The Catholic king,' Holofernes is said to have added with his Spanish arrogance, 'wants to know whether or not you are ready to remedy this problem of religion.'"

"I admire his way of expressing himself!" said my father. "Exterminating half of the population is called, in this bloody diplomacy, 'remedying this problem of religion'. And how did Jezebel respond when presented with this rebuff and this ultimatum?"

"With vague and uncertain promises, coupled with protests, caresses and infinite respects for Holofernes's master, whom she called 'my son', and who couldn't even be bothered to meet her in Bayonne."

"She's a snake grovelling in the dust at her Spanish master's feet," snarled Caumont, "and yet there's no question of any marriage between her dear little son and Doña Juana, nor between Marguerite and Don Carlos. I'm told on good authority that Holofernes sent Jezebel a categorical refusal of any such union."

Another long silence followed these words as the gentlemen breathed a modest sigh of relief through their anger and worry. This new mood did not escape my father's notice, for he said, a little hastily I thought: "And yet we must be on our guard and not reassure ourselves too easily. If Holofernes's refusal of these marriage proposals gives us some respite, this respite doesn't remove the sword hanging over our heads. It's still there, and can be swayed by any breeze that blows through the mind of this woman. It will hang there day and night, winter and summer and only Jezebel's whim will determine whether the thread will be cut or no."

He paused, and then continued gravely: "My friends, it is time to decide firmly and forthrightly to arm our allies throughout the province, to fortify our positions and to create a union among them strong enough so that no one can be attacked without the others coming to his defence."

I was greatly troubled by my father's words, for, as long as I'd had any understanding of these matters, I knew him to be a Huguenot loyalist, who had refused during the civil wars to join Condé's camp. Now he was proposing to his peers to "arm and fortify themselves" against royal power. And thinking more about it as I lay in bed that night beside the sleeping Samson, I realized with trepidation that the danger threatening our people must be immense and quite imminent for my father to have changed his position to such a degree.

On the fifteenth day of March 1566, a few days before my fifteenth birthday, little Hélix's suffering became unbearable, just as my father had predicted, and he administered small doses of opium to her. Still, her moans and cries increased in intensity and frequency, and we installed her in a small room on the ground floor. We also put in a bed for Barberine, but in fact I was the one to occupy it, justifying my presence there by my future profession and by the fact that since Barberine slept so soundly that a cannon blast wouldn't wake her, her presence at night was of but little help.

My poor Hélix had grown excessively thin and had fallen into such an extreme state of cachexia that she weighed no more than a shadow. I felt this especially when I took her in my arms to carry her into the common room when her sickness gave her some respite. It seemed that everything was going at once, her flesh, her musculature, her nerves and the vital elements that circulated in them. For she grew weaker as she grew thinner, and daily seemed more detached from life, requesting less and less frequently to be carried in to be with the others. This came almost as a relief, since every time I picked her up I was devastated by how much lighter she felt in my arms and I could scarcely hide my anguish in her presence. Worse still, when she was settled in a chair, covered to her neck (her emaciation and running fever having made her quite susceptible to cold), I noticed, in contrast to the ruddy faces, loud voices and vigorous gestures of those around her, how pale and angular her face had become, how weak her voice and how languid her poor skeletal arms.

I spent as much time with her as I could. Until the fateful day that death shall take me, I shall never forget the marvellous love that would suddenly illuminate her mournful eye when I would appear in the doorway. But it was but a flash, for she was too weakened to maintain this light. She seemed comfortable in this little room, especially when she was first moved there and still spoke of getting well and cared about her body. "Oh Pierre, when I shall be on my feet again, you won't care about me any more. I'll be too ugly. I'll have a neck like a chicken, hollow shoulders and breasts as flat as my hand."

"You'll fatten up, Hélix. As soon as your pain stops, flesh will grow back under your skin, all beautiful and firm again, just like Franchou, whom you envy so."

"But when, when, when?" she said so plaintively that my heart was like to break. "I'm so tired by this long and painful convalescence. It's nearly two years since I've run about the courtyard in Mespech. And I think that if I ever get well, it'll be too late and you'll have already left to become a doctor in Montpellier."

I thought she was going to weep, but she no longer seemed to have the strength for tears. Her thin little hand made a little movement in the hollow of mine, and, succumbing to the opium my father had given her, she slipped into a deep slumber.

One April morning she asked me, "Are those birds I hear?"

"Yes indeed! And there are hundreds of them!"

"Oh Pierre, there are leaves on the trees in the close around the moat. The new grass is all tender, and the wheat is already up. And next year I'll be in the cold dark ground."

"Silly goose," I comforted. "Next year you'll be right here at Mespech in my arms, just like today."

She answered "no" with a look, no longer having the strength to contradict me, and fell asleep, her poor head on my shoulder weighing no more than a dead bird. I fell into a deep meditation, which only made me sadder the more I thought, yet I could not escape it. In the evening of that same day, I was alone with my father in the library and asked, "Father, can you clarify something for me, please? When Christ was before Lazarus's tomb, it says in the Gospel according to St John, "And Jesus wept.""

"Is this what's bothering you?"

"Yes. I don't understand His tears. Why does Christ cry about the death of Lazarus when He has come to his tomb to resuscitate him?"

"Your question, my son, shows how carefully you have read the Scriptures. The answer to your question is that Jesus does not mourn Lazarus as the Jews who are watching him think. His tears are for the ineluctable separation of the living and the dead."

This woefully beautiful answer entered me like an arrow that cut the thread between Hélix and me, and, to my confusion and shame, uncontrollable tears burst from my eyes. Seeing this, my father rose and hugged me to his chest and whispered to me with immense tenderness: "You were nursed and raised with little Hélix and naturally you love her dearly. Your tears do not surprise me. Don't be ashamed of your sorrow, nor afraid of how long it will last. Suffering takes a very long time."

I felt I might drown in my father's delicate kindness, yet at the same time I was so strengthened by it that I dared to ask my father a question that had been troubling me deeply ever since I'd known little Hélix was failing. "Father, will she be saved?"

"Oh, Pierre! Who can answer your question except the Maker of all things? And yet," he continued after a thoughtful silence, "if there is an ounce of value in the frailty of my human judgement, I will say that I hope and believe it. She is so young to be called to her Maker."

Whenever he knew I was there, Samson would come to visit little Hélix, and sitting modestly by, illuminating the room with his copper-coloured hair, he would remain there smiling at the patient without moving or talking. Miroul also came to visit her with his viol. The instrument had been my mother's and had been given to our valet at Sauveterre's insistence, who appreciated the boy's beautiful voice. As Uncle de Sauveterre expected, Miroul had taught himself to play, having a heaven-sent gift of music. On Sundays, when we celebrated Communion at Mespech, he sang the Psalms of David, holding his viol on his knees and sweetly plucking its strings. That Sauveterre had arranged this astonished me at first. I had grown up believing that music, even religious music, was very voluptuous. But I saw that Calvin himself believed otherwise when later I read from his pen that "it had a wondrous and vigorous power to inflame men's hearts to praise God with an ever greater zeal."

Hélix's poor little face lit up when she heard Miroul, and every time he appeared she sang in a sweet, low voice: "Miroul's got bright eyes! Oh yes, but / One is blue, and the other's chestnut…"

If her head did not ache too badly, she would ask him for a psalm, always the same, the one beginning "Bless our paths, O Lord…". Miroul sang it in a most arresting voice, his viol on his knees. This psalm must have pleased Hélix because it was a song of hope and because she believed she was at the end of her voyage and gave herself over to the Lord to guide her—but she also loved it because it sang of paths and routes and because she had for so long been confined to her bed by her extreme frailty.

"Pierre, my love," she said one day, her voice so tenuous now that I could hardly hear her, "I have only to hear this psalm sung to remember the time I rode behind you on your horse on the way to the le Breuil farm three years ago."

When she was first settled in the little room on the ground floor, Barberine came to see her often, but all she could do was cry bitterly for hours at a time, which troubled little Hélix so much that my father urged her mother to make her visits shorter and less frequent. The rest of our household was urged to greet her from the door without coming into the room, especially la Maligou, who didn't cry so much, but rather tired the patient out with her endless gossip.

My little sister Catherine, her blonde braids hanging sadly about her face and a doll on her arm, came in one day to see Hélix when she was in one of her periods of remission. She asked for the doll, and hugged it and cradled it in her arms despite her age, as if it were her own little baby smiling happily all the time. Seeing this, Catherine said to her, "Hélix, I want to give her to you. She's yours!"

Whereupon, she ran off, and went to her room to cry her heart out over the loss of her favourite doll whom she loved tenderly. I went to find her as soon as I could, suspecting how aggrieved she was. She now occupied my mother's majestic room, the largest and most beautiful in Mespech, with purple and gold curtains framing its arched windows, and a richly ornamented four-poster bed. It was in this bed, so enormous for her little body, that I found her sobbing and succeeded in consoling her.

From that day on, the doll never left little Hélix's arms, who seemed ever smaller, being so thin and frail. Remembering how, one night when she was still healthy and happy, she'd awakened me to confide in me her terror of hell because of her "great sin", I worried that she might once again be feeling this fear along with the apprehension of her death. But both during her remissions and her crises, with her doll hugged tightly to her, she seemed quite serene and almost gay.

During the day, one or another of our servants would pop their heads in at the door and greet her: "Good morning, Hélix, how are you?" She could make no response when she was in one of her crises, but otherwise, she would smile sweetly and answer in a sing-song voice as she hugged her doll: "Better, better, much better!"

It has since often occurred to me that the doll was what I had once been for her when I was much younger and the object of such an immense tenderness from this childlike Eve—a love which later became a sin of the body, but never of the soul.

Little Sissy also came to see Hélix in her room, but she was quickly banished and I well remember why. Though she was a mere eleven years old, like my sister Catherine, she was after other kinds

of games than dolls, her flesh well developed already, full of flirta-
tious postures and looks, blinking her dark liquid slits of eyes at me
provocatively. Despite her excessive weakness, Hélix was well aware
of these tricks, and she whispered in my ear, "Pierre, get rid of that
little crow. She's hovering too close around you."

Of course, I did her bidding, but the Gypsy's daughter, as clever
as ten serpents, suddenly resisted, wrinkling her nose and spitting fire
and brimstone. When I in turn got angry, she seized me with both
arms around the waist and wrapped herself around me to prevent
being pushed out the door. When at last I succeeded in shoving her
out and had closed the door behind her, I saw little Hélix in tears,
her desperate eyes fixed on me.

Those were her last tears. The next morning, 25th April, she was
once again calm and very serene. At noon, when Faujanet peeked
in as usual to say hello, she said to him: "Good Faujanet, you shall
soon be making my coffin."

Hearing this, Faujanet blushed, and stood there open-mouthed,
his smile frozen on his lips, very stupid and sad, not knowing what
to say or how to leave.

That day, I know not how, despite her extreme feebleness, she
looked very beautiful again with a radiance that was not of this world.
During the evening she asked me to wash her, sprinkle perfume on
her, put some rouge on her cheeks and change her shift. I asked her
if I should call Barberine and Franchou.

"No," she said, "you. Just you!"

When I'd finished, she signalled to me to sit down on her bed,
and, leaning her light head on my shoulder, hugging her doll in
her right hand, she slipped her left hand into my open doublet (for
it was already quite hot for the season) and grasped the medallion
of Mary I wore around my neck, her poor haggard eyes begging
my permission. I remained still for quite some time, but my forced

immobility ended up by making me uncomfortable, and I got up quietly, believing she'd fallen asleep. Her head slipped towards me, and then her body. Feeling I was still somehow attached to her, I saw she was still holding on to the chain of the medallion with her left hand. I had some difficulty disengaging her fingers to free myself, and turning to look back I saw that her eyes were open and rolled back. I knelt trembling at her bedside and listened to her heart— something I'd often done in jest when hearing her tell me she'd had a great love-thought, and I would always answer that I would straightaway check, and woe betide her if she were lying—but on this day it was life that was lying, for her poor heart was no longer beating against her ribs.

No more than an hour had passed since little Hélix's death when my father sent me and Samson to help with marking the spring lambs. In fact, they could have very well done without us and on my return to Mespech the next morning, I understood that it had been a pretext to get me out of the way while my father, locked away in his ground-floor room, sawed off the cranium of the dead girl to verify his diagnosis. When I returned, little Hélix was folded into a shroud and lay in her chestnut coffin, Catherine's doll in her arms, and around her head a bandage whose purpose I understood instantly.

Faujanet had waited for me to take one last look at little Hélix before nailing on the cover which would separate her for ever from the world of the living. I made a short prayer and, walking quickly away so as not to hear the hammer blows, I went up to Catherine's room where, as I suspected, she lay on her bed in tears both for the death of her friend and the loss of her doll. Taking her in my arms, I felt a sweet warmth from her plump little body which brought me enormous relief after what I had just seen and, mingling tears and kisses, I promised her that upon my return from Montpellier I'd bring her the biggest, most beautiful doll that a girl in Sarlat had ever had.

Before going to find my father to report on the marking of the spring lambs, I took time to dry my tears, not wanting to make a spectacle of my weakness. I found him in his library, pacing back and forth, his face quite drawn. He said with a coldness that I could see was feigned: "It was indeed an abscess, as I'd thought, grown so large that it was pressing on the meninges and the nerves and drowning them in pus." I was terribly distressed, and not wishing to dwell on the gruesome image his words painted in my mind, I said, "Are you going to inform Monsieur de Lascaux?"

"No. He's not a bad man, really, but too puffed up in his vanity like a turkey, and I'd only make an enemy of him."

He lowered his eyes. "Escorgol has finished digging her grave next to Marsal on the north of the close. We'll bury her at noon according to our rites. I will make a short sermon. Do you wish to be present?"

I quickly understood that my father was not asking whether I wished to be excused from appearing but instead was requesting that I contain my feelings in the presence of our servants.

"I'll be there," I said as stiffly as I could. And, though it was implicit, I kept my promise and remained dry-eyed while they lowered her featherweight coffin into "the cold and dark of the ground", as little Hélix had said.

Our entire household was present, looking sad and mournful. My father gave the eulogy. I thought I understood, as I listened, why he had wanted to take over Sauveterre's usual duty of sermonizing: for he slipped in a quotation from Calvin, chosen, I thought, to echo the conversation we'd had a few days before about little Hélix: "Those whom God calls to his salvation," went the quote, "He receives with His bounteous mercy without regard for their station."

I noticed that my father went out of his way during the weeks that followed to keep me busy and in constant motion, often sending me outside Mespech, to le Breuil, to the les Beunes mill or to Sarlat. But though I accomplished these missions conscientiously, I found little interest in them, having lost all enthusiasm for life. I applied myself mournfully to everything I did, even with Samson, towards whom, only God knows why, I felt less loving, and I fell into a taciturn state that left him greatly troubled, but which I seemed unable to break, every word summoning up a terrible effort.

As I rode Accla around on various errands for my father, the tender new spring leaves reaching out to me neither caught my eye nor caused the usual delicious intake of breath and happy swelling of my chest, so sorrowful was I and as though drawn earthward. Not even Accla could give me pleasure, and as I rode her I could feel her astonishment that I loved her so little. However busy I might appear, I could do nothing but remember the past, chewing it over like a sad dog his leash, in thoughts that never ceased, even in bed, where I tossed and turned, burnt and shrivelled on the embers of my sorrow.

My melancholy had lasted a month already, when Samson and I were called into the library. I noticed immediately from my first glance at my father and Sauveterre that their heads were held much higher than at any time since the meeting with the Protestant lords at Mespech. My father, in particular, seemed himself again, rejuvenated, his chin raised, hands on his hips and voice sonorous:

"My rascals," he said, with his old playfulness, "the affairs of the Reformation have taken a turn for the better since the Bayonne meeting at which, as you know, Jezebel very nearly sold our blood to the Spanish. Now everything has changed. You should know that about four years ago a few hundred of our Bretons established a colony in the Americas on the coast of Florida. Just here," he said, putting his finger on a point of his globe, which Samson and I obediently leant over to study, astonished that it was so far from Sarlat. "These

Bretons," he continued, "are good sailors, good soldiers and have done some buccaneering in the Antilles. Well, Felipe II got uneasy that the French were 'nesting' so near his conquests and sent a large force to Florida, which surprised our Bretons by treachery and massacred every last one of them after promising them safe conduct if they surrendered."

"There's no limit," Sauveterre added, his voice shaking, "to the blood this very Catholic king has been willing to shed for his empire. If the truth is ever known about all the massacres he has perpetrated in the Americas, there's not a Christian would not hold him in abomination."

"But news of this particular massacre reached the French court, my rascals," said my father, "and the Florentine is gnashing her teeth and is loudly and furiously demanding justice and reparations from her son-in-law. She won't get them, and she's too contemptible, of course, to go to war over this, but for the time being, at least, her so-called holy alliance with Felipe is over. And so we are safe—for the moment at least, I must stress this—and already there seems to be a lessening of assassinations of isolated Huguenots throughout the kingdom, as if the most fanatical papists were losing heart after seeing the Spanish king ill-esteemed in France."

After a moment of silence, my father looked at each of us in turn and said with a kind of authoritative pomp: "My sons, your Uncle de Sauveterre and I have decided that the time is ripe to send you to Montpellier to begin your studies. You shall set out two days hence. Miroul, your valet, will accompany you."

I was neither happy nor sorry with this decision. I simply accepted it with the indifference I felt about everything. However, I gathered together, at my father's behest, all my worldly goods, clothing and books, which did not amount to any great volume. Three of us would be travelling, but would take four horses, the fourth a packhorse for our belongings, as well as three blunderbusses and ammunition. In our saddlebags we would each carry two pistols, as well as a sword and dagger which should never leave our sides even when we slept. At my father's insistence, we were to wear full armour and helmet while travelling and remove them only when bivouacked: a terrible burden in the summer's heat, but though well armed, our troop was awfully small for such a long voyage.

I would ride Accla and Samson Albière, his white pony. And for Miroul and the packhorse he would lead, far from giving us old nags, my father provided two rapid and tough little Arabians, arguing that, if attacked by a large band of brigands, our only chance would be to flee and that we couldn't risk losing our precious valet or our possessions.

Our journey was to take us from Sarlat to Cahors, and then Montauban. But from there my father counselled us not to take the road to Castres, which would have been shorter, but consisted of winding roads through very wild country. He preferred the longer plains route through Toulouse, Carcassone and Béziers, where the road would be more travelled.

On the eve of our departure my father and Sauveterre, remembering their days as captains of the Norman legion, inspected our equipment to the last detail: arms, harnesses, bridles, horseshoes, straps, awls and thread to repair our bridles, everything was examined.

Finally, as the day of our trip dawned, my father, greatly moved, and Sauveterre, equally so but showing it less, received us in the library when we were fully armed and helmeted.

Sauveterre spoke first, calling on us to remember to pray to God not with our lips but in our hearts; to read the Scriptures and to be mindful of them; to sing the Psalms (Miroul was bringing his viol) morning and night; and to remember the Word of God as a constant counsel in all matters of our lives, large and small.

When he had finished, my father gave us some advice bearing more on our conduct in this life than our future in the next: "My rascals," he said in a grave but warm voice, "you've scarcely got thirty years of experience between you, and yet you're going out on the highway to face the vast world. There will be innumerable pitfalls along the way. To avoid them you will need all your resources and your weapons, but you should realize that courtesy is first among these. With rich and poor, gentleman and peasant, always keep your Périgordian amiability. Bear umbrage to no man, neither in words nor in deeds. And yet let everyone know from your demeanour that you are not men to be bearded. Be slow to quarrel, especially you, Pierre, who are so quick to anger, but if you must fight, don't back off, but advance boldly. This is for you, Samson, who are so slow to unsheathe your sword and so long in concluding a fight. You must realize that your delay could cost your beloved brother his life, as it almost did at la Lendrevie. When you're on the road, avoid drinking, gambling and feasting like the devils of hell, for they will quickly ruin your purse, your soul and your health. Once in Montpellier, choose your friends for qualities which will last and not simply glitter, and choose them preferably from among the Protestants of the town, who are legion, thank God. With strangers, be chary in words but not in observation. In doubtful company, do not wave your reformer's flag, but do not hide it either, unless it is dangerous to do otherwise. Finally, at Montpellier, study diligently and follow your masters, since this is the goal of your journey and is so costly to the barony of Mespech. And try to remember as you study that the labour of your youth will be like capital from which you can draw interest for the rest of your life."

Here he paused thoughtfully.

"Samson will be the keeper of the purse, and Pierre the commander of the little troop. Miroul will be your subject and must remember who is the master. But treat him according to his merits, which are not slight, and listen to his advice. Through the hardships he knew as a child he knows more of the world than you do."

I thought my father had finished or that he was embarrassed to conclude. And indeed he was, but conclude he did, having things yet to say which he found especially delicate with Sauveterre at his side and his own life as an example. But he finally made up his mind, and continued despite Samson's innocent wide eyes and Sauveterre's grumblings and frowns, even though my father used a half-contrite tone, especially at the beginning:

"The advice which follows is for you in particular, Pierre, but I'm saying it in front of Samson so that later perhaps he may also make some use of it."

He paused again, and then continued in a manner that wasn't exactly as humble as it might have been.

"Pierre, you have, alas, inherited from me an excessive taste for the sex which is not our own. It is consequently much to be feared that throughout your life you will be 'a blazing furnace ceaselessly throwing off flames and sparks'. That is Calvin's phrase. Think about it. It vividly describes the infirmity of our nature. And to be sure, not to sin is better than to sin, but if, driven by the ardour of our blood, we must succumb," (here of course, Sauveterre raised a sceptical eyebrow), "at least show some prudence in these matters lest you lose everything. I beg you, my son, not to throw yourself blindly into traps which, in a big beautiful city like Montpellier, will be set everywhere to snare you. Don't go jumping, boots off, into bed with the first girl you see simply because she turns her head and bats an eyelash at you. Beware of diseased, wicked, crafty and avaricious women. In fact," he went on with a smile, "beware of all of 'em. But if, by chance, you happen on a good wench, be good to her, for you're not lacking in heart, nor in generosity."

This speech astonished Samson and displeased Sauveterre, but it didn't take me long to figure out why my father, who thought only of healing my sorrow, pronounced it.

Uncle de Sauveterre was the first to embrace us, then my father, so warmly and tightly that you didn't have to be a great clerk to understand that the sacrifice made to send us to Montpellier had little to do with money. Finally, François came in and, with his long face quite expressionless, embraced each of us politely.

Not wanting to drag out this goodbye into an emotional scene, my father hurried the adieux in the courtyard. Our entire household was gathered there, including those from le Breuil, the quarry and the les Beunes mill. The men stood sadly and silently by and all the women wept, la Maligou muttering her superstitions and gossip as usual, Barberine sobbing that she was losing everything since she was losing "her two bright suns". I wiped the last tear from Catherine's face, smiled at Little Sissy and, as Samson and Miroul were already on their horses, mounted mine. We walked the four horses across the three drawbridges followed by all our servants running alongside and behind us. I waved a last goodbye and, as I turned, caught sight of my father's pale face, and setting my horse to a trot, left my youth behind me.

Despite the road, it took us nearly two hours to get to Sarlat, for I kept our pace quite slow so as not to tire our horses given the length of our journey. I had no desire to talk, but it was a lively and watchful silence I kept, full of agile thoughts, no longer mired, I was happy to observe, in the swamps of the past month where my mind had sunk so morosely since little Hélix's death. As we set out from Sarlat to Cahors, I discovered a long steep road flanked by thick stands of chestnut trees on either side. I eased my black jennet into a walk, and, turning in my saddle with a hand on the pommel, I asked Miroul to sing us a psalm to soothe this long, steep and monotonous climb. Still turned, I saw him duck his head to pull on the strap of the viol, and, dropping the reins on the withers of his little Arabian as it struggled up the hill, he handed the packhorse's lead to Samson, thanking him with a look. Placing the viol across his saddle he plucked a few chords and began, either by chance, or because he, too, loved it, or because he found it so appropriate to our long journey, the same psalm little Hélix had so often requested in her last weeks: "Bless our paths, O Lord…"

At first I worried about the effects of this choice on my morale, but I discovered that it was all right. As Miroul and Samson sang, I began to hum along quietly, and for the first time I had no knot in my throat or tears or sorrow. As it was such a long hill, Miroul sang all the verses, having learnt them by heart in little Hélix's sickroom. When he reached the end of the psalm, I asked him to sing it again, which he did, and as he began, I sang out full-throated, standing and leaning forward in my stirrups while Samson watched me indulgently:

> *Bless our paths, O Lord,*
> *We follow them content,*
> *For You, Who hear our word*
> *Make our way by your intent.*
> *Whether happy paths or dreary,*
> *I walk on in faith so true,*
> *And however dark or weary,*
> *My roads all lead to you.*

The road levelled out on a plateau just as we were finishing this verse, and I asked Miroul to put his viol back on his shoulder and to take the lead of the packhorse from Samson. As soon as he had, I turned to Samson:

"Samson, can you smell the delicious odour of leaves and tender grass?"

"I thmell it," replied Samson, happy to see me at last emerged from my silence. "It'th the hot morning thun drying lath nighth dew."

"Samson, is Montpellier as big a city as Sarlat?"

"Bigger and more beautiful."

"It must be beautiful if there are wenches there who turn their heads so coyly and bat their eyelashes at you."

"Whath thith?" lisped Samson in a way that brought all my love for him rushing back.

"Samson," I said to tease him, "will you remember to draw your sword quickly if we're attacked?"

"I'll remember."

"Samson, will you dawdle when it's time to draw your pistols from their holsters?"

"I won't dawdle," Samson laughed radiantly.

"Samson, we're on the plateau and the soil is sandy. Shall we gallop?"

"Yeth, by Jove, if you want!"

And turning to Miroul, I cried, "Gallop, Miroul, are you ready?"

"My Arabians will follow you, my master, to the ends of the earth!"

I set off, with Samson following, and behind us, holding the lead in one hand and his reins in the other, galloped Miroul with his two Arabians. To our right and to our left, like arrows loosed from a bow, the branches of the trees flew by and, with Accla's warm withers galloping beneath me, I was suddenly filled with a fresh hope that shone like the new spring leaves.

PUSHKIN PRESS

Pushkin Press was founded in 1997, and publishes novels, essays, memoirs, children's books—everything from timeless classics to the urgent and contemporary.

Our books represent exciting, high-quality writing from around the world: we publish some of the twentieth century's most widely acclaimed, brilliant authors such as Stefan Zweig, Marcel Aymé, Antal Szerb, Paul Morand and Yasushi Inoue, as well as compelling and award-winning contemporary writers, including Andrés Neuman, Edith Pearlman and Ryu Murakami.

Pushkin Press publishes the world's best stories, to be read and read again. Here are just some of the titles from our long and varied list:

—————

THE SPECTRE OF ALEXANDER WOLF
GAITO GAZDANOV

'A mesmerising work of literature' Antony Beevor

BINOCULAR VISION
EDITH PEARLMAN

'A genius of the short story' Mark Lawson, *Guardian*

TRAVELLER OF THE CENTURY
ANDRÉS NEUMAN

'A beautiful, accomplished novel: as ambitious as it is generous, as moving as it is smart' Juan Gabriel Vásquez, *Guardian*

BEWARE OF PITY
STEFAN ZWEIG

'Zweig's fictional masterpiece' *Guardian*

THE WORLD OF YESTERDAY
STEFAN ZWEIG

'*The World of Yesterday* is one of the greatest memoirs of the twentieth century, as perfect in its evocation of the world Zweig loved, as it
is in its portrayal of how that world was destroyed' David Hare

JOURNEY BY MOONLIGHT
ANTAL SZERB

'Just divine… makes you imagine the author has had private access to your own soul' Nicholas Lezard, *Guardian*

BONITA AVENUE
PETER BUWALDA

'One wild ride: a swirling helix of a family saga… a new writer as toe-curling as
early Roth, as roomy as Franzen and as caustic as Houellebecq' *Sunday Telegraph*

THE PARROTS
FILIPPO BOLOGNA

'A five-star satire on literary vanity… a wonderful, surprising novel' *Metro*

I WAS JACK MORTIMER
ALEXANDER LERNET-HOLENIA

'Terrific… a truly clever, rather wonderful book that both plays
with and defies genre' Eileen Battersby, *Irish Times*

SONG FOR AN APPROACHING STORM
PETER FRÖBERG IDLING

'Beautifully evocative… a must-read novel' *Daily Mail*

THE RABBIT BACK LITERATURE SOCIETY
PASI ILMARI JÄÄSKELÄINEN

'Wonderfully knotty… a very grown-up fantasy masquerading as
quirky fable. Unexpected, thrilling and absurd' *Sunday Telegraph*

RED LOVE: THE STORY OF AN EAST GERMAN FAMILY
MAXIM LEO

'Beautiful and supremely touching… an unbearably poignant
description of a world that no longer exists' *Sunday Telegraph*

THE BREAK
PIETRO GROSSI

'Small and perfectly formed… reaching its end leaves the reader desirous to start all over again' *Independent*

FROM THE FATHERLAND, WITH LOVE
RYU MURAKAMI

'If Haruki is *The Beatles* of Japanese literature, Ryu is its *Rolling Stones*' David Pilling

BUTTERFLIES IN NOVEMBER
AUÐUR AVA ÓLAFSDÓTTIR

'A funny, moving and occasionally bizarre exploration of life's upheavals and reversals' *Financial Times*

BARCELONA SHADOWS
MARC PASTOR

'As gruesome as it is gripping… the writing is extraordinarily vivid… Highly recommended' *Independent*

THE LAST DAYS
LAURENT SEKSIK

'Mesmerising… Seksik's portrait of Zweig's final months is dignified and tender' *Financial Times*

BY BLOOD
ELLEN ULLMAN

'Delicious and intriguing' *Daily Telegraph*

WHILE THE GODS WERE SLEEPING
ERWIN MORTIER

'A monumental, phenomenal book' *De Morgen*

THE BRETHREN
ROBERT MERLE

'A master of the historical novel' *Guardian*